Extrasensory Perception

Extrasensory Perception

Support, Skepticism, and Science

Volume II

Theories of Psi

Edwin C. May and Sonali Bhatt Marwaha, Editors

Foreword by James H. Fallon, PhD

 PRAEGER™

An Imprint of ABC-CLIO, LLC

Santa Barbara, California • Denver, Colorado

Library of Congress Cataloging-in-Publication Data

Extrasensory perception: support, skepticism, and science / Edwin C. May and Sonali Bhatt Marwaha, Editors; Foreword by James H. Fallon, PhD.
  volumes cm
Includes bibliographical references and index.
Contents: Volume 1. History, Controversy, and Research.
ISBN 978–1–4408–3287–1 (hardback) — ISBN 978–1–4408–3288–8 (ebook)
1. Parapsychology. I. May, Edwin C., 1940– editor. II. Marwaha, Sonali Bhatt, 1963– editor. III. Fallon, James H., writer of foreword.
BF1031.E887   2015
133.8—dc23   2014047692

ISBN: 978–1–4408–3287–1
EISBN: 978–1–4408–3288–8

19 18 17 16 15   1 2 3 4 5

This book is also available on the World Wide Web as an eBook.
Visit www.abc-clio.com for details.

Praeger
An Imprint of ABC-CLIO, LLC

ABC-CLIO, LLC
130 Cremona Drive, P.O. Box 1911
Santa Barbara, California 93116-1911

This book is printed on acid-free paper ∞

Manufactured in the United States of America

To
Charles Honorton, a researcher way ahead of his time.

Contents

PART II: THE FUTURE OF PSI RESEARCH

Foreword

James H. Fallon

This two-volume compendium will become required reading for our first-year graduate students and highly recommended reading for our post-doctoral scholars, especially those who have let slip the rapier edge of their critical thinking. This may seem a bit odd coming from a basic sciences hard-boiled neuroscientist who has never published an article or even uttered a public word about extrasensory perception, psi, anomalous cognition, or other noms de voyage with which this field has traveled.

The general field of extrasensory perception has deep historical roots dating perhaps to the first cultural, artistic, and burial artifacts of both homo sapiens and Neanderthalensis. But the birth of scientific study in this field, starting perhaps in the "golden era" of the 1930s, is nigh only a century old. And a tempestuous history it has certainly endured, roughly paralleling the controversies and upheavals in our understanding of quantum physics and of consciousness itself. But is it time for a new summary compendium of the field? Further, have there been the requisite advancements in technique, experimental approaches and findings, and novel theory, to justify a comprehensive reanalysis and introspection of the state of this field, as detailed comprehensively in these two volumes? I wouldn't have agreed to write this foreword—being an otherwise mainstream biological and psychiatric academic—unless I was convinced the answer to these two questions is "yes."

What struck me most while reading drafts of the chapters was not the novelty of the issues brought up—although there are some startlingly unique ones—but their familiarity in my own fields of neuroscience and psychiatry. Questions of optimal experimental design; providing falsifiable hypotheses for others to, rightly so, tear apart; statistical design and testing and what those numbers really mean in one's data set; providing believable—but to whom—mechanisms of action to explain one's findings; and ensuring ethical handling of the entire experiment and the subjects recruited, and protections against fraud and conflict of interest. This was familiar territory. But what stunned me and made me shift uncomfortably in my chair was that these psi researchers were doing it better than most of my mainstream colleagues in their publications and grants. Perhaps this derives in part from being embedded in a century of blistering attacks from every enclave of science and nonscience. Relentlessly. But I do not offer up a dose of apologia here for these psi scientists, but rather a reluctant admission that a group of scientists, often kept at bay and outside the pale of "straight" science and medicine, were doing it mostly better than we were.

Virtually every scientist I have ever met has a recurring story—that they or someone close to them have experienced the seemingly impossible, most often a violation of the commonsense belief that time is asymmetric at its heart and moves in only one direction. Even with their knowledge that there is precious little in long dearly held equations in Newtonian or quantum equations that requires that time moves in a rectified, forward direction, they still claim that precognition is impossible. One of the curious sidebars to these conversations with mainstream scientists is that many will tell you that (1) we actually know little of the fundamental structure of reality, (2) we know very little of the basis of broadly accepted experiences, consciousness, and (3) that even though we think that something like psi may actually exist, we would never admit it outside of a happy hour where no other scientists are present, lest we risk our grant proposals coming up short by 0.5% in the next federal funding cycle. Beyond these common experiences are those that illuminate the problem to unreasonables; that many of us know Nobel laureates and National Academy members who are rather convinced, uncomfortably so, of the existence of psi phenomena, and at the same time know others in religious and metaphysical fields who, astonishingly, express with great certitude that precognition and all psi is an impossible and absurd idea and little more than magical wishful thinking. I'm pretty much of this latter category of mainstream scientists who is considered, even by my own science colleagues, as a "goat" although *anomalistic psychology* goat is closer to my own approach.[1]

---

[1]The terms "sheep-goat"—(believers-non believers in psi) were developed by Gertrude Schmeidler, professor of psychology at the City University of New York (CUNY) in 1942. *Anomalistic psychology* is the study of human behavior and experience connected with what is often call the paranormal, without the assumption that there is anything paranormal involved.

I should explain, lest I risk offering up a softball free pass to this wild field of science. The softening, however slight, of my stance on the existence of psi phenomena has followed on several experiences in the past decade. The first was a psi meeting entitled "A Meeting of Minds: Invitational Workshop on Anomalous Cognition" I was invited to at the University of British Columbia that included equally sheep, goats, and skeptics. I was invited as someone half in the goat and half in the skeptic cadre. More importantly, what was clear from that meeting is that the psi scientists, the leaders in the field, were most interested in critique, the sharper and pithier the better. This impressed not only me, but more importantly, the other goats and skeptics invited to the meeting, which included Nobel laureates and National Academy of Science cognoscenti. It was clear to us that this was to be a truly rare event, where open criticism and utter honesty were prized above all other considerations. In addition, one of the editors of these volumes (May) was one of the presenters.

The second event was that I was asked to review a research manuscript in 2007 on the effects of "intentional foods" on mood. This was the first, and only, time until this year that I reviewed a research paper on psi. Now, I was brought up a devout Catholic but abandoned this great world doctrine of my youth at 19 years of age and knew well the belief by Catholics, perhaps over a billion of them, in the perceived very real psychical and psychological power of the Eucharist, a reality that is transmuted from the Eucharist into the body, blood, soul, and divinity of Jesus Christ, a process called transubstantiation, which is perceived as being pure reality. I gave up such thoughts 50 years ago, but can a billion believers in the Eucharist, and perhaps another billion pancultural believers worldwide in the power of blessed foods, from chicken soup to sacrificial offerings, that is, "intentional foods," be wrong? Well, of course they can all be wrong, just as wrong as the 95% of scientists who denied the existence of adult stem cells in the brain or of the excitatory properties of dopamine in the brain. My experience after 45 years of research science, when someone tells you that 95% of scientists believe something, or conversely that 95% of scientists agree that something can't exist, take notice. These are no reasons to accept or not accept phenomena as fact, but it does draw my attention. So I agreed to critique this most outrageous of scientific claims that I ever heard. Magical chocolate? Yeah, sure.

The manuscript arrived from the editor-in-chief's office, and I settled down to read it, fully prepared to toss grenades, lob in mortar rounds, and blast away at this monstrosity with my own brand of 50mm Browning enfilade. I was so bucked up I had to do the first reading standing up. After the initial read, I sat down and thought about the paper for several hours. Something bothered me beyond what I had expected. So a second more thorough and responsible perusal was in order. Then, after a night of sleeping on it, or perhaps off it, a third quiet careful reading followed the next day. And I took notes, and read the referenced articles. And checked a statistics manual. And so on. Finally, after a fifth read, I had to take a knee. What became annoyingly clear at that point is that the authors had followed, and gone beyond, what I was used to reading, not only mainstream neuroscience articles ultimately published in rigorous journals, but also articles published in the top four science/medicine journals. In spite of the rigor of the manuscript, I gave it only a tepid "accept" to the editor, not because I believed in the reported effect—after all, it *couldn't* be true—but because structurally, the methods were sound, and the statistics derived double blind were solid. And the paper was published. Then I received a call from a science writer at *Time* magazine. I spent an inordinate length of time explaining why I accepted such an outrageous article for publication and explained to the writer that the experimental method, quality of the provenance of the data, and statistical analyses were up to par and beyond that of some articles I have read in JAMA, NEJM, *Science,* and *Nature.* My main conclusion was that this small article in a journal of healing was the clearest indictment of mainstream science I could think of. They met all requirements of the best mainstream journals but were rejected. When asked why, I guessed that since there is no generally accepted mechanism of action for such psi as this psychokinetic-type finding, bias ruled all the reviewers' judgment. Given that the findings of the vast majority of articles published in major mainstream journals are never substantiated in labs of other scientists, this all started becoming curious to me. Sure, the effect size was small, similar to some findings in major clinical studies, but to reject articles based on the negative bias of "there's no way that can happen" seemed to be a sure way of grinding science in the modern era to a certain halt.

The end of this experience was anticlimatic. After hours on the phone with the *Time* writer, speaking to the quality of the data and such, the writer finally asked me, "But do you now believe that intentional foods can actually work?" Unable to suppress the wise guy in many of us, I impulsively quipped *"So I take a rutabaga and put it close to my head, and it somehow changes the food and improves the mood of the person who ate it?" I asked. "Nah."* When the *Time* article was published, that was the only part of my interview that made it in.

The point I want to make here with regard to the first volume of this set is that the rigor, care, and attention to methodology I was exposed to in the article I reviewed is on full display by the numerous contributors. As I hinted above, psi researchers are among the best in terms of methodological excellence.

Another thing I learned from these volumes is that psi research has informed the mainstream in a variety of ways, having been among the leaders of adopting statistical quantities such as effect size and meta-analysis as well as opening new doors for investigation such as I outlined above. But I was taken aback when I realized from the volumes that the very nature of space and time themselves might well be better understood from psi research, which just might lead the way even for the physics of these pesky areas of inquiry.

Back to the article—the first part of the chocolaty experience was over, but that really wasn't the end of it. The chocolate article was followed by another one, this time on the mood-enhancing effects of—and I'm not making this up—tea that had undergone "good intentions" during a traditional Buddhist tea ceremony. The findings of the study were that those subjects who drank the treated tea had a significant improvement of mood over those who drank untreated tea but also that their belief that the tea ceremony would work further improved mood scores, perhaps in some sort of "real" effect interaction with attitude. In other words, although the tea treatment itself had significant effects, if the subject was a "sheep," there was an enhancement, and if the subject was a "goat," the effect was attenuated. In either case, untreated tea appeared to have no significant effect either way. I recoiled.

But again, after reading the article several times, everything from a scientific, statistical methodological point of view was, as in the intentional chocolate study, solid. But it made no sense to me as an actual event that could possibly occur. Then I had to take a knee one more time. The tea study sent me back to the late 1990s when we were carrying out experiments in my lab on the protective effects of growth factors on dopamine neuron survival in a rodent model of Parkinson's disease. We had found that TGFa (transforming growth factor alpha), among all the growth factors we tried, had a significant effect of protecting dopamine cells from the neurotoxic effects of the drug we used, a standard model used for decades. But a colleague contacted me and asked if I was interested in putting another panel of compounds, in this case nutriceuticals, into our neurotoxicity-cell survival pipeline. After some arm twisting, to say nothing of the guffaws of disbelief of my lab staff, which included experienced MDs and PhDs, and the stern resistance by our animal research review committee, who for the first time considered me a bit goofy for even considering testing green tea nutriceuticals in a University of California lab, I decide to go ahead with the experiment. After two months of testing, the lab chief came to me with the bad news. The green tea solution (primarily an electrolyzed solution of EGCG and vitamin B_{12}) actually had a significant effect on protecting the dopamine neurons in the neurotoxicity tests in live animals, superior to the other growth factors, save for TGFa. We tried all combinations of the electrolysis and the ingredients, and only the electrolyzed combined version worked. My lab personnel were speechless. And I wasn't sure what to do next, especially since the research funds for it were used up. But this experience highlighted something else besides the surprising efficacy of the solution, and that is the importance of funding for such research, which is always much much less than needed to do full parametric studies in hundreds if not thousands of subjects. Always underfunded, and always underpowered, such nutriceutical and alternative therapy research would be forever doomed in mainstream science.

This state of affairs may be operating in the psi field as well. Conscientious, well-meaning benefactors could never really provide the level of support necessary to "prove" any such claims, especially to skeptics, if not goats, my own lab and myself included. But this story doesn't end here, and it took a peculiar personal turn. Several years after we carried out the animal testing of the electrolyzed green tea/B_{12} solution in animals, the small biotech company that created the solution started testing it in some small, typically underfunded, human case studies that involved multiple organ systems and in some cancer patients undergoing chemotherapy and radiation therapy. At this time in 2001, my wife developed non-Hodgkins lymphoma (NHL) a form of immune system cancer. And to our horror, by the time it was detected, the tumor was already enormous, filling much of her lymphatic system. She immediately started Rituxan chemotherapy. Within a couple of weeks, she had lost all energy and confided to me that she might rather die than to continue with the chemo, considering how poorly she felt. But she is a natural fighter and kept on, and agreed to start taking daily doses of the electrolyzed green tea/B_{12} solution. But she also agreed, and this surprised me, to undergo acupuncture and Chi kung treatments with Dr. Tatsuo Hirano. It is important to note that up until this time she, as well as I, did not believe at all in "woo-woo" medicine of any sort, even eschewing meditation as too weird and affected, if not just downright ineffective. But within about a week of starting the tri- woo-woo therapies, she started feeling much better. She had developed severe anemia from the chemo and had to start taking shots for her anemia but then quickly felt so energetic that, in spite of the continuing anemia, she needed no further shots. Her blood work simply didn't line up with how she felt, which, for the rest of her ensuing months in chemo, was nothing short of startling. Now, neither she nor I could conclude that any one of these therapies ended her chemo side effects. This apparently is also a typical challenge for showing whether alternative therapies actually work. Her lymphoma has not returned now 13 years later. Why, we don't know. But follow-up adjunct therapies using this electrolyzed solution in a group of other patients with cancer also undergoing chemo and/or radiation treatments produced the same results. Patients with terminal pancreatic and breast cancer were also gaining weight, back to exercising, and playing golf up until the week they died. So in the light of day, looking at my own research experiences, perhaps these kind of food articles deserve a second look. And more. But who would fund that at the level necessary to impress skeptics, goats, and perhaps the greatest critics of all, the psi researchers themselves?

But wait, there is more. The second volume in this set is devoted entirely to possible theories of how all this might work. One of them caught my attention in that while still purporting that psi is real, it calls into question the interpretation of any psi experiment that uses statistics to come to some conclusion. For example, in the food studies above, one interpretation is that somehow food treated with "good intentions" exerts an "influence" that might improve health or a person's mood; however, in another interpretation, perhaps, someone (researcher or subject) is using their psi—in particular, precognition—in such a way as to mimic the causal effects of the food. Basically, the food itself is doing nada—all the psi action resides in the decisions the researcher or subject makes. In the digital lingua franca of today, OMG! If this is possible, and it is a mighty big *IF*, then much of the mainstream's statistically based science, including much of my own, may be called into question with regard to the mechanisms involved! The only clear response to this is YIKES!

This two-volume set presents a banquet of ideas by the greatest living minds and experimentalists in the field of psi. Replete with potential breakthrough testable and falsifiable hypotheses, the book is also a field guide for scientists of all disciplines, especially those still in the shank of their professional development, on how to productively think critically, and with a skeptical eye, and how to keep improving one's methods, experimental approaches, and statistical handling of both simple and highly complex, sometimes impenetrable, data sets. The rigor of the studies analyzed here is humbling at times and may inspire us "mainstream" types to proceed with our work under what must seem to be siege conditions. But this is exciting stuff to be sure.

I shan't ruin the telling of these for you by expanding on them. Get ready for a good read. A great ride in an academy that takes on the toughest questions of our time.

James H. Fallon, Ph.D.
Professor Emeritus, Anatomy & Neurobiology School of Medicine
Professor, Psychiatry & Human Behavior School of Medicine
University of California at Irvine

Chapter 1

Fundamental Issues for Psi Theorists

Sonali Bhatt Marwaha and Edwin C. May

> The truth may be puzzling. It may take some work to grapple with. It may be counterintuitive. It may contradict deeply held prejudices. It may not be consonant with what we desperately want to be true. But our preferences do not determine what's true.
>
> —Carl Sagan (1995)

A CATCH-22 SITUATION

Through the history of psi research, the discipline has suffered from a form of Catch-22. On one hand, the critics have said we do not believe anything you say with regard to the data because you have no plausible theory to explain your results. Such statements, however, ignore the history of the development of science and the history of psi-research. Part of the reason for this is obvious. If one has a theory that is good at explaining the current data, there is no need to look further until *new* data require a new theory. One of the most stunning examples of this comes to us via the Rayleigh-Jeans law in 1905 that provided an excellent fit, at that time, to the data of the intensity of electromagnetic (EM) radiation that was emitted by a black body as a function of its temperature and wavelength of light. Up to about the turn of the twentieth century, the formulation for this law fit the data quite well for wavelengths that could be measured with the equipment of the day. In the early twentieth century, however, the equipment for measuring light improved and became sensitive to shorter and shorter wavelengths. With that new data, something fantastic occurred; the Rayleigh-Jeans law began to fail not by a little but by orders of magnitude. This failure was so striking that it was then, and is now, referred to as the *Ultraviolet Catastrophe*—ultraviolet being short wavelength(s) of light. Here is an example of new data leading the charge for requiring a new theory. No one said at the time, we do not believe your ultraviolet measurements because you do not have a theory. Enter the current savior theory by Planck, and the birth of quantum mechanics, with what is now known as Planck's law. This theory fixed the problem in that it fit the data for small wavelengths as well as those adequately describe by the Rayleigh-Jeans law. Data came before theory.

As an illustrative aside, May's graduate school advisor in physics remarked, "Science is about truth with a *lower case* 't.' " Of course, he meant that there are very few absolutes—maybe even none—in science. Theories are always subject to change when new data require it.

We provide one more example—continental drift. In 1912, Alfred Wegner proposed that the early earth contained a single landmass consisting of the continents we recognize today. Looking at the coast of Africa and that of South America qualitatively suggested that they were together at one time. But in 1912, there was no theory to account for what—in the day—was considered nonsense. In 1958 (46 years later), Samuel Warren Cary introduced the theory of plate tectonics, and continental drift theory was established. Again, data came before theory. These are not isolated examples; rather, there are not many counterexamples where theory leads to new data.

On the other side of psi's Catch-22 is that when theories are proposed, critics brush them aside, claiming there are no valid data on which to apply any theory, so why bother. As seen in Volume I, the data are there. Moreover, as philosopher Richard Corry concludes in his chapter in Volume I of this collection titled, "ESP, Causation, and the Possibility of Precognition," "there is nothing impossible about ESP, nor is it impossible that we could find good empirical reason to believe in ESP." And physicist Daniel Sheehan in his chapter titled, "Remembrance of Things Future: A Case for Retrocausation and Precognition" (this volume), concludes, with appropriate caveats, "Insofar as retrocausation is embedded in standard physical theory, in principle, precognition appears permitted within the known time-symmetric laws of physics."

FUNDAMENTAL ISSUES FOR PSI THEORISTS

The fundamental issues that the experience of ESP raises are related to the nature of time, causality, and information. Theorists are thus challenged to address not only the nature of these fundamental concepts but also their apparent violation as seen from a person's point of view—the other view being that of the external information-centric physical world. As the work of Joseph McMoneagle, Dean Radin, and Michael Persinger in Volume I, along with the other extensive work in the psi research literature, indicates, there is more than sufficient evidence for the existence of an information transfer anomaly and the experience of perceiving this information arising from a distant point in spacetime, which is manifested as ESP or precognition. Thus, what appears to be a violation may indeed be normal functioning of the external world, and atypical above-average perceptual abilities of a few.

By "above-average," we do *not* mean "supernormal"; rather, we are referring to the 15% of the population that lies outside one standard deviation from the mean in a normal probability curve. This group of people are usually lost in our tendency in experiments to average data and determine normative ranges for any measure. Each individual exists on this vast continuum of abilities determined by their genetic and environmental makeup, which give rise to individual differences.

Traditionally, psi researchers have viewed psi as a two-stage process. The two-stage model of receptive psi was first articulated by Tyrrell (1946). Stage one, called the *process* in Tyrrell's terminology, is an unconscious process in which the anomalous information is received by the organism. Stage two, called the *product*, is the means by which the anomalous information is transformed into useful information or behavior by the organism (Broughton, 2011). As Tyrrell notes, *"The product of the paranormal cognitive process is not paranormal. . . .* The product of the paranormal cognitive process is always the product of cognitive and other processes which we are not in the habit of calling paranormal" (Tyrrell, 1946, p. 68, italics original). As Broughton states,

> Stage one is the properly anomalous part. How can information from the future travel backwards in time? How can information travel great distances with no carrier medium? . . . Stage two is not anomalous. This stage involves the normal psychological and neurophysiological processes of the human body.

We have formalized this two-stage process into the physics domain and the neuroscience domain in our multiphasic model of precognition.

However, psi is commonly perceived as a unitary experiential event. This focused early research on examining psychological aspects such as personality and beliefs as factors influencing the experience. Thus, early thinking on psi took the individual as a starting point and weaved theories around that perspective.

As we have seen in *The Fundamentals of Psi* (Volume I), the questions raised by psi address both the external world and the world of internal experiences. As Tyrrell did, this leads us to consider psi as a process rather than a unitary event. Theories thus have to address the *process* of psi—a process that incorporates all the fundamental questions raised.

This volume demonstrates that psi researchers from a variety of disciplines have been giving thought to the theory question. This volume is devoted to the exploration of a number of current proposed theories of anomalous cognition that have grown out of the data, modifications of earlier theories, and new thinking on the *how* of ESP, which are also based on advances in the mainstream sciences.

Challenges for Psi Theorists

In Volume I, we presented Joe McMoneagle's transcript of extensive remote viewing (RV) sessions. This task was carried out under the watchful eyes of the Defense Intelligence Agency (DIA) and the Central Intelligence Agency (CIA); however, this particular tasking came from the National Security Council, an advisory body to the president of the United States. This is one of hundreds of sessions that McMoneagle and other remote viewers have undertaken in the classified intelligence operations that are part of the Star Gate program. In operational tasks, the remote viewers, session monitors, and tasking authorities were all blind to the answer. After all, that is why they asked the operations part of Star Gate to help them figure out what and why something was happening—mostly with the former Soviet Union and the Peoples Republic of China during the Cold War. Of course, in laboratory experiments, standard procedures developed in the Star Gate program are used (May, Marwaha, & Chaganti, 2014).

In discussing the challenges faced by psi theorists, we will use this single operational example in Volume 1, which was provide by McMoneagle over many RV sessions, as a prime example of precognition in some part over 100 days into the future. Any complete theory of psi has to be able to account for *how* the reported remote viewing could possibly occur.

In the following section, we will first address the question of the definition of psi and state the fundamental issues that a psi theory needs to address. We address these questions in relation to the four major theoretical perspectives—dualism, psychodynamic, quantum, and classical theoretical models—and the questions that they raise for these approaches.

The Question of Definition

The scientific process, particularly in the human sciences, progresses from the observation of a phenomenon in the natural world of human experiences to defining the phenomenon, experimentation, and theory.

As researchers gain a better understanding of the phenomenon, the definitions evolve in that process. Sometimes, there are phases in which the discipline appears to be in a state of limbo when existing definitions are insufficient to address the data and the work while it is still in progress.

The field of psychology is replete with examples in which commonly accepted terms are wanting in appropriate definitions. The best examples of these are the concept of intelligence (as Edwin Boring pointed out, "intelligence is what intelligence tests measure" [Jensen, 1969, p. 8]), personality (which is defined according to the theory from which it is viewed), and consciousness, for which there still is no consensual definition.

What Arthur Jensen (1969, p. 8) stated regarding the definitional problem of intelligence may well be applicable to that of psi.

> ... the most important fact about intelligence is that we can measure it. Intelligence, like electricity, is easier to measure than to define. And if the measurements bear some systematic relationships to other data, it means we can make meaningful statements about the phenomenon we are measuring. There is no point in arguing the question to which there is no answer, the question of what intelligence really is. The best we can do is to obtain measurements of certain kinds of behavior and look at their relationships to other phenomena and see if these relationships make any kind of sense and order. It is from these orderly relationships that we can gain some understanding of the phenomena.

While there may not be a real "measure" of precognition, the experiences of many and the quantitative and qualitative research data suggest that there is reason enough to consider a continued examination of the phenomenon. For example, when the results of some experiment states that over n trials during which the target stimuli were generated after the data had been secured, positive responses were seen in k trials, amounting to a z-score (in a 1-in-5 circumstance) given by:

$$z = \frac{\mathit{hits} - \mathit{expected\ hits}}{\sqrt{np_0(1 - p_0)}} = \frac{k - p_0 n}{\sqrt{.2 \times .8 \times n}}.$$

where $p_0 = .2$ in a 1-in-5 game.

On their website, the Society for Psychical Research, UK—the oldest psi research organization (est. 1882)—extrasensory perception is defined as an "umbrella term to cover paranormal acquisition of information about persons, events or objects." It defines paranormal as "Phenomenon which is considered impossible according to the established scientific worldview." Further, it defines precognition as "paranormal (non-inferential) knowledge of a future event. If an event is interpreted as a target, then precognition becomes a form of ESP," and psychokinesis as "paranormal influence of the mind of a person upon physical objects."

The Rhine Research Center defines precognition as "knowledge of an event that has not yet occurred, or information that appears to be transferred from the future into the present" and psychokinesis as "mind interacting with matter at a distance."

Myers (2005/1903), who was among the first to use the term "telepathy," defined it as "the communication of impressions of any kind from one mind to another, independently of the recognized channels of sense" (p. 95).

Tyrell (1961, p. 6) provided a definition of ESP of very general scope "to cover all cases in which knowledge of things or events is acquired by a person, in whatever manner, without the use of the ordinary channels of sense-perception of logical inference or of memory." In defining precognition, he states:

> If knowledge is acquired of an event which has not yet happened, but which later happens as foretold; and if this knowledge could not have been obtained by logical inference from present facts, and could not result from an intention to fulfil the prediction, and is of too precise or detailed a character for its fulfilment to be attributed to chance, then the case is said to be one of Precognition. Precognition thus means the *direct* perception of events which have not yet happened. (p. 8)

Charles Tart (2009, p. 131) defines precognition as the "successful prediction of future events when such events couldn't be rationally predicted from knowledge of current conditions and the laws governing their change." Dean Radin (1997, p. 15) defines precognition as "information perceived about future events, where the information could not be inferred by ordinary means."

The definitions discussed so far are mainly from the perspective of the percipient. These circular definitions are not amenable to developing a hypothesis for testing. With these definitions, an experimenter can follow any protocol and consider the resulting observation as that of ESP. As May (2010, p. 3) has commented, the anomalous cognition (AC) definitions mean

> . . . that we define anything that happens when it shouldn't according to the known senses, as AC—a negative definition to be sure. Moreover, this definition has profound implications that are rarely discussed, at least directly, for experiments. It is rather straightforward and relatively inexpensive to design a protocol that meets the

requirement in the above definition. . . . if we cannot think of a "normal" way to account for an observation, then it must have happened by "paranormal" means.

The Star Gate team expanded on these definition by providing some qualifiers and defined precognition as "the acquisition and description, by mental means alone, of information blocked from ordinary perception by distance or shielding and thought to be secure against such access" (Puthoff, Targ, & May, 1977).

Since the 1990s, the Cognitive Sciences Laboratory, at the Laboratories for Fundamental Research, has adopted the term "anomalous mental phenomena" instead of the more widely known "psi." Likewise, they use the terms "anomalous cognition" and "anomalous perturbation" for ESP and PK, respectively. They have done so because they believe that these terms are more naturally descriptive of the observables and are neutral with regard to mechanism. Anomalous cognition (AC) is defined as the perception and cognition of information that is blocked from the usual sensory systems by distance, shielding, or time and that emerges from a distant point in spacetime. In this process, some individuals are able to gain access to information from events outside the range of their senses by a currently not understood mechanism. Several synonyms for this phenomenon are in use: remote viewing (RV), precognition, clairvoyance, and ESP. They define anomalous perturbation (AP) as a form of interaction with matter in which all known physical mechanisms are absent. In other words, some individuals are alleged to be able to influence matter by an as yet unknown process. This phenomenon is also known as psychokinesis (PK).

The new definition, built on earlier definitions, provided in our chapter in this volume titled, "The Multiphasic Model of Precognition," may be an advance in the thinking on psi and aid in developing better protocols, as in providing a framework for understanding the process and hence theory building. The underlying assumption for this definition is that ESP is not a singular event but a process. Thus, an operative definition of precognition has to incorporate a process rather than an event. With this in view, we have defined precognition as *an atypical perceptual ability that allows the acquisition of non-inferential information arising from a future point in spacetime.*

In this definition, "acquisition" refers to the persons-perspective, "information emerging from a future point in spacetime" is information-centric. The nature of the signal and carrier are presently unknown processes and hence are not indicated in the definition. As researchers determine these unknowns, they will be incorporated into the definition, as a normal process of the advancement of a science.

Considering the lacunae in the definitions, how do we know that precognition has occurred? Well thought out experimental protocols determine that. With regard to precognition, the standard protocols used in remote viewing experiments are discussed in May, Marwaha, and Chaganti (2014). In spontaneous real-life situations, only a post hoc analysis can determine whether the apparent psi experience was indeed a precognitive event or synchronous, or normal future thinking based on experience, reason, expectations, motivations, and desires.

Fundamental Issues for Psi Theories

There are four fundamental issues that a psi theory must address. These include:

1. *Causality violation.* From a person-centric view, is it possible that something can happen *before* what caused it to happen happens first?
2. *Information transfer from a distant spacetime point.* How can information transfer backward in time, and what is the carrier of such information?
3. *Perception of information emerging from distant spacetime point.* Considering we do not know the nature of the information carrier, we assume it is something that is not part of the normal human repertoire. In which case, what is the mechanism for the perception of this information carrier?
4. *Individual differences.* Can individual differences account for the presence of psi ability in only a small percent of the population?

The Experience of Psi

The experience of psi—acquiring and processing the information—rests entirely within the neuroscience domain of the percipient. It is not concerned with the nature of time, causality violation, or information transfer which are physics domain problems. There are three approaches that theorists can take in viewing this: a dualist approach, a psychodynamic approach, and a physicalist approach.

The dualist approach to psi is primarily a view from within. An adequate dualist model has to address questions of how information is acquired from the external world and processed. It also has to account for the individual differences in psi ability.

Aside from laying out the process by which a psi perception occurs, a psychodynamic approach, like the dualist approach, has to account for how information from the external world is acquired and processed before being manifested in idiosyncratic ways. Standing on the

foundation of individual differences, it has to account for what contributes to these differences that enable one to be either a psi adept or a psi
inept.

For the physicalist approach, the brain is at the center stage—the region
of activity is entirely in the neuroscience domain. The challenges facing
the physicalist psi theorists are as daunting, or even more so, than those
raised in the physics domain. Theorists taking this approach have to
address the question of how the putative psi signals are perceived, what
is the nature of the transducer that converts the signals that can be processed by the brain, what sensory pathways are involved in processing
these signals, and what is the process by which they are manifested as
coherent responses. What is the nature of the individual differences that
distinguish between those with and without a psi ability? There is sufficient evidence in mainstream cognitive sciences emphasizing individual
differences, which are the sine qua non of biological and psychological
differences.

Based on a review of literature, Whitaker and Selnes (1976, p. 844) concluded that each person's brain may be as individual as his physiognomy.
They cite Gray, who has stated, "No cortex is an exact duplicate of
another, either in the number or size of its convolutions. Indeed, it seems
likely that each roof brain is as individual to its possessor as his face ..."
This is no surprise considering the genetic variability between individuals. Tahmasebi, Davis, Wild, et al. (2012) report on the variability of functional organization relative to brain anatomy. For example, a two- to
threefold interindividual variation in size of the visual cortex is seen in
humans, a variation that could lead to substantial difference in visual ability. Similarly, variations in the number of axons in the optic nerve, the
number of retinal ganglion cells in a single eye, and the density of photoreceptors in the retina is also seen (Andrews, Halpern & Pervis, 1997;
Hofer, Carroll, Neitz, et al., 2005; Wesner, Pokomy, Shevell, & Smith,
1991), including the presence of tetra- or even pentachromacy (Neitz
et al.,1993). Using a battery of tests that included orientation discrimination, wavelength sensitivity, contrast sensitivity, vernier acuity, direction-
of-motion detection, and velocity discrimination, Halpern, Andrews, and
Purves (1999) found that there was significant interindividual differences
in visual ability, which could be the result of interindividual variation in
the amount of neural circuitry devoted to vision.

As Kanai and Rees (2011) observe, "In the neuroscience of human
behavior and cognition, inter-individual differences are often treated as a
source of 'noise' and therefore discarded through averaging data from a
group of participants" (p. 231). Individual differences are seen in grey
matter volume and white matter microstructure. Based on an extensive literature review, they report that due to anatomical variations, interindividual differences are seen in various domains. Aside from experts in specific

areas (musicians, taxi drivers, athletes), interindividual differences are seen in the general normal population in areas such as motor behavior, complex motor tasks, ability to select the correct response in the presence of response conflict, speed, accuracy, and flexibility of decision making. Interindividual variability is also seen in psychophysical thresholds for sensory discrimination, visual acuity threshold, fluctuation in subjective perception while the physical stimulation is constant, variation in subjective awareness of physically identical visual stimuli, visual awareness, synesthetic experiences, metacognitive ability, attentional networks, speed of information processing, and personality.

These variations provide a basis for considering the presence of psi ability as a normal or atypical ability, and the individual differences seen in this ability. Additionally, there are also intraindividual differences, which are influenced by the psychological status, health conditions, environmental disturbances, medication, and so on that may also affect the functional status of an individual at a given point in time, contributing to intraindividual differences in performance on a task in which he or she is proficient.

It is essential to highlight individual differences for two reasons: (1) doing so emphasizes the unique ability of each individual, and (2) this uniqueness and the accompanying abilities, for example musical ability, mathematical ability, artistic abilities, influence performance in experiments. Thus, if we were examining the relation between mathematical skills and abstract reasoning, the research protocol would require that we select a group who has good mathematical ability, instead of picking up random subjects from a general population. The same applies for psi ability. This has a direct bearing on the issue of sample selection and replicability for proof-oriented and process-oriented research in psi.

The Thermodynamic Approach and Psi

The thermodynamic approach to psi is a compelling hypothesis. As we have described in the chapter in this volume titled, "Entropy and Precognition," the second law of thermodynamics—entropy in closed systems can never decrease—informs us that at the macroscopic level (i.e., us, for example), time should and does move in a single direction. All of us are getting older by the second. Another observable is that the quality of AC in general and precognition in particular is proportional to the change of entropy of the target stimuli. Herein resides a clue to understanding how precognition may be possible.

The QM Approach and Precognition

Evan Harris Walker (1973) was among the first to apply quantum theory to the problem of psi. The laboratory data available to him at the time was primarily that of the binary card guessing type, Zener card guessing studies, and later RNG studies. Walker's model is based on the premise that consciousness, which he defined as "conscious experience" (Walker, 1984, p. 281), interacts with the microscopic quantum world to affect changes in it or to glean information from it.

Can RV data be explained by the QM model? Aside from the primary problem of determining how QM formalisms that are applicable to the microscopic world can be used to explain actions and influences in the macroscopic world, the QM models have to address the problem of retro-causation. Additionally, they have to answer the question of how activities taking place in, for instance, a remote region of Russia can be perceived by a viewer sitting in California. Can QM address the question of information transfer? Moreover, if conscious experience (consciousness) is responsible for the stable states in the external world, how do we account for the entire activity of submarine construction by the distant viewer, as seen in Joe McMoneagle's transcript in Volume I? Assuming that conscious experience is influencing the macro world, what is the means by which there is a continuous flow of information propagated to a distant point in space-time? Moreover, considering there are so many people involved in the activity, whose conscious experience is influencing the outcomes of the activities? These are some of the biggest challenges that quantum theorists of psi have to address when considering psi as it occurs in the natural world of spontaneous experiences for which remote viewing is the best approximation.

We have briefly discussed some of the crucial questions that a psi theorist has to address in his or her theory, whatever the approach he or she may choose to follow. In the following section, we provide an overview of the theories discussed in this volume. Each theory contributes much toward understanding different aspects of the psi puzzle, as much as the many more questions that they raise. What is evident from reviewing these models is that a multidisciplinary approach is required to solve this puzzle.

In this volume, we have arranged the chapters opening with models that are strictly in the physics domain, starting with a speculative multidimensional model, quantum theory models, and an entropy-based model. Subsequently, we move to models that address the neuroscience domain, to psychological models, and conclude with a dualist perspective. The concluding chapters in this volume address the challenges for the future of psi research.

THEORIES OF PSI

The theories included in this volume cover the range from physicalist to dualist theories. We start with professor of mathematics and astronomy

Bernard Carr's "Hyper-Dimensions and the Notion of Time: Implications for Psi Phenomena," which lays the foundation for the theories that follow. As Carr states, the invocation of extra dimensions beyond the familiar ones of space and time has a long history and has recently taken center stage in modern physics. The possible existence of these hyperdimensions provide the grounding on which other theories of psi phenomena are built.

In "Physics beyond Causality: Making Sense of Quantum Mechanics and Certain Experimental Anomalies," Richard Shoup discusses the time-honored "law" of cause-and-effect, and its inadequacies in dealing with quantum phenomena and other well-researched experimental phenomena. By replacing forward-only causality with symmetric relations, he arrives at a slightly modified theory that is simpler and less mysterious and that represents all known quantum phenomena in a more understandable structure, does not violate conservation laws, and does not require or invoke fundamental randomness in its explanations. In addition, the theory can serve as a basis for explaining phenomena seen for decades in well-controlled laboratory experiments in parapsychology, including those sometimes incorrectly thought to violate physical law.

Daniel Sheehan's chapter, "Remembrance of Things Future: A Case for Retrocausation and Precognition," revolves around two central axes of a physical theory of precognition: (1) causality and the thermodynamic arrow of time and (2) quantum mechanics. He first examines the experimental evidence for precognition, followed by the basic physics of retrocausation, starting with basic definitions and an examination of the *time-symmetric* nature of physical laws. Next, he considers how reality unfolds in a temporally *asymmetric* way, that is, why time appears to have a direction, an *arrow*. The most important of these is the *thermodynamic arrow*, governed by the second law of thermodynamics, which probably conditions our own perceived (*psychological*) arrow of time. Retrocausation is then examined as it pertains to mainstream quantum theory and experiment. For this, he introduces an interpretation of quantum mechanics that explicitly incorporates retrocausation and then surveys some recent quantum experiments that purport to demonstrate it. Finally, he assess precognition in light of current physics, ending with several questions that may help guide future research.

Brian Millar addresses some of the fundamental questions about the QM based observational theories of psi in the chapter titled, "What You Always Wanted to Know about the Observational Theories." In this chapter, he clarifies what psi is and is not, explains the basics of QM and the measurement problem of QM, and addresses how QM might work in the human world of psi experiments. Further, he discusses the question of experimenter psi and the role of virtuoso, so-so, and psi-challenged experimenters in the outcome of an experiment.

In the chapter titled, "Entropy and Precognition: The Physics Domain of the Multiphasic Model of Precognition," Edwin May and Joseph Depp discuss entropy and its role in the propagation of psi information. Entropy is a measure of randomness. The more random a system is, the higher is its entropy. This chapter goes into the details of how the second law of thermodynamics—an entropy concept—tells us how this happens and why at the macro level (person-perspective) time moves in only one direction. Yet, the data of precognition clearly violate this notion. Based upon the results of the Star Gate program, the quality of anomalous cognition appears to be correlated with and, perhaps, limited by, the gradient of entropy of the target stimuli. This chapter describes in detail the various aspects of these notions and shows the evidence in support of their concepts.

The next set of theories address the experiential domain of the psi problem.

The chapter titled "The Multiphasic Model of Precognition" (MMPC) by Sonali Bhatt Marwaha and Edwin C. May takes on the ambitious task of providing a process-oriented theory for precognition. Conceptually, the model begins in the physics domain at some future point in spacetime, tracks the information, or at least attempts to provide plausibility arguments, from that point to the position of the percipient. Then the MMPC shifts into the brain and *assumes* that whatever the energy transfer mechanism was that brought the information to the central nervous system (CNS), it has been transformed into electrochemical signals that the CNS understands by some unspecified transducer. Once the information is inside the head, the MMPC considers what happens then as taking place in the neuroscience domain. The neuroscience domain addresses the acquisition and interpretation of retrocausal signals across three stages: (1) perception of signals from an information carrier, based upon psychophysical variability in a putative signal transducer; (2) cortical processing of the signals, mediated by a cortical hyperassociative mechanism; and (3) cognition, mediated by normal cognitive processes leading to a apparent precognitive response. Following the detailed description of the model, the authors discuss the testable hypotheses that are generated by each stage of the model, and suggest that the model has the potential for developing a research program based on it.

In the following chapter, Dick Bierman discusses his theory called consciousness induced restoration of time symmetry (CIRTS), which focuses upon "time" rather than "information," although the two are related through the second law of thermodynamics. "Consciousness," as used in this model, is defined as "awareness." Bierman takes seriously the fact that most physical formalisms—for instance, electromagnetic theories—are inherently time symmetric, based on which he proposes that conscious observation does remove part of the constraints that prohibit time symmetry to occur. Additionally, CIRTS seeks to integrate the physical and neuropsychological aspects of paranormal phenomena. CIRTS unifies the phenomena that are known by the terms "telepathy," "clairvoyance," "presentiment," and "precognition." This framework results in straight-forward hypotheses that can easily be tested. Further, the theory gives an account of the difficulty of replicating experimental results and for the decline effects often observed in psi research.

If the mechanism of ESP operation is analogous to normal perception, that is, the percipient senses the target by ESP in some trials while producing only chance guesses in others, then the theory of probability predicts a marked asymmetry between the results of positive-aim and negative-aim sessions in forced-choice ESP experiments. That asymmetry was never found in actuality.

Zoltán Vassy discusses the activational model of ESP in which chance guessing and ESP are combined in the same way in each trial, predicting results in accord with empirical data. The model can be generalized to free-response experiments and spontaneous ESP experiences as well. Conceptually, the activational model is straightforward and is based upon results from neuroscience with regard to decision making in choosing one option from a few competing options. There are accumulators in the brain, one each for each decision option, and they compete with each other by their levels of activation and cross-accumulator inhibitions signals. The model appears to break new ground in the neuroscience domain even though it considers only forced-choice data, and it is sometimes algebraically complex.

The question of experimenter-mediated psi has been plaguing the field of psi research since the 1970s. If experimental results use statistical inference to come to some conclusion, then what that actually means is that the observed effect occurs both in the effort condition and the control condition only less often than in the effort condition. Given that it happens at all in the control condition implies that the putative effect is also, at least, part of the normal variation of the system under study. In the chapter titled, "Experimenter Psi: A View of Decision Augmentation Theory," Edwin May discusses this tested heuristic model by first discussing the psi-meditated instrumental response model of Rex Stanford of which the decision augmentation theory (DAT) is a mathematical extension. DAT essentially addresses this question, is there a micro-PK force per bit? This is followed by a discussion on the applications of DAT.

Walter von Lucadou's chapter titled, "Model of Pragmatic Information" (MPI) is a general psychological model of psi phenomena including both ESP and micro- and macro-PK, based on the quantum metaphor. The model draws from synchronicity theory initiated by C. G. Jung and W. Pauli and interprets psi phenomena not as a result of any causal influence of mind on matter or other minds, but as "meaningful coincidences" as correlations not produced by causal interaction of the kind physicists know and apply successfully, but mediated by correspondences of sense and meaning. The MPI starts from a system-theoretic viewpoint and uses concepts drawn from generalized quantum theory (GQT). The GQT had its origin in what was called weak quantum theory (Atmanspacher, Römer, & Walach, 2002), which relaxed many of the underlying requirements imposed by quantum mechanics to sharpen the often vague and metaphoric usage of originally quantum theoretical terms such as complementarity and entanglement in fields of knowledge differing from physics and to apply such concepts to the human sciences.

In the chapter titled, "First Sight: A Way of Thinking about the Mind, and a Theory of Psi," James Carpenter presents a psychological theory of psi. As a psychological theory, it attempts to account for what psi means and how it works, and how it fits in with all the rest of what we currently know about our psychological functioning. It proposes an answer to the question of what psi is for in our everyday lives. The first sight theory proposes a structure for organizing and understanding what we have already found, and gives guidance for what sorts of questions are likely to be most fruitful in the future. In this chapter, Carpenter offers guidance for a comprehensive and integrative program of research.

There is considerable discussion amongst psi researchers concerning the degree to which physicalism/materialism can eventually provide a comprehensive, testable model of psi. The counterargument is, of course, it will not be sufficient, and, therefore, requires deeper insight into the nature of dualism (i.e., generally thought of as mind not equal to brain). In philosophy, there are many subdivisions within each of the views, which make it quite confusing for those not trained in the formal discipline of philosophy. In his chapter titled, "Anomalous Cognition and Mind-Body Dualism," David Rousseau informs us that the simplistic arguments such as those stated above are woefully lacking and thus first provides an overview of the various "isms" to enable us to understand them so that we can have an informed dialogue about the issues concerned. Following this, he addresses how dualism (some form of it) can address the nature of anomalous cognition. Surprisingly, Rousseau argues that the nature of ESP does *not* threaten physicalism, nor does it provide support for the mind-body dualism as is often claimed by psi researchers. He discusses the critical questions we have raised in the context of dualism and provides his own framework for a dualist approach in AC research.

In considering the future of psi research, we first bring to you the 1975 presidential address for the Parapsychological Association annual meeting in Santa Barbara, given by the late Charles Honorton. Some of the issues he discusses include the normalization of psi research and the questions of replication that are as relevant today as they were

40 years ago. In reading his chapter, one gets an idea of what has changed, what has not changed, and what needs to change in psi research.

We conclude this volume by examining the future directions for psi experimenters in the chapter titled, "Next Step: Process-Oriented Research: Guidelines for Experimenters." In this chapter, we identify the classes of experiments that we no longer need to conduct for proof-of principle. We emphasize the need for process-oriented research, suggest research questions for experimenters, and provide a guideline for developing a research program.

As you read these volumes, we hope that it gives you a greater understanding of the science of psi.

REFERENCES

Andrews, T. J., Halpern, S. D., & Purves, D. (1997). Correlated size variations in human visual cortex, lateral geniculate nucleus, and optic tract. *Journal of Neuroscience, 17*(8), 2859–2868.

Atmanspacher, H., Römer, H., & Walach, H. (2002). Weak quantum theory: Complementarity and entanglement in physics and beyond. *Foundations of Physics, 32*, 379–406. http://arxiv.org/abs/quant-ph/0104109

Broughton, R. (2011). An evolutionary approach to anomalous intuition. *8th Symposium of the Bial Foundation: Behind and Beyond the Brain: Intuition and Decision-making, –Porto, Portugal, April 7–10, 2010.* Porto, Portugal: Fundação Bial.

Halpern, S. D., Andrews, T. J., & Purves, D. (1999). Interindividual variation in human visual performance. *Journal of Cognitive Neuroscience, 11*(5), 521–534.

Hofer, H., Carroll, J., Neitz, J., Neitz, M., & Williams, D. R. (2005). Organization of the human trichromatic cone mosaic. *Journal of Neuroscience, 25*(42), 9669–9679.

Jensen, A. R. (1969). How much can we boost IQ and scholastic achievement? *Harvard Educational Review, 39*(1), 1–123. http://eric.ed.gov/?id=EJ008537.

Kanai, R., & Rees, G. (2011). The structural basis of inter-individual differences in human behaviour and cognition. *Nature Reviews Neuroscience, 12*(4), 231–242.

May, E. C. (2010). Guest Editorial: Technical challenges for the way forward. *Journal of Parapsychology, 74*(2), 2–11.

May, E. C., Marwaha, S. B., & Chaganti, V. (2014). Anomalous cognition: Two protocols for data collection and analyses. In E. C. May & S. B. Marwaha (Eds.), *Anomalous cognition: Remote viewing research and theory,* pp. 18–37. Jefferson, NC: McFarland.

Myers, F. W. H., & Smith, S. (2005). *Human personality and its survival of bodily death.* Mineola, N.Y: Dover Publications.

Neitz, J., Neitz, M., & Jacobs, G. H. (1993). More than three different cone pigments among people with normal color vision. *Vision Research, 33*(1), 117–122.

Puthoff, H., Targ, R., & May, E. C. (1977). *Advanced Threat Technique Assessment,* Final Report Project 7403. Menlo Park, CA: SRI International.

Radin, D. I. (1997). *The conscious universe: The scientific truth of psychic phenomena.* New York: HarperEdge.

Sagan, C. (1995, January–February). Wonder and skepticism. *Skeptical Enquirer, 19*(1). www.csicop.org/si/show/wonder_and_skepticism/

Tahmasebi, A. M., Davis, M. H., Wild, C. J., Rodd, J. M., Hakyemez, H., Abolmae-sumi, P., & Johnsrude, I. S. (2012). Is the link between anatomical structure and function equally strong at all cognitive levels of processing? *Cerebral Cortex, 22*(7), 1593–1603.

Tart, C. T. (2009). *The end of materialism: How evidence of the paranormal is bringing science and spirit together.* Oakland, CA: Noetic Books, Institute of Noetic Sciences.

Tyrrell, G. N. M. (1946). The modus operandi of paranormal cognition. *Proceedings of the Society for Psychical Research, 48*(173), 65–120.

Tyrrell, G. N. M. (1961). *Science and psychical phenomena: Apparitions.* New Hyde Park, NY: University Books.

Walker, E. H. (1973). Application of the quantum theory of consciousness to the problem of psi phenomena. In W. G. Roll, R. L. Morris, & J. D. Morris (Eds.), *Research in parapsychology, 1972* (pp. 51–53). Metuchen, NJ: Scarecrow.

Walker, E. H. (1984). A review of criticisms of the quantum mechanical theory of psi phenomena. *Journal of Parapsychology, 48*(4), 277–332.

Wesner, M. F., Pokorny, J., Shevell, S. K., & Smith, V. C. (1991, January 1). Foveal cone detection statistics in color-normals and dichromats. *Vision Research, 31*(6), 1021–1037.

Whitaker, H. A., & Selnes, O. A. (1976). Anatomic variations in the cortex: Individual differences and the problem of the localization of language functions. *Annals of the New York Academy of Sciences, 280,* 844–854.

Part I

Theories of Psi

Chapter 2

Higher Dimensions of Space and Time and Their Implications for Psi

Bernard Carr

Science assumes that the world is governed by natural laws, so psychical research can become acceptable to the rest of the scientific community only if psi is also subject to such laws. Another essential feature of science is that it must involve some *theory* to explain the observations, which is why understanding the properties of psi is more important than just accumulating statistical proof of its existence. As Henry Margenau (1985, p. 120) has urged:

> No amount of empirical evidence, no mere collection of facts, will convince all scientists of the veracity and the significance of your reports. You must provide some sort of model: you must advance bold constructs. . . . in terms of which ESP can be theoretically understood.

Since there are many branches of science (psychology, neuroscience, biology, chemistry, physics), there can be different levels of theory. However, according to *reductionism*, these branches form a hierarchy with physics at the base, thereby providing a "bottom-up" explanation of the world. This implies that physics is the most *fundamental* branch of science, so it is particularly important to have a physical theory of psi.

This would be good not only for psychical research but also for physics. For the history of physics is full of the inexplicable becoming explicable and—even though rare anomalous phenomena are often received skeptically at first—studying them has nearly always led to useful insights. Indeed, one reason physicists figured so prominently among early psychical researchers was that they saw in the phenomena evidence for some new type of physics (Noakes, 2004).

But how feasible is it that physics can accommodate psi, and are all forms of psi amenable to a reductionist brain-based explanation, or do some "rogue" phenomena suggest that the physics required is not of the usual materialist kind (Kelly et al., 2006)? Physics in its *classical* mechanistic form cannot even explain the *normal* mental phenomena because there is a basic incompatibility between the localized features of mechanism and the unity of conscious experience (James, 1890). However, the classical picture has now been replaced by a more holistic *quantum* one, and some people have argued that this *can* include consciousness. Indeed, E. H. Walker (1984, p. 26) has argued that *only* quantum theory can explain psi:

> This must lie at the heart of the solution to the problem of psi phenomena; and indeed an understanding of psi phenomena and of consciousness must provide the basis of an improved understanding of quantum mechanics.

Certainly, quantum effects such as entanglement, nonlocality, and zero-point fluctuations are often invoked to explain psi, with observational theory (discussed by Brian Millar in this volume) having many advocates.

Unfortunately, the attempt to extend physics to accommodate psi engenders antipathy from both physicists (who are skeptical of its reality) and psychical researchers (who are generally wary of attempts to explain it in physicalistic terms). An important factor in both these antipathies is the status of reductionism. Physicists see psi as a threat *to* reductionism, while psychical researchers see physicalistic explanations of it as a threat *from* reductionism. However, I believe that this antipathy is misconceived and that a new paradigm—involving a radically different sort of physics (which I term "hyperphysics")—may eventually reconcile psi and physics and shed light on both of them.

The plan of the rest of this chapter is as follows. I will first give a brief overview of the general attempts to link psi and physics, commenting briefly on the transmission and quantum models. Thereafter, I will focus exclusively on models that invoke higher dimensions. After reviewing the history of the topic, I describe my own theory, which involves a higher dimensional model of perception, focusing first on its application to ordinary physical percepts and then extending the discussion to nonphysical ones. The theory was first described some time ago (Carr, 2008) but this is its most up-to-date exposition. Finally, I highlight some general issues raised by the hyperspatial approach.

CONNECTING PSI AND PHYSICS: GENERAL CONSIDERATIONS

In deciding whether psi can connect with physics, we first need to decide which class of phenomena we are trying to explain, since some clearly present a greater challenge to theorists than others. This raises the question of whether there are different *levels* of psi, requiring increasing modifications to physics. For example, one might assume that macro-PK poses more of a challenge than micro-PK because more energy is involved; and that precognition is more problematic than clairvoyance, and retro-PK more problematic than PK, because they involve time as well as space displacement. There is also the question of whether mind-mind interactions (such as telepathy) are fundamentally distinct from mind-matter interactions (such as PK) or whether they are aspects of a single unitary phenomenon (Roe et al., 2003; Thalbourne, 2004).

Most physicists interested in psi would probably agree that one should try to obtain as unified a description of psychic phenomena as possible, without invoking a new feature of physics for each one. Indeed, the introduction of the single term "psi" (although loosely defined) might be thought to anticipate that. In particular, it is important to have a unified description of psi as it appears in the laboratory and in the field. For example, there has been a large amount of laboratory work on micro-PK (the influence of psi on a system that is intrinsically probabilistic), with associated theoretical attempts to explain this in terms of quantum effects. However, there has been rather little attempt to apply these models to the much more dramatic macro-PK manifestations that arise in (say) poltergeists cases. Indeed, some theorists seem to accept micro-PK but remain skeptical of macro-PK, although one might hope that these phenomena are two extreme forms of a single psychokinetic interaction.

A similar dichotomy arises when we consider ESP. In laboratory experiments, we do not usually know which "hits" are due to chance and which are due to psi—indeed, some theorists have argued that no transmission of information need be involved at all (Lucadou, 1995). However, it is unclear whether such a model can be extended to some real-life situations (e.g., crisis apparitions), in which genuine information seems to be conveyed (see Lucadou's chapter in this volume). Likewise, one might hope that presentiment effects observed in the laboratory (Bierman & Radin, 1997; Spottiswoode & May, 2003), involving time displacements of a fraction of a second, somehow relate to spontaneous premonitions involving much larger displacements. Since the study of laboratory psi was prompted by observations in the field, it seems unsatisfactory to reject the latter and explain only the former.

Next, one needs to decide which psi process is most *fundamental*, and there are differing views on this. Supporters of observational theory would argue that all psi could be explained in terms of observation-induced collapse of the quantum wave function (which might be regarded as PK). On the other hand, proponents of decision augmentation theory (DAT) attribute psi to precognition (May et al., 2014/1995a,b), as do some models relating psi to neuronal patterns in the brain (Taylor, 2007). There is a similar controversy over the relative roles of clairvoyance and telepathy in ESP. At one extreme, it has been argued that clairvoyance is the primary phenomenon, with telepathy being attributed to clairvoyant scanning of the agent's brain-state. At the other extreme, it has been proposed that telepathy is primary, with clairvoyance being explained in terms of (precognitive) telepathy with the future state of the mind of the person who confirms the target.

It is important to distinguish physical *theories* of psi from physical *dependencies* of psi or physical *consequences* of psi. As regards the dependencies, various physical influences have been claimed to modify the efficacy of psi—for example, geomagnetic effects (Persinger, 1985; Wilkinson & Gauld, 1993) or local sidereal time (see Ryan & Spottiswoode in Vol. I of this work). However, this may just reflect the sensitivity of the psychic organ (possibly some part of the brain) to such influences and may have nothing to do with the mechanism of psi. On the other hand, geomagnetic effects could still be relevant to the mechanism if one attributed psi to extremely low-frequency radio waves (Irwin & Watt, 2006).. Sometimes, as with the claim that sound of a particular frequency can produce apparitions (Tandy, 2002), it is not clear whether the physical effect is triggering psi or some nonpsychic process (like a hallucination). As regards the consequences of psi, ESP may trigger various physical reactions in a subject—such as an electrodermal response—even if this is not recognized consciously. But again, this may have nothing to do with the mechanism of psi.

On the other hand, some physical features of psi clearly have important implications for its nature. For example, it has been argued that the presentiment effect may reflect some form of time-symmetry effect (Bierman, 2010), and a similar idea arises in attempts to link precognition (precall) with memory (recall). This touches on a profound puzzle: Even though our conscious experience of the world entails a time asymmetry, all the equations of physics are time symmetric. In particular, the solutions of wave equations may involve both "retarded" and "advanced" parts (corresponding to propagation along the future and past light cones, respectively). Although the latter are usually rejected as being acausal (in the sense that they would allow the present to affect the past and the future to affect the present), nothing in known physics precludes them. What is particularly exciting is that quantum experiments now provide a possible way of searching for them (Cramer, 2006). If retrocausal effects were demonstrated, it could have profound implications for psi.

Another interesting issue arises in the context of the sort of micro-PK experiments carried out by the PEAR group (Jahn & Dunne, 1987). It is usually assumed that micro-PK operates by shifting the mean of a supposedly random distribution, and this seems to be indicated by at least some meta-analyses (Radin & Nelson, 2002; Dobyns et al., 2004). On the other hand, Fotini Pallikari (1998) suggests that—over sufficiently long runs (including control periods)—there is no shift in the mean but merely a "gluing" effect, whereby micro-PK enhances the clustering of both hits and misses. She claims to find evidence for this "balance effect" from a fractal analysis of existing data (Pallikari, 2001). A subsequent meta-analysis (Bosch et al., 2006) also gives no shift in the mean, although this has been disputed (Radin et al., 2006). Pallikari's claim is controversial but if confirmed, it would imply that micro-PK is not simply a force. In this case, macro-PK is either spurious or has a completely different explanation (despite the desirability of a unified model). For example, the sort of rotating force field invoked in metal-bending (Hasted, 1981) and recurrent spontaneous psychokinesis (RSPK) outbreaks (Roll et al., 1973) can have nothing to do with this.

It should be stressed that the balance effect does not constitute a full theory of psi, since it does not explain how the interaction with consciousness actually arises. The same criticism could be levelled at many other purported theories of psi. This emphasizes that there are different *levels* of explanation. In particular, one must distinguish between physical and psychological levels of explanation. For example, there has been much interest in whether sensory models (Irwin, 1979) or memory models (Roll, 1966) best explain ESP and in the psi-mediated instrumental response model (Stanford, 1974) or first sight model (Carpenter, 2004). Psi researchers are also interested in identifying the personality characteristics of subjects who score highly in laboratory experiments. However, none of this may have any bearing on the more fundamental question of how ESP works from a physics perspective. Sometimes, of course, it is not clear whether a feature is physical or psychological. For example, does the decline effect reflect the fact that subjects get bored, or does it relate to the balance effect (Pallikari, 2003)?

Finally, in producing a physical theory of psi, we need to decide whether we are demanding a new paradigm of physics or merely tinkering with the current one. It is natural to start by trying the second (less radical) approach, and there are many reviews of "tinkering" models (Rush, 1986; Stokes, 1997; Dobyns, 2000; Beichler, 2001). However, the danger is that one will end up grafting so many extra bits onto the old paradigm (like adding epicycles to the Ptolemaic model of the Solar System) that it becomes hopelessly complicated. There is also the problem of *testability*. There are actually many models for psi, and by adding enough bits to the standard paradigm, one can doubtless explain anything. However, a crucial requirement of a scientific theory is that it should be *falsifiable* (Popper, 1959) and, as emphasized by Stokes (1991), many paraphysical theories are inadequate in this respect.

It is useful to group the physical theories of psi into three general categories: field or signaling models, quantum models, and higher-dimensional models. Most of the focus of this chapter will be on the third approach, but I will complete this section by considering the first two. A more comprehensive discussion of some of the theories in these two categories is provided by Rush (1986) and Stokes (1997).

Field or Signaling Models

Many physical theories of psi can be viewed as "signaling" models, in the sense that they involve the transmission of information or energy via some sort of particle or field (these concepts being linked in modern physics). Often, the field involved is already part of the current paradigm. This includes, for example, explaining ESP in terms of electromagnetic waves (Sinclair, 1930; Vasiliev, 1976; Kogan, 1968; Taylor, 1975; Persinger, 1975, 1979; Becker, 1992) or neutrinos (Ruderfer, 1980). It also includes explaining PK in terms of electrostatic forces (Lucas & Maresca, 1976; Roll, 2003).

One serious criticism of all these models is that our bodies have no obvious transmission or reception organs (Braude, 1979a). If psi works like a mental radio, there is also the problem of encoding and decoding the signal (Beloff, 1980). Indeed, the claim that psi does not attenuate with distance (while questionable) may be incompatible with any information-theory approach (Frieden, 1998), an argument made forcefully by John Palmer (1978, p. 77):

> Generally speaking, the experimental evidence indicates that ESP can occur at great distances and does not decline with distance. These findings do not fit well with most hypotheses that physical energies mediate the transmission of extrasensory information. Indeed, the information transmission model may itself be erroneous.

However, as discussed later in this chapter, even if signaling models cannot work in four dimensions, they may still be viable in higher dimensions, since the viewer and the viewed may become contiguous in the higher-dimensional space. The multiphasic model of precognition discussed later in this book incorporates hyperdimensional space in its theoretical premise.

Quantum Models

Quantum theory provides some scope for an interaction of consciousness with the physical world, and it also completely demolishes our normal concepts of physical reality, so it is not surprising that some paraphysicists have invoked it to explain psi. For example, Jahn (1982) argues that consciousness has two complementary aspects: one particle-like (localized) and the other wave-like (nonlocalized).

The most concrete realization of the quantum approach is the observational theory, according to which consciousness not only collapses the wave function but also introduces a bias in how it collapses (Walker, 2000). In this picture, all psi is interpreted as a form of PK, which results from the process of observation itself (i.e., there must be some kind of feedback). Observational theory has the virtue that it can make *quantitative* predictions. For example, one can estimate the magnitude of PK effects on the basis that the brain has a certain information output (Mattuck, 1977, 1984), and the results seem comparable with what is observed in macro-PK effects. On the other hand, observational theory also faces serious criticisms. One can object on the grounds that psi sometimes occurs without any feedback. For example, John Beloff (1988) has pointed out that there are pure clairvoyance experiments in which only a computer ever knows the target. One can also question the logical coherence of explaining psi merely on the grounds that one observes it (Braude, 1979b). Finally, David Bohm (1986) has cautioned that the conditions in which quantum mechanics apply (low temperatures or microscopic scales) are very different from those relevant to the brain.

Nevertheless, many physicists interested in psi back some form of quantum approach (Oteri, 1975; Costa de Beauregard, 1979; Jahn & Dunne, 1987). Some proposals exploit the nonlocality of quantum theory, as illustrated by the famous Einstein-Podolsky-Rosen (EPR) paradox. An atom decays into two particles, which go in opposite directions and must have opposite (but undetermined) spins. If at some later time one measures the spin of one of the particles, the other particle is forced instantaneously into the opposite spin-state, even though this violates causality. This nonlocality effect is described as "entanglement," and Bohm (1951) tried to explain this in terms of hidden variables, which he invoked as a way of rendering quantum theory deterministic. Experiments later confirmed the nonlocality prediction (Aspect et al., 1982) and thereby excluded at least a large class of models involving hidden variables.

Dean Radin (2006) has argued that entanglement is fundamental to psi. This is because he regards elementary-particle entanglement, bio-entanglement (neurons), sentient-entanglement (consciousness), psycho-entanglement (psi), and socio-entanglement (global mind) as forming a continuum, even though there is an explanatory gap (and skeptics might argue an evidential gap) after the second step. If the Universe were fully entangled like this, he argues, we might occasionally feel connected to others at a distance and know things without use of the ordinary senses. This idea really goes back to Bohm (1980), who argued that there is a holistic element in the Universe, with everything being interconnected in an implicate order, which underlies the explicit structure of the world. This implicit order is perhaps mediated by psi (Pratt, 1997). Most mainstream physicists regard such ideas as an unwarranted extension of standard quantum theory, but one clearly needs some sort of extension if one wants to incorporate mind into physics.

Although quantum entanglement has now been experimentally verified up to the scale of macroscopic molecules, it must be stressed that it is not supposed to allow the transmission of *information* (i.e., no signal is involved). For example, attributing remote viewing to this effect would violate orthodox quantum theory. Theorists have reacted to this in two ways. Some have tried to identify what changes are necessary in quantum theory to allow nonlocal signaling (Valentini, 1991). For example, Brian Josephson and Pallikari-Viras (1991) have a model in which entanglement can be utilized biologically. Others accept that there is no signaling but invoke a "generalized" quantum theory (Atmanspacher et al., 2002) that exploits entanglement to explain psi acausally. This is also a feature of Lucadou's model of pragmatic information (see this volume), which interprets psi effects as meaningful nonlocal correlations between a person and a target system. Lucadou claims that this model accounts for many of the observed features of psi, including the difficulty of replicating psi under laboratory conditions.

There are various other quantum-related approaches to explaining psi. Some of these exploit the effects of "zero point fluctuations" (Puthoff, 1989) or "vacuum energy" (Laszlo, 1993). This is a perfectly respectable physical notion, with many tested physical predictions, so it is not surprising that some people have tried to relate it to the traditional metaphysical notion that there is some ubiquitous energy field (*chi, qi, prāṇa, élan vital,* etc.) that connects living beings. Hal Puthoff (2007) has recently assessed the possibility that vacuum fluctuations might offer some synthesis of physical and paraphysical phenomena. He views the zero point energy sea as "a blank matrix upon which coherent patterns can be written," such information corresponding to particles and fields at one extreme and living structures and memory at the other extreme.

Although these ideas might be regarded as being on the fringe of the standard paradigm, the recent discovery that 70% of the mass of the Universe is in the form of "dark energy"—most naturally identified with vacuum energy—is stimulating interest in this sort of approach. For example, Jack Sarfatti (2006) regards both consciousness and gravity as emerging from the vacuum fluctuations associated with dark energy. Others invoke "subtle energy fields," which allegedly involve some form of unified energy of such low intensity that it cannot be measured directly (Tiller, 1993). A generalization of this idea relates subtle energy fields with the radiation associated with zero point energy (Srinivasan, 1988).

Although quantum theory is likely to play some role in a physical model for psi, my own view is that a full explanation of psi will require a paradigm that goes beyond it. Of course, nobody understands quantum theory anyway, so claiming that it explains psi is not particularly elucidating—it just replaces one mystery with another one. Also, many of the aforementioned proposals already deviate from standard quantum theory, so this raises the question of how radical a deviation is required to qualify as a new paradigm. In my view, none of those mentioned above is sufficiently radical, and one needs a new approach—perhaps of the kind envisaged by Bohm—that can explain *both* psi and quantum theory.

HYPERSPATIAL APPROACH

A key ingredient of the unification proposed in this chapter is the invocation of extra dimensions beyond the familiar ones of space and time. This notion has a long history but only recently has it taken center stage in modern physics. Physicists no longer adopt the simplistic view that space is three-dimensional (as posited by Newton) or even four-dimensional (as posited by Einstein). A unified understanding of the forces that operate in the Universe suggests that there are extra "internal" dimensions, which are either wrapped up so small that they cannot be seen or geometrically warped so that normal matter cannot access them.

Although this proposal is supposed to explain certain aspects of the physical world, the key idea of this chapter is that mental experiences may also involve some form of higher-dimensional space and that this space may relate to the one of physics. The argument is most easily understood in the context of ordinary physical perception, where there has been a long-standing philosophical debate over the relationship between phenomenal space (in which percepts reside) and physical space (in which objects reside). The reductionist view is that phenomenal space is just an internal reflection of physical space, with no intrinsic reality. However, the view advocated here is that the phenomenal world (or at least its geometrical aspects) and material world are merely different cross-sections of a five-dimensional structure. I then argue that other types of mental experiences also involve such a space and possibly one of more than five dimensions. The higher-dimensional reality structure is called the

Universal Structure, and it combines aspects of (external) physicality and (internal) mentality.

This proposal implies that percepts of the physical world are no longer unique in representing an external reality. The idea of higher levels of reality is hardly new. It features prominently in ancient occult traditions and, from a modern perspective, in the work of the many people reviewed in this chapter. What *is* new is the greater mathematical sophistication that can be brought to bear on the proposal from modern physics. Although the higher-dimensional paradigm is still in a fairly primitive form, I regard it as offering the best hope of linking matter and mind in a single mathematical structure. Of course, such speculations are not mainstream, and most of my physics colleagues—even those sympathetic to incorporating mentality into physics—would be uncomfortable with the notion that extra dimensions have any connection with consciousness. Nor has this idea been widely welcomed by psi researchers, many of whom are opposed to any physicalistic approach. On the other hand, the idea has at least some prominent supporters in the field. Ian Stevenson was "convinced that a further understanding of the existence of two spaces, or perhaps multiple spaces, is necessary for the solution of many problems in parapsychology," while Michael Whiteman professed that "everything hinges for me on the admission of other spaces" (Poynton, 2011).

An Overview of Previous Hyperspatial Approaches

The space perceived by our ordinary physical senses appears to be three-dimensional (3D) in the sense that it extends in three mutually perpendicular directions. This means that points can be identified by three coordinates, with the distance between them being given by Pythagoras's theorem. This 3D space provided the arena for Newtonian dynamics and was the basis of classical physics for 250 years. Events can also be assigned a time coordinate, but time is absolute in a Newtonian model, in the sense that it flows at the same rate for everybody, so the time and spatial coordinates of an event are independent.

The notion that there could be extra dimensions that are not revealed by our physical sensory systems—that ordinary physical reality could be a pale reflection of some deeper higher-dimensional reality—might be said to go all the way back to the parable of Plato's cave. Observers in the cave see only the 2D shadow of objects, projected on the wall by a fire behind them, and so mistake shadows for real objects. This proposal was met with derision by Plato's contemporary, Aristotle, but provides a powerful metaphor for modern-day arguments that reality may be more than meets the eye. The idea that there could literally be a fourth dimension (in some sense perpendicular to the other three dimensions) seems to have first come from Henry More. His 1671 book *Enchiridion Metaphysicum* associated spirits with the extra dimension, although his contemporary John Wallis regarded this suggestion as unimaginable, "a monster in nature, and less possible than a chimera or centaur."

In the following few centuries, mathematicians began to consider the implications of a fourth dimension more rigorously. In 1754, Jean d'Alembert considered the possibility that time is a fourth dimension, thereby anticipating Einstein by 150 years. In his 1773 book *Prolegomena to any Future Metaphysics*, Immanuel Kant considered how the handedness of a 3D object in 4D space would depend on which side it is viewed from in the fourth dimension. This idea was taken further in 1827 when August Möbius contemplated transforming 3D objects into their mirror image by turning them over in a fourth dimension. In 1846, Gustav Fechner speculated about the effect of the encounter of a 3D being on 2D "shadow men." In 1854, the notion that 3D space could be curved in some higher-dimensional space, so that the separation between points deviates from the Pythagoras expression, was explored by Bernhard Riemann and later by many others.

The occult applications of an extra dimension resurfaced in 1880 when the astronomer Johann Zöllner invoked a fourth dimension in *Transcendental Physics* to explain some of the spiritualistic phenomena associated with the American medium Henry Slade. For example, Slade's spirits allegedly tied knots in cords whose ends were sealed together, and this should be impossible in ordinary 3D space. The implications of an extra dimension were explored further in 1884 (by analogy) when Edwin Abbott described the effects of a third dimension on the inhabitants of a 2D world in his book *Flatland.* He showed how the intersection of a 3D body with a 2D world would generate anomalies for its inhabitants reminiscent of spiritualistic phenomena. So the notion that such phenomena might arise in a 3D world as a result of interactions from a fourth dimension (as in Zöllner's proposal) seemed natural. Indeed, the period from 1890 to 1905 was a golden age for the fourth dimension, and the notion that spirits (or even God!) resided there became particularly fashionable.

Everything changed in 1905 when Einstein showed that a fourth dimension really does exist but that it is not appropriate for the more exotic purposes envisaged in the pre-relativistic period. Nevertheless, I will now describe how the invocation of extra dimensions in physics and philosophy over the past century has led to a renewed interest in the link between mind and higher dimensions and put the hyperspatial model of psi on a more rigorous footing.

Einstein's theory of special relativity showed that space and time measurements are not absolute but depend on the velocity of the observer and transform in such a way that the speed of light is the same for everyone. A few years later, Minkowski interpreted this to mean that space and time are amalgamated into four-dimensional (4D) "spacetime," with time

playing the role of the fourth dimension and material objects corresponding to "world lines." This means that the 4D distance between two events
resembles the Pythagoras formula except that the time component has a
negative sign (the time coordinate being imaginary). As illustrated in Figure 2.1(a), with two spatial dimensions suppressed, different observers
have different time and space axes, but they all agree on the speed of light,
since photons travel at 45 degrees. In a 3D representation (with one spatial
dimension suppressed), a crucial role is played by the light cone, as illustrated in Figure 2.1(b). We observe events only on our past light cone, all
points on this surface having zero 4D distance from us. While all observers agree that events within the future or past light cone are in the future
or past, respectively, they disagree on the order of events in the "elsewhere" region because there is no absolute present.

In 1915, Einstein's theory of general relativity showed that spacetime is
curved by the presence of matter (i.e., the 4D distance no longer has the
Minkowski form). One can envisage spacetime as a curved surface
embedded in a Euclidean space with yet more dimensions. This explains
the origin of gravity geometrically and describes how objects move in a
gravitational field.

The idea that there could be an extra *spatial* dimension—a fifth physical
dimension—was introduced in 1919 by Theodor Kaluza in an attempt
to provide a geometrical explanation of electromagnetic interactions
analogous to the geometrical explanation of gravitation provided by general relativity. In 1926, Oskar Klein added a further ingredient by suggesting that the fifth dimension is wrapped up on the Planck length of
10^{-33} cm. This is too small to observe, but its existence neatly explains

Figure 2.1
**The amalgamation of space and time into 4D spacetime (a) and the light-cone
structure in special relativity (b)**

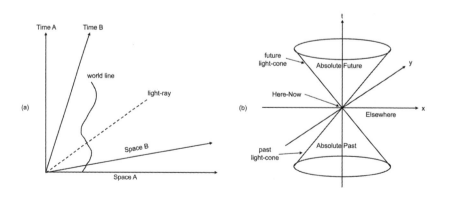

Figure 2.2
The construction of a 3D reality structure (a) and a 4D reality structure (b) for physical percepts and its extension to a reality structure with D dimensions for nonphysical percepts (c).

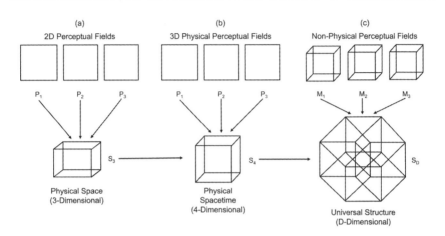

the quantization of the electric charge. Despite the attractions of this idea, it was forgotten by mainstream physics for the next 60 years.

Nevertheless, it was during this period that the notion of higher dimensions was explored by philosophers in an attempt to understand the relationship between the physical space of objects and the phenomenal (experienced) space of percepts. That these spaces are ontologically different was first stressed by Freddie Ayer (1940) and Bertrand Russell (1948), and perceptual psychologists now routinely study the geometry of phenomenal space. More radically, C. D. Broad (1923) suggested that these two spaces could be merged into a single space of more than three dimensions in which sensations of all kinds exist. H. H. Price (1953) also took this view and envisaged these two spaces as causally related parallel universes. The notion that phenomenal space should be afforded equal status to physical space was taken further by John Smythies (1956), who explored the relationship between these spaces implied by recent developments in neurology and introspectionist psychology. He argued that physical and phenomenal spacetime should be regarded as different cross-sections of a single higher dimensional space, an idea developed subsequently in various works. (Hart, 1965; Dobbs, 1965; Smythies, 1988, 1994, 2003, 2012). This proposal relates to my own approach and is discussed in more detail later.

The role of higher dimensions in physics changed dramatically in the 1980s when it was realized that all interactions between elementary particles can be accounted for by invoking further wrapped-up dimensions.

In these modern versions of Kaluza-Klein theory, one distinguishes between the 4D "external" space and some higher-dimensional "internal" space. The number of internal dimensions depends on the model. In "superstring" theory—which became very topical in 1984—the total number of dimensions is 10, so one has a 4D external space and a 6D internal space. There were originally five different versions of superstring theory, but then Ed Witten (1995) suggested that all of these are part of a more embracing 11D picture called *M-theory*. Nina Arkani-Hamed et al. (1998) proposed a variant of this model in which some of the extra dimensions are extended rather than compactified. In a later version of this idea, with just one extended dimension, proposed by Lisa Randall and Raman Sundrum (1999), the physical world can be regarded as a 4D "brane" in a 5D "bulk," confinement to the brane being ensured by warpage of the 5D geometry. The sequence of higher dimensional paradigms is summarized as follows: 3D (Newton) → 4D (Einstein) → 5D (Kaluza-Klein) → 10D (Superstrings) → 11D (M-theory).

Alongside these mainstream developments, a few physicists were considering less orthodox applications of higher dimensions. The 1970s saw the birth of paraphysics (the subject that tries to relate parapsychology to physics) and in the 1980s paraphysicists began to consider the possibility of still more dimensions. In particular, a series of papers studied 8D models in which one complexifies the four coordinates of space and time. This means that there are real and imaginary space and time axes, so that the higher-dimensional separation can be zero even when the 4D separation is not. This model was first proposed in standard relativity, as a way of unifying Einstein's equations for gravity with Maxwell's equations of electromagnetism (Newman, 1973). The paraphysical application of this idea was proposed independently by Russell Targ et al. (1979) and Elizabeth Rauscher (1979). Whiteman (1977) invoked a 6D model, with three real times, claiming that this leads to the Maxwell and Dirac equations. Ceon Ramon and Rauscher (1980) suggested a 12D model, with three complex space and three complex time dimensions, while another particle physics motivated 12D model was proposed by Burkhard Heim (1988). All these extensions of relativity theory suppose that points can be contiguous in higher-dimensional spacetime (i.e., with zero higher-dimensional separation) even though they are separated in ordinary spacetime. This contiguity is supposed to explain how events at remote locations or times can be present in consciousness (Schmeidler, 1972).

Perhaps the most mathematically sophisticated attempt to connect matter and consciousness through higher dimensions has come from Saul-Paul Sirag (1993). The key to his approach is group theory: He proposes that there is a hierarchy of consciousness associated with the hierarchy of what mathematicians term "reflection spaces." In particular, an important role is attributed to 7D reflection space, the symmetry group of one of the Platonic solids.

A mathematically simpler approach invokes a single extra spatial dimension (analogous to the Zöllner proposal). In principle, a fifth dimension can take on the same role as that attributed to the fourth dimension in pre-relativistic physics. For example, John Ralphs (1992) claims that this can explain such diverse phenomena as spirit communications, movements of objects through space and time, clairvoyance, and dowsing. The most detailed 5D model of this kind comes from Jim Beichler (1998). He assumes that points in spacetime extend into a fifth dimension as what he terms "axial A-lines" and that the existence of material objects reflects the curvature of spacetime in this dimension. For animate objects (and Beichler regards life as more fundamental to psi than consciousness), biochemical reactions are associated with field density patterns along these lines, and nonphysical interactions between them occur via what he terms "lateral A-lines." These extend in both space and time, and provide a signaling mechanism for telepathy, clairvoyance, precognition, and memory. In this picture, the existence of the fifth dimension means that the mind extends beyond the brain, so the 4D body is merely the scaffolding of a more complex 5D structure.

In recent decades, a number of people have emphasized the possible relevance of higher dimensions to paraphysics. Jean-Pierre Jourdan (2010) invokes a 5D model of this kind to account for the remarkable changes in the perception of the physical world reported in some near-death experience (NDE) cases. He argues that the brain restricts consciousness to 4D space (resulting in normal perception), but NDEs give some "height" in the fifth dimension, with the degree of perceptual anomaly depending on this height. Robert Brumblay (2003) reports similar changes of perception in out-of-body experiences (OBEs). William Tiller (1993) claims that the higher dimensions of psi are more supported by experience than the ones associated with particle physics, and his scheme also associates these dimensions with different frequencies (i.e., with objects having different rates of vibration). Claude Swanson (2003) advocates a similar scheme, his "synchronized universe principle" envisaging parallel universes as sheets in a higher dimension. Two "unsynchronized" systems can exist side by side in the same space and time, yet be unaware of each other because of their different frequencies and phases.

Christian Hallman (2007) has also invoked multidimensional models of consciousness. He associates waking sensations with three space dimensions (a cube) and one time dimension (a circle) but dreaming space with an outer cube connected to an inner cube by the fourth dimension of a hypercube. In later papers, he extends this proposal to more exotic experiences. Vernon Neppe and Edward Close (2012) have written extensively about what they call the "Vortex N-dimensional Pluralism paradigm." This features an infinitely extended N-dimensional space with vortices allowing communication across the extra dimensions. This model emphasizes the informational and communication elements associated with consciousness that cannot be translated into space and time. They favor a 9D model, with three dimensions of space, three of time, and three of consciousness. This model has several features in common with those of Whiteman and myself.

None of these proposals could be regarded as mainstream physics, and they vary in their mathematical sophistication. Also, while all such models are here classified as "paraphysics," the higher-dimensional model has implications for all fields. Thus, Neppe and Close claim their model provides a philosophical-scientific alternative to mind-body theories, linking parapsychology, theology, and philosophy. I would make the same claim for my own model, which is the focus of discussion for the rest of this chapter.

LINKING MATTER AND MIND THROUGH EXTRA DIMENSIONS OF SPACE AND TIME

The key question addressed in this section concerns the relationship between the material world, which we encounter in our normal waking state, and the mental world, which we encounter in our memories, dreams, and altered states of consciousness. The usual assumption is that the material world is "external," "objective," or "public" and constrained by physical laws, whereas the mental world is "internal," "subjective," or "private" and less lawful. However, one might be suspicious of this dichotomy because even our experience of the material world is ultimately mental. It is certainly important to appreciate that there is a subset of percepts associated with the physical world, so we might term these "physical percepts," but percepts themselves are always mental. This links to a long-standing philosophical controversy about the relationship between our perception of the world and the world itself. Some people have adopted the *direct realist* (or *naïve realist*) view, in which percepts are a direct apprehension of reality, while others have adopted the *representative* (or *indirect realist*) view, in which percepts are just an internalized mapping of reality. However, this controversy originally arose in the context of the 3D Newtonian paradigm, and we will see that it takes on a different form in the context of the 4D relativistic paradigm. It will also be necessary to extend the discussion to include percepts not generated by the physical world, which we term "nonphysical percepts." In any case, the resolution of this controversy plays a key role in my own proposal.

Phenomenal Space and 3D Reality Structure

The term "phenomenal space" here refers to the space associated with those percepts that appear to be generated by the physical world via physical sensors (i.e., the only ones associated with an external reality in the standard view). Since we well understand the physical and physiological processes whereby an object emits a signal, which is then registered by the sensory system and transformed into a pattern of neuronal firing in the brain, very few people would nowadays support the *direct realist* view in which phenomenal space *is* physical space. Also, it is clear that perception is a creative process, with higher-order brain processes filling in gaps or even overriding the raw sensory data. All this ostensibly supports *representative theory*, in which phenomenal space is just an internal construct of the brain.

The crucial assumption of representative theory is that there is an external reality, which reconciles how different observers perceive the world. But what is the nature of this consensual reality? If one were to ask a philosopher of the pre-relativistic age in what sense the physical world is real, he might have replied as follows: There exists a 3D space in which are localized both the sensors through which we observe the world and the physical objects themselves. Each observer has only partial information about that space because of the limitations of his sensory system (his eyes providing him with a projection of the space that is essentially 2D) and the nature of the objects themselves (only their surfaces being visible). However, the crucial point is that, given his location and the direction in which he is looking, one can always predict how he ought to see it. One may say that the physical world is a 3D structure that consistently reconciles how everybody within that structure perceives it. This is what is meant by stating that the physical world is real. The situation is depicted in Figure 2.2(a), which represents three perceptual fields (P_1, P_2, P_3) by squares and the reality structure (S_3) by a cube. So perception corresponds to what I term an *aspect map* Π_i from 3D to 2D such that $\Pi_i S_3 = P_i$ for each observer i.

On the other hand, this picture does not provide a complete picture because the phenomenal world certainly *seems* to be "outside," and it is very improbable that extensive probing of the brain would ever locate the images themselves "inside" (like some sort of filmstrip). This gives rise to the classic mind-body problem (Chalmers, 1995). Indeed, some people have argued that phenomenal space may not be required at all on the grounds that physical space alone can explain the geometrical aspects of perception (Decock, 2006). More importantly, the description above assumes the 3D Newtonian paradigm, whereas we have seen that physicists now adopt a description of the world that involves at least four dimensions and possibly many more. This suggests that the "real" world

Figure 2.3
The relationship between object and percept in a model that involves observation along the past light cone (a) and a more general model of perception with consciousness being associated with the nexus of signaling world lines connecting spacetime events to the brain (b). Two spatial dimensions are not shown.

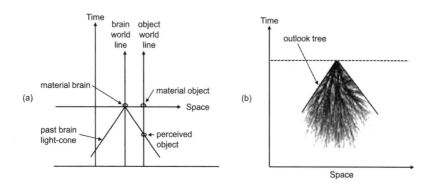

bears very little resemblance to the 3D world we actually experience and that our biological sensory systems reveal only a very limited aspect of reality. Indeed, the version of reality assumed by old-fashioned representative theory is itself a representation.

Phenomenal Space and 4D Reality Structure

As a first step to confronting this problem, let us see how the above discussion changes in the 4D paradigm. The construction of S_3 applies only at a particular time. From a Newtonian perspective, time is absolute, so the 3D structures at successive moments can be patched together to incorporate the flow of time. However, this does not give a precise description of the physical world; it is merely an approximation that applies when objects move at much less than the speed of light. A modern-day philosopher, mindful of the implications of special relativity, would argue that the physical world is a 4D structure, denoted by S_4, with the objects and sensors being represented by world lines. Nevertheless, the notion that the world is real because there is a structure of some dimensionality, which reconciles our perceptions of it, is the same. Indeed, the prime message of relativity is that one can *only* reconcile how different observers perceive the world if it is 4D.

Figure 2.2(a) is now replaced by Figure 2.2(b) provided we interpret P_i appropriately. To address this issue, let us consider the 4D interpretation of perception in more detail. Since an observer's visual field at any moment corresponds to part of his past light cone, one must distinguish between the *material* object (which is the intersection of the object's world-line with a spatial hypersurface of constant time) and the *perceived* object (which is the intersection of the worldline with the brain's past light cone), as illustrated in Figure 2.2(a). The controversy between direct realism and representative theory takes on a different form with this perspective. For since *both* the object and the percept are lower-dimensional sections of a 4D structure, neither is primary and so the standard view of representative theory is superseded. The identification of a percept with some cross-section of a 4D object may seem simplistic, since it excludes secondary aspects (qualia), but for now we are considering only the geometrical aspects.

Of course, perception is generally more complicated than indicated in Figure 2.3(a). Not even visual perception is restricted to the past light cone—it may also involve mirrors, lenses, TV cameras, photographs and so on—and there are also nonvisual modes (sound and touch) that involve signals traveling much slower than the speed of light. So while the percept is 2D in the 3D model of reality, being just a geometrical projection, it is at least partly 3D in the 4D model because of all the extra information that can propagate from objects to sensors off the light cone. The distinction between the 3D and 4D models may be summed up as follows:

$$3D \text{ view: } 3D \text{ object} \rightarrow 2D \text{ percept}$$

$$4D \text{ view: } 4D \text{ structure} \rightarrow 3D \text{ object} + 3D \text{ percept}$$

Physical perception is also dependent upon brain processes and higher-order cognitive functions, but even electrical signals between neurons can be described in terms of (albeit very complicated) world lines. As illustrated in Figure 2.2(b), this suggests that all perception can be represented in terms of spacetime connections of some sort. So perception still corresponds to an aspect map $\Pi_i S_4 = P_i$, but it now goes from 4D to 3D.

With this description, it no longer seems natural to locate percepts—and hence consciousness itself—within the brain. Rather, one has a sort of *extended mind* in which conscious experience is associated with the parts of spacetime to which the brain is linked through a causal nexus of signaling world lines. Perception should be associated with the *entire* 4D process, and the brain is just one end of the chain. This is reminiscent of the "spacetime reductive materialism" model of James Culbertson (1976), in which consciousness is contained within what he terms the "spacetime outlook tree" of the brain.

While this does not resolve the issue of direct versus indirect realism decisively, because any philosophical model of perception could probably be represented in 4D terms, it does obscure the distinction between the two views. Representative theory applies in the sense that: (1) there is a distinction between S_4 and P_i; (2) some percepts may be generated by the part of the nexus within the brain itself; (3) one cannot identify 3D perceptual space with 3D physical space. However, direct realism applies in the sense that physical and perceptual space are naturally merged as part of a 4D reality structure, so phenomenal space need not reside within the head.

The Flow of Time and 5D Reality Structure

The 4D description of perception given earlier is still incomplete because it makes no reference to *experience*. While the 4D reality structure may describe the *contents* of consciousness associated with the physical world, it does not describe consciousness itself and so hardly warrants the description "mental." This leads me to take a more contentious step.

What is missing relates to a long-standing problem on the border of physics and philosophy: how to describe the flow of time. The point is that relativity theory alone does not describe the basic experience of "now" that is such an essential ingredient of our perceptual world. For in the "block" universe of special relativity, past and present and future coexist; the 3D object is just the "constant-time" cross-section of an immobile 4D worldline, and we come across events as our field of consciousness sweeps through the block. However, nothing within the spacetime picture describes this or identifies the particular moment at which we make our observations. So if I regard my consciousness as crawling along the world line of my brain, like a bead on a wire, as illustrated in Figure 2.4(a), that motion itself cannot be described by relativity theory.

Thus, there is a fundamental distinction between physical time (associated with special relativity and the outer world) and mental time (associated with the experience of "now" and the inner world). This point was first emphasized by Arthur Eddington (1920) and Hermann Weyl (1922) and later by numerous others. Indeed, the status of the "now" has been the focus of a huge philosophical debate between the *presentists* and the *eternalists* (Savitt, 2014). The problem of the flow of time also relates to the problem of free will. In a mechanistic universe, a physical object (such as an observer's body) is usually assumed to have a well-defined future world line. However, one intuitively imagines that at any particular experiential time, there are a number of possible future world lines, as illustrated in Figure 2.4(b), with the intervention of consciousness allowing the selection of one of these. The impression of choice may be illusory, but that is how it *feels*. The middle line in the figure shows the unchanged (mechanistic) future, while the other lines show two alternative (changed) futures.

Another question that arises is how the "beads" of different observers are correlated. If two observers interact (i.e., if their world lines cross),

Figure 2.4
The three problems of consciousness in relativity: the passage of time (a), the selection of possible futures (b), and the coordination of time for separated observers (c)

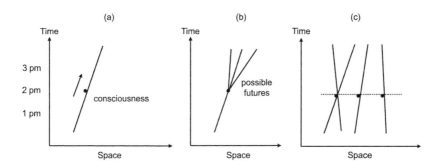

they must presumably be conscious at the same time (i.e., their "beads" must traverse the intersection point together). However, what about observers whose world lines do not intersect? Naïvely identifying contemporaneous beads by taking a constant time slice, as illustrated by the broken line in Figure 2.4(c), might appear to be inconsistent with special relativity, since this rejects the notion of simultaneity at different points in space. However, this notion is restored in general relativity because the large-scale isotropy and homogeneity of the Universe singles out a special time direction.

Figure 2.5
How the problems in Figure 2.4 may be resolved by invoking a fifth dimension (a), this relating to the notion of the physical world as a 4D brane in a 5D bulk (b) and to a unified psychophysical model in which phenomenal space and physical space are different slices of a 5D space (c)

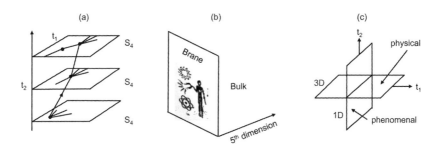

The failure of relativity to describe the process of future becoming past and different possible future world lines may also relate to quantum theory. This is because the collapse of the wave function to one of a number of possible states entails a basic irreversibility. The problem of reconciling relativity theory and quantum mechanics may therefore connect to the problem of understanding consciousness (Penrose, 1989). Note that one also needs some concept of simultaneity at different points in space in quantum mechanics to describe nonlocal effects associated with quantum entanglement.

One way of describing the flow of time, described most cogently by Broad (1953), is to suppose that there is a *second* type of time (t_2), or at least a higher dimension, with respect to which our motion through physical time (t_1) is measured. Physical time is then amalgamated with space into spacetime, while mental time describes how the field of observation moves through spacetime. At any moment in t_2, a physical object will have either a unique future world line (in a mechanistic model) or a number of possible world lines (in a quantum model). The intervention of consciousness allows the future world line to change in the first case or to be selected from in the second case. This is illustrated in Figure 2.5(a) and is one interpretation of what is termed a "growing block universe." This can also be related to "brane cosmology", as illustrated in Figure 2.5(b), and the "many worlds" interpretation of quantum mechanics (Everett, 1957).

The crucial implication of this step is that a unified psychophysical description must involve a 5D reality structure, S_5, rather than a 4D one. As illustrated in Figure 2.5(c), which is a modified version of Figure 2.5 (a), physical spacetime (x,t_1) and phenomenal spacetime (x,t_2) are just different slices of (x,t_1,t_2) space (where x denotes spatial coordinates). Indeed, physical and phenomenal space are on an equal footing from a 5D perspective. This is a psychophysical model in the sense that it describes the passage of time, which is the basis of all conscious experience. However, to avoid terminological confusion, I will describe S_5 as a *hyperphysical* space and reserve the term "physical space" for S_4, since this is only accessible by physical sensors.

This model might be compared with that of Smythies (1956). In his original model, physical and phenomenal spacetime have a separate set of spatial dimensions but a common time dimension, so he requires seven dimensions. Also, his original model makes no connection between the phenomenal spaces of *different* observers, so if there are n observers, he needs $3n + 4$ dimensions. But the whole point of the present approach is that the different phenomenal spaces are supposed to be different projections of a single 5D space. In fact, his latest model is also 5D and differs from mine only in that he does not identify the fifth dimension with t_2 (Smythies, 2012). While he envisages the phenomenal plane moving through the physical plane, this motion is not itself described by the model because he chooses not to spatialize t_2, so his fifth dimension is just an extra space.

These considerations suggest that the problem of the flow of time is intimately related to the problem of the relationship between matter and mind, so the problems must be solved together. The introduction of t_2 may seem to be the first step toward an infinite regress (Dunne, 1967/1927), but t_2 is not introduced to describe the flow of time per se; it is just required to distinguish between mental and physical time.

The 5D model has interesting implications for the nature of memory. The mainstream view is that all memories are stored in the brain, but this is hard to demonstrate because we do not yet understand the process of memory storage. The view encouraged by the 5D model is that memories of physical events reflect the direct access of consciousness to the physical spacetime that contains those events. For if percepts of objects are not inside the head, the same may apply to memories of objects. In this case, the brain need not store the memory itself but only some link to the original spacetime event, so it contains a tag rather than a trace. This accords with Culbertson's model of memory.

The Universal Structure and a Space for Nonphysical Percepts

The discussion up to now has covered only those percepts that derive from the physical world. But what about the nonphysical percepts that have no physical counterparts? They may be grouped into three classes—normal, paranormal, and transpersonal—and each class comprises four types of percept.

- Normal percepts include (1) physical sense data, (2) physical memories, (3) visualizations, and (4) dreams.
- Paranormal percepts include (1) ESP, (2) retrocognition/precognition, (3) apparitions, and (4) threshold effects on the border of sleep.
- Transpersonal percepts include (1) OBEs/NDEs, (2) pre/postlife imagery, (3) higher planes, and (4) mystical experiences.

The earlier discussion pertains to only the first two types. Although the breakdown into 12 is somewhat arbitrary, since one could merge or subdivide the phenomena in various ways, the order of the sequence will turn out to be significant. The crucial point is that one needs a model accommodating all three classes.

The controversy between direct realism and representative theory takes on a different significance in the context of nonphysical percepts. One might argue that the percept is now primary and that there is no outside world to be represented. However, there still seems to be a space, Whiteman (1986, p. 6) stating that "in all kinds of non-physical sensing, objects have extension, position, direction and shape, and are capable of being moved about in that space relative to other objects there." Furthermore, the existence of psi hints that this space is collective in some sense: clairvoyance and psychokinesis suggest that mental space *contains* physical space, while telepathy suggests that even nonphysical percepts may reside in some communal space, albeit different from physical space. Transpersonal experiences suggest the existence of even "higher" spaces. So, just as S_5 merges physical and phenomenal space for physical percepts, maybe one can envisage some form of merged space for all types of percepts.

This possibility motivates an extension of the 5D model of perception in which the reality structure has extra dimensions. The application of the model to specific phenomena is discussed elsewhere (Carr, 2015); here I merely present the idea in a formal way. With the addition of each dimension, the number of "objects" and "sensors" incorporated increases, so one generates a hierarchy of reality structures of increasing dimensionality (S_4, S_5, S_6 ...). One eventually reaches a maximum dimensionality D, at which point one has extended the reality structure as much as possible. The final one (S_D) is termed the *Universal Structure* and is represented symbolically in Figure 2.2(c) by a hypercube (the 4D analogue of a cube). The lowest member of the hierarchy is taken to be the 4D reality structure of special relativity (S_4), since S_3 excludes time. The dimensionality of a nonphysical perceptual field is unclear, so it is represented by a cube in Figure 2.2(c).

Any percept contained within this reality structure is said to possess "actuality" and in principle, all percepts could be included. One can formally regard the extra percepts that are incorporated as one introduces successive dimensions as defining a sequence of "actuality planes" (A_r with $1 < r < D\text{-}3$), where the term "plane" is not used in the usual 2D sense but turns out to have geometrical significance. It is implicit here that all perception involves some form of sensor that is itself associated with an actuality plane and cannot receive signals from any higher one. Indeed, there should be a hierarchy of signaling mechanisms: Just as a physical sensor on A_1 accesses a 4D outlook tree, so a sensor on A_2 should access a 5D outlook tree and so on.

The precise nature of the extra dimensions is not specified at this point, but our model for S_5 suggests that the extra dimensions are time-like, there being a separate time t_r for each actuality plane. However, there is only one *experiential* time in this model, the different t_r just representing its projections in the different actuality planes. It is as though consciousness perceives the world through a number of windows, each with its own clock. The key point is that there is a hierarchical relationship between the different times, such that the past, present, and potential future of t_r are contained within the present of $t_r + 1$.

The interpretation of clairvoyance within the hyperspatial model is that S_5 already *contains* physical space. I have also suggested that S_5 contains memories, so this implies a unified model of clairvoyance and memory. Since future world lines in physical time (t_1) coexist in mental time (t_2), precognition is also allowed but not in the sense of an absolutely predetermined future. As illustrated in Figure 2.5(a), at any point in t_2, the past in t_1 is uniquely prescribed, but there are many potential futures, and these are successively selected with respect to t_2. So, the futures glimpsed in S_5 are alterable, Whiteman (1986) terming this "provisional potentiality." The interpretation of telepathy is that even percepts of nonphysical origin possess some attributes of *externality*. However, it is not clear that this can be described in terms of S_5, and I argue elsewhere that at least some psi experiences require a space of higher dimensionality (Carr, 2015).

The focus of the preceding discussion has been primarily on the visual sense mode. However, all our experiences of the world must be equivalent to each other in an informational sense, so data obtained through different sensory modes must presumably be compatible. Indeed, one might interpret the Universal Structure as an *informational space*, with D (in some sense) specifying the dimensionality of its information content.

The crucial step in this proposal is the identification of the Universal Structure with the higher-dimensional space of modern physics. In particular, I relate it to the Randall-Sundrum version of M-theory, illustrated in Figure 2.5(b), in which the physical Universe is regarded as a 4D brane in a higher-dimensional bulk. For if physical objects occupy only a limited part of that higher-dimensional space, it is natural to ask whether anything else exists there. Since the only nonphysical entities we experience are mental ones, and since it has been argued that all mental experiences have to exist in some sort of space, it seems natural to associate this with the "bulk."

The fact that I adopt the phrases "bulk" and "brane" need not imply commitment to M-theory itself. Indeed, the extra dimensions are usually space-like rather than time-like in M-theory. Also, there is only one extended dimension in the Randall-Sundrum model, although the picture can be generalized to allow more. However, I do require some form of higher-dimensional model, and the term "hyperphysical" is generally used to describe such models. It should be stressed that the higher actuality planes are not strung out along the fifth dimension in this model; rather, they correspond to a hierarchy of branes of increasing dimensionality. So, they are packed inside one another like Russian dolls rather than being like slices through a cake. However, the key point is that both percept and object are viewed as the projections of some higher-dimensional structure, which might be described as "hyperphysical matter," so the distinction between matter and mind becomes blurred. For this reason, the Universal Structure might be interpreted as a Universal Mind.

The next step is to formulate a theory of how the different elements in the Universal Structure interact with each other. This is a very ambitious task. The Randall-Sundrum picture confines attention to the interaction of objects on the brane, whereas the full theory must also consider the interactions of objects in the bulk. So, not only must one provide a model for how objects on A_1 interact (i.e., a complete theory of physics), one must also describe how objects on higher actuality planes interact. This is also necessary if one wants to extend the discussion from the passive aspects of mind involved in perception to more active ones.

The model involves a formulation of what I call transcendental field theory. The name indicates, first, that all the interactions are assumed to proceed via fields and second, that the fields involved are more extensive than the usual physical ones in that they do not only involve space and time. We also assume that all interactions can be interpreted *geometrically*. In the context of objects on the first actuality plane (i.e., physical objects), this interaction corresponds to gravity, which is a manifestation of the fact that spacetime is curved. Thus, we can think of A_1 as a 4D sheet within the Universal Structure, with the existence of a physical object being reflected in the fact that it induces curvature of the sheet (cf. Beichler's model). We then extend this idea to higher dimensions, with A_r being associated with an $(r + 2)$ brane in the Universal Structure. The Universal Structure interprets the matter-mind interface as some form of "hyperdimensional" interaction. It is not yet clear how transcendental field theory explains this, but it does at least offer the conceptual hope of unifying matter and mind within an extension of current physics. The nature of the unification is summarized in Figure 2.6 and its caption.

MORE SPECULATIVE CONSIDERATIONS

The Universal Structure proposal raises many issues that are common to all hyperspatial models. In this section, I will highlight some of these issues and then discuss some speculations about the nature of time and subtle matter. However, it must be stressed that all these ideas are very preliminary, providing more questions than answers.

- The focus of the preceding discussion has been on the perceptual aspects of mind and other aspects would need to be included in a full treatment—for example, cognition, emotion, volition, and dispositional factors. I would not anticipate that all such aspects can be reduced to hyperphysics, since it seems likely that some forms of mental experiences have no connection to physics at all. Also, the preceding discussion has certainly not resolved the problem of

Figure 2.6
The relationship between matter and mind in the proposed model. Individual mind has a number of attributes, but we have focused mainly on its perceptual aspects. Both percepts (in the first person domain) and the objects from which they derive (in the third person domain) are contained in some higher-dimensional Universal Structure, which comprises a hierarchy of actuality planes {A$_i$}. Physical objects (i.e., matter) are associated with the lowest plane {A$_1$}, which corresponds to a 4D brane. Hyperphysical objects (usually classified as mental) are associated with higher actuality planes, and these correspond to higher-dimensional branes, which interact via higher-dimensional fields. The total dimensionality D is unspecified but determines the number of actuality planes (D-3).

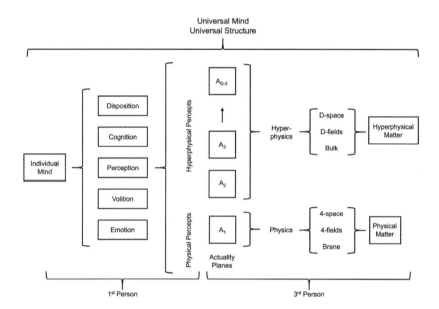

consciousness. So this approach does not aspire to provide a complete theory of mind. Nevertheless, it does offer the conceptual hope of unifying matter and mind within an extension of current physics.

- In any theory purporting to unify matter and mind, the real challenge is to explain the phenomena in the overlap of these domains. In a sense, all the phenomena labelled as "paranormal" come into this category, which is why psychical research plays such a key role in bridging these two domains (Carr, 2008). A common feature of these phenomena is that they involve what Michael Grosso (2014) terms a "dream bubble," a fusion of public and private space, in which the ordinary laws of physics do not apply. The Universal Structure purports to provide this fusion.

- With many rogue phenomena, it can be argued that psi provides an alternative hypothesis to the hyperspatial one. But if psi can itself be interpreted in hyperspatial terms, how can one decide whether psi explains mental space or mental space explains psi? The answer hinges on the nature of psychic perception. In the Universal Structure proposal, all perception is channeled through some form of sensor, but this need not be physical. Indeed, there should be a hierarchy of sensors associated with the hierarchy of actuality planes.

- One interesting issue is whether we do not observe an extra dimension because it is compactified on too small a scale to be seen (as in the Kaluza-Klein model) or because we are confined to a thin slice of the extra dimension by the warpage of the higher-dimensional geometry (as in the brane model). In the first case, an "internal" space is associated with each point of "external" space. In the second case, the extra dimension looks compactified *locally*, but it is extended *globally*.

- Another important issue is whether the extra dimensions are space-like or time-like (i.e., whether they have a positive or negative sign in the expression for the distance between points in the higher-dimensional space). In the context of 5D models, the extra dimension is often assumed to be space-like because of the Flatland analogy, but we have seen that a second time dimension might elucidate the passage of time. In fact, all the extra dimensions are time-like in my own model. Time-like and space-like dimensions have very different manifestations and could potentially be distinguished by phenomenological reports.

The Specious Present, Personal Identity, and Consciousness

The motion of S_4 through the fifth dimension, depicted in Figure 2.5(a), permits the animation of spacetime only in a *global* sense. It corresponds to a sort of *universal* consciousness but does not explain *individual* consciousness or clarify the distinction between the "first person" and "third person" perspectives in Figure 2.6. Another problem is that we have discussed only t_1 and t_2; the roles of the higher times have not yet been considered. Here I make a very speculative proposal, which links these two problems.

We first note that the conscious experience of time—and hence the existence of personal identity—makes sense only within certain bounds because we could not be aware of time scales which were too short or too long. The problem on the short time scale is that our physical sensory systems have a finite time resolution and so we cannot observe processes shorter than this. Indeed, it has been suggested that consciousness is associated with a brain frequency of 40 Hertz, corresponding to a time of 0.025 seconds (Gold, 1999). This minimum time scale of consciousness (τ) is called the *specious present*, a term first introduced by Robert Kelly (1882) and then elaborated by William James (1890). The problem on the long time scale is that our brains do not register changes that are too slow (e.g., on a time scale longer than that associated with short-term memory). So there is a sense in which the conscious flow of time exists only between these upper and lower limits. Of course, we can still *intellectualize* about longer and shorter time scales, but we cannot *experience* them.

In the usual waking state, the value of τ is presumably determined by brain processes. However, a striking feature of mental experience is that the specious present appears to change in some circumstances. This applies even in "normal" experiences, is more accentuated in "paranormal" experiences, and is most dramatic in "transpersonal" experiences. This may be partly explained in terms of brain processes, since there is a huge neuroscientific literature on time perception and its variability. On the other hand, in any "filter" theory of consciousness (in which consciousness is not generated *by* the brain but merely perceives the world *through* it), one might expect τ to change dramatically if consciousness can be decoupled from the brain. This raises the question of whether there could be other levels of consciousness in the Universe, not necessarily associated with brains, operating with a different specious present and perceiving the world through organs sensitive to a different frequency range. Such notions have also been advocated by Josiah Royce (1904) and Henri Bergson (1946).

Variations in the specious present may also relate to psi. Thouless and Wiesner (1947) suggest that the focus of the mind is usually on the brain but that processes termed "psi-gamma" (receptive) and "psi-kappa" (expressive) occasionally operate on the surrounding "penumbra." The aforementioned considerations suggest that the penumbra should extend over a time scale τ. Because there is no distinction between past and future within the specious present, this implies that precognition and retrocognition should be possible on time scales below τ, and this may relate to the notion of consciousness induced restoration of time symmetry (Bierman, 2010). With the usual brain-based specious present, τ is only a fraction of a second, but this might still suffice to explain the (short time scale) "presentiment" effect (Bierman & Radin, 1997). The penumbra should also have a length scale cτ (where c is the speed of light), so one might also anticipate clairvoyance within a range of around 10,000 kilometers. Longer time scale premonition or wider range clairvoyance would require an increase of the specious present. One possible model of PK invokes the transfer of information from the mind to the physical system (Mattuck, 1977). However, the wide spatial range associated with the usual specious present makes PK very weak. One needs to decrease τ to enhance this, so receptive and expressive effects require an increase and decrease in the specious present respectively.

What sort of model could describe this concept? Since the specious present is a feature of mental time, which is associated with the fifth dimension in this model, I suggest that the perceptual field of an observer must extend in this dimension by an amount identified with the specious present. Indeed, there should be a hierarchy of specious presents, one for each actuality plane, corresponding to an extension in each time dimension. This proposal has important implications for the nature of personal identity because the fragmentation of Universal Consciousness into individual consciousness presupposes a certain spatial and temporal resolution, which would no longer pertain for a consciousness with a much longer or shorter specious present. Indeed, as one increases the dimensionality, one can envisage a hierarchy of progressively more inclusive selves: supraliminal, subliminal, and beyond (cf. Myers, 1903). This has obvious implications for the survival hypothesis.

Subtle Matter, Subtle Bodies, and Subtle Perception

The hyperspatial approach implies that some form of "subtle matter" occupies the higher dimensional space. A crucial issue concerns the nature of the subtle matter and how it interacts with ordinary matter. Let us first consider a 5D model, with the extra dimension being space-like and extended. By definition, physical matter is confined to the first actuality plane A_1, this corresponding to a slice whose thickness is the confinement scale. One could envisage three different models for subtle matter: (1) it is 4D but can move in the extra dimension (like another brane in the bulk) and may in principle intrude into physical space; (2) it has some extension in the fifth dimension and has a lower dimensional manifestation when it transits physical space (like the intruding sphere in Flatland); (3) it has a *large* extension in the fifth dimension and always overlaps with the brane. Since even physical objects have a small thickness in the fifth dimension, the distinction between these cases really depends upon how the higher-dimensional extent of subtle matter compares to this.

If the fifth dimension is time-like, both physical and subtle matter are associated with 5D world lines in S_5, just as ordinary matter is associated with a 4D world line in S_4, so situation (3) applies. However, there is a distinction between the *experienced* dimensionality of an object and the dimensionality of the space in which it resides. If there are many time-like extra dimensions, one might argue that subtle matter involves the same space as ordinary matter but operates in a different frequency range. This notion arises in various esoteric traditions, as well as more modern approaches (Tiller, 1993; Swanson, 2003).

By analogy with the physical body, I assume that a subtle body is a form of subtle matter possessing subtle sensors through which consciousness can *experience* parts of the Universal Structure. A subtle body on A_r

can observe objects on its own and any lower actuality plane but only affect objects on its own plane. During normal consciousness, this should be collocated with the physical body and have a specious present determined by the brain, but during altered states of consciousness, it may extend further into the fifth dimension, thereby allowing access to a larger domain of space and time. It is also claimed that it may separate from the physical body altogether in some circumstances (e.g., during an OBE). If one can extend this concept to higher actuality planes, there should be a hierarchy of subtle bodies with a hierarchy of specious presents.

CONSEQUENCES OF THE HYPERSPATIAL APPROACH

Implications for the Nature of Reality

The proposed paradigm is very much in the spirit of Paul Brunton (1941), who urged that we must learn to mentalize space and spatialize mind. The benefit of this is that physical percepts are no longer unique in representing an external reality. However, the price one pays is that the space required is not the usual physical one; it is a higher-dimensional space with a complicated hierarchical structure. I would argue that this higher-dimensional space—with its multiple levels of reality—is a vital component of any model for psi. This idea will attract opposition from various quarters. Materialists will want to reject it—along with the evidence for psi—at the outset because they assume that there can be only one level of reality. Even some people who accept psi may not be enamored with the multilevel approach.

On the other hand, Poynton (2001) compares physicalistic one-level thinking to "the flat-earth paradigm that once held sway in geography and is incapable of providing a rounded understanding," while Pratt (1974) warns:

> If we insist upon carrying out experiments on the assumption that psi is simply another process in a one-level universe of impersonal cause and effect relations, failure is built into the very approach to the phenomena.

Of course, the idea of higher levels of reality also features prominently both in ancient occult traditions and, from a more modern perspective, in the seminal work of Whiteman (1986), which has been cogently summarized by Poynton (1994). In particular, Whiteman uses a "reality index" to classify a range of separative experiences—going from fantasy to waking to mystical states—and this index might be associated with different actuality planes.

The proposed model has important implications for the relationship between our perception of the world and the world itself. In particular, the old-fashioned dichotomy between direct realism and representative theory no longer applies, because "common sense" three-dimensional reality is itself a representation. The phenomenal world (at least its geometrical aspects) and material world are merely different cross-sections of a single higher-dimensional structure. In its most ambitious form, the model regards any experience as being contained in the Universal Structure, but consciousness can access this only through some form of sensor.

Implications for Physics and Reductionism

Physics has progressed through a sequence of paradigm shifts, so it would be perverse to believe that it will not go through further ones. Although it is not inevitable that a future paradigm will incorporate mind (let alone psi), it is worth recalling the prognosis of Radin (1997, p. 291):

> It may be that just as we were shocked to learn at the dawn of the twentieth century that matter and energy were essentially the same, perhaps at the dawn of the twenty-first century we are in the midst of discovering that mind and matter are essentially the same.

A similar notion has been expressed by the cosmologist Andrei Linde (1990), and there have been several other attempts to draw a link between mind and recent ideas in modern physics (Le Shan, 1974; Heim, 1988; Wasserman, 1993; Sirag, 1993; Bryan, 2000; Pavsic, 2001; Sarfatti, 2006; Bockris, 2005). Because of the progressive nature of paradigm shifts, I would anticipate the new paradigm being a step *forward* from the current ones, in the sense that it builds on relativistic or quantum physics, and the higher-dimensional approach is a good example of this.

Regardless of the details, if the hope of an extended theory of physics is fulfilled, an important semantic issue is whether we should call this sort of approach "physics," since doing so will certainly antagonize an appreciable fraction of both physicists and psychical researchers. It is certainly not the sort of physics that describes material objects, so I prefer to call it "hyperphysics" (the term "paraphysics" having negative connotations for some people). The formal distinction is that one might associate normal physics with the brane and hyperphysics with the bulk. However, the important point is that it is the same sort of physics, which derives from studying the material world. It emerges naturally from normal (albeit ultraspeculative) physics, and its focus is not psi alone (which is another reason the term "paraphysics" is less appropriate).

This is just as well, since physicists will probably never take psi seriously unless it can be shown to be an outcome of their own "final theory." Of course, string theorists never intended their higher dimensions to be used in this way, so they may not welcome the introduction of a term that links them with paraphysics in this way. Indeed the scientific status of string theory is itself a matter of debate (Smolin, 2006; Woit, 2006), so any proposal of the kind advocated here is likely to intensify the skepticism of the critics. People who dismiss string theory as mathematics rather than physics would doubtless regard the present proposal as the *reductio ad absurdum* of the approach.

We have seen that an issue of great current interest is whether quantum theory—in particular, nonlocal entanglement—can explain psi. This is certainly a popular view in some quarters (cf. Radin, 2006), but I do not believe quantum theory can be the whole answer. Since we have interpreted the Universal Structure as an information space, one suspects that the paradigm required will also involve some new insight into the link between matter, mind, and information. To quote Anton Zeilinger (2008):

> In the history of physics, we have learned that there are distinctions that really we should not make, such as between space and time . . . It could very well be that the distinction we make between information and reality is wrong . . . that we need a new concept that encompasses or includes both.

This is reminiscent of the views of Brian Josephson, expressed in an interview with Halcomb Noble (1988, p. 179):

> You ask whether parapsychology lies within the bounds of physical law. My feeling is that to some extent it does, but physical law, itself, may need to be redefined. It may be that some effects in parapsychology are ordered-state effects of a kind not yet encompassed by physical theory.

There is also the issue of whether the approach advocated here is reductionistic. Since reductionism means "reducing to physics," this depends on what one means by physics. If one means old-fashioned classical physics, then even orthodox physicists would acknowledge that reductionism cannot work. However, if one means the sort of higher-dimensional hyperphysics advocated here, then it might still be viable.

Implications for Psi

If our concept of physics may have to change to accommodate psi, so too may our concept of the paranormal, for the relationship between normal and paranormal clearly reflects the relationship between physics and paraphysics. Of course, how one defines the "paranormal" inevitably depends on one's preconception as to its nature. If paranormal phenomena are fundamentally anarchic in nature, as advocated by Beloff (1980), then it would make sense to regard paranormal phenomena as the ones that will *never* be explained by physics.

But if psi were ever incorporated into physics (or hyperphysics), would it still be regarded as paranormal? This is essentially a semantic issue, and one might argue that all phenomena become "normal" once they have been explained. However, there will always be a qualitative distinction between psychic phenomena and normal physical phenomena, if psi necessarily involves mind. Indeed, this would then provide a qualitative criterion with which to distinguish psychic phenomena from the more general class of anomalous phenomena. There will always be a qualitative distinction between hyperphysics and physics, so the distinction between normal and paranormal just reflects this. In this context, note that the change from physics to hyperphysics required to accommodate mental phenomena is not a gradual change, achieved by adding a sequence of embellishments to the standard picture. It is a fundamental (discontinuous) change, in which mind is suddenly incorporated at the most basic level. It corresponds to a sudden shift in what Beichler (2006) describes as the Cartesian boundary.

CONCLUSION

In this chapter, I have argued that a large class of mental phenomena involve some form of space, although this is not the usual space of classical physics, since it involves extra dimensions. The notion of extra dimensions has also been proposed as an explanation of certain aspects of the physical world, so it seems natural to relate these two ideas. They are amalgamated in what I term a "Universal Structure," which can be interpreted as a higher- dimensional psychophysical information space. This space has a hierarchical structure and includes both the physical world at the lowest level and the complete range of mental worlds—from normal to paranormal to transpersonal—at the higher levels. The assumption that mental phenomena require a communal space is tantamount to positing some form of Universal Mind, which is controversial but central to the Universal Structure proposal. While this approach cannot claim to provide a complete theory of mind, it does demonstrate a unifying link between a wide range of phenomena that are usually regarded as disparate, with each one providing an extra piece in the jigsaw of what might constitute a complete theory. Although some basic questions about the nature of hyperphysical interactions in this model remain unclear, I believe this approach offers the possibility of a paradigm in which matter and mind are merged at a very fundamental level.

Acknowledgments. This chapter contains some material from a chapter written for another volume (Carr, 2015) and from my SPR presidential address (Carr, 2008). I thank the editors concerned for permission to reproduce this material.

REFERENCES

Abbott, E. A. (1983/1884) *Flatland: A romance of many dimensions*. New York: Barnes & Noble.

Arkani-Hamed, N., Dimopoulos, S., & Dvali, G. (1998). The hierarchy problem and new dimensions at a millimeter. *Physical Letters B, 429*, 263–272.

Aspect, A. J., Dailibard, J., & Roger, G. (1982) Experimental test of Bell's inequalities using time-varying analyzers. *Physical Review D, 49*, 1804–1807.

Atmanspacher, H., Romer, H., & Walach, H. (2002) Weak quantum theory: Complementarity and entanglement in physics and beyond. *Foundations of Physics, 21*, 221–232.

Ayer, A. J. (1940). *The foundations of empirical knowledge*. New York: Macmillan.

Becker, R. O. (1992). Electromagnetism and psychic phenomena. *Journal of the American Society for Psychical Research, 86*, 1–17.

Beichler, J. E. (1998). Strange facts find a theory: A new dimension for psi. *Yggdrasil: Journal of Paraphysics, 1*, 567–596.

Beichler, J. E. (2001). To be or not to be! A paraphysics for the new millennium. *Journal of Scientific Exploration, 15*, 33–56.

Beichler, J. E. (2006). Science at the Cartesian crossroads: Mind and matter or a ghost in the machine. In *Mind, Man and Machine, U.S. Psychotronics Association Proceedings, 15*, 1–16.

Beloff, J. (1980). Could there be a physical explanation for psi? *Journal of the Society for Psychical Research, 50*, 263–272.

Beloff, J. (1988) Parapsychology and physics: Can they be reconciled? *Theoretical Parapsychology, 6*, 23–30.

Bergson, H. (1946). *The creative mind* (M. L. Andison, trans.). New York: Philosophical Library.

Bierman, D. J. (2010) Consciousness induced restoration of time symmetry (CIRTS): A psychophysical theoretical perspective. *Journal of Parapsychology, 74*, 273–299.

Bierman, D. J., & Radin, D. (1997). Anomalous anticipatory response on randomized future conditions. *Perceptual & Motor Skills, 84*, 689–690.

Bockris, J. O. (2005). *The new paradigm: A confrontation between physics and paranormal phenomena*. Texas: D & M Enterprises.

Bohm, D. (1951). *Quantum theory*. New York: Prentice-Hall.

Bohm, D. J. (1980). *Wholeness and the implicate order*. London: Routledge & Kegan Paul.

Bohm, D. J. (1986). A new theory of the relationship between mind and matter. *Journal of the American Society for Psychical Research, 80,* 113–136.

Bösch, H., Steinkamp, F., Boller, E. (2006). Examining psychokinesis: The interaction of human intention with random number generators: A meta-analysis. *Psychological Bulletin, 132,* 497–523

Braude, S. E. (1979a). Objections to an information-theoretic approach to synchronicity. *Journal of the American Society for Psychical Research, 73,* 179–193.

Braude, S. E. (1979b) *ESP and psychokinesis: A philosophical examination.* Philadelphia: Temple University Press.

Broad, C. D. (1923). *Scientific thought.* London: Routledge & Kegan Paul.

Broad, C. D. (1953). *Religion, philosophy & psychical research.* New York: Harcourt-Brace.

Brumblay, R. J. (2003). Hyperdimensional perspectives in out-of-body and near-death experiences. *Journal of Near-Death Studies, 21,* 201–221.

Brunton, P. (1941). *The hidden teaching beyond yoga.* New York: E. P. Dutton.

Bryan, R. (2000). What can elementary particles tell us about the world in which we live? *Journal of Scientific Exploration, 14,* 257–274.

Carpenter. J. C. (2004). First sight: Part I. A model of psi and the mind. *Journal of Parapsychology, 68*(2), 217–254.

Carr, B. J. (2008). Worlds apart: Can psychical research bridge the gulf between matter and mind? *Proceedings of the Society for Psychical Research, 59,* 1–96.

Carr, B. J. (2015). Hyperspatial models of matter and mind. In E. Kelly, A. Crabtree, and P. Marshall (Eds.), *Beyond physicalism: Toward reconciliation of science and spirituality.* Blue Ridge Summit, PA: Roman & Littlefield.

Chalmers, D. J. (1995). The puzzle of conscious experience. *Scientific American, 273,* 62–68.

Costa de Beauregard, O. (1979). Quantum paradoxes and Aristotle's two-field information concept. In C. T. Tart, H. E. Puthoff, & R. Targ (Ed.), *Mind at large,* pp. 177–187. New York: Praeger.

Cramer, J. G. (2006). Reverse causation and the transactional interpretation of quantum mechanics. In D. P. Sheehan (Ed.), *Frontiers of time: Retrocausation. Experiment and theory.* AIP Conference Proceedings for the 87th Meeting of AAAS Pacific Division.

Culbertson, J. C. (1976). *Sensations, memories and the flow of time.* Santa Margarita, CA: Cromwell.

Decock. L. (2006). A physicalist reinterpretation of phenomenal space. *Phenomenology and the Cognitive Sciences, 5,* 197–225.

Dobbs, H. A. C. (1965). Time and ESP. *Proceedings of the Society for Psychical Research, 54,* 249–361.

Dobyns, Y. H. (2000) Overview of several theoretical models. *Journal of Scientific Exploration, 14,* 163–194.

Dobyns, Y. H., Dunne, B. J., Jahn, R. G., & Nelson, R. D. (2004). The mega-REG experiment: Replication and interpretation. *Journal of Scientific Exploration 18,* 369–398.

Dunne, J. W. (1927/1967). *An experiment with time.* London: Faber & Faber.

Eddington, A. S. (1920). *Space, time and gravitation: An outline of the general relativity theory.* Cambridge: Cambridge University Press.

Everett, H. (1957). Relative state formulation of quantum mechanics. *Reviews of Modern Physics, 39,* 454–462.

Frieden, B. R. (1998). *Physics from Fisher information: A unification*. Cambridge: Cambridge University Press.

Gold. I. (1999). Does 40-Hz oscillation play a role in visual consciousness? *Consciousness and Cognition, 8*, 186–195.

Grosso. M. (2014). *The strange case of St. Joseph of Copertino: Ecstasy and the mind-body problem*. New York: Oxford University Press.

Hallman, C. J. (2007). Part I: A multidimensional model of the dreaming state of consciousness. *Subtle Energy & Energy Medicine, 18*(2), 75–91; Part II: A multidimensional model of the released state of consciousness. *Subtle Energy & Energy Medicine, 18*(3), 89–111; Part III: A multidimensional model of the deceased state of consciousness. *Subtle Energy & Energy Medicine, 19*(2), 57–90.

Hart, H. (1965). Towards a new philosophical basis for parapsychological phenomena. *Parapsychological Monographs No. 7*. New York: Parapsychology Foundation.

Hasted, J. (1981). *The metal-benders*. London: Routledge & Kegan Paul.

Heim, B. (1988) *Postmortale Zustande? Die Televariante Area Integraler Weltstrukturen*. Innsbruck: Resch.

Irwin, H. J. (1979) *Psi and the mind: An information processing approach*. Metuchen, NJ: Scarecrow.

Irwin, H. J., & Watt, C. (2006). *An introduction to parapsychology* (5th ed.). London: McFarland.

Jahn, R. G. (1982). The persistent paradox of psychic phenomena: An engineering perspective. *Proceedings of IEEE, 70*, 136–170.

Jahn, R. G., & Dunne, B. (1987) *Margins of reality: The role of consciousness in the physical world*. Orlando: Hartcourt Brace Jovanovich.

James, W. (1890). *The principles of psychology* (Vols. 1–2). New York: Henry Holt.

Johnson, R. (1953). *The imprisoned splendour*. London: Hodder & Stoughton.

Josephson, B. D., & Pallikari-Viras, F. (1991) Biological utilization of quantum nonlocality. *Foundations of Physics, 21*, 197–207.

Jourdan, J-P. (2010). *Deadine: Derniere limite*. Paris: Pocket.

Kaluza, T. (1921). Zum Unitatsproblem in der Physik. *Sitzungsber. Preuss. Akad. Wiss. Berlin (Math. Phys.)*, 966–972.

Kelly, E. R. (1882). *The alternative: A study in psychology*. London: Macmillan & Co.

Kelly, E. F., Kelly, E. W., Crabtree, A., Gauld, A., Grosso, M., & Greyson, B. (2006). *Irreducible mind: Towards a psychology for the 21st Century*. Blue Ridge Summit, PA: Roman & Littlefield.

Kogan, I. M. (1968) Information theory analysis of telepathic communication experiments. *Radio Engineering, 23*, 122–130.

Laszlo, E. (1993). *The creative cosmos*. Edinburgh: Floris.

Le Shan, J. (1974). *The medium, the mystic and the physicist*. London: Turnstone Press.

Linde, A. (1990). *Particle physics and inflationary cosmology*. Chur, Switzerland: Harwood Academic.

Lucadou, W. von (1995). The model of pragmatic information. *European Journal of Parapsychology, 11*, 58–75.

Lucas, D., & Maresca, N. (1976). Some current Soviet theories of psi. *Journal of Parapsychology, 40*, 60–61.

Margenau, H. (1985). *The miracle of existence*. Woodtribe, CT: Ox Bow.

Mattuck, R. D. (1977). Random fluctuation theory of psychokinesis: Thermal noise model. In J. D. Morris, W. G. Roll, & R. L. Morris (Eds.), *Research in Parapsychology 1976*, pp. 191–195. London: Scarecrow.

Mattuck, R. D. (1984). A quantum mechanical theory of the interaction of consciousness and matter. In M. Cazenave (Ed.). *Science and consciousness: Two views of the universe*, pp. 49–65. New York: Pergamon.

May, E. C., Utts, J. M., & Spottiswoode, S. J. P. (2014/1995a). Decision augmentation theory: Toward a model for anomalous mental phenomena. In E. C. May & S. B. Marwaha (Eds.), *Anomalous cognition: Remote viewing research and theory*, pp. 222–243. Jefferson, NC: McFarland.

May, E. C., Spottiswoode, S. J. P., & Utts, J. M. (2014/1995b). Applications of decision augmentation theory. In E. C. May & S. B. Marwaha (Eds.), *Anomalous cognition: Remote viewing research and theory*, pp. 244–267. Jefferson, NC: McFarland.

Myers, F. H. W. (1903). *Human personality and its survival of bodily death*. London: Longmans.

Neppe, V. M., & Close, E. R. (2012). *Reality begins with consciousness: A paradigm shift that works*. Seattle, WA: Brainvoyage.com, Brainquest.

Newman, E. T. (1973). Maxwell's equations in complex Minkowski space. *Journal of Mathematics and Physics, 14*, 202–213.

Noakes, R. (2004). The "bridge which is between physical and psychical research": William Fletcher Barrett, sensitive flames, and spiritualism. *History of Science, 42*, 419–464.

Noble, H. B. (1988). *Next: The coming era in science*. Boston: Little, Brown.

Oteri, L. (1975) *Quantum physics and parapsychology*. New York: Parapsychology Foundation.

Pallikari, F. (1998). On the balancing effect hypothesis. In N. Zingrone (Ed.), *Research in Parapsychology*, pp. 102–103. Metuchen, NJ: Scarecrow.

Pallikari, F. (2001). A study of the fractal character in electron noise processes. *Chaos, Solitons and Fractals, 12*, 1499–1507.

Pallikari, F. (2003). Must the "magic" of psychokinesis hinder a precise scientific measurement? *Journal of Consciousness Studies, 10*, 199–219.

Palmer, J. (1978), Extrasensory perception: Research findings. In S. Krippner (Ed.), *Advances in parapsychological research 2*, pp. 59–243. New York: Plenum.

Pavsic, M. (2001). *The landscape of theoretical physics: A global view*. Dordrecht, The Netherlands: Kluwer Academic.

Penrose, R. (1989). *The emperor's new mind*. Oxford: Oxford University Press.

Persinger, M. (1975). ELF field meditation in spontaneous psi events. Direct information transfer or conditioned elicitation? *Psychoenergetic Systems, 3*, 155–169.

Persinger, M. (1979). ELF field mediation in spontaneous psi events. In C. T. Tart, H. E. Puthoff, & R. Targ (Eds.), *Mind at large*, pp. 191–204. New York: Praeger.

Persinger, M. (1985). Geophysical variables and human behaviour. *Perceptual and Motor Skills, 61*, 320–322.

Popper, K. (1959). *The logic of scientific discovery*. New York: Basic Books.

Poynton, J. C. (1994). Making sense of psi: Whiteman's multilevel ontology. *Journal of the Society for Psychical Research, 59*, 401–412.

Poynton, J. (2001). Challenges of out-of-body experiences: Does psychical research fully meet them? *Journal of the Society for Psychical Research, 65*, 194–206.

Poynton, J. (2011). Many levels, many worlds and psi: A guide to the work of Michael Whiteman. *Proceedings of the Society for Psychical Research, 59,* 109–139.

Pratt, D. (1997). Consciousness, causality and quantum physics. *Journal of Scientific Exploration, 11,* 69–78.

Pratt, J. C. (1974). Some notes for the future Einstein of parapsychology. *Journal of the American Society for Psychical Research, 68,* 133–155.

Price, H. H. (1953) Survival and the idea of another world. *Proceedings of the Society for Psychical Research, 50,* 1–25.

Puthoff, H. E. (1989). Gravity as a zero-point-fluctuation force. *Physical Review A* 39, 2333–2342.

Puthoff, H. E. (2007). Physics and metaphysics as co-emergent phenomena. In S. Savva, (Ed.), *Life and mind: In search of the physical basis.* Victoria, B.C: Trafford.

Radin, D. (1997). *The conscious universe: The scientific truth of psychic phenomena.* New York: Harper & Collins.

Radin, D. (2006). *Entangled minds: Extrasensory experiences in a quantum reality.* New York: Simon & Schuster.

Radin, D., & Nelson, R. (2002) Meta-analysis of mind-matter interaction experiments, 1959–2000. In W. Jonas & C. Crawford (Eds.), *Spiritual healing, energy, medicine and intentionality.* Edinburgh: Harcourt Health Sciences.

Radin, D., Nelson, R., Dobyns, Y., & Houtkooper, J. (2006). Reexamining psychokinesis: Comment on Bosch, Steinkamp and Boller. *Psychological Bulletin, 132,* 529–532.

Ralphs, J. (1992). *Exploring the fourth dimension.* London: Quantum.

Ramon, C., & Rauscher, E.A. (1980). Superluminal transformations in complex Minkowski space. *Foundations of Physics, 10,* 661–669.

Randall, L., & Sundrum, R. (1999). An alternative to compactification. *Physical Review Letters, 83,* 4690–4693.

Rauscher, E. A. (1979). Some physical models potentially applicable to anomalous phenomena. In A. Puharich (Ed.), *The Iceland Papers.* Amherst, WI: Essentia Research Associates.

Roe, C., Davey, R., & Stevens, P. (2003). Are ESP and PK aspects of a unitary phenomena? *Journal of Parapsychology, 67,* 343–366.

Roll, W. G. (1966). ESP and memory. *International Journal of Neuropsychiatry, 2,* 505–521.

Roll, W. G. (2003). Poltergeists, electromagnetism and consciousness. *Journal of Scientific Exploration, 17,* 75–86.

Roll, W. G., Burdick, D., & Joiner, W. T. (1973). Radial and tangential forces in the Miami poltergeist. *Journal of the Society for Psychical Research, 67,* 267–281.

Royce, J. (1904). *The world and the Individual.* London: Macmillan.

Ruderfer, M. (1980). Neutrino theory of psi phenomena. In B. Shapin & L. Coly (Eds.), *Communication and parapsychology,* pp 121–149. New York: Parapsychology Foundation.

Rush, J. H. (1986). Physics and quasi-physical theories of psi. In H. L. Edge et al. (Eds.), *Foundations of parapsychology: Exploring the boundaries of human capability,* pp. 276–292. London: Routledge & Kegan Paul.

Russell, B. (1948). *Human knowledge: Its scope and limits.* London: Allen and Unwin.

Sarfatti, J. (2006). *Supercosmos.* Bloomington, IN: Authorhouse.

Savitt, S. (2014). Being and becoming in modern physics. In E. N. Zalta (Ed.), *The Stanford Encyclopaedia of Philosophy* (Summer 2014 ed.). http://plato.stanford.edu/archives/sum2014/entries/spacetime-bebecome

Schmeidler, G. (1972). Respice, adspice, prospice, *Research in Parapsychology, 1971*, 117–143.

Sinclair, U. (1930). *Mental radio.* Springfield, IL: Thomas.

Sirag, S. P. (1993). Consciousness: A hyperspace view. In J. Mishlove (Ed.), *The roots of consciousness*, pp. 327–365. Tulsa, OK: Council Oaks Books.

Smolin, L. (2006). *The trouble with physics.* New York: Houghton-Mifflin.

Smythies, J. R. (1956). *Analysis of perception.* London: Routledge & Kegan Paul.

Smythies, J. R. (1988). Minds and higher dimensions. *Journal of the Society for Psychical Research, 64*, 242–244.

Smythies, J. R. (1994). *The walls of Plato's cave.* Aldershot: Avebury.

Smythies, J. R. (2003). Space, time and consciousness. *Journal of Consciousness Studies, 10*, 47–56.

Smythies, J. R. (2012). Consciousness and higher dimensions of space. *Journal of Consciousness Studies, 19*, 224–232.

Spottiswoods, S. J. P., & May, E. C. (2003). Skin conductance presentiment response: Analysis, artefacts and a pilot study. *Journal of Scientific Exploration, 17*, 617–642.

Srinivasan, T. M. (1988). *Energy medicine around the world.* Phoenix, AZ: Gabriel Press.

Stanford, R. G. (1974). An experimentally testable model for spontaneous psi events: I. Extrasensory events. *Journal of the American Society for Psychical Research, 68*, 34–57.

Stokes, D. M. (1991). Mathematics and parapsychology. *Journal of the American Society for Psychical Research, 85*, 251–290.

Stokes, D. M. (1997). *The nature of mind.* Jefferson, NC: McFarland.

Swanson, C. (2003). *The synchronized universe.* Tucson, AZ: Poseidia.

Tandy, V. (2002) A litmus test for infrasound. *Journal of the Society for Psychical Research, 66*, 167–174.

Targ, R., Puthoff, H. E., & May, E.C. (1979). Direct perception of remote geographic locations. In C.T. Tart, H. E. Puthoff, & R. Targ (Eds.). *Mind at large*, pp. 78–106. New York: Praeger.

Taylor, J. (1975). *Superminds.* New York: Warner.

Taylor, J. (2007). Memory and precognition. *Journal of Scientific Exploration, 21*, 553–571.

Thalbourne, M. A. (2004). *The common thread between ESP and PK*, Parapsychological Monograph No. 19. New York: Parapsychological Foundation.

Thouless, R. H., & Wiesner, B. P. (1947). The psi process in normal and paranormal psychology. *Proceedings of the Society for Psychical Research, 48*, 177–196.

Tiller, W. A. (1993). What are subtle energies? *Journal of Scientific Exploration, 7*, 293–304.

Valentini, A. (1991). Signal-locality, uncertainty and the subquantum H-theorem. *Physics Letters A, 158*, 1–8.

Vasiliev, L. L. (1976). *Exploration of distant influences.* New York: Dutton.

Walker, E. H. (1984) Quantum mechanics and parapsychology. *Journal of Indian Psychology, 4*, 21–26.

Walker, E. H. (2000). *The physics of consciousness: The quantum mind and the meaning of life.* Cambridge, MA: Perseus.

Wasserman, G. (1993). *Shadow matter and psychic phenomena.* Oxford: Mandrake.

Weyl, H. (1922). *Space-time-matter.* London: Constable.

Whiteman, J. H. M. (1977). Parapsychology and physics. In B. Wolman (Ed.), *Handbook of parapsychology*, pp. 730–756. New York: Van Nostrand Reinhold.

Whiteman, J. H. M. (1986). *Old and new evidence on the meaning of life: Vol. 1. An introduction to scientific mysticism*. Gerrards Cross, UK: Colin Smythe.

Wilkinson, H., & Gauld, A. (1993). Geomagnetism and anomalous experiences, 1868–1980. *Proceedings of the Society for Psychical Research, 57*, 275–310.

Witten, E. (1995). String theory dynamics in various dimensions. *Nuclear Physics B, 443*, 85–126.

Woit, P. (2006). *Not even wrong: The failure of string theory and the continuing challenge to unify the laws of physics*. New York: Basic Books.

Zeilinger, A. (2008). The reality tests. http://seedmagazine.com/content/article/the_reality_tests/P3/

Zöllner, J. C. F. (1880). *Transcendental physics* (C.C. Massey, trans.). London: W. H. Harrison.

Chapter 3

Physics beyond Causality: Making Sense of Quantum Mechanics and Certain Experimental Anomalies

Richard Shoup

> The law of causality, I believe, like much that passes muster among philosophers, is a relic of a bygone age, surviving, like the monarchy, only because it is erroneously supposed to do no harm.
>
> —Bertrand Russell

Given that the dynamic equations of physics are time symmetric, why can we send a message from past to future (evidently), but not from future to past? More generally, why do we steadfastly believe that experiments cause their results *and not vice-versa as well*?

Are all phenomena ruled by the traditional, deeply ingrained forward cause-and-effect principle, or do some well-controlled, well-documented experiments clearly demonstrate retrocausal influence, as suggested later in this chapter? And if some retrocausal effects have been demonstrated, does this necessarily demand a major revision of the extremely successful theories of relativity and quantum mechanics?

I will attempt to show here that all of these questions can have clear answers if only we will look deeply enough and reconsider (only) one or two of our deepest assumptions about the foundations of physics. If quantum phenomena appear to us as "weird" and violate "common sense," then perhaps we should take this as an indication that our underlying assumptions are faulty—that our common sense itself could benefit from some re-examination and revision. In addition, we may be able to shed some light on some experimental results and anomalies that appear to involve both distant and backward-in-time signaling.

There are two matters that I wish to address here: (1) the confusing and seemingly weird nature of quantum physics and (2) the anomalous phenomena known as *psi* or psychic phenomena. These two, as perhaps should be expected, turn out to be deeply related.

Toward these ends, this writing presents my theory and slightly idiosyncratic view of quantum physics, not ignoring orthodoxy, and with only slight departures from it. I then apply this theoretical viewpoint to both conventional quantum experimental situations and to psi phenomena such as telepathy, clairvoyance (remote viewing), and particularly precognition. The discussion here will be mostly in an informal style to focus on the deeper underlying concepts that are at issue, rather than on the standard formal mathematics that requires specialized knowledge and that often carries unrecognized and possibly unwise assumptions.

ABOUT QUANTUM PHYSICS

> We may say that there is at present no occasion and no reason to speak of causality in nature—because no [macroscopic] experiment indicates its presence and . . . quantum mechanics contradicts it.
>
> —John von Neumann

Quantum physics as taught today is still somewhat mysterious and incomprehensible. The theory works well, but almost no one claims to fully understand it. Students are admonished to not question the fundamentals but just "Shut up and calculate." Quantum mechanics (QM) is still famously incompatible with Einstein's relativity. In this section, we review two standard quantum experiments in order to ask whether the traditional concept of unidirectional cause and effect is inadequate, part of the problem, and in fact counterproductive, to a full understanding of quantum phenomena.

Classic Quantum Experiment I: EPR (Einstein, Podolsky, Rosen)

We may start with the simplest EPR configuration (Bell, 1964) shown in Figure 3.1 (left), where two particles are each put into a state of *superposition*

Figure 3.1
In a simple EPR configuration (left), two particles are each superposed and then entangled (E), move apart, and are later measured separately at A and at B. By relativity, an observer can move in such a way (center) that he sees A measured before B. An observer moving oppositely (right) sees B measured before A in the same situation. The two measurements always correlate, so ordinary causality is not arguable as an explanation.

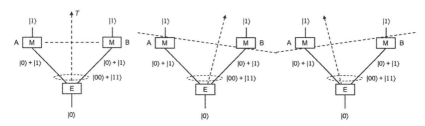

of two binary states (spin up or down, for example), then *entangled* (coupled via an interaction into a combined inseparable state) and sent off in different directions. The entangled particles are later measured independently at two distant locations. As has been well confirmed by experiments, the two measurements will give random but highly correlated (opposite or identical) up-down results, despite being unable to communicate with each other in the conventional sense. No information passes from one to the other during measurement, yet the particles retain their correlated relationship because of the earlier entangling interaction.

Literally dozens of interpretations of the formalism of QM (some are actually extrapolations or extensions) have been proposed to make "sense" of the entanglement phenomenon. See a summary in Omnes (1994) and examples such as Aharonov, Bergmann, and Lebowitz (1964) and Costa de Beauregard (1998). The fact that none of these interpretations is fully and widely accepted after more than 80 years of discussion suggests again that something is lacking in our deeper conceptualizations of physical reality and interactions, and specifically that our common-sense notion of causality is flawed.

Somewhat disturbing to newcomers and most experts alike is that the EPR phenomena seems to violate the foundational principle of causality—that causes must precede their effects—and that what happens locally seems to affect something very far away (sooner than a light signal could transit). Even more disturbing is the realization that under certain relative motions (by special relativity), two observers could differ on their judgment of which measurement happened first (Figure 3.1 center and right). Since neither measurement is in the forward light cone of the other, there is no canonical ordering. The order is, in fact, observer dependent, and thus there can be no causal relationship between them in the usual sense. The two measurements remain independently random and yet-perfectly correlated, and the outcomes seem to be linked by some mechanism that is beyond causality.

Classic Quantum Experiment 2: Interferometer with Delayed Choice

John Archibald Wheeler's famous delayed choice thought experiment (Wheeler, 1978) puts a very fine point on the issue of causality (Figure 3.2). In this optical interferometer experiment, and in careful experimental confirmations (Jacques, 2007), a future action can apparently determine the entire prior history of the transiting photon.

Two beam splitters, BS1 and BS2, each pass or reflect an incident photon on its path toward detectors D1 and D2. If both beam splitters are in place, and paths are of equal length, an incoming photon will take both paths (in superposition) and will interfere with itself at BS2, thus arriving at D2 exclusively. If BS2 is removed, however, photons will take one or the other path from BS1 (supposedly at random) and be detected at both D1 and D2 equally. Since beam splitter BS2 can be removed after the photon has already passed BS1 (the "delayed choice"), BS2's presence or absence appears to determine what happened previously at BS1. Again, our traditional concept of causality seems to be inadequate to describe this phenomenon.

Wheeler dramatically amplified the impact of this situation by proposing that such an interferometer could be composed using two paths of light bent around a distant star or galaxy by gravitational lensing, thus allowing the final beam splitter's presence or absence to seemingly determine what happened billions of years previously.

From these two experiments alone (and many others, see Radin, 2006) we can infer that the traditional idea of forward-only causality has little meaning or explanatory power, especially where the correlation of entangled quantum variables is concerned. Something deeper is needed within physical theory—and experimental results in parapsychology make an even stronger case. For a current account of time-entangled states, see (Aharonov et al. [2012] and Moreva et al. [2014]).

ABOUT PARAPSYCHOLOGY

Despite its antiquated and awkward name, the field of parapsychology has much to offer physics and science as a whole. Elusive but persistent phenomena such as telepathy, clairvoyance, precognition, and psychokinesis (collectively known as psi phenomena) have been observed repeatedly in carefully controlled laboratory experiments by numerous experimenters over decades. Unfortunately, a great deal of nonsense

Figure 3.2
Wheeler's delayed choice experiment. With both beam splitters in place, all photons are detected at detector D2 due to interference at BS2. But if BS2 is absent, photons arrive equally and randomly at D1 and at D2. Wheeler observed that the decision about the presence or absence of BS2 could be made after a photon had already passed BS1.

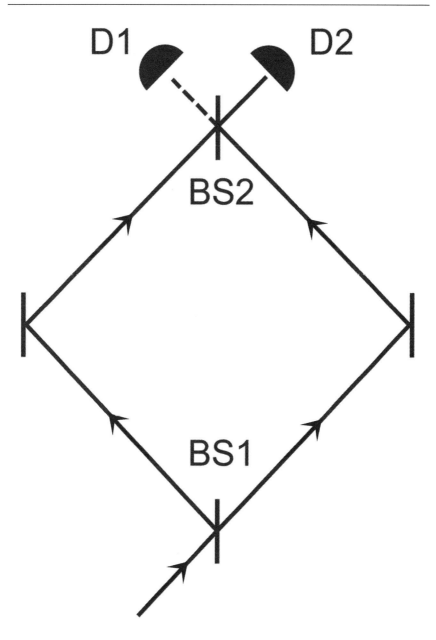

surrounding "paranormal" experiences in the general culture has tended to obscure and drown out this important scientific research.

There is highly credible evidence for these phenomena, with obvious significant implications, and these data should be seriously examined and studied by every forward-looking physicist interested in a deeper understanding of reality. Excellent introductions to this body of research along with extensive source references may be found in books such as Radin (1997, 2006), Broughton (1992), Krippner and Friedman (2010), Carter (2012), and in peer-reviewed journals such as the journal of the AAAS-affiliated Parapsychological Association *Journal of Parapsychology*, the *Journal of the Society for Psychical Research*, and the *Journal of the Society for Scientific Exploration*.

Until recently, most physicists have assumed—largely without examination—that these experimental data cannot be taken seriously because they appear to violate well-tested and accepted physical laws, and especially offend our base assumption of cause and effect. In fact, it has been believed and asserted by some scientists that a complete rewrite of physics would be necessary if these phenomena were real (Gell-Mann, 1994). But as we strongly suggest later in this chapter, and as some physicists are beginning to recognize (Elitzur, Dolev, & Zeilinger, 2002), this is simply not so, and only modest changes in the foundations of quantum theory are needed to allow and to explain many of the phenomena that have been observed in parapsychology experiments for many years.

Characteristics of Psi Phenomena

From the significant body of experimental evidence, a few important properties of these anomalous psi phenomena have emerged. We list a few of them here to provoke interest, and for reference later, but without thorough discussion.

1. *Time/order independence (clairvoyance vs. precognition)*. Evidence suggests that an experimental target symbol or image can be (randomly) chosen before *or after* the subject's response with nearly equal success.
2. *Complexity independence (goal orientation)*. Evidence suggests that the complexity of the task does not matter very much, only the desired outcome.
3. *Experimenter effect (belief, audience)*. Evidence suggests that some experimenters routinely observe significant psi effects, while others do not, even when employing the same experimental protocol. (Note relation to 2 above.)

4. *Selectivity.* Evidence suggests that a subject can "tune in" to a particular target, often at a distance in space or in time or both.
5. *Small effect, elusive.* Evidence suggests that while these effects are well confirmed in many careful laboratory experiments, they remain small and elusive, and mitigating variables are yet to be fully identified and understood.

Perhaps the most shocking and problematic—and thus the most pregnant—characteristic of psi phenomena listed is their apparent independence of time order (1 above). Experimentally, for example, it does not

seem to matter much whether a remote viewing takes place before, during, or after the viewed event (Radin, 1997). Persistent evidence suggests strongly that thinking about these phenomena in terms of the usual notions of cause and effect is likely to be counterproductive and may in fact be a major impediment to a deeper understanding.

Importance of Challenging the Law of Causality

Psi phenomena represent both a very significant challenge and an opportunity, surely important for their own explanation, and for science as a whole, and thus should be of great interest to any technological society. With the stakes as high as causality, randomness, and time, it is difficult to overstate the importance of research into psi phenomena. Progress in this area may well lead to a reformulation and reinterpretation of quantum theory, as suggested later in this chapter, and thus to deep reconsideration of some parts of physics. Even the scientific method itself, based largely on a concept of limited causality and forward influence, may be in need of reexamination. However, it does appear that a major rewriting of physics is *not* indicated or necessary, and would be highly implausible in any case.

ABOUT SCIENTIFIC PROGRESS

Science resolutely and formally rests on the experimental *evidence*, not merely our current beliefs and theories. We are permitted to ask questions of Nature, and must accept her answers, even when—*especially* when—we do not like them. It is exactly that evidence that does not fit our current paradigm that holds the keys to new learnings and breakthroughs. The conundrum that remains quantum physics today—after the better part of a century since its formulation, the theory works very well, but no one really understands it—clearly indicates that there is something wrong with our deepest assumptions about Nature. The evidence from parapsychology makes an even stronger case for rethinking foundational assumptions. This chapter presents our best attempt to show what is wrong and how to fix it, and it touches on some of the implications of a new viewpoint.

Characteristics of a Revised Theory

As strongly suggested earlier in this chapter, a new theory is needed. As computer pioneer Carver Mead has remarked, "The [quantum revolution] got stuck about a quarter of the way around" (Mead, 2013). We strive to finish this job by developing a new and revised theory with the following characteristics:

Sensibility

The theory must "make sense" in that it should be comprehensible and explainable without great recourse to ungrounded assumption or taking refuge in isolated mathematical description. This may, and almost certainly will, require the reader to give up certain deeply held assumptions —formerly "common" sense—and readjust his or her viewpoint rather than accept radical new assumptions or principles.

Compatibility

The theory must be compatible with well-established existing physics and experimental results to a very great degree. Most likely, this will be accomplished not by rewriting existing theory but by discovering and developing new and deeper foundations to the physics that we already have.

Explanatory Power

The new theory must explain (provide a plausible basis for) both existing and known phenomena as much as possible, and predict new ones. In particular, we desire here (1) a better way of understanding QM and (2) a way to understand psi phenomena such as telepathy, clairvoyance, and precognition. In these cases, testable hypotheses should suggest themselves such that new experiments may be designed and performed. Ideally, a revised theory will provide new foundations for existing physics as well as significant implications for future physics.

A SLIGHTLY REVISED QUANTUM THEORY

> The man who cannot occasionally imagine events and conditions of existence that are contrary to the causal principle as he knows it will never enrich his science by the addition of a new idea.
> —Max Planck

To materially approach the issue of causality and its place in quantum theory, we need to reconsider some of the most basic elements of such a theory, including states, values, relations among variables, and then to re-examine our understanding of the concepts of superposition, entanglement, and measurement.

Values and Superposition

Omne possibile exigit existere.
(Everything that is possible demands to exist.)

—G. Leibniz

The most significant problem in understanding quantum theory is not the mathematical formulation, it is in our conceptualization of what a "value" or "state" is, and in our classical macroscopic assumptions about causality and the nature of time (Price, 1996).

Quantum physics is often described as strange or nonsensical because it permits an object to be "in two places at the same time" or allows a particle to "go through both slits simultaneously." To sidestep this conceptual difficulty, we recommend thinking of the value of a variable as the solution to a set of constraints or boundary conditions. (As discussed later in this chapter, some of these constraints may lie in the past, the present, or even the future.)

In this view, variables, and entire configurations or states, can have *multiple values*, that is, multiple solutions to the constraints that are placed on them, whether in abstract mathematics or in physical "reality." For example, in the delayed choice arrangement mentioned earlier, there are two possible paths after the first beam splitter. The photon in this case can be described as going both ways—in a sense, taking both paths—in a combined state called *superposition*.

To mitigate the strangeness of this concept, consider the more familiar and yet entirely analogous example of a real polynomial equation with multiple roots, such as

$$x^2 - 1 = 0, \text{ whose roots are } x = \{+1, -1\}.$$

This equation may be considered as a *constraint* on the value of x, distinguishing those several values that are valid or possible in the given situation from those that are not. Multiple solutions are, of course, nothing surprising in the case of real-world situations represented by polynomials.

By direct analogy to the aforementioned polynomial equation, we could have a physical arrangement that included a quantum binary variable, or *qubit*, in a superposition of two values (in Dirac notation $|0\rangle$ and $|1\rangle$, e.g. spins or polarizations or paths). A vector in Hilbert space is often used to represent a composite of the two possible outcomes, equally weighted, yielding probabilities when measured of $p(0) = p(1) = 0.5$. (For simplicity, we omit all normalizing constants in this and subsequent discussion.)

$$|0\rangle + |1\rangle$$

The point here is that a polynomial or other constraining equation with multiple solutions—a situation frequently encountered in engineering and science—is no different or stranger or less definite than a superposition

of values in a quantum state variable or wave function. In both cases, a constraint serves to restrict or reduce the domain of values that would otherwise be available, whether mathematical and abstract, or physical and "real." These composite values can be distinguished equivalently by a description of the constraint system itself, by a multiset of enumerated values, or by a formalism, as is typical in QM using vectors in a multidimensional space. The difference is that in a classical configuration modeled with a polynomial, a root is typically chosen by convention to match the physical situation, whereas in the quantum case, a value is the unique result of measurement and is thought to be random.

The concept of a superposed or composite value is analogous to our commonsense notion of several distinct possible outcomes. In everyday life, of course, we as macroscopic creatures will see only singular classical values. Everything we experience has a single position, takes only one path, and has only one outcome. Still, there are many paths from San Jose to San Francisco, even though we drive along only one of them on any given trip.

It is a useful extension of "common sense" to consider multiple solutions to a constraint system as one value, though possibly composite. In the delayed choice configuration, for example, the particle does not itself move along both paths in the usual classical sense, but both paths are included in a single *set of possibilities*, and these are captured in the corresponding Dirac vector or wave function. One way to state what distinguishes quantum from classical mechanics—and what our common sense must be extended to include—is that *in the quantum realm, possibilities are "real" and can interact to have real effects.*

Quantum mechanics is about possibilities, not just actual completed interactions in the usual classical sense. Superposition may be thought of as an underconstrained combination of the possible classical outcomes of a measurement and not something mysterious. Through superposition, nature takes advantage of all opportunities open to it, those defined by the constraints imposed by a physical experimental configuration, both past and future. This is the core of the physicist's path integral or sum-of-histories approach (Schulman, 1981). Speaking of the real effects of these possibilities, we might say informally, *"Everything that can be, is, and everything that can happen, does."*

As Steven Pinker has pointed out (2002, p. 220), we tend to function based on our inherent intuitions about the way the world works. He provides a tentative list of such core intuitions that include intuitive physics, intuitive biology, intuitive engineering, intuitive psychology, a spatial sense, a number sense, a sense of probability, intuitive economics, a mental database and logic, and language. Thus, we find it difficult to learn Newtonian physics until we have unlearned intuitive physics (p. 223). QM falls further outside the domain of our naïve intuitive physics,

making it an even more perplexing subject to understand. Thus, *if what happens in the real physical world conflicts with our common sense, it is our common sense that must yield.*

Relations and Functions

> It is contrary to the mode of thinking in science to conceive of a thing . . . which acts itself, but which cannot be acted upon.
> —Albert Einstein

If we abandon the time-honored "law" of cause and effect, what replaces it? Configurations, including several variables, are best thought of as embodying one or more bidirectional *relations* among the variables. A relation is defined here as *a restriction on joint values* of two or more variables and is usually expressed as an equation. For example, if integer variables x and y are constrained by the equation $x + y = 0$, then x and y are each singly completely unconstrained, able to individually take on any value in their domain; their *joint* values, however, are restricted to pairs satisfying the given equation—a much more limited set than all pairs of independent values. In this case, when one variable has been chosen or fixed, the other is also determined uniquely.

Entanglement, similarly, is a quantum state that typically involves a constraint on joint values of two or more variables together but not on the variables individually. In the basic EPR setup mentioned earlier in this chapter, for example, each particle when measured appears to give a completely random result, yet the two will be strongly correlated, showing the presence of a joint constraint. The difference in the quantum situation is again that neither value is determined until one of them is measured.

Several existing interpretations of QM, including Cramer's quite successful transactional interpretation (1988), for example, utilize both forward and backward "waves" or other imagined communication to establish the total relationship between entities in a quantum interaction. It is suggested here that these two aspects be combined into a single relation, a nondirectional constraint on joint values, *neither solely causal nor retrocausal*. Causality (in either direction) in these situations should be replaced by bidirectional relational concepts such as *influence, dependence,* and *correlation.*

With the following simple conversion between Fahrenheit and Celsius temperatures, we illustrate the usual forward *conversion function* or process with two algorithms (sets of computational steps) to be executed depending on the desired direction. (This form of the conversion takes advantage of the fact that the two scales coincide at –40 degrees.)

$$°C = (°F + 40) \times \frac{5}{9} - 40$$

$$°F = (°C + 40) \times \frac{9}{5} - 40.$$

Tradition and algebraic habits have caused us to write equations in this functional way, with the algebraic expression (the computation) on one side and the "result" on the other. Computer programming languages have evolved to mirror this process. But the true symmetry of this relation can be seen clearly if it is written a bit differently:

$$5 \, (°F + 40) = 9 \, (°C + 40).$$

Computation can proceed in either direction in this conversion *relation*, and the two variables are thus mutually constrained. When the two variables are linked together in this way, no directionality is implied until one of F and C is chosen as "open" (undetermined, the dependent variable), and the other is given a particular fixed value (the independent variable). Then only might it be said that the fixed value "causes" the open value to become fixed as well. It is this symmetry that precludes the usual notion of causality and that we need to emphasize in thinking about physical configurations, especially in quantum mechanics.

Preparation, Measurement, and Randomness

> [QM] yields much, but it hardly brings us closer to the Old One's secrets. I, in any case, am convinced that He does not play dice.
>
> —Albert Einstein, letter to Max Born

The most controversial aspect of QM from its inception through to today has been *measurement* of a quantum variable. Typically, the initial state of a qubit is *prepared* (manipulated) into a balanced superposition of states, say $|0\rangle$ and $|1\rangle$. (Many different implementations are possible, including polarizations, spins, etc.) This qubit may then undergo some processing or *hermitian* (lossless, reversible) interaction with other qubits. Eventually, it will undergo *measurement*—an interaction that is considered in orthodox QM to be a "projection" or "collapse" of the wave function to a classical value and thus nonhermitian, irreversible, and nondeterministic (i.e. random, causeless, and unpredictable in principle) (Omnes, 1994).

Without detailed justification here, we strongly subscribe to the view that *quantum measurement is a unitary transformation* like any other evolution of the wave function. (This is in some ways similar to several well-known interpretations of QM such as decoherence [Zurek, 2003] as well as to Wheeler-Feynman [1945] absorber theory.) In this view, in the simplest case, *measurement is just the time-reverse of preparation* and consists only of *unitary* (i.e., lossless, reversible) operations like every other change of state. There is no mysterious "collapse of the wave function," no information loss, and no randomness inherent in this process. By this model and new understanding of measurement, a better name for it might be "postparation."

It should be pointed out that if measurement were really a fundamentally random "collapse"—in principle, causeless and unpredictable—then *something* would still be required to determine the outcome, for example, 0 or 1 in a binary system. To extend Einstein's famous complaint slightly, do we think that God himself not only rolls his dice but also reaches down and sets the result of each and every measurement? In a more mundane but real sense, one bit of information would have to be supplied from *somewhere* to make this binary determination each time. Ultimately, it must be concluded that *the idea of a truly causeless event has no meaning* and furthermore would violate conservation of information and energy were it possible.

In the absence of continual divine intervention, *the necessary determining information can come from only one place—the measurer* and the future dependencies (receivers, absorbers) to which it is connected (Aharonov, Bergmann, & Lebowitz, 1964; Aharonov & Rohrlich, 2005; Cramer, 1988), including measurement equipment, the experimenter, and observers. A constraint or boundary condition in the future can (and must) determine an otherwise underconstrained value, just as can an initial boundary condition in the past, or both can have effects. This symmetry and the unitarity of measurement follows directly from conservation principles and from giving up the orthodox *assumption* of nonunitary measurement derived from Bohr's statistical interpretation of the wave function and von Neumann's "collapse" hypothesis, sometimes called process 1 (von Neumann, 1955).

However, if no dice are involved, why do quantum measurements typically give random-appearing results, in keeping with the usual assumption of quantum theory, and yet still governed by the coefficients of the wave function? Perhaps the outcomes of measurements typically made in our macroscopic, room-temperature world *appear* highly random because the measurement device and the future to which it is connected are highly complex and disordered. This suggests that such *a measurement event—and thus the theory itself—is not fundamentally random or statistical in nature at all* but usually seems so when a large number of particles are involved. Typical measurement instruments, and even a human observer, are complex macroscopic objects and thus must see (and in many cases partially determine) classical but random-appearing results.

Furthermore, if the measurement apparatus and the future to which it is connected include more possibilities for one outcome than another, a *bias* will exist toward that result, just as the preparation can supply unequal coefficient to the wave function, for example,

$$\alpha \,|0\rangle + \beta \,|1\rangle.$$

Rather than the uniform random distribution typically found with macroscopic measurement devices in the laboratory, an unbalanced distribution or an unexpected correlation could be seen, even if the source is a "quantum-random" process such as nuclear particle decay.

Ultimately, by this theory, all such measurement outcomes must be determined by combined influences from the past *and* the future, including (by backward influence) the observers and their dependencies *and biases*. Acceptance of such a time-symmetrical and unitary view of measurement within the physics community is sparse today, but the supporting evidence has become difficult to ignore, and the implications are quite significant when this theory is fully unfolded and appreciated. As examples, later in this discussion we consider some situations in which seemingly random measurement outcomes appear to have been deliberately manipulated via future conditions to produce interesting phenomena.

APPLICATIONS AND IMPLICATIONS

Adoption of a relational rather than causal approach has various significant implications for quantum physics, most especially for phenomena often seen in parapsychology.

In Quantum Physics

Even the great initial success of the Quantum Theory does not make me believe in the fundamental dice-game, although I am well aware that our younger colleagues interpret this as a consequence of senility. No doubt the day will come when we will see whose instinctive attitude was the correct one.

—Albert Einstein, letter to Max Born

Any other implications aside, we contend that this theory captures a simpler yet fully capable theory of quantum mechanics without major injury to that theory or to the greater foundations of science. Giving up the unnecessary and inappropriate assumption of forward-only cause and effect is the key element and is long overdue, as some others have also concluded (Aharonov, Bergmann, & Lebowitz, 1964).

In this theory, QM no longer presents a conundrum, and the major source of supposed indeterminacy and "weirdness" is removed at its root. With a better understanding of the nature of superposition and entanglement, all quantum evolution is seen to be unitary—a vast simplification and return to sensibility. By combining the two arrows of influence, forward and backward also seen in several other popular interpretations (Cramer, 1988; Vaidman, 2007), we can benefit from the further simplification of a single bidirectional relation.

Taking full account of future constraints that may influence present events (or possibilities of present events), we model and predict all the usual quantum phenomena but with a much simpler logical structure. Standard examples such as the two-slit experiment, EPR, delayed choice, and so on are explained plausibly. Spooky action at a distance is no longer, and Einstein and Aharonov are vindicated.

By the same token, the supposed randomness of quantum processes, and thus the implied statistical character of all quantum interactions, is called into question (and denied). Both the new theory and abundant evidence suggest that assumed random processes are in fact mutable and that anomalous phenomena that appear to violate causality do indeed happen. When investigating these phenomena, it is generally assumed that physical random processes such as true random number generators (RNGs) produce definite values in a completely noncausal way and thus represent the gold standard for independence in experimental sciences. In contrast (and ironically, according to the present theory), a true RNG appears instead to be the *least* definite, most open, most malleable device possible. Having no bias whatsoever of its own, by design, it is completely subservient to incoming influences from its connections in the future, the very clients it purports to serve.

While the theory presented in this discussion shows promise, it should be clear that we have just scratched the surface of understanding and interpreting it, particularly in the experimental explorations undertaken thus far in this area. The potential implications for science and society of a deeper understanding of causality, randomness, and time are quite broad and consequential, and thus further research is strongly indicated.

In Parapsychology

If you haven't found something strange during the day it hasn't been much of a day.

—John A. Wheeler

We cannot say that all or even some psi phenomena *must* be due to and explained by this theory. However, we can show that some of them *can* be so explained, and thus the orthodox complaint that psi phenomena violate existing physics is repudiated.

Consider a highly simplified ESP forced-choice guessing experiment of the form shown in Figure 3.3. The subject makes his guess (perhaps a card, a number, a picture, etc., given by symbol S) trying to match that of a target generator (symbol T), and the results are tallied (the result R, a hit or a miss).

Suppose an experiment of this type has been conducted, and the results show a hit rate higher than that expected by chance, as is the case in many published examples in the literature (Rhine, 1934, 1936; Honorton & Ferrari, 1989; Radin, 1997, 2006). We assume the experimental situation is carefully controlled and that all forms of ordinary signaling or leakage between subject and the target generator have been prevented and ask how this physical anomaly could be explained. Consider four general possibilities as highlighted in the figure:

1. *Influence from T to S in the present.* The subject was somehow able to sense the target symbol and adjust his guesses accordingly. This is the simplest explanation for either clairvoyance (S chosen after T) or precognition (S chosen before T). The associated mechanism would have to include a previously undetected means of

Figure 3.3
Possible paths to bring about extrachance correlation between subject and target. Direct interactions in the present (1) (2); prior interactions or common cause (3); and backward influence from bias on results due to future constraints or interactions (4).

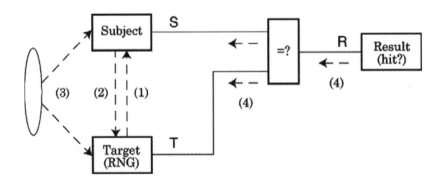

information transfer utilizing an undiscovered human sensitivity or sense organ. This does not seem very plausible, yet it is still a commonly assumed hypothesis about how these phenomena must work. Moreover, if the target is chosen after the guess, then the subject must possess some precognitive ability, and this would require information flow backward in time, contrary to relativity and the "law" of cause and effect.

2. *Influence from S to T in the present.* The subject was somehow able to affect the target generator directly. This is the usual psychokinetic explanation, difficult to accept, yet apparently supported by many careful real-world experiments, for example, Schmidt, (1978) and Jahn and Dunne (2005). Quantum processes that are now considered to be fundamentally random would have to be influenceable, and information would have to be conveyed in some currently unknown way. A new or unnoticed force or field would seem to be necessary—unlikely in the face of existing and well-tested physical theory.

3. *Influence via the past (common cause or prior interaction).* The subject was somehow able to make use of prior correlations or entanglement between himself and the target generator to make or adjust his guesses, similarly to (1) above but conditioned by some connection from the past. After all, real RNGs have a physical history, and their performance may not be entirely isolated from past events, as is usually intended and assumed. Also, it is generally thought that any residual correlations between well-separated objects would have been erased long ago by unavoidable decoherence at ordinary temperatures, but this seems far from conclusively established.

4. *Influence via the future.* Anomalous results in the future were reflected backward through the equality constraint to affect the target generator by *future* influence, similarly to (3) above but relying on a future *biased* interaction. It is this hypothesis that has been almost uniformly unnoticed or ignored, and in which we are most interested.

With hypotheses (1) and (2) above, an additional unknown path of influence or information flow would be necessary between S and T, and this seems to be in serious conflict with current well-explored physical theory. However, alternatives (3) and (4) do not require any direct or indirect information transfer between S and T, instead relying on correlation, and thus do not imply a mysterious path nor the difficulties associated with it.

In particular, hypothesis (4) (correlation due to future interactions) can readily account for many if not all of the so-called clairvoyant, precognitive, and psychokinetic anomalistic effects apparently exhibited in such experiments. Furthermore, it is in good agreement with the afore-mentioned psi characteristics as well, *without* requiring new paths or mechanism or any major insult to well-accepted physical law. If we allow time-symmetric (bidirectional) influence as argued earlier in this discussion, no information is transferred retrocausally, yet unexpected correlations may appear just as if it had been. In other words, the *freedom inherent in the RNG is constrained by influence from the future* (a bias on the results), and correlation with the subject is seen as a consequence.

Note that the uniform distribution of targets generated by the RNG is still completely preserved so long as the distribution of the subject's guesses is relatively uniform. The case of extrachance results with biased subject guesses is discussed in Shoup (2002).

SUMMARY AND FREQUENTLY ASKED QUESTIONS

Informally: *Events in the past and in the future conspire to create the present.* Perhaps the simplest way to summarize this approach to quantum physics and its implications is in the form of a list of frequently asked questions:

Q: Can future events influence the present?
A: Yes, in effect, *if* the present is underconstrained by the past. This is most clearly demonstrated in the basic quantum experiments such as Young's two-slit, EPR, and delayed choice.

Q: Does God play dice?
A: No! By this theory, nothing is fundamentally random or causeless, which would imply a violation of conservation of energy and information. Einstein was right.

Q: Does the wave function really "collapse"?
A: Not at all. It is all unitary evolution, measurement included. By this theory, measurement is seen as an entirely time-symmetrical reflection of preparation.

Q: Are RNG outputs really random and causeless?
A: No. According to this theory, nothing is fundamentally random or causeless. Processes considered "quantum random" are in superposition or underconstrained (by the past) until future constraints due to interactions such as measurement resolve them to unique values. They appear random because these interactions are often highly complex. An RNG is best thought of as a reflection of its future, not itself an independent source.

Q: Isn't this theory thus deterministic, so free will is ruled out?
A: It is, but most of what we think of as free will is psychological and is not threatened.

Q: Are psi phenomena possible and real?
A: Yes. The evidence is quite extensive and consistent, and new theory predicts it, but the effects are usually small and elusive with today's knowledge and techniques.

Q: Do psi phenomena require rewriting physics?
A: No, but some modest changes to the assumptions and formalism of QM are needed. These allow the quantum realm to be much better understood as well.

Q: Do psi phenomena imply information transfer?
A: Not necessarily. Correlation due to past *or future* entanglement can *appear* to be information transfer if underdetermined events are involved. Future constraints can have an effect if the past does not determine the future completely, that is, when a superposition exists via the inclusion of a random process as a source. Examples include telepathy, clairvoyance, precognition, and even psychokinesis in some cases. For example, in a precognition experiment, random determination of the targets by the RNG may correlate with the subject's guess more often than chance, thus making it appear that information has propagated backward from the future.

Q: Can a message be sent into the past?
A: Yes. In general, one can *send* a message into the past via superposition or entanglement and have an effect on *extant possibilities* there—where there is still some freedom. But *the message cannot be received there* (i.e., have a direct effect on the past) because doing so would affect the superposition, remove some open possibilities, and in effect "send" a conventional message *to* the future instead.

Q: Can psi effects be made large and controllable?
A: Yes, in principle, by biasing future interactions significantly toward the desired outcomes. But it would apparently require manipulating *many* particles to do this.

To summarize, in this chapter, we have reviewed the time-honored "law" of cause and effect and its inadequacies in dealing with quantum phenomena and other well-researched experimental phenomena. By replacing forward-only causality with symmetric relations, we arrive at a slightly modified theory that is simpler and less mysterious, that represents all known quantum phenomena in a more understandable structure, that does not violate conservation laws, and that does not require or invoke fundamental randomness in its explanations. Future constraints can influence what happened in the past *if* there is some freedom available, for example, by superposition of possibilities generated by a random source.

In addition to simplifying and clarifying standard quantum theory, this theory can serve as a basis for explaining phenomena seen for decades in well-controlled laboratory experiments in parapsychology, including those sometimes incorrectly thought to violate physical law.

REFERENCES

Aharonov, Y., Bergmann, P., & Lebowitz, J. (1964). Time symmetry in the quantum process of measurement. *Physical Reviews, 134*, B1410–B1416.

Aharonov, Y., Cohen, E., Grossman, D., & Elizutr, A. C. (2012). Can a future choice affect a past measurement's outcome? arXiv:1206.6224v5

Aharonov, Y., & Rohrlich, D. (2005). *Quantum paradoxes: Quantum theory for the perplexed*. Weinheim, Germany: Wiley-VCH.

Bell, J. (1964). On the Einstein Podolsky Rosen paradox. *Physics, 1*, 195–200.

Broughton, R. (1992). *Parapsychology: The controversial science*. New York: Ballantine.

Carter, C. (2012). *Science and psychic phenomena*. Rochester: Inner Traditions.

Costa de Beauregard, O. (1998). Timelike nonseparability and retrocausation. arXiv:quant-ph/9804069v1

Cramer, J. (1988). An overview of the transactional interpretation of quantum mechanics. *International Journal of Theoretical Physics, 27*. http://mist.npl.washington.edu/ npl/int_rep/toc.html

Elitzur, A., Dolev, S., & Zeilinger, A. (2002). Time-reversed EPR and the choice of histories in quantum mechanics. *Quantum Computers and Computing, Proceedings of 22nd Solvay Conference in Physics*. World Scientific. See also arXiv:quant-ph/0205182.

Gell-Mann, M. (1994). *The quark and the jaguar*. New York: Holt and Co.

Honorton, C., & Ferrari, D. C. (1989). "Future telling": A meta-analysis of forced-choice precognition experiments, 1935–1987. *Journal of Parapsychology, 53*, 281–301.

Jacques, V. (2007). Experimental realization of Wheeler's delayed-choice gedanken experiment. *Science 315*, 966–968. See also arXiv:quant-ph/0610241v1.

Jahn, R. G., & Dunne, B. J. (2005). The PEAR proposition. *Journal of Scientific Exploration, 19*(2), 195–246. http://www.princeton.edu/~pear.

Krippner, S., & Friedman, H. L. (2010). *Debating psychic experience: Human potential or human illusion?* Santa Barbara, CA: Praeger.

Mead, C. (2013). *The evolution of technology*. Retrieved from ISSCC conference 2013 plenary address: http://isscc.org/media/2013/plenary/Carver_Mead

Moreva, E., Brida, G., Gramegna, M., Giovannetti, V., Maccone, L., & Genovese, M. (2014). Time from quantum entanglement: An experimental illustration. *Physical Review A, 89*(5), 052122.

Omnes, R. (1994). *The interpretation of quantum mechanics*. Princeton, NJ: Princeton University Press.

Pinker, S. (2002). *The blank slate: The modern denial of human nature.* New York: Viking.

Price, H. (1996). *Time's arrow and Archimedes point.* New York: Oxford University Press.

Radin, D. (1997). *The conscious universe.* New York: HarperEdge.

Radin, D. (2006). *Entangled minds.* New York: Paraview.

Rhine, J. B. (1934). Extra-sensory perception of the clairvoyant type. *Journal of Abnormal and Social Psychology, 29,* 151–171.

Rhine, J. B. (1936). Some selected experiments in extra-sensory perception. *Journal of Abnormal and Social Psychology, 31,* 216–228.

Russell, B. (1913). On the notion of cause. *Proceedings of the Aristotelian Society, 13,* 1–26.

Schmidt, H. (1978). Observation of a psychokinetic effect under highly controlled conditions. *Foundations of Physics, 8* (5/6). http://www.fourmilab.ch/rpkp

Schulman, L. S. (1981). *Techniques and applications of path integration.* New York: John Wiley & Sons.

Shoup, R. (2002). Anomalies and constraints: Can clairvoyance, precognition and psychokinesis be accommodated within known physics? *Journal of Scientific Exploration, 16*(1), 3–18.

Vaidman, L. (2007). The two-state vector formalism. arXiv:0706.1347v1

von Neumann, J. (1955). *Mathematical foundations of quantum mechanics.* Princeton, NJ: Princeton University Press.

Wheeler, J. A. (1978). The "past" and the delayed-choice double-slit experiment. In A. R. Marlow (Ed.), *Mathematical foundations of quantum theory.* New York: Academic Press.

Wheeler, J. A., & Feynman, R. P. (1945). Interaction with the absorber as the mechanism of radiation. *Reviews of Modern Physics, 17,* 157–161.

Zurek, W. H. (2003). Decoherence and the transition from quantum to classical: Revisited. arXiv:quant-ph/0306072

Chapter 4

Remembrance of Things Future: A Case for Retrocausation and Precognition

Daniel P. Sheehan

Time's passage is an irreducible condition of our existence. Consciousness plays in the present, memories order the past, while speculation and uncertainty cloud the future. In physics, time is essential to defining and interpreting virtually everything, while it remains poorly defined itself. Its unidirectional progression represents perhaps the starkest asymmetry in nature and one of the great explanandums of science. In what sense do the past and future exist? Does the future have an equivalent ontological status to the past? If so, why is this not evident to us, and if not, why not and how is it different? The past shapes the present through memories and relics, but does the future also have a say? More to the point, although the fundamental laws of nature are time symmetric in their formulations, and so admit equally solutions in which time runs in both directions, why do we experience time running in just one direction? Though these questions can be simply posed, science offers no satisfactory answers—and even largely eschews the questions.

Over the past seven decades, a significant body of experimental evidence has accumulated to indicate that information from the future can be accessed from the present, via so-called *precognition*; however, this evidence is not widely accepted by the scientific community. There are at least two overarching reasons for this. First, there is no explanatory theory for precognition that is acceptable to mainstream science (physics). Second, it implicitly violates causality, a concept so familiar in everyday experience that it is virtually unquestioned by the scientific community. Taken together, they place precognition not only outside the scientific mainstream but beyond the pale of polite discussion.

The theoretical resources applied to the phenomenon of precognition have thus far been miniscule compared with those applied to other, more acceptable, problems like dark energy, dark matter, or high-temperature superconductivity, and this lack might be the decisive impediment to a viable theory; however, an even more fundamental question must be faced first: Is precognition, even in principle, approachable within the current paradigm of physics? Can precognition be described within its current language and formalism, for example, wave functions, mass-energy, and spacetime, or is it a phenomenon that will require a restructuring of the foundations of the field and a new vocabulary? Will it involve a metaphysical reorientation from the pure materialism, which currently structures science, to maybe a broader Cartesian dualism or, perhaps even more radically, to idealism? Precognition cannot be located solidly within any of these; nonetheless, for this discussion, it will be assessed from the purely materialist viewpoint, focusing on the following question: Can precognition be accommodated within the current materialist paradigm of mainstream physics? Precognition will be approached through the more primary phenomenon of retrocausation. Note that retrocausation is a necessary but insufficient condition for precognition; the latter also requires consciousness, another physical conundrum, but one that lies (far) beyond the scope of this work.

It is hoped that this inquiry will expose theoretical shortcomings of precognition and, therefore, help in developing a viable theory as well as to suggest new experiments by which to illuminate it. This inquiry will revolve around two central axes of physical theory: (1) causality and the thermodynamic arrow of time and (2) quantum mechanics. These will be unpacked in stages. First, the experimental evidence for precognition will be surveyed, followed by the basic physics of retrocausation, starting with basic definitions and an examination of the *time-symmetric* nature of physical laws. Next, I consider how reality unfolds in a temporally *asymmetric* way, that is, why time appears to have a direction, an *arrow* (Reichenbach, 1956; Davies, 1974; Mackey, 1991; Halliwell et al., 1994; Savitt, 1995; Price, 1996; Schulman, 1997; Zeh, 2007; Sheehan, 2006, 2011a). The most important of these is the *thermodynamic arrow,* governed by the second law of thermodynamics, which probably conditions our own perceived (*psychological*) arrow of time. Retrocausation will then be examined as it pertains to mainstream quantum theory and experiment. For this, we introduce an interpretation of quantum mechanics that explicitly incorporates retrocausation and then survey some recent quantum experiments that purport to demonstrate it. Finally, I will assess precognition in light of current physics, ending with several questions that may help guide future research. To keep this discussion tractable, the topic of consciousness will be put aside entirely. I begin with a brief survey of evidence supporting precognition.

EXPERIMENTS IN PRECOGNITION

Precognition is the apprehension of anomalously detailed knowledge or awareness about the future by conscious beings. It can be roughly divided into near-term ($\tau \sim 1$ to 10^{-2} s) and long-term ($\tau \sim 10^4$ to 10^8 s) forms.

Precognition can be either conscious or unconscious (Sheehan, 2006, 2011b; Radin, 2006a,b, 2013; Bierman & Radin, 1997; Mossbridge, Tressoldi, & Utts, 2012). Experimental tests of the former historically involve forced-choice guessing of outcomes of randomly chosen future events, for example, randomly programmed blinking lights. A meta-analysis from 309 forced-choice experiments conducted between 1935 and 1987 provides very strong statistical evidence for conscious precognition (Honorton & Ferrari, 1989). More recently, measurement of unconscious precognition, called *presentiment* or prestimulus response in the literature, has been inferred via the physiological responses of test participants (e.g., skin conductance, heart rate, blood oxygenation levels, or electrical potential in the brain) as they are subjected to randomly chosen dichotomous stimuli (e.g., loud noise versus silence, bright light flashes versus darkness, emotionally charged pictures versus calm pictures). It has been found consistently and with high statistical significance in numerous studies and by many independent laboratories that subjects can respond subtly in advance of strong stimuli, though no obvious cue has been provided. In some studies, the random stimuli are not even chosen until after the subjects respond (Radin, 2006b; Houtkooper, 2006; Bierman, 2006, May et al., 2005). It is emphasized that no single trial can establish the existence of precognition; rather, experiments rely on averaging of responses from multiple subjects over multiple trials. (This is similar to how quantum mechanical expectation values are experimentally determined—from many measurements over an ensemble of quantum states, none of which individually need coincide with the actual expectation [average] value.) Experimental protocols are among the most stringent in the sciences, seeking to eliminate all possible confounds and alternative explanations for the results; these might include sensory or statistical cues to the participants, anticipatory strategies taken by them, or hardware flaws. Experiments have become so solid that, despite mainstream science's hardened disbelief in precognition, results have been published in top-tier peer-reviewed journals (Bem, 2011).

On longer time scales ($\tau \sim 10^4$ to 10^5 s), one can look to the Global Consciousness Project (GCP; Nelson & Bancel, 2006; Bancel & Nelson, 2008) and remote viewing. The GCP maintains a global network of several dozen random event generators (REGs) that continuously output random numbers (in the form of 1s and 0s), which are collected from each REG in 200-bit increments per second. Considering the well-established random output from REGs, the cumulative data from the worldwide GCP network should be entirely random, with a well-defined Gaussian mean, variance, kurtosis, and so on. While this is usually the case, as established from careful calibration studies, there are also limited periods when the statistical structure of the data stream deviates significantly from Gaussian expectations, particularly in its variance.

It is proposed that these anomalous REG events are correlated with world events in which large numbers of people share a common focus of attention, for instance, during religious festivals, New Year celebrations, earthquakes or other natural disasters, and terrorist attacks. Most salient to the subject of retrocausation and precognition are "impulse" events that have no prior warning, for example, earthquakes and terrorist attacks. Arguably the most statistically significant REG anomaly observed over the past 15 years occurred in the hours surrounding the September 11, 2001, airliner attacks on the East Coast of the United States. Nelson and Bancel (2006) claim that these impulse events often have precursors in the data up to 10^4 to 10^5 seconds in advance of the event, suggesting that humans en masse might have presentiments or premonitions of future events. Although an explanative theory is entirely wanting—after all, why should a network of inanimate REGs respond to human affairs?— the data are compelling. No satisfactory alternative physical explanations for these statistical anomalies have been advanced—for example, spurious electromagnetic fields, power grid fluctuations, or REG malfunctions—although other psi-based explanations have been proposed (May & Spottiswoode, 2014/2011).

Remote viewing (RV), a method for obtaining information across space-time, has been studied extensively for nearly five decades. Evidence indicates RV human operators can access information up to about 10^6 seconds into the future (P. S. Cyrus, private communication). At the longest time scales ($\tau \sim 10^4$ to 10^8 s), precognition, *premonition*, has been a celebrated part of human experience throughout history. Although not currently substantiated or quantified by laboratory studies to the degree of other types of precognition (e.g., presentiment, GCP's REG data, remote viewing), premonitions are difficult to dismiss, especially given the many well-documented, sensational anecdotal accounts. Further, for those who have experienced them personally, they can seem as objective as any other experimental evidence; of course, one must be cautious in interpreting them because first-person experiences can be unreliable. As for presentiment, the origin and nature of premonition remain unexplained, but it may be likely that the difference between precognition and premonition is purely academic.

TIME IN PHYSICS

We now turn to mainstream science for its account of retrocausation, which is a physically necessary but insufficient condition for precognition. Before plunging into the physics, we define our terms because the terminology surrounding discussions of time are often confused and imprecise. Here we define some commonly used (and misused) terms.

Determinism is the circumstance in which the present state of a system is uniquely calculable from either a past or a future state. Determinism presumes correlations but does not presume interactions mediated by any particular physical laws (i.e., causes or retrocauses). By definition, it presumes temporal symmetry. All the fundamental equations of physics are deterministic.

Causation is the proposition that a present event has a *cause* in the past but not necessarily one in the future. Like determinism, it implies correlations, but unlike determinism, it assumes law-mediated interactions (causes) and temporal asymmetry (i.e., forward direction only).

Retrocausation (RC) is the temporal mirror of causation: a present event has a *retrocause* in the future but not necessarily one in the past. Like causation, it involves law mediated interactions, correlations, and temporal asymmetry (i.e., reverse direction only).

Time-symmetric causation (*bicausation* or *equicausation*) is an amalgam of the previous two cases: determinism with (retro) causes at both temporal endpoints.

Rounding things out, *acausation* is the circumstance in which events simply occur, having neither causes nor retrocauses. (The collapse of the wave function in orthodox quantum mechanics can be viewed as acausal.)

The distinction between *causation* and *correlation* is critical. Correlations are descriptive and empirical, while causation requires an additional explanation (e.g., a physical interaction).

Temporal Symmetry in Physical Laws

The fundamental laws of physics are time symmetric; that is, they equally admit forward-time and reversed-time solutions. In everyday parlance, Nature is not particular about the direction of time.

In classical physics, for example, Newton's famous equation for force can be written:

$$F = ma = m \frac{d^2x}{dt^2} = m \frac{d^2x}{d(+t)^2} = m \frac{d^2x}{d(-t)^2}.$$

Notice that if forward (positive) time ($+t$) is replaced by reversed (negative) time ($-t$), Newton's equation remains the same. In other words, a system governed by this equation is equally well described either by forward or reverse time. For a deterministic system, then, the present can be calculated equally well either from its past with time running forward ($+t$) or from its future with time running backward ($-t$). Furthermore, because Newton's equation is time symmetric, its solutions must also be time symmetric. Consider, for instance, a mass (m) bobbing at the end of a spring with stiffness k. (Think of a baseball suspended by a rubber band.) In one dimension, its equation of motion is:

$$F = m\,\frac{d^2x}{dt^2} = -kx,$$

and its solution is that of a harmonic (sinusoidal) oscillator, that is, a mass bobbing without damping:

$$x(t) = A\cos\left(\sqrt{\frac{k}{m}}\,t\right).$$

Here A is the amplitude of oscillation. Substituting $-t$ for $+t$ in 3 does not change the solution because cosine is an even function; that is, $\cos(\omega t) = \cos(\omega(-t))$. In practical terms, this means that if you were shown a movie of the ball bobbing up and down at the end of the rubber band, you could not tell *a priori* whether the film was running forward or backward, since both temporal directions look equally reasonable from a physical perspective. In other words, the motion of this mass-spring system is time symmetric.

This temporal symmetry holds not only in the everyday classical, macroscopic realm but also in the microscopic, quantum mechanical realm. For example, the one-dimensional Klein-Gordon equation, which describes spin-zero elementary particles, can be written:

$$\left[\frac{1}{c^2}\frac{\partial}{\partial t^2} - \frac{\partial}{\partial x^2} + \frac{2\pi\,m^2c^2}{h}\right]\Psi = 0.$$

Again, as for Newton's equation discussed earlier, the same Klein-Gordon equation results for $+t$ as for $-t$; thus, time-forward and time-reversed solutions should be equally admissible. A similar demonstration can be made for the celebrated Schrödinger equation with appropriate mathematical caveats.

Given this pervasive time symmetry in physical law, how can cause or retrocause be assigned? Consider a ball on a hill rolling under gravity, as in Figure 4.1(a). If, presently, the ball is in the middle of the hill, is it correct to say that the *cause* of the ball rolling down the hill *now* is that it *was* at the top of the hill *earlier*, or is it correct to say that the *retrocause* is that it *will be* at the bottom of the hill *later*? From a formal physical perspective, the answer is "yes." From a pure physics perspective, both explanations are equally good; therefore, neither is preferred. And yet, we prefer the former, the causative explanation, rather than the retrocausative. This leads us to the great asymmetry of existence: *time's arrows*.

A Quiver of Arrows

The ostensive unidirectionality of time is often called the arrow of time, a term coined by Authur Eddington (1929), one of the pre-eminent physicists of the early twentieth century. Several arrows are commonly distinguished, including (1) psychological, (2) quantum mechanical, (3) charge parity violation, (4) radiation, (5) cosmological, and (6) thermodynamic. This subject is considered in many fine treatises (Reichenbach, 1956; Davies, 1974; Mackey, 1989; Halliwell et al., 1994; Savitt, 1995; Price, 1996; Schulman, 1997; Zeh, 2007).

The *psychological arrow*, which orients each of us personally in time, derives from the sequential ordering of events in our lives, running from past toward future. This arrow is the most experiential and the most persuasive, and is therefore potentially the most misleading and deceptive. When considering the other arrows—and time in general—we must guard against its commonsense prejudices because it deeply colors our perceptions, reasoning, and intuition. It is believed this arrow is ultimately directed by the thermodynamic arrow; continuing research attempts to make this link more physically explicit (Mlodinow & Brun, 2014).

The *quantum mechanical arrow* pertains to the so-called *irreversible collapse* of quantum wave functions. Quantum systems are often in superposition states, meaning roughly that they are combinations of multiple discrete states. When measured, however, either by a conscious observer or by nature, quantum superpositions must disappear (collapse), leaving just one of the original discrete states. The collapse is irreversible—it cannot be undone—thereby pointing uniquely the direction of time.

The *charge parity* (CP) *violation arrow* arises from the temporally asymmetric decay of certain rare elementary particles like the neutral kaon and the B meson (Lees et al., 2012). Decay processes such as these, which violate CP (charge parity) symmetry, must also violate T-symmetry (time symmetry) to conform to the overarching CPT symmetry, which all elementary processes obey. This arrow is tangential to precognition but is believed to be central to the observed matter-antimatter asymmetry of our universe—an asymmetry for which all of us should be truly thankful.

The *radiation arrow* is founded in the observation that light, sound, and other forms of radiation tend to spread out from their sources, rather than concentrating into them. For instance, light shines out, away from a light bulb; never does light in a room spontaneously converge into the bulb, although this is a perfectly acceptable physical possibility. If one examines the equation governing radiation (the wave equation), it is time symmetric and hence has two solutions: the expected time-forward solution (the *retarded* solution) and a time-reversed solution (the *advanced* solution). In general, we observe the retarded but not the advanced one. Ultimately, the radiation arrow can probably be traced to the specialness of boundary conditions working in concert with the second law of thermodynamics. Similarly, the psychological arrow, which involves biochemical reactions in the brain, is also usually considered derivative of the thermodynamic arrow.

The *cosmological arrow* is defined via the Hubble cosmological expansion. Einstein's general relativistic field equations forbid the cosmos from being static; rather, it must either expand or contract, since stasis is not an option under the purely attractive force of gravity. Presently, the universe is expanding rather than contracting, as evidenced by the dispersive Hubble flow of galaxies. This fundamental asymmetry defines an overall temporal arrow for the universe. At local levels (planetary, solar, and galactic), the thermodynamic arrow still rules, but even it ultimately depends on the continued existence of a nonequilibrium universe, which cosmological expansion guarantees.

In our everyday existence, the *thermodynamic arrow* is by far the most important. This arrow—predicated on the monotonic increase in disorder (entropy) in the universe, as dictated by the second law of thermodynamics—pertains to almost every aspect of our lives, from the moment of our conceptions, through the innumerable biochemical reactions of our lives, to the final diffusive mixing of our last breaths as we die. It has been called "*the supreme law of nature*" (emphasis added) (Eddington, 1929).

According to the second law, the reason time runs forward rather than backward (as for retrocausation) is because it is far more *likely* to run forward than backward, just as it is far more likely for your living room to get more chaotic as the week wears on, rather than more orderly. At the microscopic level, individual molecular interactions remain time symmetric; however, in moving from the microscopic to macroscopic realm, the second law emerges from molecular motions en masse. The reason for this does not lie with the fundamental equations of physics, which are time symmetric, but instead with the so-called boundary conditions of the system, which support and particularize the solutions of the equations.

By mathematical necessity, the solutions to the differential equations expressing physical laws require boundary conditions in space and time. The equations alone are quite general, and the boundary conditions narrow the equations' solutions to the particular one that apply to the particular system in question. For instance, for the mass-spring (ball-rubber band) system in Equation 2, one might specify the initial (or final) position and velocity of the ball so that the solution (Equation 3) gives the instantaneous position of that particular ball at every moment forever into the future (or past). By specifying boundary conditions for these general equations, one gets exact solutions that apply to particular systems under particular circumstances. Physical law operates somewhat like human laws in that human laws are also quite general, but they find real-world meaning when they are applied to particular circumstances—their boundary conditions.

The equations of physics are strict but at the same time flexible enough (via their initial and boundary conditions) to describe the rich diversity of physical situations seen in the world. For simple systems like a ball on a rubber band or one rolling down a hill (Figure 4.1(a)), the solution equations (e.g., Equation 3) are simple and time symmetric, but when there are lots of particles, for instance, in the case of the countless gas molecules in a typical room, the complete solutions are too complex to describe in detail, so approximate (probabilistic) solutions must be used. By probability theory, these solutions have a one-way temporal direction—thus breaking time symmetry—and thereby establish the thermodynamic arrow, which points in the temporal direction of maximum disorder (entropy), in accordance with the second law.

Figure 4.1
Ball rolling on hill (a) and transactional Interpretation of viewing light from the star Betelgeuse (b).

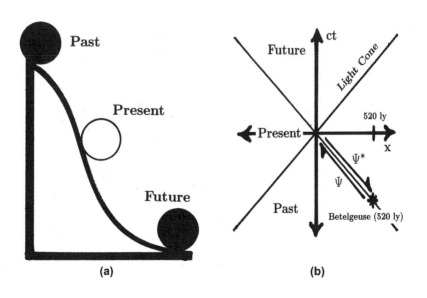

(a)   (b)

The thermodynamic arrow, however, holds a secret: It requires a low entropy past for the universe such that the second law's entropy increases are possible in the first place. The origin of this low entropy past remains a mystery. It is particularly disturbing because if one takes it seriously, then one must admit that, from a purely probabilistic point of view, it is far more likely that all our yesterdays—even the entire history of the universe—never actually occurred. (See Notes for details.)

In summary, several temporal arrows can be identified, the most influential of which appear to be the quantum mechanical at small scales and the thermodynamic at the macro scale and in everyday life. These several arrows, however, do not settle the mystery of retrocausation and precognition; rather, they deepen it.

QUANTUM RETROCAUSATION: THEORY

At a macroscopic level, where the second law holds sway and most events are *irreversible*, temporal asymmetry is obvious, and causation dominates. In the microscopic regime, however, where individual processes are *reversible*, one might expect retrocausation to be more evident. Indeed, many interpretations of quantum theory allow for retrocausation; some even depend on it.

Arguably, quantum theory is the best tested, most precise and accurate theory in science, boasting agreement between experiment and theory with precision sometimes better than one part in a trillion. Quantum phenomena have been experimentally studied on length scales from 10^{-18} to 10^5 m; they are predicted to remain intact down to the Planck length (10^{-35} m) and, in principle, up to the length scale of the universe (10^{26} m). However, despite its scope and ability to quantitatively predict the outcome of experiments, the physical reality and meaning behind its equations remain obscure. Simply put, quantum mechanics lacks an unambiguous metaphysics. There are roughly a dozen mainstream *interpretations* of quantum theory that attempt to put the flesh of meaning on the abstract theoretical skeleton of its equations. Although each viable interpretation coherently explains the same well-known experimental facts about the world, the underlying ontology of each can be radically different. For instance, whether the quantum wave function ψ is physically real remains contentious, even more than 80 years since it was introduced. It is perhaps unsurprising, then, that the nature of time also remains unsettled. In fact, a number of quantum models and interpretations admitting retrocausation have been developed, including ones by Schottky (1921); Costa de Beauregard (1953); Watanabe (1955); Aharonov, Bergmann, and Lebowitz (1964); Cramer (1980, 1986); Kastner, (2013); Wharton (2007); and Elitzur (2006).

Transactional Interpretation

Of the several interpretations and models of quantum mechanics that admit the possibility of retrocasuation, one that explicitly invokes it is the transactional interpretation (TI), advanced by Cramer in 1986. In TI, unlike in the orthodox Copenhagen interpretation and most other interpretations, the quantum wave function ψ is ontologically real, rather than merely an abstract mathematical tool. Quantum events, from which all of reality is presumably forged, are handshake agreements between the past and the future, mediated by the mutual exchange of time-forward *retarded* waves ψ and time-reversed *advanced* waves ψ^*. In this sense, both causation and retrocausation operate simultaneously, thereby creating the present. TI bears resemblance to the two state vector formalism pioneered by Watanabe (1955) and, later, more successfully by Aharonov, et al. (1964, 2011), Cramer (1980, 1986), Kastner (2013). It was inspired by the Wheeler-Feynman (1945) absorber theory of radiation.

Consider the quantum event of seeing the first twinkling of the star Betelgeuse in the constellation Orion on a clear winter's night (Figure 4.1 (b)). Betelgeuse is located about 520 light years from Earth, so the light you see was emitted a hundred years before Shakespeare penned his last sonnet or Francis Drake sailed against the fearsome Spanish armada. For your seeing to occur, Betelgeuse emitted a retarded *offer* wave (ψ) in about 1500 CE, which propagated forward in time in a typically causal fashion. Upon arrival in the present, the absorber (your eye) returns an advanced *response* wave (ψ^*) backward in time to the emitter (Betelgeuse) in a retrocausal manner. The *transaction* is completed when a stochastic choice is made on the outcome of quantum variables and then repeated until completion when all necessary conserved quantities (e.g., energy, momenta, spin) are transacted and agreed upon by the absorber (eye) and emitter (star). Until the transaction is complete, the photon is neither emitted nor absorbed. Only when this 520-year transaction is successful is the photon seen. *Fiat lux! Let there be light!*

The transaction is instantaneous or, more aptly, it is *atemporal* since no time elapses during these processes. The retarded and advanced waves contribute equally; thus, causation and retrocasuation can be considered to play equivalent, symmetric roles in creating reality. (If one wishes, one can invert the order of the offer and response waves without harm to the theory; that is, the offer wave can originate in the future while the response wave originates in the past.) The time symmetry of TI, even with what amounts to wave function collapse, obviates the quantum arrow.

TI has many attractive features beyond this egalitarian view of causation. It has been successful in cleanly resolving a number of so-called quantum paradoxes that have accumulated over the years—including Schrödinger's cat, EPR, Wigner's friend, and Wheeler's delayed choice—

without invoking unsettling EPR-like correlations and entangled states. It can explain the exponential speed-up of quantum computers (Castagnoli, 2013). It also gives meaningful ontological status to the central characters of quantum theory, the wave function (ψ) and its complex conjugate (ψ^*), which traditionally have been considered mere mathematical tools of the trade. In TI, they are the time-forward (retarded) and time-reversed (advanced) solutions to the Schrödinger equation, thus finally giving some physicality to the otherwise mysterious Born probability amplitude, $\psi^*\psi$. Precognition might even be accommodated within TI by considering transactions between a subject in the present with his future self. This amounts to *self-interactions,* as in other standard interpretations of quantum mechanics. Despite its compelling ontology, TI remains only one of many viable interpretations of quantum mechanics. Quantum reality remains, it seems, largely a matter of taste.

Let us turn now to purported experimental signatures of retrocausation in mainstream quantum physics.

QUANTUM RETROCAUSATION: EXPERIMENTS

Experimental support for retrocausation can be found at time scales ranging from the shortest measurable ($\tau \sim 10^{-23}$ s) to literally years ($\tau \sim 10^8$ s). Evidence at the shortest time scales (10^{-7} to 10^{-23} s) are exclusively quantum, while longer time scales (10^{-2} to 10^{-8} s) are dominated by human precognition. This section will briefly survey notable well-studied examples from the quantum regime. By no means is this survey complete, nor is it claimed that retrocausation is the sole explanation advanced for these experimental results; however, *in toto,* it perhaps provides the simplest, most compelling explanation.

Elementary Processes

Undergirding everyday activities, for instance, enjoying a fresh Lorna Doone cookie, are countless elementary quantum mechanical events. These elementary events often transpire over subatomic length and time scales (e.g., $l \sim 10^{-15}$ m and $t \sim 10^{-23}$ s).

Embodying Gell-Mann's totalitarian principle—*anything not forbidden is compulsory*—a quantum event can be written as the sum of all possible ways in which the event can be realized. As an everyday (nonquantum) example, consider the various ways you might go to the store to purchase your Lorna Doones. You could walk, jog, run, bike, hop-skip-and-jump, pogo-stick, long jump, crawl on your hands and knees, bounce on your left foot, pirouette around the block three times, ride a rhinoceros, as well as an infinite number of other possible ways. Surely, some are easier than others and hence are more likely to be realized. Analogously, in calculating the probability amplitude for a quantum event, one adds up the probabilities of all possible ways it might occur. Usually, there are just a handful of dominant terms. Interestingly, these usually involve both time-forward and time-reversed processes.

As an example, consider the well-studied phenomenon of electron Compton scattering ($\tau \sim 10^{-21}$ second), wherein an x-ray photon collides with an electron, exchanging energy and momentum. To connect this with an everyday activity, let the electron be a basketball player and the photon a basketball. In a collision event, the high-speed ball (photon) is caught by the player (electron) then is quickly thrown away again at a lower speed in an arbitrary direction.

To calculate the probability of Compton scattering, one must add up the probabilities from all possible ways to describe the event. Consider two dominant terms. In the first, the incoming photon strikes the incoming electron, is absorbed, then after a brief time is re-emitted as a lower-energy photon. This is quite reasonable and expected. The sports analog is clear: The high-speed basketball is caught by the player then thrown away again at a different speed. The second dominant term, however, is more interesting. Here the incoming electron first emits a low-energy photon, waits a bit, then absorbs a high-energy photon to complete the scattering process. The analogous basketball play is bizarre: The player throws the ball away before even catching it! One might be tempted to discard this second process as unphysical because it not only flouts normal temporal ordering but also what one expects from conservation of energy. Nevertheless, it must be included in the calculation to achieve agreement between theory and experiment. Apparently, subatomic processes do not respect the unidirectional forward progression of time but require both temporal directions be considered at once. Causation and retrocausation, it seems, command equal standing in the subatomic realm.

Defenders of pure causality can claim the details of the scattering process are hidden behind the veil of the Heisenberg time-energy uncertainty relation. That is, because the scattering occurs over such a brief time interval, the details of the collision's energy cannot be determined experimentally. Or one might claim that individual quantum processes (e.g., as depicted in Feynman diagrams) should not be taken too literally. Perhaps so, but this is cold comfort, since it undermines the model tying experiment successfully to theory. Furthermore, invoking this preferred temporal direction is not indicated by the underlying formalism—it must be done by caveat—thus, it amounts to a new (and unnecessary) physical axiom. If the history of science teaches us one thing, it is this: While scientists may have their preferences about how nature should be, nature is what it is; we must conform to it, not it to us. Just as quantum mechanics required a radical shift in worldview, perhaps retrocausation requires another.

Wheeler Delayed Choice Experiment

A central tenet of quantum theory is the principle of complementarity which, glibly stated, is: *A wave is a wave, a particle is a particle, and never the twain shall meet.* Operationally, this means that the outcome of a quantum measurement on a wave function ψ will render either a particle (e.g., a photon) or a wave (e.g., an interference pattern), but not both at once. This wave-particle duality highlights the central position played by the experimenter in determining reality: The experimenter is free to ask questions (and this entails the choice of apparatus), and Nature is free to provide answers (often with probabilistic outcomes). The observer and the observed are flip sides of the same coin: reality.

The archetypal apparatuses for measuring the particle and wave aspects of wave functions—be they photons, electrons, neutrons, or large molecules—are depicted in Figure 4.2. A wave function passes through a slitted screen from left to right and is detected on the far right surface (the detector). A wave function impinging on the single-slit screen has only one option to pass and therefore goes straight through, generating a well-localized signal on the detector. On the other hand, a wave function passing through the double-slit screen has two options and so—following Yogi Berra's famous driving advice, *When you come to the fork in the road, take it*—penetrates both slits at once to create an interference pattern at the detector. (Wave function here is meant an ensemble of identically prepared waves passing through the slits individually.) The distinct patterns at the detectors, either interference (Figure 4.2(b)) or non-interference (Figure 4.2(a)), have been verified in numerous experiments with photons, electrons, neutrons, and even large molecules, like buckminsterfullerenes (C_{60}).

These complementary behaviors—wave or particle—can be realized experimentally in a single apparatus: a Mach-Zehnder interferometer (Figure 4.2(c)). It consists of two beam splitters (half-silvered mirrors that reflect half the incoming signal and let through the other half, designated BS), two regular mirrors (designated M, one of which can be moved so as to create a variable path length along one of the interferometer's arms), and two detectors (D). The output beam splitter (BS2) is removable from the apparatus, thereby determining the nature of the measurement. When BS2 is present, wave-like behavior (interference) is observed; when it is absent, particle-like behavior is observed at the detectors (D1, D2).

Light from a single-photon source enters the interferometer from the bottom left and is split by BS1. It will take Path 1, Path 2, or both paths simultaneously depending on the presence or absence of BS2. If BS2 is present, there are two paths from input to output; therefore, taking Yogi Berra's advice, the light will take both paths at once and produce an interference pattern, as it would through a double-slit screen (Figure 4.2(b)).

Figure 4.2
Wavefronts (left) impinging on single-slit and screen (a), wavefronts impinging on double-slit and screen (b), and schematic of Mach-Zehnder interferometer (c). BS = beamsplitter; M = mirror; D = detector.

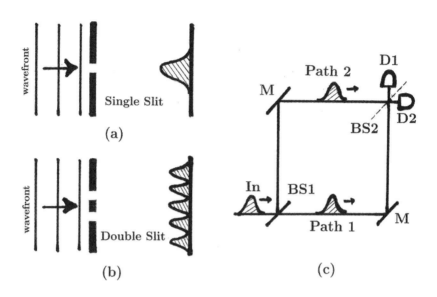

(The lower-right mirror can be moved to generate the equivalent of an interference pattern at the detectors.) In contrast, if BS2 is absent, only one path is possible at the output, so no interference pattern is observed, as in the case of the single-slit screen (Figure 4.2(a)).

Note that for interference to occur in the first case (BS2 present), the light traverses both paths, whereas in the second case with no interference (BS2 absent), the light traverses either Path 1 or Path 2, but not both. In the first case, light acts as a wave, while in the second it acts as a particle. Thus, the choice by the experimenter of having BS2 either present or absent determines the outcome of the measurement as a wave or particle.

Now comes a dirty trick that leads to a temporal paradox: Wheeler's delayed choice. In this experiment, BS2 is inserted or removed *after* the light has entered the interferometer but before it reaches the detector. In effect, the experimenter tries to confuse the light by switching the nature of the apparatus after it has supposedly made a choice of going along either a single path or a double path toward the detector. In this scenario, using classical physical reasoning, one expects the detected pattern to be that set up by the original BS2 configuration; after all, once the light has started along one path or two, it is too late to go back and change things. Quantum mechanically, however, according to both theory and experiment, this is not what happens. Instead, the detected pattern corresponds to the BS2 arrangement set up during the flight of the light through the interferometer, before reaching the detector.

A definitive experimental realization of Wheeler's experiment was conducted by Jacques, Wu, Grosshans, et al. in 2007. The single-photon source was a nitrogen-vacancy color center in a diamond nanocrystal that could be selectively stimulated. The path length of the Mach-Zehnder interferometer (L = 48 m) was such that the light travel time through it was L/c 160 ns. The delayed choice regarding BS2 (its presence or absence) was made during this 160-nanosecond interval by a random number generator, based on sampling amplified shot noise from a white light source. The results of the experiments strongly supported quantum mechanical predictions.

There are two pronounced, competing explanations for these results. The orthodox interpretation is to assert that the state of the light in the interferometer (whether particle or wave) is indeterminate until a measurement has been made at the detector, that it is improper to claim the light has taken any particular path through the interferometer because it is not subject to measurement during its flight. Once measured by the detector, however, the photon takes into account the configuration of the entire apparatus. In a sense, the light's flight through the interferometer is atemporal; it becomes real only at the instant of measurement. Though this explanation is certainly coherent and acceptable, it carries with it the baggage of entanglement and superluminal correlations inherent in the famous Einstein-Podolsky-Rosen (EPR) experiments.

A second interpretation of the experimental results invokes retrocausation. Here the measurement at the detector can "rewrite" history for the 160 nanoseconds of the light travel time through the interferometer. In the transactional interpretation, similarly to the starlight example, the retarded (offer) wave from the nitrogen-vacancy color center reaches the detector, which then emits an advanced (response) wave backward in time to the color center. The response wave completes the transaction in accord with the status of the beamsplitter (BS2 present or absent), thus responding to any changes made to the apparatus by the delayed-choice protocol. This retrocausal "rewriting" of history spans roughly 10^{-7} seconds, which though brief compared with everyday time scales, is quite long compared with elementary quantum processes, which also seem to involve retrocausal behavior (10^{-7} second/10^{-23} second = 10^{16}).

Again, it is emphasized that retrocausation need not be invoked to explain these results, but it is as reasonable an interpretation as the orthodox one. Furthermore, it seems to have the advantage over the traditional explanation both in terms of parsimony and in honoring the fullness of the physical theory that undergirds it. Moreover, as one moves beyond short time scales and up from quantum mechanical to wholly classical systems, the orthodox accounts of time become increasingly strained, as evidenced in Figure 4.2.

DISCUSSION

Precognition faces multiple challenges to acceptance by the mainstream scientific community. Foremost, it is crippled by the lack of a comprehensive physical theory even though experimental evidence for it is statistically robust and repeatable. This deficiency, however, is only half the story because, after all, many well-accepted physical phenomena lack comprehensive theory, for example, dark matter, dark energy, high-temperature superconductivity. While any of these might require a fundamental rethinking of physical theory, none on their face contradicts a cherished paradigm—but this is not so for precognition. It flouts our most basic intuitions and sensibilities regarding time, and it undermines our *ur-paradigm* of causation, upon which most of science is built. Precognition puts the nature of time itself on trial, as well as the very meaning of macroscopic causality.

Indeed, precognition conflicts with commonsense notions of memory and time passage, which strongly inform our interpretation of physical law. Surprisingly, or perhaps presciently, however, the primary equations of physics are time symmetric, thereby, in principle, permitting retrocausation and precognition. If one takes physical law at face value, free from human perspective and prejudice, precognition is not surprising; rather, it is expected, and yet, it appears to be a rare phenomenon, one that is currently validated by statistical inference and only under well-controlled laboratory conditions.

Perhaps the deeper, more salient question is not "Does precognition exist?"—for it has ample experimental support (§2)—but rather, "Why is it apparently so rare?" The answer seems to be connected with the second law of thermodynamics and perhaps also with wave function collapse. Overshadowing both, however, is the experiential (psychological) arrow of time. Insofar as our physical reality is apprehended via our psychological arrow, it is difficult to see past the prejudices and misconceptions it overlays on our perceptions. Like fish that cannot perceive the water in which they swim, we—as creatures immersed in time possessing unidirectional psychological and thermodynamic arrows—have difficulty grasping its underlying bidirectional symmetry.

So long as the psychological arrow is aligned with the external *local* arrow (e.g., thermodynamic, radiation, quantum), regardless of the direction of the overall *global* arrow, the world will be perceived (psychologically) as unfolding in the normal time-forward fashion. In other words, if all particle trajectories and fields were locally reversed so as to locally reverse the local temporal arrow—including that of the brain—one would not know; time would still appear to run forward.

The primary physical deal breaker to acceptance of precognition is causation, underwritten by the second law, which governs all macroscopic processes in everyday life (and is probably also responsible for the psychological arrow). Causation comports with the second law because it involves the same *event ordering* as the second law's requisite entropy increases, which are overwhelmingly probable (see Notes.) In contradistinction, retrocausation, though it is equally deterministic as causation, posits event ordering that is in the opposite direction to that demanded by the second law; hence, insofar as the second law is absolute, retrocausation is physically impossible. This, however, does not settle the matter.

Over the past 20 years, the absolute status of the second law itself has faced unprecedented scrutiny (Čápek & Sheehan, 2005; Sheehan 2002, 2007b, 2011b). More than two dozen theoretical and experimental challenges have been proposed by multiple research groups worldwide and have been detailed in more than 70 peer-reviewed articles, many in top-tier journals. Taken together, these indicate the second law should not be considered an absolute law. While it pertains to everyday systems quite well, the second law appears to fail in some thermodynamic regimes, as demonstrated in recent theory and experiment (Sheehan, 2013; Sheehan, Mallin, Garamella, & Sheehan, 2014).

If the second law is not absolute, then the thermodynamic constraint on its temporal arrow is loosed; macroscale retrocausation cannot be dismissed out of hand, and perhaps, by extension, neither can precognition. If the second law can be violated in the laboratory, as has been recently claimed (Sheehan, Mallin, et al., 2014), then it becomes plausible that life itself might also have devised mechanisms by which to subvert it. Certainly, at present, there is no experimental evidence for this; however, if an organism could "peer" into its own future so as to gain information advantageous to its survival and reproduction, natural selection would seem to favor it. Theoretical proposals for biological second law subversion have been advanced (Sheehan, 2007a).

The second major obstacle to the acceptance of precognition is quantum mechanics, although it has yet to be proven that the two are actually linked. It has been widely suggested that precognition might be explained in terms of quantum entanglement and EPR-like correlations; however, a clear, formal case for this has not been made. Human-based precognition is not amenable to standard quantum mechanical interpretation, specifically, to EPR-like correlations, without requiring substantial revision of the mainstream conception of consciousness and its relation to the physical world. Inasmuch as precognition involves macroscopic thermodynamic conscious beings, enabled by chemical and electrical activity in the brain, in the mainstream view, it should be classical and thermodynamic in nature, not quantum mechanical. Compelling cases have been made for the quantum nature of consciousness, but they are neither established nor mainstream (Schwartz, Stapp, & Beauregard, 2005; Hameroff, 2007). On the other hand, one cannot invoke EPR-like correlations to explain strong correlations between consciousness and future events, as was done for the delayed choice experiments, without upgrading the classical model of consciousness to a quantum one.

Recent results from the nascent field of quantum biology have extended quantum phenomena to living systems beyond the familiar territory of chemical bonding and ionization to nontrivial phenomena such as superposition, entanglement, quantum computation, tunneling, and nonlocality. Well-known examples of nontrivial quantum biological processes include (1) energy transport within the photosynthetic complex (quantum coherence and entanglement), (2) magnetoreception (ability to detect the direction one is facing based on the earth's magnetic field) using cryptochrome (a class of flavoproteins that are sensitive to blue light, found in plants and animals), (3) quantum measurements in hearing and sight and, perhaps, smell.

That environmental sensing would utilize subtle quantum processes should not be surprising given that survival often turns on subtle environmental clues. In the case of cryptochrome, it appears that one sense (sight) has extended into another: magnetoreception. Too little is known about the scope and limits of quantum biology to exclude the possibility that precognition might be an extension of traditional (possibly quantum) processes in the brain or elsewhere in the body.

Mainstream quantum phenomena (e.g., superconducting currents, superfluids, lasers) have for decades been demonstrated on time and distance scales comparable to those at which the human brain operates, so quantum consciousness cannot be ruled out on this basis. Their time and length scales fit comfortably with those speculated to be pertinent to quantum precognition. Mainstream quantum phenomena have been investigated from subnuclear size scales (10^{-18} m) up to roughly 10^5 m (entangled photons for secure communications) and are believed to extend down to the Planck length (L_p 10^{-35} m), the shortest distance within the purview of accepted physics. Thus, in logarithmic terms, *quantumness* extends over nearly two-thirds the length scales of the known universe (10^{26} m)—that is, $[\text{Log}(10^5/10^{-35})]/[\text{Log}(10^{26}/10^{-35})] = 0.66$—easily subsuming all biologic length scales. Likewise, retrocausal processes have been measured or presumed to extend from the Planck time (L_p/c - 10^{43} s) up to about 10^8 s (premonition), thereby spanning more than 80% of the logarithmic scale of the universe's age ($\approx 10^{18}$ s); that is, $[\text{Log}(10^8/10^{-43})]/[\text{Log}(10^{18}/10^{-43})] = 0.84$.

CONCLUSIONS AND FUTURE DIRECTIONS

In this essay, I have attempted to show that retrocausation arises naturally, even forcefully, from accepted physical theory and that a wide range of microscopic and macroscopic experiments, from short to long time scales ($10^{-23} \leq \tau \leq 10^8$ s), appear to support it. Several interpretations of quantum mechanics not only permit it, but even rely upon it. Precognition is a particular biological instance of retrocausation that has strong experimental support while lacking clear theoretical explanation. It is not clear whether precognition can be understood classically or quantum mechanically within the current paradigms of science. The quantum behavior of complex, nonequilibrium multiparticle systems, like life, are not sufficiently well understood at present to definitely rule in or rule out macroscopic (spatial and temporal) quantum processes in life, the brain, and consciousness (Hameroff, 2014), especially as it concerns precognition.

Retrocausation and precognition enjoy a wealth of outstanding theoretical and experimental questions and challenges, including:

1. To what degree, if any, can the future influence the past? If it is possible, what is the physics and what are the limits of influence?
2. If retrocausation holds similar standing as causation in the world, why is it so less evident?
3. Should retrocausation be regarded simply as epistemic (explanatory), or can it be established as ontological (real) in the same way as causation? What experiments could firmly establish this?
4. Why do conscious beings appear to have special access to the future, or does the future have special access to us? What aspects of consciousness or neurophysiology make this possible?
5. Is consciousness quantum mechanical in nature and, if so, can this help explain precognition?
6. What are the spatial and temporal limits of precognition, that is, how far into the future can one see and how far away?
7. Is it possible to create a nonconscious apparatus that mimics human precognition, a forward-directed time machine? Would it be wise to build such an oracle?

In summary, precognition has compelling experimental support but lacks a comprehensive physical theory. Insofar as retrocausation is embedded in standard physical theory, in principle, precognition appears permitted within the known time-symmetric laws of physics; however, it faces at least two perceived physical roadblocks: the second law and the constraints of quantum mechanics. The second law is probably no longer absolute, thus raising the possibility that life has discovered ways to subvert it. Second, it is not known if or whether life can or does exploit quantum processes on a macroscopic scale such as to incorporate them into precognition. In total, then, given the strong experimental evidence for precognition and the lack of any clear physical prohibition, precognition should be taken seriously by the scientific community.

A Modern Fable

According to legend, in 1928, the physicist Paul Dirac derived his celebrated relativistic wave equation after staring deeply into an after-dinner fire. While investigating the energy states predicted by his revolutionary equation, he found two sets of solutions: one with positive energies and another, mysterious, mirror set with negative energies. Most other physicists would have thrown away the second set as being unphysical—after all, negative energy states make no physical sense—but Dirac, true to his aesthetics and to the mathematics, kept both solution sets, ascribing to the second a new type of particle. In 1932, Carl Anderson discovered the positron (a positively charged electron), the first example of antimatter (matter's mirror), thereby confirming Dirac's prediction.

Today, we are faced with a similar choice. For three centuries, the fundamental equations of physics have predicted both "positive-time" and "negative-time" solutions and, by proper extension, both causation and retrocausation. Despite this, the scientific community has rejected the negative-time retrocausal solutions as unphysical. However, as experiment and theory probe more deeply into the physical world, it becomes increasingly evident that these negative-time solutions may, in fact, play a largely hidden but perhaps equal role in establishing reality. Precognition stands as the foremost exemplar of retrocausation at the macro scale. Our reluctance to embrace retrocausation and precognition has probably more to do with our commonsense prejudices about time, conditioned by the time-asymmetric thrall of the second law, than they have with physical reality, per se.

Retrocausation and causation seem to be complements of one another, necessary halves of a unified temporal whole. Likewise, precognition complements our native knowledge and memory. Should we one day consider them on equal footing, we will have done nothing more than honor what has always been before us, both in our experiences and in the equations of physics. Time will tell.

Notes: To get an idea of how unlikely our past really is, let us estimate the statistical mechanical probability that yesterday even occurred, based on the ratio of its number of microstates (Ω) of yesterday versus today, calculated via the Einstein-Planck formula: $\Omega = \exp[S/k]$, where S is the entropy and k is the Boltzmann constant (Penrose, 1989). We crudely approximate cosmic entropy production as solely due to stellar nucleosynthesis, exhausted as heat into the cosmic microwave background reservoir ($T_{\text{CMB}} = 2.7$ K) and expressed via the Clausius relation $dS = (1/T)dQ/dt$. If so, the ratio of the change of the number of cosmic microstates since yesterday is roughly

$$\frac{\Delta\Omega}{\Omega} \simeq e^{\frac{P_{stellar}\tau_{day}}{kT_{CMB}}} \simeq e^{10^{76}} \simeq e^{10^{76}},$$

where P_{stellar} is the power production of the visible universe's 10^{22} stars, and τ_{day} is the number of seconds in a day.

If we interpret this ratio of microstates ($\Delta\Omega/\Omega$) as a measure of the configurations' relative probability, as is commonly done, then the probability that yesterday occurred is about $10^{-10^{76}}$ that is, roughly zero. In other words, it is far more likely—astronomically so—that the universe in all its complexity spontaneously began in the present moment (with our faux memories intact) than that there was so highly an ordered yesterday as we assume. Although this is unpalatable to most of us, it highlights one of several fundamental problems squaring the nature of time with the laws of physics. Our universe, it seems, is a very unlikely place to be—at every moment.

Even assuming—against almost all odds—that yesterday did in fact happen, the implication of this analysis is that it is *highly* probable that time advances in the direction of the thermodynamic arrow, not just for the cosmos, but even for the smallest systems, for example, biologic cells. The second law governs the thermodynamic arrow for almost every system consisting of more than just a few particles, from nuclei to galactic superclusters. Thermodynamic time runs forward because the universe is out of equilibrium and is continuously moving toward it, eternally increasing its disorder. As a child, I once argued with my mother that it would be better if I did not clean up my room so as to spare the universe a further entropy increase due to the second law. My argument went nowhere; I should have appealed to his father, a physical chemist.

Acknowledgments. The author thanks Edwin May and Sonali Marwaha for their kind invitation to contribute to this volume, for their patience, and for his editorial suggestions. The author also thanks P. S. Cyrus and A. L. Pirruccello for helpful discussions.

REFERENCES

Aharonov, Y., Bergmann, P., & Lebowitz, J. (1964). Time symmetry in the quantum process of measurement. *Physical Reviews, 134*, B1410–B1416.

Aharonov, Y., Popescu, S., & Tollaksen, J. (2011). A time-symmetric formulation of quantum mechanics. *Physics Today, 63*, 27–32.

Bancel, P. A., & Nelson, R. D. (2008). The GCP event experiment: Design, analytical methods, results. *Journal of Scientific Exploration, 22*, 309–333.

Bem, D. (2011). Feeling the future: Experimental evidence for anomalous retroactive influences on cognition and affect. *Journal of Personality and Social Psychology, 100*, 407–425.

Bierman, D. J. (2006). Empirical research on the radical subjective solution of the measurement problem. Does time get its direction through conscious observation? In D. Sheehan (Ed). *Frontiers of time: Retrocausation experiment and theory*, pp. 238–259. American Institutes of Physics.

Bierman, D. J., & D. I. Radin. (1997). Anomalous anticipatory response on randomized future conditions. *Perceptual and Motor Skills, 84*, 689–690.

Čápek, V., & Sheehan, D. P. (2005). *Challenges to the second law of thermodynamics: Theory and experiment.* Vol. 146 in Fundamental theories of physics series, Dordrecht, Netherlands: Springer.

Castagnoli, G. (2013). Highlighting the mechanism of the quantum speedup by time-symmetric and relational quantum mechanics. arXiv:1308.5077v6

Costa de Beauregard, O. (1953). Une réponse à l'argument dirigè par Einstein, Podolsky et Rosen contre l'interpretation bohrienne de phénomènes quantiques. *Comptes Rendus 236*, 1632–1634.

Cramer, J. G. (1980).Generalized Absorber theory and the Einstein-Podolsky-Rosen paradox. *Physics Review D, 22*, 362.

Cramer, J. G. (1986). The transactional interpretation of quantum mechanics. *Reviews of Modern Physics, 58*, 647.

Davies, P. C. W. (1974). *The physics of time asymmetry.* Berkeley: University of California Press.

Eddington, A. (1929). *The nature of the physical world*, London: Everyman's Library (J. J. Dent).

Elitzur, A. C. (2006). Retrocausal quantum measurement: Some recent findings and their theoretical implications. Invited paper, read at "The Second Law of Thermodynamics: Foundations and Status." Invited lecture, read at *Annual Meeting of the Pacific Division of the AAAS University of San Diego*, June 18–22, 2006.

Halliwell, J. J., Peìrez-Mercader, J., & Zurek, W. H. (1994). *Physical origins of time asymmetry.* Cambridge: Cambridge University Press.

Hameroff, S. R. (2007). The brain is both neurocomputer and quantum computer. *Cognitive Science, 31*(6), 1035–1045.

Hameroff, S. R. (Ed.) (2014). *Toward a science of consciousness. The Tucson Conference 2014: 20th Anniversary, April 21–26, 2014 Tucson-University Park Marriott under the direction of the Center for Consciousness Studies*, University of Arizona.

Honorton, C., & Ferrari, D. C. (1989). "Future telling": A meta-analysis of forced-choice precognition experiments, 1935–1987. *Journal of Parapsychology, 53*(28), 281–308.

Houtkooper, J. M. (2006). Retrocausation or extant indefinite reality? In D. Sheehan (Ed.), *Frontiers of time: Retrocausation experiment and theory, American Institutes of Physics, AIP Conference Proceedings, 863*, 147–168.

Jacques, V., Wu, E., Grosshans, F., Treussart, F., Grangier, P., Aspect, A., & Roch, J. F. (2007). Experimental realization of Wheeler's delayed-choice gedanken experiment. *Science, 315*(5814), 966–968.

Kastner, R. E. (2013). *The transactional interpretation of quantum mechanics: The reality of possibility.* Cambridge: Cambridge Univrsity Press.

Lees, J. P., Poireau, V., Tisserand, V., Tico, J. G., Grauges, E., Palano, A., . . . & Schumm, B. A. (2012). Observation of time-reversal violation in the B 0 meson system. *Physical Review Letters, 109*(21), 211801.

Mackey, M. C. (1991). *Time's arrow: The origins of thermodynamic behavior.* New York: Springer-Verlag.

May, E. C., Paulinyi, T., & Vassy, Z. (2005). Anomalous anticipatory skin conductance response to acoustic stimuli: Experimental results and speculation upon a mechanism. *Journal of Alternative and Complementary Medicine, 11*(4), 695–702.

May, E. C., & Spottiswoode, S. J. P. (2014/2011). The Global Consciousness Project: Identifying the source of psi. In E. C. May & S. B. Marwaha (Eds.), *Anomalous cognition: Remote viewing research and theory,* pp. 268–277. Jefferson, NC: McFarland.

Mlodinow, L., & Brun, T. A. (2014). Relation between the psycho-logical and thermodynamic arrows of time. *Physics Review E, 89,* 052102.

Mossbridge, J., Tressoldi, P. E., & Utts, J. (2012). Predictive physiological anticipation preceding seemingly unpredictable stimuli: A meta-analysis. *Frontiers in Psychology, 3,* 390. doi: 10.3389/fpsyg.2012.00390

Nelson, R. D., & Bancel, P. A. (2006). Anomalous anticipatory responses in networked random data. In D. Sheehan (Ed.), *Frontiers of time: Retrocausation experiment and theory,* pp. 260–272. American Institutes of Physics.

Penrose, R. (1989). *The emperor's new mind: Concerning computers, minds and the laws of physics.* Oxford: Oxford University Press.

Price, H. (1996). *Time's arrow and Archimedes' point: New directions for the physics of time.* Oxford: Oxford University Press.

Radin, D. (2006a). *Entangled minds: Extrasensory experiences in a quantum reality.* New York: Paraview.

Radin, D. (2006b). Psychophysiological evidence of possible retrocausal effects in humans. In D. Sheehan (Ed.), *Frontiers of time: Retrocausation experiment and theory.* American Institutes of Physics.

Radin, D. (2013). *Supernormal.* New York: Deepak Chopra Pub.

Reichenbach, H. (1956). *The direction of time.* Berkeley: University of California Press.

Savitt, S. F. (Ed.). (1995). *Time's arrows today: Recent physical and philosophical work on the direction of time.* Cambridge: Cambridge University Press.

Schottky, W. (1921). Das Kausalproblem der Quantentheorie als eine Grundfrage der modernen Naturforschung uberhaupt. *Naturwissenschaften, 9*(25), 492–496.

Schulman, L. S. (1997). *Time's arrows and quantum measurement.* Cambridge, U.K: Cambridge University Press.

Schwartz, J. M., Stapp, H. P., & Beauregard, M. (2005). Quantum physics in neuroscience and psychology: A neurophysical model of mind-brain interaction. *Philosophical Transactions of the Royal Society B: Biological Sciences, 360*(1458), 1309–1327.

Sheehan, D. P. (Ed.). (2002). *First International Conference on Quantum Limits to the Second Law,* San Diego, CA, July 2002, AIP Conference Volume 643.

Sheehan, D. P. (Ed.) (2006). *Frontiers of time: Retrocausation – Experiment and theory.* AIP Conference Series, Volume 863, Melville, NY: AIP Press.

Sheehan, D. P. (2007a). Thermosynthetic life. *Foundations of Physics*, 37(12), 1774–1797.

Sheehan, D. P. (Ed.). (2007b). The second law of thermodynamics: Foundations and status. *Special Issue of Foundations of Physics*, 37(12). Proceedings of AAAS Symposium, June 19–22, 2006, University of San Diego, CA.

Sheehan, D. P. (Ed.) (2011a). *Quantum retrocausation: Theory and experiment.* AIP Conference Series, Volume 1408, Melville, NY: AIP Press.

Sheehan, D. P. (Ed,). (2011b). Second law of thermodynamics: Status and challenges. *Proceedings of symposium at 92nd Annual Meeting of Pacific Division of AAAS*, June 14–15, 2011, University of San Diego, CA; AIP Conference Volume 1411.

Sheehan, D. P. (2013). Nonequilibrium heterogeneous catalysis in the long mean-free-path regime. *Physical Review E*, 88(3), 032125.

Sheehan, D. P., Mallin, D. J., Garamella, J. T., & Sheehan, W. F. (2014). Experimental test of a thermodynamic paradox. *Foundations of Physics*, 44(3), 235–247.

Watanabe, S. (1955). Symmetry of physical laws: Part III. Prediction and retrodiction. *Reviews of Modern Physics*, 27(2), 179.

Wharton, K. B. (2007). Time-symmetric quantum mechanics. *Foundations of Physics*, 37(1), 159–168.

Wheeler J. A., & Feynman, R. P. (1945). Interaction with the absorber as the mechanism of radiation. *Reviews of Modern Physics*, 17, 157.

Zeh, H. D. (2007). *The physical basis of the direction of time.* (5th Ed.). Berlin: Springer.

Chapter 5

What You Always Wanted to Know about the Observational Theories

Brian Millar

The observational theories (OT; Schmidt, 1975; Walker, 1975) have the reputation of being something difficult, something only for big eggheads and little nerds (Houtkooper, 2002; Millar, 1978; Stokes, 1987). My intention here is to shatter this false impression. Most everyone can master the ideas involved in short order. I restrict my remarks here to a short presentation of the ideas. While a single lesson is sufficient to learn the essentials, like driving a car, this will not make you a formula one driver. One thing is needed above all: can you believe six impossible things before breakfast? Try—things get heavier as they go faster. "Easy: my nurse taught me relativity while changing my diaper." Then how about—an electron can go through two holes *at the same time.* "Hokey: That's in the "double-slit" verse of the old nursery rhyme on quantum mechanics." Good, if you can believe such-like things, you are ready for OT.

WHAT PSI IS NOT AND A LITTLE ABOUT WHAT IT IS

Parapsychology is the scientific study of psi. Psi comes in both *in* and *out* varieties: extrasensory perception (ESP) and psychokinesis (PK). ESP looks like a kind of perception—just without the senses—and PK seems to be a kind of push or pull—just without using the muscles. It appears obvious that in ESP, a signal passes from (say) a sender to a receiver, like with radio; the only unknown is the nature of the signal. In PK, likewise, some kind of unknown force must be exerted by the agent. Only one problem with this—*it's dead wrong!* ESP is *not* signal based, and PK is *not* a force. Like a weasel and a stoat—a stoat is (s)totally different.

Now it is known what psi *isn't*, there just remains a minor detail—what *is* it then? According to the observational theories, ESP is a *"memory" of things future.* "Of course, why didn't I think of that?" Consider guessing the top card of a well-shuffled pack. After the guess is made, turn it over to see what it actually is (feedback): Your earlier guess is partly determined by what you physically see at feedback. The process involves two steps. In the first, a random number generator (RNG) in the brain is (unconsciously) consulted in the process of making a guess. When the target card is seen later, the output of the RNG is observed. Parapsychological experiments have yielded some evidence that QM-based RNG machine outputs can be affected by wishing at the later time of observation; this is sometimes (awkwardly) conceptualized as "retro-PK." (Alternatively, it may be regarded as a precognition-based selection effect, but this is not treated further here). The individual doing the guessing need not actually be the same one doing the retro-PK-ing, so long as he knows what choices the guesser made so that he can "wish for them." (Surprisingly, I have been unable to locate any straight experimental comparison in a retro-PK experiment between a QM-based RNG and a human guesser.)

The reader is likely, at this point, to protest with Alice: "*I can't remember things before they happen.*" But the ever-contrary Queen opines: "*It's a poor sort of memory that only works backwards.*" I confess I can't either, but then I don't have a single psychic bone in my whole body. Is this all "down the rabbit hole" talk? Is it logically possible to have something that looks like retrocausation? The answer (Braude, 1979, 1988; Millar, 1988) appears to be that in a (Newtonian) world, a future *event* can NOT (retro-) cause an earlier event. If you try, everything disappears in a puff of logic. The quantum world must be visited to enquire anew if it is possible there.

At this point, I take leave of the level of "This is the gas pedal. Press it to go faster": instead, the hood must be opened a fraction to learn a little about internal combustion. The quantum stuff can get a bit technical, so if you feel your head spinning, skip over this material. It's not necessary if all you want to do is drive the car, it's important only if you want to understand it how it runs.

Enter the Quantum

A classical force acts on each particle causally, one for one. It is often useful to calculate the probabilities of different outcomes; but there is no more information in this representation than the sum over individual particles. Events are basic and probabilities just a convenient mathematical summary. Quantum physics is different; think probabilities instead. Quantum mechanics (QM) is basically a calculus that calculates the *probabilities* of all possible outcomes for a specified quantum system. In QM, each particle typically *does not have* an individual trajectory. The probability distribution is everything and events, (say) flashes on a luminescent screen, are no more than (noisy) indicators of this underlying probability distribution.

For completeness, I am forced to mention in passing that QM uses an intermediate construct, state vector (or wave function), density matrix and so on, that is a "quantum state." This quantum state is represented mathematically using a matrix in a (high-dimensional) complex Hilbert space, with appropriate symmetry (Hermitian). This matrix represents wave properties: The "normal" classical result is on the diagonal (itself alone), while all the rest (the off-diagonal terms) represent Einstein's spooky stuff (wave interactions). This is regarded by most quantum physicists as the "hard ground" of reality. The probabilities are a simple function (a kind of square) of the quantum state. However, it is hard to get your head around a state vector that does not even exist in normal (3D) space. This material, while fascinating, is "far under the hood" and not too relevant for the topic of this essay. If you really want to get into this, take QM 1.01.

In classical physics, the only way things can be made to happen in the world is by "kicking it" (exert a force)! In quantum physics, nonlocal coupling (entanglement) is also possible. A system breaks into two similar particles going in different directions, subject to the conservation laws (Einstein, Podolsky, Rosen, 1935) (EPR). Systems of (two) particles that have interacted in the past can continue to behave, in some respects, as a single entangled state even though the two constituent particles are now far apart (Einstein's "spooky action at a distance"). Importantly, no information can be transferred between them: There is a *correlation* but *no signal*. Classical and quantum influence are radically different.

Is it possible in practice to simulate ESP with the resources of the quantum lab of today? Some theoretical work, such as Wheeler's (1978, pp. 9–48) quantum self-eraser raises hopes. But something more is needed than just simple EPR. Long ago, I suggested a hypothetical new quantum effect, Walker-Schmidt (WS) coupling (Millar, 1988). In conventional EPR, a past interaction induces a nonlocal (NL) coupling between two particles that extends (continues) some way into the future (until this is shaken back to two classical particles by the noisy environment—decoherence). Walker-Schmidt coupling is the hypothetical time-reversed analog of this: a *future* interaction induces an NL coupling that extends some way into the *past*.

Quite recently, there has been some evidence for WS coupling from purely physical experiments, and what's more, a practical way has been found to implement it by "delayed-choice entanglement swapping." Such experiments are based on the pure physics concept of Perez (2000), rather than from (contentious) parapsychological material. According to Ma, Zotter, Kofler, et al. (2012), nonlocal coupling can, in fact, be induced by a *future* interaction. In this experiment, the "reverse time" was small by human terms (less than half a microsecond), and a great deal more work needs to be done on these lines before anything much can be said about it. It is just possible, though, that time-reversed correlations are going on quietly all the time; it's just that no one took this seriously enough before to take the trouble of looking for them.

The measurement problem in QM asks at what point does a system cease to be described as a superposition of quantum waves and where do classical laws take over. In this jargon, the wave changes to an event with the "collapse" of the wave function. Conscious observation by a human was once conjectured to determine this point (Wigner, 1961). However, the term "observation" is used by physicists today for any interaction of a (quantum) system with anything macroscopic (and warm), not just a human. In conventional QM, the observer's influence is limited to bringing about definite events: It cannot collapse the distribution of a pre-prepared 50:50 quantum mixed state to anything other than 50:50 events. Both Walker and Schmidt agree that psi is to be considered a variant on this: There are at least a few human observers who *can* upset the balance, and this is PK. The standard solution of the measurement problem is represented by EPR, a one-way street from quantum system to observer, while the hypothetical Walker-Schmidt coupling represents a (tiny) back reaction of observation on the quantum system.

Back to the Human World

With the booty brought back from the quantum world, more can be said about what psi is. The basic effect is retro-PK. The spill around which it turns is normal feedback from the RNG to the individual (quantum observation)—no feedback, no psi. The effect is not a force on individual bits; rather, it works on the global level of the *probability distribution*. There are no "true" psi hits and misses; it's just that the whole probability distribution is shifted. ESP is the same, only the retro-PK works on a wetware RNG in the percipient's brain. According to the OTs, psi effects are correlations only, not signals. This means that any attempt to use psi as if it were a signal (e.g., to make money by gambling) is doomed to long-term failure: Causal coupling to the (noise of the) external world eventually breaks up the labile quantum state on which the effect depends.

This is still abstract, and more concrete representations are needed. These are generally known as Schmidt diagrams (Figure 5.1). They resemble the schematics of electronics, since they are effectively elementary *psi circuits*. These consist of three elements:

1. The *random generator* (RG) represents chance and is a straightforward idealized version of a hardware RNG. This may be discrete or continuous, with any number of output lines. For illustration only, the simplest case, with $p = .5$ is considered.
2. The *psi-source* (PS) represents "magic" without intelligence, a psi machine, stripped of all psychology. It is modeled after an idealized successful PKer; but unlike a real PKer, the PS scores at a constant rate. This is the novel nonconventional element: Its nature is to change the probability distribution of any RG to which it is connected. From the point of view of the psi-source, it is *irrelevant* what random elements in the external world are connected to it. All the PS machine does is change the probabilities at its *own* terminals (from $p = .5$ to (say) .51), and it neither "knows nor cares" to what (quantum noise) it is connected.
3. The *feedback channel* (FC) represents deterministic systems. It is a one-way communication channel (Shannon, 1948) from RG to PS. The feedback channel is the link between randomness in the RG and the magic of the PS, both of which are "dumb machines." It is the business element of the OT circuit, which determines what is PKed and how. The feedback channel is generally of considerable complexity and as it incorporates the logic of the circuit, it is convenient to model it as a computer. In addition to its normal duties, it couples RG and PS together to form a (temporary) single system. This total system displays properties that neither of these two parts have when apart, a quantum connection.

In any experiment with humans, two feedback channels can be distinguished. The *external* feedback channel can be directly manipulated by the experimenter (the experimental setup). The human has an *internal* feedback channel between his senses and his in-built psi source. This is known by psychologists as the *cognitive system* and is the locus of the individual's psychology. It lies outside the scope of this basic chapter to delve into the computational approach of cognitive psychology within the context of OT. Here are listed only the tools, wrench, hammer, screwdriver; the beginnings of how to use them is given elsewhere (Millar, 2015).

The curious misconception has somehow sprung up that the OTs' feedback must be trial-by-trial to be psi effective. But the retro-PK effect works directly on a *probability distribution*: Physically, it can work

Figure 5.1
Schmidt Diagrams: PK with straight-through and crossed feedback channel.

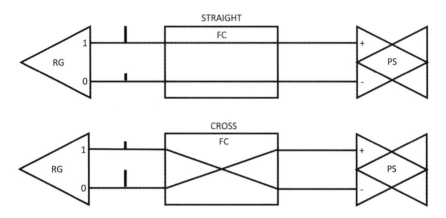

on any probability distribution at any level, from trial-by-trial up to the total (global) score of the whole experiment. The different OTs do differ somewhat on the relative size of the effect expected at different levels. I am unwilling here to make yet another quantitative "guess" to add to those of Walker and Schmidt. I expect only that higher levels may be somewhat less susceptible to psi influence than the trial-by-trial level.

Two particular factors influence which level is "chosen" to affect in any particular case. The first is the feedback that is provided. The second is the interest of the individual. Thus, the participant may be expected to target his own trial-by-trial scores or his overall total: The experimenter, however, is most likely interested in the result of the experiment as a whole. It should be possible to distinguish the level of psi input experimentally. If this is trial-by-trial the significance (z-score) grows in a well-known $\sqrt{N}$ way with the number of trials. On the other hand, if psi information is input to the experiment as whole (likely by the experimenter), then the significance is unaffected by the number of trials (and subjects, etc.). This is quite remarkable: A big experiment is apparently no better than a little one. Decision augmentation theory (DAT; May et al., 2014a,b) makes the same prediction and actually beat the OTs to the punch here. DAT shares much ground with the OTs, save for the central role of observation in the OTs.

THE CENTRAL QUESTION: WHO DUNNIT?

In contentious parapsychology, it seems only right to let the reader know "where I'm coming from." When I arrived in John Beloff's

Edinburgh parapsychology lab in the 1970s, I tried all the then most promising lines of investigation one after the other—ganzfeld, EEG evoked potentials, thermistor PK, RNG-PK, and so on. My results were consistent: no psi. I began to read the *Journal of Parapsychology* with the same "voluntary suspension of disbelief" as I had with the *Arabian Nights*. Psi was something that occurs only in books and not in my own real-life experience. This was something personal that could not be ignored: A parapsychologist who (almost) never sees psi is about as much use as a pub without beer.

I am well aware that successful experimenters find my psi-free experience of the world quite incredible, even perverse. Virtuoso experimenters such as Martin Johnson, Charles Honorton, and Helmut Schmidt must imagine I do dreadful things to my experimental participants to suppress all the superabundant psi they see everywhere they look. The conventional theory then (as now) was that success is all due to social interaction: Some experimenters can "coax" psi out of participants, and others cannot. That can be; so I began informally using students with proven social skills to do the actual interaction with participants. What happened then? *Still no psi*: another beautiful theory felled by an ugly fact!

Perhaps I am a natural "psi-buster," actively inhibiting psi (on some psi level)? A fellow worker, Adrian Parker, who overlapped briefly with me at Edinburgh, did produce significant results and had recently found a high scoring percipient, SB. Adrian generously turned him over to me to test, just to see what would happen. The cosmic joke was that SB then scored significantly with me as experimenter but less (nonsignificant) with Adrian (Parker & Millar, 2014). It wasn't long, however, until decline set in, and he was no longer able to score with either of us. Anyway, strike one for me being a psi-buster!

Were my successful colleagues (both Adrian and later Richard Broughton for a longer period) actually "messing up" their experiments in some way, or were their results real psi? Both careful workers messing up is really hard to believe. The social skills idea seemed unlikely because of the (lack of) results of my informal use of popular student experimenters as a buffer. Further, just looking at how these two experimenters interacted with participants did not seem particularly different from my own ways. We shared the same participant pool. The suspicion arose—were they perhaps producing their results by means of their *own* psi, as OT claims?

If I were a singular example of the "psi-challenged" experimenter, I would readily concede that it is me who is weird. But Britain had by then a long tradition of "no psi": Since Rhine, people had looked for comparable results in vain. The first real contender was Soal, who seems to have become so desperate that he ended up faking his results (Markwick, 1978). Donald West spent decades looking for psi—no sign until he teamed up with George Fisk, who "elicited" psi in participants assigned to him, but not in West's (West & Fisk, 1953). My own mentor was John Beloff, who was notorious for pure chance results. The story was told of an eminent American parapsychologist of those days who, part way across the Atlantic for a conference, announced, "And here, Gentleman, is the psi line, like the Mason-Dixon line back home. Any nearer to Britain and psi ceases to exist." At that time, psi was an almost exclusively American phenomenon.

It was with this background that I first began looking at OT. Dominant experimenter psi not only fits within the framework of the OTs but is actually to be expected. The continuing prosperity of the gambling industry already suggests that the usual subject pool of 20 randomly selected student participants contains negligible psi talent. It is not too difficult for experimenters, who are highly self-selected for success, to out-gun that. This implies that the usual parapsychological assumption of weak, normally distributed psi ability is "out the window" (Millar, 1979).

Agency

The psychologist usually has a really easy time in deciding who is responsible for a (psychological) effect. All he has to do is look: Anna presses buttons, Fred presses buttons, and so on. For the parapsychologist, however, this is a really big deal: There is no obvious way of telling who does the psi. Of course, in an ESP setup, it is known who is guessing; but in the two-step process of the OTs, this need not be the person who is doing the heavy (psi-)lifting (retro-PK). If only humans were equipped with a little red lamp that lights up when psi-ing! The obvious question is: "Why don't you ask them?" The answer in the usual explicit kind of PK experiment is: "I'm just wishing, and that's it!" It seems this alone is sufficient: All the subsequent processing involved in psi-ing is unconscious and cannot be made conscious by introspection (preconscious) either. In fact, wishing too actively seems to be actually counterproductive.

This is already pretty slim fare, but is conscious "wishing" really necessary either? At the time the OTs were just emerging, Stanford (1974a,b), not an OT man, thought deeply about psi from a psychological, rather than a physical, viewpoint. Stanford talked, somewhat opaquely, about a "disposed system." (He did not want to exclude the possibility that purely inanimate systems can exhibit psi-like behavior.) In terms of humans, he considered that conscious wishing is *not necessary*: If some possible futures are of greater *benefit* to the organism than others, the good ones are *automatically* psi-selected. If an RNG produces a 1 (instead of 0), then a brick is dropped on the participant's toes: According to Stanford, this may psi-reduce the frequency of 1s. This insight led to quite a bit of successful experimentation in which people did not even know they were part of a psi experiment—nonintentional psi.

But if this is so, then it makes a lot of sense to ask who stands to benefit most from a psi experiment. The participants typically merely earn course credits and satisfy their curiosity. For the experimenter, however, a successful result may mean renewed research grants, a whole improved career: He and his starving family won't be thrown off campus into the cold, cold snow. Hands down, *the experimenter* has the most to gain. Even virtuoso experimenters were impressed by this argument. Stanford's ideas were later to be incorporated in DAT (May et al., 2014a,b).

This kind of view fits well into the OT framework (and Stanford said it so much more clearly than any of the OTists). Psi is applied, quite unconsciously and automatically, to every observation, every moment of every day. Each individual continually optimizes his own "benefits" landscape, and all this without even so much as the need to think (i.e., unconsciously). Here too, the experimenter has the most to gain. Furthermore, only the experimenter (and analyst) have feedback of the final results (statistical test[s]) of an experiment, which is necessary on the OTs for a psi effect on the level of the experiment.

In the standard psychology model, the experimenter is regarded as an ideal objective recorder of participant results. To achieve this in standard psychology experiments, it is straightforward to cut off all sensory contact between experimenter and participants. Once psi is introduced, though, and this model breaks down, the psychologist knows no way to cut off psi influence. In the OT picture, there is actually no difference in principle between all the personnel involved in the experiment, provided they get feedback of the results: *All are observers.* They may be participants, experimenter, data analyst, and so on—or conceivably even the lab dog, who is petted and fed more treats when things are going well (Schmidt, 1983).

Experimenter Groups

Empirically, three distinct groups of experimenters seem to exist:

1. *Virtuoso.* Only a handful of experimenters *regularly* report large effects and roundly significant statistics. This virtuoso group overwhelmingly represents the public face of parapsychology. On the OT basis, these are likely people with appreciable psi-strength, who under other circumstances might be psychics.
2. *So-so.* The majority of experimenters (and published studies) report "so-so" results that, even if nominally significant, are not convincing unless one believes in psi already. Furthermore, with these experimenters, the results are typically inconsistent, for example, positive scoring one time and negative the next.

I am not at all sure what to make of this group. It seems possible that some just make different mistakes in successive experiments. It is a rare experiment that tests only a single statistical hypothesis; if there are four independent tests, then the chance of getting "significance" is not 5% but 20%. (For comparison, the going rate of significant results in psi experiments is about one in three [Kennedy, 2013].) If the number of tests is known, then a (Bonferroni) correction can be made. But typically, this is not reported, and one wonders how many go "cherry-picking" until they find a significance to report. On the other hand, in the OTs, some may be experimenters with weak and fluctuating psi strength, here today, gone tomorrow.

3. *Psi-challenged.* A third group comprises those experimenters who (almost) never get results (such as me). It is difficult to estimate the frequency of the "psi-challenged" group, since—unless they are singularly masochistic—they rapidly give up. The current most visible representative is Wiseman (Wiseman & Schlitz, 1998, 1999). It seems likely that this group is considerably larger than appears on the surface. It might even be that the majority of new psychology graduates are psi-challenged: This would account neatly for the prevalence of psi-skepticism in such circles.

Virtuosos *Uber Alles*

It is not generally realized how much of parapsychology is due to the handful of virtuoso experimenters, while the so-so group acts as mere chorus. Seldom have so many owed so much to so few! There is a great danger that current parapsychology has become the ultimate in projective tests. Pictures not only *seem* to be in the glowing embers but *really are* present in the otherwise random events of the physical world. For the virtuoso experimenter, every experiment may be no more than a "selfie," the results of which are determined by his fancy of the moment.

Rex Stanford, a virtuoso, whose brother is a psychic, presciently saw where the wind is blowing when he questioned, "Are we Shamans or Scientists?" (Stanford, 1981). The OTs support the view that successful experimenters are quite likely shamans. Where have all the great psychics of yesteryear gone? They now call themselves successful psi experimenters. I can hardly escape the impression, however, that some virtuoso experimenters would be most unhappy to lose the status of "scientist" and be demoted to the level of a mere "Palladino."

In the OTs, experimenters are no longer objective reporters of participant psi: they are just Observer Joes, part of the action like everybody involved. I see no rush of virtuoso experimenters investigating on this basis. And why should they? Their psi already brings them high in the benefits landscape.

Perhaps the long-term answer is that they cannot remain high forever: some time, they have to come down. One of the factors bringing parapsychology down is crazy-sounding New Age–type ideas: some of these are remarkably being supported by experiments using sophisticated parapsychological methodology. The prime example is the Global Consciousness Project (GCP, Bancel & Nelson, 2008). It is possible that global consciousness is an objective fact of Nature. To many (particularly outsiders), though, it looks suspiciously like the kind of daydream that might be brought on by overexposure to the beguiling and numinous notion of Tielhard de Chardin's (1959) noosphere. GCP is very much a test case: if it turns out that the great majority of experimenters can independently replicate the original findings, the effect is in the external world; if only a few can, it is psi experimenter effect. If, as I and others (May & Spottiswoode, 2014/2011) suspect, the latter is the case, then there is a chance that other virtuoso experimenters may seriously consider treating themselves as the valuable psi resource the OTs suggest they are.

It would be unfair to give virtuoso experimenters the blame for failing to follow up on experimenter-psi. The fact is that established institutions tend to go for conservative work. Each of the few actually employed in parapsychology is under considerable (subtle) pressure *not* to research anything so "way out" as experimenter-psi, however much he might personally wish to do so. Investors expect the good old signal-based parapsychology they can understand, not the "topsy-turvy" world of OT in which everything seems turned on its head.

If the results of psi experiments are primarily dependent on the experimenter, rather than the nominal participants, this explains the recurrent cycle that has bedeviled parapsychology since its inception. A new experimenter has an idea, does a whole series of successful experiments, and proclaims the "repeatable experiment," then others attempt the same experiment but without the same success.

RETROSPECT AND PROSPECT

I have now achieved the limited goal I set, namely to explain the basic ideas of OT, briefly and (hopefully) clearly. Divested of technicalities, these are few and simple. Only the notion of a kind of quantum retroaction is, at first sight, quite shocking. That PK works primarily on such an apparently abstract thing as a probability distribution (or the quantum state underlying it) also initially takes a bit of swallowing, particularly for the psychologist. But if precognition really exists, it is necessary to acknowledge "that's just how the world is." There is, of course, much more to the OTs. What is the experimental evidence? Has much of parapsychology really slipped into an experimenter-driven self-fulfilling prophecy mode? Can that be determined by hard experiment? If so what can be done about it?

The OTs state that feedback is necessary for psi. A corollary is that if this is true, psi can be manipulated by manipulating the feedback. It may even be possible to construct that psi "insulator" that has eluded parapsychology to date. Considerable additional material is to be found in Millar (2015).

If there is any truth in the OTs, it would be unfortunate if parapsychologists just continue to treat psi in the same way as any other psychological effect, hoping against hope someday to stumble blindly upon a *truly* repeatable experiment. The OTs offer possible *systematic* ways of surmounting the current impasse. If they are not widely tried in practice, it will certainly never be known whether they work or not.

Acknowledgments. This chapter is partly based on Millar (2015).

REFERENCES

Bancel, P. & Nelson, R. (2008). The GCP event experiment: Design, analytical methods, results. *Journal of Scientific Exploration, 22*(3), 309–333.

Braude, S. E. (1979). The observational theories in parapsychology: A critique. *Journal of the American Society for Psychical Research, 73,* 349–366.

Braude, S. E. (1988). Death by observation: A reply to Millar. *Journal of the American Society for Psychical Research, 82,* 273–280.

Einstein, A., Podolsky, B., & Rosen, N. (1935). Can quantum-mechanical description of physical reality be considered complete? *Physics Review, 47,* 777.

Houtkooper, J. (2002). Arguing for an observational theory of paranormal phenomena. *Journal of Scientific Exploration, 16*(2), 171–185.

Kennedy, J. E. (2013). Can parapsychology move beyond the controversies of retrospective meta-analyses? *Journal of Parapsychology, 77,* 21–35.

Ma, X., Zotter, S., Kofler, J., Ursin, R., Jennewein, T., Brukner, C. & Zeilinger, A. (2012). Experimental delayed choice entanglement swapping. *Nature Physics, 8,* 479–484.

Markwick, B. (1978). The Soal-Goldney experiments with Basil Shackleton: New evidence of data manipulation. *Proceedings of the Society for Psychical Research, 56,* 250–277.

May, E. C., & Spottiswoode, S. J. P. (2014/2011). The Global Consciousness project: Identifying the source of psi. In E. C. May & S. B. Marwaha (Eds.), *Anomalous cognition: Remote viewing research and theory,* pp. 268–277. Jefferson, NC: McFarland.

May, E. C., Spottiswoode, S. J. P., & Utts, J. M. (2014a/1995). Applications of decision augmentation theory. In E. C. May & S. B. Marwaha (Eds.), *Anomalous cognition: Remote viewing research and theory,* pp. 244–267. Jefferson, NC: McFarland.

May, E. C., Utts, J. M., & Spottiswoode, S. J. P. (2014b/1995). Decision augmentation theory: Toward a model for anomalous mental phenomena. In E. C. May &

S. B. Marwaha (Eds.), *Anomalous cognition: Remote viewing research and theory,* pp. 222–243. Jefferson, NC: McFarland.

Millar, B. (1978). The observational theories: A primer. *European Journal of Parapsychology, 2,* 304–332.

Millar, B. (1979). The distribution of psi. *European Journal of Parapsychology, 3*(1), 78–110.

Millar, B. (1988). Cutting the Braudian loop: In defense of the observational theories. *Journal of the American Society for Psychical Research, 82,* 253–271.

Millar, B. (2015). Quantum theory and parapsychology. In E. Cardeña, J. Palmer, & D. Marcusson-Clavertz (Eds.), *Parapsychology: A handbook for the 21st century.* Jefferson, NC: McFarland.

Parker, A. & Millar, B. (2014). Revealing psi secrets: Successful experimenters seem to succeed by using their own psi. *Journal of Parapsychology, 78*(1), 39–55.

Perez, A. (2000). Delayed choice for entanglement swapping. *Journal of Modern Optics, 47,* 139–143.

Schmidt, H. (1975). Toward a mathematical theory of psi. *Journal of the American Society for Psychical Research, 69,* 301–319.

Schmidt, H. (1983). Superposition of PK efforts by man and dog. In R. White & R. Broughton (Eds.), *Research in Parapsychology,* pp. 96–98. Metuchen, NJ: Scarecrow.

Shannon, C. E. (1948). A mathematical theory of communication. *Bell Systems Technical Journal, 27,* 379–423.

Stanford, R G. (1974a). An experimentally testable model for spontaneous psi events: I. Extrasensory events. *Journal of the American Society for Psychical Research, 68,* 34–57.

Stanford, R. G. (1974b). An experimentally testable model for spontaneous psi events: II. Psychokinetic events. *Journal of the American Society for Psychical Research, 68,* 321–356.

Stanford, R. G. (1981). Are we shamans or scientists? *Journal of the American Society for Psychical Research, 75,* 61–70.

Stokes, D. M. (1987). Theoretical parapsychology. In S. Krippner (Ed.), *Advances in parapsychological research, 5,* pp. 77–189. Jefferson, NC: McFarland.

Teilhard de Chardin, P. (1959). *The phenomenon of man.* New York: Harper Perennial.

Walker, E. H. (1975). Foundations of paraphysical and parapsychological phenomena. In L. Oteri (Ed.), *Quantum physics and parapsychology.* New York: Parapsychology Foundation.

West, D. J., & Fisk, G. W. (1953). A dual experiment with clock cards. *Journal of the Society for Psychical Research, 37,* 185–197.

Wheeler, J. A. (1978). The past and delayed choice double slit experiment. In A. R. Marlow (Ed.), *Mathematical foundations of quantum theory,* pp. 9–48. New York: Academic Press.

Wigner, E. P. (1961). Remarks on the mind-body question. In I. J. Good (Ed.), *The scientist speculates.* London: Heinemann.

Wiseman, R., & Schlitz, M. (1998). The remote detection of staring and the experimenter effect. *Proceedings of 22nd International Conference of the Society for Psychical Research.* York: University College.

Wiseman, R. & Schlitz, M. (1999). Experimenter effects and the remote detection of staring. *Journal of Parapsychology, 61,* 197–207.

Chapter 6

Entropy and Precognition: The Physics Domain of the Multiphasic Model of Precognition

Edwin C. May and Joseph G. Depp

The multiphasic model of precognition (MMPC), as discussed in the following chapter, identifies two distinct phases of precognition. Phase I, the physics domain, addresses the question: how is it possible for information to traverse from one spacetime point to another? We suggest that the solution might be found within entropic considerations. Phase II, the neuroscience domain, hypothesizes that the acquisition and interpretation of retrocausal signals is via three stages: (1) perception of signals from an information carrier, which is based upon psychophysical variability in a putative signal transducer; (2) cortical processing of the signals, which is mediated by a cortical hyper-associative mechanism; and (3) cognition, which is mediated by normal cognitive processes that lead to a precognitive response. In this chapter, we expand the discussion on the physics domain of the MMPC.

ENTROPY

What might the concept of entropy hold for psi research? To answer this question, it may be useful to review entropy and its changes. The

Oxford English Language Dictionary has a number of different definitions of entropy:

- *Physics*. A thermodynamic quantity representing the unavailability of a system's thermal energy for conversion into mechanical work, often interpreted as the degree of disorder or randomness in the system.
- Lack of order or predictability; gradual decline into disorder.
- *Information theory*. A logarithmic measure of the rate of transfer of information in a particular message or language.
- The equations for information and thermodynamic entropy are equivalent except for a constant multiplier.

Building upon the pioneering work of Leó Szilárd (Szilárd, 1964; Szilárd & Feld, 1972a,b), Shannon and Weaver (1949) developed what is now called information theory. This theory formalizes the intuitive idea of information that there is more "information" in rare events, such as winning the lottery, than in common ones, such as taking a breath. Shannon defined the entropy for a given system as the weighted average of the probability of occurrence of all possible events in the system. Entropy, used in this sense, is defined as a measure of our uncertainty, or lack of information, about a system. Suppose, for example, we had a fair die (i.e., each of the six sides is equally likely to come up). This system is, in fact, the maximum possible entropy for this system—the most uncertain with regard to what face will face up after a toss. If, on the other hand, the die were completely biased so that the same side always came up, the entropy would be zero. In other words, if each outcome is equally likely, then each event has the maximum surprise. Conversely, there is no surprise if the same side always lands facing up.

Brian Greene (2003) in his book *The Elegant Universe* and on a NOVA production (Greene, 2012) spells out in very understandable terms why physics appears not to care whether time moves forward or backward, yet we all experience the arrow of time flying in one direction, only— towards the future. As he shows, entropy is the answer to this conundrum.

In one example on the NOVA show, Greene drops a wine glass full of wine, shows it in slow motion and comments that it seems unlikely there is a way to put the shattered glass and splashed wine back again—not unlike "Humpty Dumpty sat on a wall. / Humpty Dumpty had a great fall. / All the king's horses and all the king's men / Couldn't put Humpty together again." In simple terms, the laws of physics tell us that all we have to do is reverse the velocity of each tiny fragment of broken glass and each micro drop of wine, all the atoms in the table and in the air, and we end up with a full, intact glass of wine. Since the laws of physics allow this to happen, how do we square these laws with the everyday experience of time marching on? The answer, of course, is entropy, or more precisely, the second law of thermodynamics, which states that isolated systems must evolve to greater and greater disorder. Suppose we start with a bound book as Greene does in the NOVA presentation—the pages are all in order; then we rip the book apart and toss them into the air. What results is a chaotic scrambling of the pages all over the ground. The reason is simple; there is only one possible way for the pages to land in order and a huge, almost countless number of ways not to land in order. This is the second law at work. Thus, as the world moves forward toward more and more disorder, we can tell that macroscopic time moves in only one direction. Entropy gives us the single direction of the arrow of time.

Yet, in some psi experiments during which the target stimulus is randomly generated *after* a response, we have a fundamental problem. This begins to look exactly like a violation of all we have discussed thus far and often is the underlying reason there is so much, and quite valid, skepticism about psi in general and precognition in particular. Causality violation—things that happen only happen *after* the events that caused them to happen happened first and not before.

This chapter will demonstrate a possible way out of this very troubling dilemma.

PSI EXPERIMENTS AND CHANGES OF ENTROPY

Relating psi to entropy did not happen in a flash of wise insight—rarely does the progress of science happen that way. Rather, a series of clues along the way began to stack up to point the research in that direction.

Clues toward an Entropy Model of Precognition

During the time of the Star Gate program, we noticed that there were a class of operational anomalous cognition (AC) missions (i.e., involving intelligence gathering or simulations thereof) that appeared never to fail (May & Lantz, 2014/2010). These included underground nuclear tests, electromagnetic pulse devices, static and dynamic rocket motor tests, and rocket launchings. One possible explanation might be that these target types shared a common physical attribute; they all involve enormous expenditures of energy in a short period of time. Of course, the first thing that comes to mind is that somehow these short bursts radiate energy in such a way that the central nervous system of the participants responds accordingly—a traditional sensory explanation. However, this cannot account for the numerous examples when the AC was carried out precognitively, *before* the actual event had occurred and, thus, another possible example of macroscopic causality violation. That is, something happened before the thing that caused it to happen, happened first!

To account for the success of such trials, instead of the energy considerations, we chose a different direction: this class of operational targets seem to share another physical property besides rapid energy release—a dramatic and rapid increase in thermodynamic entropy. For example, in an underground nuclear test, the bomb material is ordered in a small package, and the surrounding earth is all stable and quiet—a state of relatively low entropy. Then, kaboom! What happens next is total chaos and disorder—a huge increase of entropy. What is left of the bomb material is scattered, and a bubble of earth may rise many meters in the air before settling back to form a huge dust cloud.

This, of course, has the added advantage in that the changes of thermodynamic entropy are also related to the macroscopic single direction of time as described by Greene (2003).

We will illustrate this kind of target with a single example of a task from a counter-nuclear terrorism group with the responsibility of finding nuclear material on U.S. soil under a terrorism scenario. We were asked to participate in a Nuclear Emergency Search Team (NEST) exercise. In June 1994, we met the NEST team coordinator, who gave us his photograph. We were asked to provide AC data for an exercise that was to take place somewhere in the continental U.S. territory on October 17, 1994; however, we were required to have the data in his hand by July 31, 1994—clearly a precognitive AC task. We found out after the exercise had taken place that on this date, a substantial amount of radioactive material was hidden somewhere in New Orleans, Louisiana.

One of our participants described in detail with words and drawings that the site involved a large drum of sensors, sensor feeds, a drum filled with gas or liquid, an airborne platform collector, and the repositioning of satellites.

The sponsor informed us that the drawings were reasonably correct and that accompanying written statements that claimed satellites were being repositioned for the exercise was also correct. Additionally, there was enough information in the response to identify the city in which the radioactive material was hidden. It is important to note here that unlike a controlled laboratory experiment in which a quantitative analysis can be conducted, operational or simulated operational sessions (like in this case) requires a different and qualitative kind of analysis. It is presented here only to lend support to the laboratory anecdotal discussion above.

Besides the thermodynamic changes of entropy illustrated here, another kind of entropy comes to us from information theory and is called informational entropy. Leó Szilárd, the famous Hungarian physicist of whom we spoke earlier, demonstrated a connection between thermodynamic and informational entropy by showing that both types of entropy have the same equations except for a constant multiplier (Leff & Rex, 1990).

Target Stimuli and Their Entropic Content

We will only outline this computation here because such computations are common in vision research and can be found in the psi research literature (May & Lantz, 2014/2010) as well.

Imagine a three-color bit-mapped photograph wherein each color is eight bits deep; that is, each color can take on 256 intensity values from zero to 255. Each pixel is, therefore, 24 bits deep. So the entropy is given by:

$$H = -\sum_{c=1}^{3} \sum_{j=1}^{255} p_{j,c} \log_2 (p_{j,c}),$$

where c represents the color number (i.e., $c = 1,3$ for red, green, blue, respectively) and $p_{j,c}$ is the probability of a color pixel, c, with intensity j. These probabilities are easily obtained from constructing a pixel histogram of the whole photograph for each color. Suppose, for example, the photograph was half white and the other was half green, but in a checkerboard layout. Suppose further that this photograph is 800×600 pixels for each color. Then in this simple example, the number of single full green (intensity of 255) pixels is half of 800×600 pixels, or 240,000 pixels. So the j in the equation is a single value of one; $p_{1,green} = .5$. One way to think of this probability is to suppose that we throw a dart (random toss) at a paper print of the picture. Then $p_{1,green} = .5$ represents the chances that the dart will hit a green pixel. We have called this the "frame" entropy in our work when we consider a photograph of some natural scene and do all the appropriate summations indicated by the equation.

We also use this equation to compute the average of the absolute value of the spatial gradient for the photograph. For example, consider a patch of 20×20 pixels in an 800×600 pixel photograph. For our standardized photograph of this size, there are 40×30 such nonoverlapping patches. An entropy, $h_{i,j}$ ($i = 1,40, j = 1,30$), is computed for each patch as above. This produces an entropy map for the photograph. A standard technique is used to compute the spatial entropic gradient across the photograph (May & Spottiswoode, 2014/1994). Then the average of the absolute magnitude of the spatial gradient is used to arrive at a single number for any given photographic stimulus.

It is clear from maps of differing photographs that target stimuli with the high entropic gradients show tall "hills" and deep "valleys" in entropy space, whereas a low gradient map is much flatter. These maps are not unlike topological survey maps that graphically show hills and valleys in physical space. As it turns out, the absolute magnitude of the spatial gradient of the highest gradient target stimulus (i.e., a bridge over a stream in the forest) is 327% larger than that for the smallest (i.e., the main pyramid in Giza) in our set of 300 photographs. So, if an AC response is sensitive to the entropic gradient of the target stimulus, this would predict the bridge stimulus should be much easier to "see" by AC than the pyramid. Since this computation is strictly a color mapping, the final average gradient number for each photograph is independent of the cognitive content of the photograph—a photograph of a flower, for example, may have a higher average entropic gradient than one of a nuclear explosion; it depends only upon the distribution of colors. More-over, this gradient is also independent of the contrast of the photograph. The easiest way to see that is to understand that changing the contrast of a photograph stretches or compacts the pixel histogram; however, it keeps the relative color probabilities ($p_{c,j}$ above) constant (May, 2014/2011).

May, Spottiswoode, and Faith (2000) tested the hypothesis that the average of the absolute magnitude of the spatial gradient of a target pho-tograph will correlate with quality of the AC as measured by the figure of merit (FoM) assessment of the quality of the match with the intended target stimulus. The FoM is the product of the session accuracy—what fraction of the target was described correctly—times the reliability—what fraction of the response was correct. To obtain a high FoM, a parsimonious response (i.e., not much incorrect information) should correspond to a large fraction of the target material. In 75 trials, they found a Spearman-Rank correlation of 0.212 for the entropic gradient, with the figure of merit statistically significant ($p = .034$); whereas the correlation with the entropy itself was near zero ($\rho = 0.042$, $p = .362$). This is what we might expect if AC were mediated by some sensory system, since all five of our sensory systems are better gradient detectors than they are steady state detectors.

To date, there have been seven laboratory studies (four published and three unpublished) involving 229 individual trials that have tested the concept that AC is correlated with entropic gradients. The combined cor-relation (Spearman's rho) between the entropic gradient and the FoM was 0.211 ($z = 3.22$, $p = 6.4 \times 10^{-4}$; 95% confidence interval for the correla-tion of [0.084, 0.332]); whereas correlating the same data with the entropy itself gave rho of 0.028 ($z = 0.37$, $p = .36$; 95% confidence interval for the correlation [-0.120, 0.175]). Thus, the detection of AC acting just like a sen-sory system is as we suggested earlier in this discussion.

At this juncture, this sensory-like finding of an AC correlation with the change of entropy and not with the entropy itself remains speculation. In evolutionary terms, we cannot say whether the putative sensory system is new, old, or some combination of the five known systems.

We seem to have a number of pieces of a puzzle that suggest a way forward. These are, so far:

- The second law of thermodynamics gives rise to our perception of time's arrow pointing in only one direction.
- In a growing number of studies, the quality of AC is statistically correlated with changes of entropy of the target stimuli.
- Precognition (i.e., gaining noninferential information from a future unrealized event) appears to violate macroscopic causality.

Taken together, this is likely to be a huge clue as to how to proceed.

TOWARD THERMODYNAMICS AS A MODEL OF PRECOGNITION IN THE PHYSICS DOMAIN

We begin with what appears to be an anomaly. It is possible to borrow from information theory a simple equation for binary sequences relating to changes in Shannon entropy as a function of the fractional number of ones in a sequence. The total change in entropy/bit for a sequence with any probability of a binary one is given by:

$$\Delta H = 1 + p \log_2 (p) + (1 - p) \log_2 (1 - p),$$

where p is the fractional number of 1s in the sequence. Of course, this equation is completely independent of AC or the Shannon entropy of AC targets; rather, it is simply a theoretical expression drawn from traditional information theory. Yet, if we reinterpret ΔH to be the entropic gradient of AC targets and p to be the overall psi result (transformed to a binary representation) of an AC experiment, a surprising result emerges. Figure 6.1 shows a number of AC studies in a graphical representation plotted over this equation.

The smooth U-shaped curve in Figure 6.1 is the graphical representation of the change of entropy formula. The seven AC studies cluster around a gradient value near 0.06. The horizontal error bars represent one standard error of the mean. The data shown near the gradient value of 0.04 represent the results from a different form of AC called forced-choice guessing wherein the target is randomly chosen from a limited set, and the participant is aware of all possible targets within the set. Of course, the studies are conducted under double-blind conditions.

A common set of targets, called Zener cards, were used extensively for research in the 1930s through 1980s (Honorton & Ferrari, 1989). A deck of Zener cards consists of five each of the symbols square, circle, wavy lines, star, and cross for a total of 25 cards.

Figure 6.1
All anomalous cognition experiments in which entropic gradients are available are shown with their 1-σ standard errors (near 0.06 entropic gradients) and selected Zener card guessing results shown near 0.04.

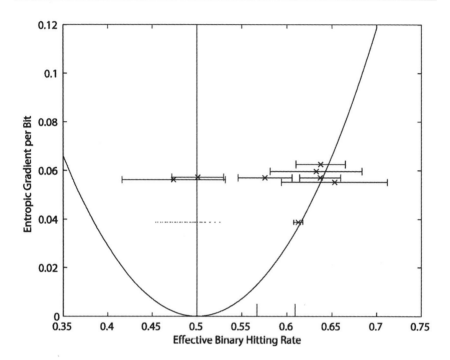

Some of the Zener card AC data were randomly taken from the literature and are shown clustering around an effective binary hitting rate of 0.5 (i.e., mean chance expectation). However, there is a single study with a small error bar (i.e., 2,500 trials) shown near a hitting rate of 0.61 (or the equivalent of 0.43 in a one-in-five Zener card game in which chance expectation is 0.20) that was chosen from the literature because it was the largest number of trials we could find with the highest hitting rate. (Special thanks to Richard Broughton for finding these data sets.)

What we find remarkable in Figure 6.1 is that the unrelated information-theoretic curve looks like some kind of a limit for high-quality AC. Although it is only one study, the highest quality Zener card study with a substantial number of trials appears to be bounded by the curve. We note that in a Zener card study, the mean chance expected hit rate is 0.2; however, the apparent limit for Zener cards is a hit rate of 0.43 (i.e., equivalent to the 0.62 binary hit rate shown in Figure 6.1). We emphasize once again that this putative limit is a statistical one. For example, there are rare cases reported that a participant got all 25 cards correct in a single one-deck trial (Rhine, 1963), which would be plotted at a binary hit rate of one—way outside the suggested limit; however, the probability of seeing such a high score is extremely small. The way to think of the limit is as the mean of normal curves with, as yet, unknown variances.

We were able to explore Zener card data in much more depth by examining the card-guessing literature in much greater detail. One of two data sets consisted of 7,167 runs of a single deck of 25 cards each. These data span from August 1933 through August 1938 and include a large number of different participants. The second data set came from primarily one high-scoring individual and consisted of 3,662 runs of a single deck, and it spanned from October 1930 to April 1939 (May, 2011, 2014/2011).

Thus, for a total of 10,829 decks of Zener cards corresponding to 270,725 individual card guesses, the limit as shown earlier in this discussion appears to hold. Keeping in mind that such a limit must be, by its nature, a statistical one, we estimated what we would expect under a null hypothesis of no psi using a standard technique of a Monte Carlo estimate. We found that only 0.03% of Zener card decks would exceed the putative statistical limit implied in Figure 6.1; yet, using the actual data, only 0.78% did exceed the limit. In both cases, we might expect that the highest scoring card guessing data or the highest scoring AC studies would exceed the arbitrary (i.e., with regard to AC) limit curve shown in Figure 6.1. Yet, even with this high-quality data, the supposed independent (of AC) information-theoretic curve is acting like some kind of a statistical limit as it also appears to do with the free-response AC data as well. The important question at this point is, why is this the case?

DISCUSSION

It is not unreasonable to expect some limit to an AC ability. If it turns out that it is mediated via some sensory system—which is strongly suggested in that AC correlates with the gradient of Shannon entropy and not with the entropy itself—then a limit would be expected. After all, all of our known sensory systems have limits. For example, we cannot directly detect γ- or x-rays, we do not have the sensory range of some other organisms (such as a dog's sense of hearing or smell), and so forth. The simple relationship of the informational entropy in a binary sequence as shown in Figure 6.1 appears at this stage to be such a limit, albeit a statistical one, and the number of AC cases is small. Perhaps there are psychological or demographic reasons for the apparent limit in the data used here.

To answer whether psychological or demographic factors are responsible for the limit, or whether entropic gradients can account for the limit, more AC data are needed to fill in the space near entropic gradients of 0.06 in Figure 6.1.

Entropy might be a productive concept for developing a physics model for macroscopic retro-causality (precognitive anomalous cognition), since it is well understood in classical thermodynamics that the apparent unidirectional nature of the arrow of time arises from the second law of thermodynamics.

From a signal perspective, we do not know if the putative limiting factor has its origin at the source of the information, the channel through which the information propagates somehow, (i.e., called the channel capacity in engineering terms) or, finally, in the CNS detector system itself.

Suppose that the limit arises ostensibly in the central nervous system. In the CNS, thinking about anything involves the activity of a huge number of neurons that otherwise are relatively inactive; thus, thinking represents an increase of entropy. Tononi (2008) expands this notion as an entropic model call integrated information theory as a description of consciousness itself. We will describe his ideas later in this chapter.

Event-related desynchronization—the squelching of alpha production as a result of a stimulus, thought, or movement—is a clear example of entropy at play. Alpha rhythms are regular, approximately 10 hertz oscillations and therefore are relatively low in entropy. But when the alpha is interrupted to attend to a stimulus, a thought or movement of a body part, more random brain-wave patterns emerge, at least temporarily—an obvious increase of entropy. So, maybe what sets the limit is the amount of entropic increase the brain can tolerate. Roughly speaking, classical thermodynamics might suggest an answer for such a limit. The CNS is immersed in a constant heat bath nominally at 37° C (i.e., 98.6° F). Temperatures much higher than that are dangerous and can quickly lead to brain damage. In thermodynamic terms, a change of entropy is a ratio of the amount of the change of heat in an isolated system divided by its temperature. A reasonable speculation is that evolution would impose a limit of the increase of the entropy such that the brain would not suffer damage. While this might appear plausible, there is a problem with it: clearly, the information arriving at the CNS via the normal visual system is many orders of magnitude greater than even the best AC examples, yet that information does not appear to be limited in the same way. Clearly, more theoretical investigations are needed, as are more experimental data.

The American Institute of Physics hosted a symposium on Quantum Retrocausation: Theory and Experiment, which was sponsored by the American Association for the Advancement of Science in San Diego (Sheehan, 2011). The basic question under consideration was whether it is possible for some unrealized future event to causally influence the present. Note that this is different from saying "can the present influence the past." A general consensus in physics is that the past (when viewed from the present) is the past and stays that way. Most all the papers from mainstream physicists that addressed the issue of time's arrow or space-time issues from the future to the present ended up with some discussion of entropy. This, of course, suggests further that entropy and its changes cannot be ignored if we are to understand precognition.

In the multiphasic model of precognition, we address the problem of understanding precognition by defining two areas of interest: the physics domain (all aspects of the problem outside the head) and the neuroscience domain (all aspects of the problem inside the head). Based, in part, upon the data described earlier in this chapter, we pointed the physics domain problem primarily at entropy. In addition, the concept is a current topic in theoretical physics (Verlinde, 2011; Wissner-Gross & Freer, 2013). Besides being able to derive some of the most fundamental equations of physics starting from entropic principles, Verlinde goes so far as to suggest that perhaps gravity itself should be downgraded from the status of a force, since it, too, can be derived from entropic considerations. Additionally, a number of papers appeared relating entropy to fundamental issues of the universe (de Boer, Cheng, Dijkgraaf, et al., 2006; Dijkgraaf, Verlinde, & Verlinde, 1997; Savonije & Verlinde, 2001; Verlinde, 2000), including an important contribution by Lee (2011), who showed that it was possible to relate quantum information theory and classical information theory.

The point of all this current theoretical physics is to indicate how fundamental the concept of entropy is with regard to spacetime geometry This will provide the foundation of a possible physics theory as to how information moves on a carrier from one spacetime point to another, especially if not enough time has elapsed to make causal relations between the two points.

Another important aspect of entropy is definitional with regard to what is meant by consciousness itself (Tononi, 2008). Although a discussion of consciousness seems not to be relevant with regard to psi and entropy, as it turns out, it is in that there is a continuing dialogue in the psi research community about the degree to which psi is part of consciousness (Cardeña, 2014; Varvoglis, 1996).

It seems to us quite obvious that any living, sentient human has experiences including psi, all of which fit into a generic definition of consciousness. In his straightforward and elegant paper, Tononi (2008) describes a theory of consciousness as integrated information theory (IIT). The IIT of consciousness claims that at a fundamental level, consciousness is integrated information and that its quality is given by the informational relationships generated by a complex of elements. Tononi separates information into two categories, the first of which is not at all related to consciousness. Consider the light sensor in a one-megapixel digital camera. Tononi (2008, p. 218) comments on this example:

Clearly, taken as a whole, the camera's detectors could distinguish among $2^{1,000,000}$ alternative states, an immense number, corresponding to 1 million bits of information. Indeed, the camera would easily respond differently to every frame from every movie that was ever produced. Yet few would argue that the camera is conscious. What is the key difference between you and the camera?

The camera's sensor is a large number of independent elements each of which has no information about what happened with its neighboring elements, so the sensor chip is not capable of integrating or interpreting what it "sees." By contrast, a human looking at the same scene is capable of a rich internal experience invoked not by the individual pixel data, but the integrated information the observer's brain brings in addition.

It is beyond the scope of this chapter to provide a detailed analysis of integrated information theory; however, it is important to realize that Tononi (2008, p. 220) describes this difference as a relative entropy. Clearly, according to this model, consciousness and entropy are intertwined.

Max Tegmark (2014) placed the work of Tononi on a physics basis, asserting that consciousness can be considered as just another state of matter:

> Generations of physicists and chemists have studied what happens when you group together vast numbers of atoms, finding that their collective behavior depends on the pattern in which they are arranged: the key difference between a solid, a liquid and a gas lies not in the types of atoms, but in their arrangement. In this paper, we conjecture that consciousness can be understood as yet another state of matter. Just as there are many types of liquids, there are many types of consciousness. However, this should not preclude us from identifying, quantifying, modeling and ultimately understanding the characteristic properties that all liquid forms of matter (or all conscious forms of matter) share. (p. 1)

This concept echoes to some degree the geometric idea put forward by Tononi (2008, p. 224) describing experience as shapes in qualia space.

FURTHER THEORETICAL CONSIDERATION FOR THE PHYSICS DOMAIN

There are no examples in physics in which information goes from point A to point B and that information can be used (i.e., "can do work" in physics jargon), that do not have a concomitant energy carrier. Therefore, *it seems unlikely that psi will be the first example wherein a carrier is not required.* Yet, this notion is extremely troubling with regard to classical physics. From a simple signal perspective, an energy carrier that is responsible for precognition cannot be electromagnetic (EM). Why? The solution to the famous Maxwell's equations involve EM waves moving forward in time, which is how we all expect radio waves to behave. Your favorite radio station sends a signal to the transmitter and for amplitude modulation stations (AM), 50,000 watts of power sends that information to your radio. Suppose you live 100 km from the tower. Then the radio signal reaches you at the speed of light (i.e., 299,792.458 km/s) in 0.000334 seconds, but the key point is that even though it is a short time later, it *is* later. The other solution to Maxwell's equations tells that if you were 100 km from the antenna, you could use precognition to get the signal in advance, but only 0.000334 seconds in advance. Clearly, all the data supporting the existence of precognition are of the order of human time scales and thus rule out advanced EM waves as a possible energy carrier for psi.

As far as physics knows now, there are only four forces in nature: gravity—the weakest; strong nuclear—the strongest; EM—the next strongest; and weak nuclear—responsible for radioactive decay. Each of these are associated with energy, but the two nuclear forces are very short ranged. That is, they extend at best over a few nuclear diameters (e.g., 2.5×10^{-15} m). So now we have ruled out three of the four possible forces as candidates for a carrier for psi.

Revisiting Entropy and Information

Modern physics does not distinguish in any significant way between informational entropy and thermodynamic entropy. Recognition of the close relationship between thermodynamic entropy and informational entropy has given rise to an explosion of papers on the subject of quantum information during the past decade. According to a survey by Schlosshauer, Kofler, and Zeilinger (2013), three quarters of the physicists interviewed regarded quantum information theory as a major advancement in our understanding of quantum mechanics.

Many recent papers suggest that quantum information is inextricably linked to quantum gravity and that quantum gravity must play a major role in the underpinnings of any fundamental description of our universe. Twenty years ago, Leonard Susskind (1993, 1995) recognized that everything in the three spatial dimensions of the universe could be regarded as information stored on a two-dimensional surface that bounds the volume of the universe. This concept is similar to the well-known fact that the interior solutions to linear partial differential equations are completely determined by the values at the boundaries. His work has given rise to hundreds of papers that have resulted in a new field, quantum information theory, as mentioned earlier in this chapter.

Verlinde (2011) published the first of several papers suggesting that gravity and information theory are closely related. Verlinde's paper caused a flurry of associated papers, including one by Lee (2011), who showed that it was possible to relate quantum information theory and classical information theory by considering what happens to information at a Rindler horizon for accelerating observers. (A Rindler horizon is a hyperbolic surface that is, for practical purposes, the equivalent of a light cone in special relativity.)

Entanglement

Quantum entanglement has been a feature of quantum mechanics since the founding of the discipline nearly a hundred years ago. Most work on quantum entanglement has addressed only the spatial entanglement. However, about 50 years ago, it was shown theoretically that the Lorentz symmetry between space and time required that there should also exist time-entangled states. The issue was examined again recently by Aharonov, Cohen, Grossman, et al. (2012), and an experiment was proposed. (Aharonov uses the term "past" to mean measurements made in the present that are affected by measurements made in the future. He does not mean measurements made in the past with respect to the present.) At the time of this writing, the preliminary experimental results seem to confirm the hypothesis that future choice can affect past measurements (Moreva, Brida, Gramegna et al., 2014).

Recently, physicists have developed a theory for the mechanism that implements entanglement. The theory posits that two entangled particles are connected, at the time of entanglement, by a wormhole that exists in a higher dimensional space (Maldacena & Susskind, 2013; Jensen & Karch, 2013; Sonner, 2013; Susskind, 2013). The wormhole is nontraversable, which means that energy/mass cannot be sent through the wormhole from one terminus to the other. However, Butcher (2014) has put forth a theory that suggests that it may be possible to send a pulse of light through a wormhole that is otherwise nontraversable because Casimir force may hold the wormhole open just long enough for the pulse to transit the wormhole. (The Casimir force is a consequence of zero-point energy).

However, information *can* be communicated by the wormhole. Current theory holds that the information is communicated from the interior of one event horizon to the interior of the other event horizon. If valid, this theory has two very important implications. First, information is a tangible entity independent of the object that it describes. Second, a medium for information transport exists in the higher-dimensional space.

Other recent work, building on Susskind's papers (1993, 1995), has also suggested to physicists that information is a tangible entity. (The term "tangible entity" is of our own choosing. Like the terms "dark energy" and "dark matter," it is meant to be a placeholder for something that we currently do not understand.) Work on the fate of information associated with energy/mass falling into a black hole has produced the concept that information resides on the surface of the black hole and is stored in holographic form.

The mechanism for information transport in the higher-dimensional space remains speculative, but there is no reason to think that such a mechanism violates any of the physical laws that describe our universe in a four-dimensional spacetime. Current string theory suggests that the transport mechanism is gravitational, with "gravitational" taken in the broadest sense of the word. The reasoning behind the theory is that gravitation is the only effect thought to extend into hyperdimensional space, and it is gravitational effects that create a wormhole. It has been shown that there is a tachyonic soliton solution for the Higgs field (Sen, 1998). Educated speculation suggests that the soliton field may provide the medium for information transport. (Soliton: a quantum or quasiparticle propagated as a traveling nondissipative wave that is neither preceded nor followed by another such disturbance.)

Hyperdimensional Space

Most current "theories of everything" require that there exist a hyperdimensional space in which our four-dimensional spacetime is embedded. The suggested number of spatial dimensions varies wildly among theories, but all of these theories have in common the need for at least one extra spatial dimension.

Very recent work (Arkani-Hamed & Trnka, 2013) has shown that four-dimensional spacetime is not necessary for calculating scattering amplitudes for quarks. Scattering amplitudes were previously calculated by using relativistic quantum field theory, quantum chromodynamics (QCD). Such computations were very difficult to perform even for relatively simple interactions. The new theory completely eliminates time in favor of using a geometric object that is defined in hyperdimensional space. It allows scattering amplitudes to be quickly calculated for four-quark and eight-quark interactions. Previously, four-quark interactions could be calculated only on a supercomputer, and eight-quark interactions could not be calculated at all. The fact that we can do such calculations in a much simpler form in hyperdimensional space reinforces the idea that hyperdimensional space will be a necessary part of any new physics.

Moreover, each of these "theories of everything" views the history of events that occur in our four-dimensional spacetime as a sequence of three-dimensional "images" that all coexist and are separated by some small, possibly Planck length, distance in the hyperdimensional space. (The Planck length is thought to be the quantum of distance in our spacetime. It is approximately 1.6×10^{-35} m.)

The implication is that time as we know it in our four-dimensional spacetime does not exist in the hyperdimensional space (Wesson, 2010). All events that have happened, are happening, or ever will happen in our spacetime exist simultaneously in the hyperdimensional space.

Tononi (2008) developed his integrated information theory suggesting that consciousness is the ability to integrate information. He went on to put the theory on a mathematical footing within the framework of classical physics through the use of set theory. His work was expanded by Tegmark (2014) and developed in the framework of quantum physics using rigorous application of Hilbert operators applied to quantum factorization. One of the most important findings of Tegmark's work is the idea that it is possible to find certain quantum states that minimize the decoherence in complex systems. He goes on to suggest that consciousness is the state in which the decoherence is at a minimum. He also suggests, but does not prove, that the emergence of consciousness and the emergence of time are related.

As was mentioned earlier in this discussion, current theory holds that it is gravitation (in the broadest sense) that provides the mechanism for information transfer. Gravitation is intimately involved in the very definition of our spacetime, and it is gravitation that affects all energy/mass within our spacetime. Therefore, it should also not be a surprise to us if we were to find a mechanism based on gravitation that links the information in an observer to information in the "images" of events found in the hyperdimensional space.

If gravity waves exist, and are eventually seen, they may have properties that might suggest that they are good candidates for the carrier of psi, including precognition. Attractive aspects of gravity waves with regard to psi include:

- Very long range, even to the edge of the known universe. Current psi experiments appear not to have distance restrictions associated with the acquisition of the data.

- Very long periods (i.e., very low frequency). It is difficult to parse in a psi experiment which portion of the data arises from some putative psi signal compared to a psi trigger of relevant information that is already part of the memory/experience of the percipient. A crude measure of the channel capacity (i.e., how much information can flow via a carrier) is a few millibits per second—at least in qualitative agreement of a gravity wave with a low frequency.

But the problem remains: how can gravity waves reach across two separated points in spacetime and, therefore, act as a carrier for precognition? One answer might be wormholes.

Wormholes

According to Einstein and Rosen (1935), a wormhole, also known as an Einstein–Rosen bridge, is a hypothetical topological feature of spacetime that would fundamentally be a "shortcut" through spacetime. A wormhole is much like a tunnel with two ends, each in separate points in spacetime. Notice that this shortcut connects *any* two points in spacetime regardless as to where they are in that four-dimensional space. This odd configuration appears in the formalism of Einstein's general theory of relativity, but as yet, they have not been detected.

One problem with wormholes is that a tube-like wormhole needs at least one additional spatial dimension to work. We will illustrate with a two-dimensional analogy. Consider a universe that has only two dimensions—east/west, north/south but no up/down. So, to move from one point in "flatland" to another, the shortest distance was given to us by Pythagoras—the square of the hypotenuse is equal to the sum of the squares of the other two sides in a right triangle.

$$d = \sqrt{\Delta East^2 + \Delta North^2},$$

where $\Delta east$ means the distance you move east or west and similarly for $\Delta north$, and d = the distance traveled. So, if we were going to connect two points in this flatland via a wormhole tunnel, we would need to construct it above or below flatland and therefore would require an unknown dimension to the flatlanders—up/down. So also would we need more dimensions in order to have a shortcut in spacetime.

Hypergeometries

We need more dimensions and fortunately for us, there is considerable theoretical research in this arena. These are addressed in detail by Bernard Carr in the chapter titled, "Higher Dimensions of Space and Time and Their Implications for Psi" in this volume.

FINAL REMARKS

Entropy is an important concept in all branches of physics. Variations of an entropy concept even appear in the human sciences. While there is a growing literature on this topic, Bailey (1993) illustrates the point of how entropy concepts might apply to matters of human affairs. As we said at the beginning of this chapter, entropy considerations lead to our understanding as to why we are firmly convinced that at our everyday level, time clearly moves in only one direction yet at the atomic level, it does not. However, it is not clear at this juncture if entropic concepts by themselves are sufficient to provide a mechanism for precognition.

Perhaps an additional way to square the circle of macroscopic causality violation is to invoke higher dimensions as Carr suggests. We will illustrate with a fantasy world called *flatland*. The people who inhabit this world experience north/south and east/west but cannot even conceive of the possibility of up/down existing. Here you are one day strolling along in your flatland, and all of a sudden, out of nowhere appears a round blob blocking your path. You are frightened but curious as you watch the blob shrink in size, vanish, and suddenly appear behind you! This strange behavior appears to violate all the well-established rules of flatland physics, yet it happens. Then as a flatland physicist, you realize that if, and it is a very big if, there were an extra spatial dimension (i.e., up/down), as difficult as it would be to imagine, it could provide an explanation for the weirdness. Some extradimensional (now three dimensions) object has touched your world—the blob appearing out of nowhere; vanishing—by lifting off into the third dimension; and reappearing behind you by the same mechanism that caused it to appear in the first place.

Similarly, by considering an extra dimension(s) we can hope to understand what in our three-dimensional (north/south – east/west – up/down) world is the impossibility—an apparent violation of the rules of macroscopic causality.

Thus, we close this chapter with two possible (and mutually compatible) theoretical ways forward to understand the physics of precognition—entropy and hyperdimensionality.

REFERENCES

Aharonov, Y., Cohen, E., Grossman, D., & Elizutr, A. C. (2012). Can a future choice affect a past measurement's outcome? arXiv:1206.6224v5

Arkani-Hamed, N., & Trnka, J. (2013). The amplituhedron. arXiv preprint arXiv:1312.2007

Bailey, K. D. (1993). Social entropy theory: An application of nonequilibrium thermodynamics in human ecology. *Advances in Human Ecology, 2*, 133–161.

Butcher, L. M. (2014). Casimir energy of a long wormhole throat. arXiv preprint arXiv:1405.1283

Cardeña, E. (2014). A call for an open, informed study of all aspects of consciousness. *Frontiers in human neurscience, 8*(Article 17), 1–4.

de Boer, J., Cheng, M. C., Dijkgraaf, R., Manschot, J., & Verlinde, E. (2006). A farey tail for attractor black holes. *Journal of High Energy Physics, 2006*(11), 024.

Dijkgraaf, R., Verlinde, E., & Verlinde, H. (1997). BPS quantization of the five-brane. *Nuclear Physics B, 486*(1), 89–113.

Einstein, A., & Rosen, N. (1935). The particle problem in the general theory of relativity. *Physical Review, 48*(1), 73–77.

Greene, B. R. (2003). *The elegant universe: Superstrings, hidden dimensions, and the quest for the ultimate theory.* New York: W. W. Norton.

Greene, B. R. (Producer). (2012, 14 March. Illusion of time: The fabric of the cosmos. *NOVA.* https://www.youtube.com/watch?v=Kbyjjw_oLFk

Honorton, C., & Ferrari, D., C. (1989). "Future telling": A meta-analysis of forced-choice precognition experiments, 1935–1987. *Journal of Parapsychology, 53,* 281–301.

Jensen, K., & Karch, A. (2013). Holographic dual of an Einstein-Podolsky-Rosen pair has a wormhole. *Physical Review Letters, 111*(21), 211602.

Lee, J.-W. (2011). Quantum mechanics emerges from information theory applied to causal horizons. *Foundations of Physics, 41*(4), 744–753.

Leff, H. S., & Rex, A., F. (Eds.). (1990). *Maxwell's demon: Entropy, information, computing.* Princeton, NJ: Princeton University Press.

Maldacena, J., & Susskind, L. (2013). Cool horizons for entangled black holes. *Fortschritte der Physik, 61*(9), 781–811.

May, E. C. (2011). Possible thermodynamic limits to anomalous cognition: Entropy gradients. *Journal of the Society for Psychical Research, 75.2*(903), 65–75.

May, E. C. (2014/2011). Toward a classical thermodynamic model for retrocognition. In E. C. May & S. B. Marwaha (Eds.), *Anomalous cognition: Remote viewing research and theory,* pp. 327–338. Jefferson, NC: McFarland.

May, E. C., & Lantz, N. D. (2014/2010). Anomalous cognition technical trials: Inspiration for the target entropy concept. In E. C. May & S. B. Marwaha (Eds.), *Anomalous cognition: Remote viewing research and theory,* pp. 280–298. Jefferson, NC: McFarland.

May, E. C., & Spottiswoode, S. J. P. (2014/1994). Shannon entropy: A possible intrinsic target property. In E. C. May & S. B. Marwaha, (Eds.), *Anomalous cognition: Remote viewing research and theory,* pp. 299–313. Jefferson, NC: McFarland.

May, E. C., Spottiswoode, S. J. P., & Faith, L., V. (2000). Correlation of the gradient of Shanon entropy and anomalous cognition: Toward an AC sensory system. *Journal of Scientific Exploration, 14*(1), 53–72.

Moreva, E., Brida, G., Gramegna, M., Giovannetti, V., Maccone, L., & Genovese, M. (2014). Time from quantum entanglement: An experimental illustration. *Physical Review A, 89*(5), 052122.

Rhine, J. B. (1963). Special motivation in some exceptional ESP performances. *Paper presented at the 6th Annual Parapsychological Association Meeting.*

Savonije, I., & Verlinde, E. (2001). CFT and entropy on the brane. *Physics Letters B, 507*(1), 305–311.

Schlosshauer, M., Kofler, J., & Zeilinger, A. (2013). A snapshot of foundational attitudes toward quantum mechanics. *Studies in History and Philosophy of Modern Physics, 44*(3), 222–230.

Sen, A. (1998). Tachyon condensation on the brane antibrane system. *Journal of High Energy Physics, 1998*(8), 012.

Shannon, C., & Weaver, W. (1949). *The mathematical theory of communication.* Urbana: University of Illinois Press.

Sheehan, D. P. (2011). *Quantum retrocausation: Theory and experiment. Paper presented at the Quantum Retrocausation Symposium,* San Diego, CA.

Sonner, J. (2013). Holographic Schwinger effect and the geometry of entanglement. *Physical Review Letters, 111*(21), 211603.

Susskind, L. (1993). String theory and the principle of black hole complementarity. *Physical Review Letters, 71*(15), 2367.

Susskind, L. (1995). The world as a hologram. *Journal of Mathematical Physics, 36*(11), 6377–6396.

Susskind, L. (2013). Butterflies on the stretched horizon. arXiv preprint arXiv:1311.7379

Szilárd, L. (1964). On the decrease of entropy in a thermodynamic system by the intervention of intelligent beings. *Behavioral Science, 9*(4), 301–310.

Szilárd, L., & Feld, B. T. (1972a). On the decrease of entropy in a thermodynamic system by the intervention of intelligent beings *The collected works of Leo Szilárd: Scientific papers,* pp. 103–129. Boston: MIT Press.

Szilárd, L., & Feld, B. T. (1972b). On the extension of phenomenological thermodynamics to fluctuation phenomena. *The collected works of Leo Szilárd: Scientific papers,* pp. 34–102. Boston: MIT Press.

Tegmark, M. (2014). Consciousness as a state of matter. arXiv preprint arXiv:1401.1219

Tononi, G. (2008). Consciousness as integrated information: A provisional manifesto. *Biological Bulletin, 215*(3), 216–242.

Varvoglis, M. (1996). Nonlocality on a human scale: Psi and consciousness research. In S. R. Hameroff, A. W. Kaszniak, & A. C. Scott (Eds.), *Toward a science of consciousness,* pp. 589–596. Boston: MIT Press.

Verlinde, E. (2000). On the holographic principle in a radiation dominated universe. arXiv preprint hep-th/0008140

Verlinde, E. (2011). On the origin of gravity and the laws of Newton. *Journal of High Energy Physics, 2011*(4), 1–27.

Wesson, P. S. (2010). Time as an illusion. In V. Petkov (Ed.), *Minkowski spacetime: A hundred years later,* pp. 307–318. Dordrecht [Netherlands: Springer.

Wissner-Gross, A., & Freer, C. (2013). Causal entropic forces. *Physical Review Letters, 110*(16), 168702.

Chapter 7

The Multiphasic Model of Precognition

Sonali Bhatt Marwaha and Edwin C. May

INTRODUCTION

The Rhinean paradigm for psi research was fundamentally dualist in nature. Based on the science of the day, Rhine (1950, p. 146) reasoned, "... the physical world is the world of the senses. Sense data are the foundations of physics; and so the physical world is the world reported to the human mind by the sense and inferred from the data collected by the sense," and since ESP is not like normal sensory perception, there can be no discoverable relationship between ESP and the physical world. In his view, the ESP data were evidence of the transcendent nature of the human mind. He rejected the idea of a "sixth-sense," as in ESP, "there is no *experience of localization* [emphasis original] as there is with the senses" (p. 100). As he further states:

> I am more inclined to expect the final explanation to come from a fundamental readjustment of our view of mind and its relation to the world of the sense. ..... we have been trying to fit mind into the materialistic world of sensation. If it does not wholly fit in, perhaps this is because it has properties which are just as reliable and lawful, but different. (p. 101)

Contrary to this early view, our analysis of the data of precognition research points to a physicalist perspective, which may be in line with the way other sensory systems function. If we consider psi to be a normal, albeit atypical, ability, there is no apparent reason we should desist from exploring and ruling out a physicalist bases for it before invoking an alternative reality (Marwaha & May, 2015a). In this chapter, we present a signal-based, process-oriented *multiphasic model of precognition*, which we believe opens the door to a new research paradigm in the exploration of *how* precognition occurs.

The term anomalous cognition (AC) was developed in 1994 by May, Spottiswoode, and James (2014/1994) and has found favor since, as it refers to the insufficient understanding of the psi phenomenon, rather than the veracity of the data. AC research, particularly in the past 30 years, has accumulated sufficient evidence to establish the existence of information transfer through processes that we are now just beginning to understand, as evidenced by the newer theories and models in this field, many of which are presented in this volume.

In our analysis, precognition is the *only* form of ESP or cognitive anomaly as, within the framework of the definition provided, it can subsume within it all categories of ESP such as telepathy, clairvoyance, statistically based micro-PK, and maybe even postmortem survival as indicated by the super-psi hypothesis. It is beyond the scope of this work to go into details about this, but suffice to say that until we are sure that precognition can be ruled out in an event, it is difficult to consider any other form of ESP as a distinct event (May & Marwaha, 2015b; Marwaha & May, under review).

In our view, an information-centric perspective has the potential to yield answers to the question of *how* precognition occurs. We use the term *retrocausal signals* (RC-signal) to refer to the temporal, information-centered perspective for putative signals that originated from a space-like separated point in spacetime. The term *retrocausation*, which is used in physics today, posits that a future event can influence the present (Sheehan, 2011; Chapter 4 in this volume). This information-centric perspective is premised on the transmission and detection of information as in the visual and auditory system. Given that all information in the natural world is perceived in this manner, there seems to be no reason to assume that putative psi signals will behave differently. Precognition (PC), on the other hand, refers to a present-centered person-centric perspective. Based on the proposed model, we offer a formal definition of precognition:

> *Precognition is an atypical perceptual ability that allows the acquisition of noninferential information arising from a future point in spacetime.*

For two future points in spacetime insufficient time has elapsed between them to allow for any causal relationship. Procedurally in PC experiments, it means that target stimuli are randomly generated *after* data collection is complete.

Remote viewing (RV) protocols are used to determine the RC/PC aspect of an information bit. In a standard double blind RV study, an experimenter asks a participant to provide a description in words and drawings of a location that they would visit within an hour. In PC trials, after the response has been obtained and the data secured, an assistant randomly chooses a stimulus site. Blind, rank-order quantitative analysis that compares each response to the set of preselected targets is carried out to assess the degree to which there is statistical evidence for PC.

Expanding upon the preceding description, let us assume that at 10:00 a.m., a participant and the experimenter, called a monitor, are sequestered in a laboratory. Both individuals are blind to any stimulus at this point because one has not yet been generated. For approximately 15 minutes, the monitor is free to question the participant as to what is in her mind with regard to a photograph she will be shown shortly. This interview is quite structured and designed specifically to illicit as much information as possible (in words and drawings) yet at the same time not lead the participant. Once completed, the data are secured, and a computer then randomly selects one of 300 photographs, which is then shown to the participant as feedback. This feedback, of course, is not an analysis. That involves blind assessments. Confidence calling, that is, to state in advance of feedback how good the session will turn out to be, is generally problematic; however, a recent approach using *fuzzy sets*[1] when coupled with an estimate of the figure of merit null distribution has shown promise (May, 2007; Zadeh, 1965). (See May, Marwaha, & Chaganti, 2014/2011 for a detailed description of the protocol and analysis.)

Key Questions in Precognition Research

The key questions in PC research, and the most difficult ones are *when*, *where*, and *how* does this information transfer from a distant point in spacetime occur? *What* is the information carrier, and what are its properties? Answers to these will help determine in which sensory system,

---

[1]Initially, fuzzy sets were developed to provide a mathematical tool to allow quantitative evaluation of ambiguous material (Zadeh, 1965). Fuzzy sets are used in AC research to provide mathematical representations of the target material and of the AC response. Three concepts emerge from this analysis: accuracy—the fraction of the target material that was described correctly, reliability—the fraction of the response that was correct, and the figure of merit—accuracy × reliability. The figure of merit is a sensitive measure of anomalous cognition in that to obtain a high figure of merit, the participant must describe a large part of the intended target in a parsimonious way (May et al., 2014).

if any, the carrier energy is being converted to electrochemical signals. Further, what is the transmission rate (bits/symbol) of the data, and what are its limits? At what point does the apparent stochastic nature of the information occur? By stochastic nature, we mean unknown variability in the quality of the PC. Is it at the source, transmission, or at the detection point?

VanRullen and Koch (2003) have asked similar questions for normal perception:

> How do percepts and their neural representations evolve over time, both when the outside world is standing still or when it is abruptly changing, such as during an eye movement? Do we experience the world as a continuous signal or as a discrete sequence of events, like the snapshots of a Multimedia Component camera? Although the subjectively seamless nature of our experience would suggest that the relevant underlying neuronal representations evolve continuously, this is not the only possibility. Conscious perception might well be constant within a snapshot of variable duration. (p. 207)

Additionally, other questions include who possesses PC ability and why? As experience over the years has shown, PC training beyond an inherent talent level is not effective; why is this so? Why do we not see stable CNS correlates for PC? Are personality correlations something fundamental to the process, or do they appear more as procedural artifacts? These and more questions have emerged in the 130 years of research in this field.

Developing a model with so many blank spaces in the data is a challenging task. Irwin (1994) distinguishes two theoretical problems: (1) How are psi phenomena at all possible? This is called the problem of the mediation of psi, or the physical problem of psi. (2) How are people able to produce psi? This is called the problem of the manifestation of psi, or the psychological problem of psi phenomena. This view is expanded in the multiphasic model of precognition (MMPC) presented in this chapter. In the following, we (1) define the problem space, (2) present the physics and neuroscience domain in detail, (3) address the challenges posed by the MMPC, and (4) discuss the predictions based upon the model.

THE MULTIPHASIC MODEL OF PRECOGNITION (MMPC)

Defining the Problem Space

As a starting point for the multiphasic model of precognition, we have defined and expanded the problem space of AC by considering two domains: the *physics* and *neuroscience* domains.

The physics domain (PD) falls exclusively within the purview of physics. It addresses this question: How is it possible that information can go between two spacetime points and can be used, especially if the two points[2] separated, such that, not enough time has passed between their occurrences for there to exist a causal relationship? This is related to how information is carried from an external source, which is distant in time and space, to the percipient. Challenging questions such as how the information is processed by the human recipient, who are good participants and why, and what are the personality factors that govern their participation are simply irrelevant in the physics domain and properly belong to the neuroscience domain.

The neuroscience domain (ND) resides internally to the human percipient. It addresses the experiential part of the problem, that is, how is the information acquired by a putative sensory system, how is this information processed in the brain, and how is it expressed? We define the acquiring mechanism as a transition between the physics and neuroscience domains.

Using vision as an analogy, phase I consists of an electromagnetic (EM) carrier providing informational signals at the speed of light. Photons strike the retina (i.e., transition between PD and ND for vision), which converts the EM energy into electrochemical signals that are processed by the brain (phase II).

These domains divide the problem space within which a solution for the complex problem of PC can be addressed. These further consist of multiple discrete stages that can be examined independently. Intrinsic to this perspective is that different processes are involved at different stages, which finally result in PC. The MMPC, then, addresses both the physics and the neuroscience domains by considering the well-established laws of the physical world and what we currently know about brain-behavior relationships. We now consider the two domains in detail.

Figure 7.1 visually displays some of the basic ideas behind the multiphasic model of precognition (MMPC), that is, a hidden and distant stimulus becomes available in some spacetime location. How that information ends up with the participant is strictly a physics problem, as we indicate with the *physics domain*. How this information is represented by electrochemical activity in the central nervous system (i.e., a transducer as indicated by a single-headed arrow; stage 1) remains a mystery. Then we propose what happens at stages 2 and 3. The bidirectional arrows demonstrate that the brain is trying to figure out what the "sensory" input is. For example, in the visual system, when we look at a cup and a piece of paper on the desk and we reach for the cup, our brain does a considerable amount of work (unconsciously) so that we do not have to consciously think about how cups differ from paper. In Figure 7.1, then, the implicit information bubbles

---

[2]This concept holds for both time-like and space-like separated points in future spacetime.

Figure 7.1
Graphical abstract of the multiphasic model of precognition.

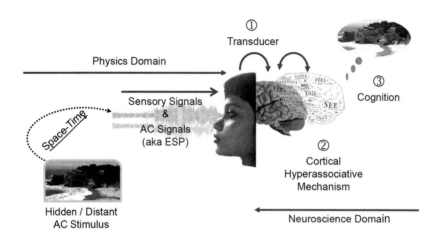

up to a conscious cognition that is reported. In this figure, the participant ends up with a representation of the distant in spacetime stimulus.

PHASE I: THE PHYSICS DOMAIN (PD)

The physics domain (PD) falls exclusively within the purview of physics. It addresses the question: how is it possible that information residing in one spacetime point may be acquired and used from a second spacetime point? The case of particular interest is when the two points are separated such that, not enough time has passed between their occurrences for there to exist a causal relationship between them. From the information-centric perspective, information from a future separation between two events, as discussed earlier, means retrocausation. Challenging questions such as how the information is processed by the human recipient, who are good participants and why, and what are the personality factors that govern their participation are simply irrelevant in the physics domain and properly belong to the neuroscience domain.

The Primacy of Entropy

As with any model development, we first must consider what data the model must be capable of explaining. Since experiments show that the quality of precognition is significantly correlated with changes of entropy of the target systems (May, & Spottiswoode, 2014/1994; May, Spottiswoode, & Faith, 2000; May & Lantz, 2014/2010), we propose that some aspect of entropy or its gradients will eventually yield an understanding of the physics domain.

The data of RC itself provides support for entropy being the prime candidate for the physics model. These data, discussed in the previous chapter on "Entropy and Precognition: The Physics Domain of the Multiphasic Model of Precognition," suggest that at the macroscopic level, it is possible to obtain information from some noninferential event in the future. This, of course, appears to violate the rules of macroscopic causality and the profound understanding that time moves in one direction only. Yet, at the microscopic level (i.e., atoms, molecules), the equations of motion are all symmetric in time. In other words, time could move forward or backward, and the collisions of molecules stay the same. This apparent paradox has been resolved now for a century. At the macroscopic level, time moves in one direction as a consequence of the second law of thermodynamics, which holds that the entropy of a closed system may never decrease. This law has not yet been violated.

The argument for entropy as a PD candidate can be summarized as follows:

- The quality of retrocausal data correlates significantly with entropic gradients of the target stimuli.
- The laws of physics tell us that the second law of thermodynamics (i.e., related to changes of entropy) can account for the apparent paradox of time between the micro- and macroscopic perspectives.

In addition to the RC data, which suggest that entropy is important, as it turns out, entropy gradients are used extensively to understand two traditional forms of information transfer—visual and acoustic. In the area of audio research, for example, an index of speech intelligibility is cochlea-scaled entropy (Stilp, Kiefte, Alexander, & Kluender, 2010). Additionally, spectral change, as measured by cochlea-scaled entropy, predicts speech intelligibility better than the information carried by vowels or consonants in sentences (Chen & Loizou, 2012). High Shannon entropy of musical phrases affects the uncertainty of determining musical pitch (Hansen & Pearce, 2012). In the visual arena, it appears that neuronal structures in the CNS take advantage of statistical aspects of subareas of the visual scene to enhance visual recognition (Gerhard, Wichmann, & Bethge, 2013); that is, sensory representations are adapted to the statistical regularities in sensory signals and thereby incorporate knowledge about the outside world. Additionally, entropy masking of a visual stimulus is related to learnability; that is, high entropic masks make it difficult to understand visual stimuli (Delaigle, Devleeschouwer, et al., 2002).

In a recent article, Stephens, Mora, Tkačik, and Bialek (2013) relate thermodynamic entropy to images. Their brief abstract in *Physical Review Letters* states:

> The scale invariance of natural images suggests an analogy to the statistical mechanics of physical systems at a critical point. Here we examine the distribution of pixels in small image patches and show how to construct the corresponding thermodynamics. We find evidence for criticality in a diverging specific heat, which corresponds to large fluctuations in how "surprising" we find individual images, and in the quantitative form of the entropy vs energy. We identify special image configurations as local energy minima and show that average patches within each basin are interpretable as lines and edges in all orientations.

Norwich (2005) provides a succinct summary of the tight relationship between physical entropy and the sensory systems:

> With reference to two specific modalities of sensation, the taste of saltiness of chloride salts, and the loudness of steady tones, it is shown that the laws of sensation (logarithmic and power laws) are expressions of the entropy per mole of the stimulus. That is, the laws of sensation are linear functions of molar entropy. In partial verification of this hypothesis, we are able to derive an approximate value for the gas constant, a fundamental physical constant, directly from psychophysical measurements. The significance of our observation lies in the linking of the phenomenon of "sensation" directly to a physical measure. It suggests that if the laws of physics are universal, the laws of sensation and perception are similarly universal. It also connects the sensation of a simple, steady physical signal with the molecular structure of the signal: the greater the number of microstates or complexions of the stimulus signal, the greater the magnitude of the sensation (saltiness or loudness). The hypothesis is currently tested on two sensory modalities. (p. 167)

These references concerning entropy and the visual and auditory systems are not exhaustive and are presented only as representative samples to illustrate the importance of entropy considerations in the understanding of the signal characteristics to the normal sensory systems.

We have noted that there is considerable experimental evidence that suggests entropic gradients may be important in understanding the physics domain; however, with regard to mechanisms, information carriers, and transducers, the evidence is circumstantial. Clearly, more work is needed. For example, there is a critical test of these ideas underway in 2013-2015. In this study, we treat thermodynamic entropic gradients as physical targets (as opposed to photographic targets) as an independent variable and the quality of the resulting PC as a dependent variable (May, Hawley, & Marwaha, in-preparation). This experiment will add valuable insight to the physics domain. The chapter titled "Entropy and Precognition: The Physics Domain of the Multiphasic Model of Precognition" in this volume discusses this domain in detail.

PHASE II: THE NEUROSCIENCE DOMAIN (ND)

Background to the Development of the ND

Since the early 1940s, numerous attempts have been made to correlate laboratory-based AC performance with individual differences in participants' personality and attitudinal characteristics to identify the underlying processes. Researchers have extensively explored various dimensions, such as beliefs and attitudes, moods, states of mind, and personality. Extroversion has been one of the most widely explored dimensions of personality in relation to ESP. In a meta-analysis of 60 independent studies examining the relationship between extraversion and ESP, Honorton, Ferrari, and Bem (1998) found a small correlation ($r = 0.09$) that was significant ($z = 4.43$, $n = 2,963$) mainly due to the large n. Even that correlation was thought to arise only due to the free response data, in that extraverted participants did better than introverted participants did. In addition, cognitive processes such as memory and subliminal perception have been examined for their relation to AC (see Rao, 2011 for review). The correlations of psi with personality variables as reported are unstable in that they have not shown to be effective in a participant selection process. That is, they are not systematic, are not easily replicable, and contain a confound in the data collection methodology. In our analysis, the participant pool is biased toward extroverts, as most of the studies use self-selected volunteers as participants.

Since the Star Gate program was tasked for applications of AC, the need to develop an effective tool to identify people with good AC skills was of paramount interest. In initial studies, the Myers-Briggs Type Inventory, Q-sort (Block, 1961) and Personality Assessment System (Krauskopf & Saunders, 1994), which uses the Wechsler Adult Intelligence Scale as a behavioral measure of personality, were investigated for their potential use as screening tools. None of these methods was predictive of AC ability; the general conclusion was that the best measure for identifying people with AC skills is assessing them on precognition tasks. This finds support in a meta-analysis of 309 forced-choice AC experiments by Honorton and Ferrari (1989, p. 281), who report "studies using subjects selected on the basis of prior testing performance show significantly larger effects than studies using unselected subjects."

Neurophysiological studies, using technology of the day, including electroencephalograph (EEG) and magnetoencephalograph (MEG; see May & Marwaha, in-preparation), and functional magnetic resonance imaging (fMRI; Moulton & Kosslyn, 2009) have been used to determine the cortical correlates of PC. To summarize the results: (1) there was no concomitant neural activity that seemed to occur during the time when perception of a RC signal is supposed to have occurred. As our understanding of the phenomena increased, we realized that this was probably due to the fact that we could not determine *when* exactly the participant had received the information that he was providing, i.e., before or during the test situation; and (2) we were, and are, still not sure about the form of energy carrier for RC signals. This implies that we were, and are, essentially searching for the proverbial needle in the haystack of neural pathways. (See the chapter titled "Neuroscientific Investigation of Anomalous Cognition" by Michael Persinger in Volume 1.)

The implications of this understanding are: (1) There is no distinguishing feature of the PC signal that can be observed in a MEG, surface EEG, or fMRI. Until we can determine this, we will not know where in the brain to look for a signal-to-perception-to-cognition correspondence. (2) As the signal may be erratic and weak, there may not be a steady flow of perception of PC signals to permit detection of the stimulus pattern. (3) The *where* and *when* of perception makes it a confounding factor in using the currently known brain mapping technologies, hence (4) making it difficult to determine whether the fMRI or EEG patterns are emerging specifically from a RC signal perception. Analyzing these observables led us to consider the process of PC as occurring in the three stages of the neuroscience domain (ND).

The ND refers to the processes that occur once the information from any external source, including RC signals, has reached the percipient's sensory system, and the processes that occur from perception to cognition of that data—a process that may take as long as 200 to 400 ms. The MMPC deconstructs this domain into three fluid stages: (1) stage 1—sensory perception of RC signal; (2) stage 2—cortical processing of the RC signal; and (3) stage 3—cognition of the information. One aspect of our model is that stages 1 and 2 are critically different in PC, following which, in stage 3, normal processing occurs as it does for any other sensory input.

Stage 1: Sensory Perception

An important element in the process of PC is the presence of a signal transducer to serve as an interface between the incoming bits of information and the cortical processing of that data. For example, the visual receptors in the retina are the transducers for information from the visible spectrum. We can keep the nature of a putative PC transducer an open question until we have a better understanding of the physics domain. Nevertheless, we can work under the assumption that PC information is processed internally in the same manner as is information impinging on other sensory systems, as noted in the PD. As the nature of the RC signal is presently unknown, we have to assume that the putative RC signal is different from the normal thresholds perceived by us. This requires us to consider a possible variation in the transducer and the processing mechanisms.

Hypothesis of Psychophysical Variability in a Signal Transducer (Hypothesis 1.1)

This hypothesis poses that psychophysical variability both in CNS extent and function can account for variation in the reception of PC information. In our analysis, PC ability is seen in varying levels of proficiency, much like the varying levels of music ability.

This hypothesis suggests that individuals with PC ability are different from those without it at the level of sensory input as follows. The RC signal is acquired by those with PC ability due to a variation in a putative biological transducer, which is the point where external signals are transformed into biochemical/bioelectrical sensory signals and transmitted to the cortical structures where cognition occurs. These signals are connected and processed across multiple cortical areas, which is part of Stage 2 of the MMPC as described in the following section. The question of what the transducer is will be determined by our understanding of the physics domain. (We note that this is the only part of the neuroscience domain that is dependent upon the physics domain. From stage 2 onward, the ND is independent of any PD considerations.)

Research in individual variations in the visual domain lends theoretical support for this hypothesis. Tahmasebi, Davis, Wild, et al. (2012) report on the variability of functional organization relative to the brain anatomy. A two- to threefold inter-individual variation in size of the visual cortex is seen in humans, a variation that could lead to substantial difference in visual ability. (While this in itself cannot account for PC, we have to consider the possibility of a signal, which may not necessarily be in the visual domain.) Similarly, variations in the number of axons in the optic nerve, the number of retinal ganglion cells in a single eye, and the density of photoreceptors in the retina is also seen (Quigley et al., 1990; Wesner et al., 1991; Varma et al., 1994; Andrews, Halpern, & Pervis, 1997; Kee et al., 1997; Roorda & Williams, 1999; Carroll et al., 2000; Hofer et al., 2005), including the presence of tetra- or even pentachromacy (Neitz et al., 1993, 2002). Using a battery of tests that included orientation discrimination, wavelength sensitivity, contrast sensitivity, veneer acuity, direction-of-motion detection, and velocity discrimination, Halpern, Andrews, and Purves (1999) found that there was significant interindividual difference in visual ability, which could be the result of interindividual variation in the amount of neural circuitry devoted to vision. These variations in the cortical structures and the retina—the visual system transducer—provide a basis for considering the presence of PC ability and the individual differences seen in this ability.

As experimental results have shown, the RC signal carrier is not mediated by EM (Targ et al., 1976). Nevertheless, we open this door slightly to permit the possibility of variations in the traditional sensory transducers, in that perhaps CNS structures that are adjacent to expanded sensory sensitivity are involved in the detection of RC signals.

The final processing of information thus obtained occurs in the brain, just as the brain is the final frontier for color perception. This leads us to stage 2 of the ND of the MMPC.

Stage 2: Cortical Processing

Stage 2 of the model involves the processing of RC signals received as hypothesized in Stage 1.

Hypothesis of Cortical Hyperassociative Mechanism (Hypothesis 2.1)

Considering the possible variation in the nature of an RC signal, we may assume that it has characteristics that are different from the known signals, and thus we propose that RC signals are processed via a cross-modal mechanism leading to a PC experience. We consider this notion by formulating the hypothesis of cortical hyperassociative mechanism (Hypothesis 2.1).

We borrow the term *hyperassociative mechanism* as used by Simner (2012) for describing the possible underlying mechanisms for synesthesia. As Simner states:

> [there may be] one of any number of possible neurological processes that might give rise to the "open channel" between different brain regions, which allows sound to be interpreted as colour, taste as touch, touch as smell, and so on. In fact, this neutral term should cover not one of several possible mechanisms, but rather, one or more of these possibilities ... Whether a functional connection is established by hyper-connectivity, by disinhibited pathways, by other means, or indeed, a combination of these, the outcome is the opening of a communication between regions that would otherwise not directly interact to produce a conscious experience in the average person. (p. 25)

Simner and Hubbard (2013) define synesthesia as a

…neuropsychological condition which gives rise to extraordinary sensation. As well as the usual impressions one would experience from everyday stimuli such as music, writing, eating foods, and so on, *synesthetes* (i.e., individuals with synesthesia) experience additional, otherwise unrelated sensations such as colors, moving shapes, unusual textures, and so on. Synesthesia is often defined as a 'merging of the senses,' suggesting that the stimulus itself and the unusual second unstimulated experience must both be sensory in nature. (p. xxi)

Simner (2012) informs us that "synaesthetic sensations derive not only from sounds, touch, tastes, words, and so on, but also from more unexpected sources, such as the act of decision making, or very fine-grain motor movements, or navigating social interactions, and so on." Sagiv, Ilbeigi, and Ben-Tal (2011) have summarized the features of synesthesia: (1) it is present in 4% of the general population, (2) is induced automatically, (3) there is permanence and regularity of synesthetic experiences, (4) synesthetes take the experience for granted, (5) the experience shares much in common with ordinary perception, and (6) it may merely represent an augmentation of normal propensities for cross-modal interactions.

Synesthetes and nonsynesthetes appear to lie on a continuum, both with respect to their neurological characteristics and in certain aspects of their cross-modal behavior (Simner, 2012). Martino and Marks (2001) distinguish between strong and weak forms of synesthesia. "Strong synesthesia is characterized by a vivid image in one sensory modality in response to stimulation in another one. Weak synesthesia is characterized by cross-sensory correspondences expressed through language, perceptual similarity, and perceptual interactions during information processing." Pointing to a genetic basis, Eagleman (2012) has found five families with color-sequence synesthesia.

Cortical hyperconnectivity has recently been associated with atypical perceptual abilities such as synesthesia (Ramachandran & Hubbard, 2001; Rouw & Scholte, 2007; Whitaker et al., 2014) and savant skills in autism (Wallace, Happe, & Giedd, 2009). Loui, Li, Hohmann, and Schlaug (2011) showed that people with the ability to recognize absolute pitch (AP) possess higher white matter connectivity in temporal lobe regions responsible for the perception and association of pitch. These hyperconnected regions include the posterior superior and middle temporal gyri in both left and right hemispheres. AP possessors had significantly higher tract volume than non-AP individuals. Bermudez and Zatorre (2009) suggest that AP performance exists along a continuum. In a recent paper, Elmer, Rogenmoser, Kuhnis, and Jancke (2015) report that functionally the left auditory cortex and the left dorsal frontal cortex are already strongly linked in a dormant state. As Elmer explains, "This coupling enables an especially efficient exchange of information between the auditory cortex and the dorsal frontal cortex in people with absolute pitch, which means that the perception and memory information can be exchanged quickly and efficiently" (University of Zurich, 2015). Ashwin, Ashwin, Rhydderch, et al. (2009) report that significantly enhanced perceptual functioning, about 2.79 times better than average, and attention to detail, also known as eagle-eyed visual acuity, is seen in some persons with autism spectrum conditions. The mechanism for this may be at the level of neural hyperexcitation and is likely governed by factors that give rise to normal variation in visual acuity in typically developing individuals. They speculate that this may be due to atypically high numbers of foveal cone cells or to dopamine receptors at the retinal or neural level (and perhaps increased levels of dopamine in these areas), which may be caused by hypomethylation.

Such observations provide theoretical and experimental support for the hypothesis in Stage 2 of the ND. As the aforementioned examples illustrate, individual variations in cortical structure and functioning give rise to cognitions that are out of the ordinary. By no means are these considered "abnormal;" rather, they are on a continuum of the repertoire of behaviors that arise from a complex mix of genetic, sensory, and cortical architecture, and personal experiences that go into making each individual experience unique. Similarly, PC ability may also be on one such continuum. Thus, we hypothesize that cortical hyperassociative mechanisms permit the processing of information acquired from a synesthesia-like coupling to an extended sensory variability through a presently unknown transducer, following which the implicitly acquired data are further processed in the brain. Thus, there may be variability at the point of sensory perception (e.g., neurotransmitters at the retinal level) (Hypothesis 1.1), and structural variability at the processing level (Hypothesis 2.1).

Further support for the hypotheses put forth for stages 1 and 2 is found in experimental and applied research. Using neuroprostheses, Thomson, Carra, and Nicolelis (2013) report a study with rats in which they augmented the normal perceptual range to include the infrared EM spectrum, which is well outside the rat photoreceptors' spectral sensitivity. Via intracortical microstimulation, the rats were able to transcend the limitation of perceiving only those stimuli that can activate their bodies' native sensory transducers. This lends experimental support to the possibility of perceiving an extended signal, EM spectrum in this case, as proposed by the MMPC. In addition, sensory substitution devices (SSDs), which aim to compensate for the loss of a sensory modality, typically vision, by converting information from the lost modality into stimuli in a remaining modality, lend support to the possibilities proposed in stage 2. There is increasing speculation that SSD perception is an artificially induced synesthesia (e.g., see Farina, 2013; Ward & Wright, 2012). As Proulx (2010) points out, many forms of expertise depend on cross-modal contingencies.

To summarize stages 1 and 2, RC signals are acquired by an individual with PC ability due to psychophysical variability in signal transducer (Hypothesis 1.1). By means of an implicit information acquisition process, these signals are then processed in accordance with stage 2. The cortical hyperassociative mechanism (Hypothesis 2.1) takes advantage of a possible increase in spectral range of EM and/or the perception of the RC signals that the brain can process, which may lead to acquisition of information that is bidirectional in time.

Stage 3: Cognition

Implicit cognition is the normal process of acquiring information from the external world. It is characterized by two critical features: (1) it is an unconscious process and (2) it yields abstract knowledge. As Lewicki, Hill, and Czyzewska (1992, p. 796) state, "... the ability of the human cognitive system to nonconsciously acquire information is a general metatheoretical assumption of almost all of contemporary cognitive psychology." They further state that the "final products of perception (i.e., subjectively encoded meanings of stimuli) is functionally independent from the information-processing algorithms and heuristics responsible for generating those subjective meanings."

Following an extensive review of studies on ESP and brain waves, EEG and functional imaging correlates of precognition and presentiment, cerebral lateralization and ESP, Williams and Roll (2008) concluded that there is considerable evidence that similar brain processes are used in ESP (a.k.a., AC) as for normal perception and behavior. Thus, in concurrence with Williams and Roll (2008), Tyrrell (1947), Roll (1966), and Broughton (2006), we hypothesize that in stage 3, cognition occurs in the same manner as for other sensory inputs. No special conditions are necessary for the cognitive processing of RC signals at this stage. Influence of emotions, memory, thinking, decision making and so on through the metacognitive processes occurs as it does for other non-PC activity for eliciting a precognitive response. Thus, we propose that in stage 3, there is no distinguishing characteristic that differentiates the cognition of RC signals from that of normal sensory signals. Precognitively obtained information is influenced by the regular psychological processes and manifested through unconscious and conscious means such as feelings, dreams, language, art, decisions, etc.

As stated in the introduction to this chapter, we strive to keep what is known in physics, psychology, and neuroscience as intact as possible.

Therefore, it seems reasonable to assume that the processes involved in cognition of signals from normal sensory modalities will also be involved in the cognition part of RC signals. We have indicated in stage 1 and stage 2 of the ND that high variability of sensorial systems connected with a synesthesia-like coupling to other CNS structures may be the pathway of RC signals into the CNS. Once there, the cognitive correlates of RC signals may be indistinguishable from those of normal sensory signals. This would suggest that it might not be possible to observe CNS correlates to RC inputs simply because they would be indistinguishable from other CNS correlates. This is particularly so because we are unable to determine what signals to look for or when the RC signals were received. For instance, the percipient may have received them before being connected to the EEG or fMRI hardware.

From our current understanding, RC signals are generally not robust and are difficult to detect. Moreover, they also appear to be statistically nonstationary; that is, statistical properties vary with regard to when they are measured. Where that apparent nonstationary aspect arises is unknown; however, there are only three possibilities—at the source, in the transmission channel, or in the detection mechanism. Therefore, the cognition resulting from PC is unreliable. Normal psychological influences, such as memory formation/retrieval, emotional overlays, lack of attention or intention, ill health, and effects of medications will interfere with PC response formation as they do with other forms of cognitive activities (McMoneagle & May, 2014/2004).

Blackmore (1981) and Broughton (2006) have reviewed the memory-based models of ESP: Roll (1966), in his "memory theory of ESP," proposed that psi responses consisted of ". . . the percipient's own memory traces and that the effect of the external (ESP) stimulus is to activate memory traces rather than supply new ideas or images" (p. 505); Irwin (1979), in his information processing model, proposed that the PC-evoked memory information goes through several stages of unconscious or preconscious processing that will determine whether it emerges into consciousness in much the same way that sensory information would be processed. Blackmore (1980, 1981) examined various aspects of memory in relation to ESP and found no significant relation between the two.

The crucial difference in the approaches between these early examinations of memory and stage 3 of MMPC is that unlike Roll's analysis, the MMPC states that the most crucial aspects in the PC process are the physics domain and stages 1 and 2 of the neuroscience domain. The MMPC proposes that once bits of information (RC signals—new ideas or images) have been implicitly received, they are stored in the memory in the same way as is information to the other sensory systems. They are retrieved when the need for the information arises. Thus, the stimulus is stored and retrieved, rather than an external stimulus activating a memory trace, as proposed by Roll. The external stimulus for retrieving the stored PC information is the key word, for example, "target," during a controlled laboratory remote viewing procedure.

Factors such as attention, emotions, beliefs, memory, creativity, uncontrolled random thoughts, intellectual decisions, and linguistic influences (May & Hecker, 1982) will interfere with PC responses as they do for the other senses. In the parlance of remote viewing protocols, they are referred to as "overlays." Thus, in a normal protocol in an RV session at our laboratory, a participant is asked to first note down/illustrate the thoughts/images that are on the top of his or her mind before the session begins. In this manner, the cognitive overlays—the personal memories—are brought to the conscious level, and RC information can be recognized by the percipient as being distinct from what is his "own." An experienced PC-abled individual can determine information that is emerging from his or her own frame of reference as compared to that which is from newly acquired RC information.

Familiarity with a certain variety of objects is potentially problematic. On one hand, it may make it easier for a participant to identify something for what it actually is; on the other hand, such familiarity invokes responses that arise from that familiarity and not from RC information (i.e., filling in cognitive blanks) from previous experience and not from data. Experienced participants utilize normal metacognitive processes to provide further details about the site. Thus, they may respond with two categories of data from a distant space/time event: (1) technical details derived from PC and (2) information arising from technical knowledge from his or her own database of information. On the other hand, a viewer who is not familiar with a submarine, for example, and its relevance for the task at hand, may not pay attention to the information about the submarine that is being received and thus bypass it, much like normal inattentional blindness. It is also true that participants will describe an unfamiliar scene by referring to similar situations with which they are familiar.

CHALLENGES POSED BY THE MMPC

The merit of this model rests in viewing the seemingly unified process of precognition as two distinct domains of physics and neuroscience. This divides the problem space and enables investigating each aspect of the problem independently, as each aspect requires different processes and expertise to understand it. We can identify some challenges that each domain poses.

The primary challenges are seen in the PD. Physicists are considering the possibility that the thermodynamic-derived single direction of time's arrow might be reversed on local or global scales (Sheehan, 2006a). Various hypotheses, such as the entropy model and quantum retrocausation

(Plaga, 1997; Sheehan, 2006b, 2011) are being investigated. The biggest challenge, however, is determining the nature of an RC signal carrier.

Intrinsically dependent on the carrier is the nature of the RC signal transducer that can convert the energy from the carrier into a form that can be processed by the CNS. The nature of the transducer can provide clues to its location, just as the auditory receptors serve as a signal transducer for audio signals that can be subsequently processed by the central auditory system. Identifying the transducer in PC ability may aid in exploring the physics domain for appropriate carriers and vice versa. Recent research has further identified the integration of touch and sound signals at the secondary stage of the auditory cortex (Foxe et al., 2002; Fu et al., 2003; Kayser, Petkov, Augath, & Logothetis, 2005; Macaluso, 2006). This opens the door for considering a variety of possible signals that can be processed and perceived by the human brain. Experimental evidence for EM or acoustic signals as possible carriers for PC has been ruled out. However, the MMPC allows us to consider these channels with regard to their sensory CNS structures that may be optimized for RC signal detection.

The challenges in the ND are, comparatively, not as onerous as in the PD. Having bifurcated the problem space, ND experimenters need not concern themselves with the challenges posed in the PD. As outlined, the primary problem for the ND is determining the nature of an RC signal transducer and its cortical connectivity. This, in itself, will lead to a breakthrough in our understanding of the PD as well as the ND.

The basic process outlined in the MMPC opens the door for exploratory research, particularly for stages 1 and 2 of the ND, which require expertise from a host of specialties. It is our sincere hope that experts from relevant disciplines take up the challenges posed and take precognition research forward. We strongly believe that there is no need for any further evidential studies for precognition—a task that has been fulfilled amply and successfully by ESP researchers over more than 150 years.

Predictions Based upon the MMPC

The task for the next phase in precognition research is well laid out in the structure of the MMPC. In our view, the two domains and three stages provide guidelines for further research.

An experiment is currently underway (2014-15) to test the entropy hypothesis put forth in the PD. Because of the supremacy of entropy, the MMPC predicts that this experiment will show better PC when target stimuli are demarked with higher entropic gradients than those that are not (May, Hawley, & Marwaha, in process). A collection of papers for work done so far in entropy can be found in May and Marwaha (2014), in the section titled, "Entropy: A Fundamental Model of Anomalous

Cognition." The PD section of the MMPC would predict a successful outcome of this experiment; namely, that a burst of thermodynamic entropy at a future remote site acts like a flashlight in a dark room, allowing the participant to have a better understanding of what is at the target stimulus.

In our view, the stages outlined in the ND are stable components of the model. While we have proposed our hypotheses for each stage, there is scope for introducing new and fine-tuned hypotheses within each stage. The basic premise of the MMPC is that precognition is an innate atypical ability, with varying levels of proficiency, seen in individuals who possess a variation in an existing signal transducer and have atypical connectivity in cortical structures.

Stage 1. Hypothesis of psychophysical variability in a signal transducer. This stage is primarily an exploratory one. The crucial condition for this hypothesis is that individuals with known and tested precognition ability should be examined for possible variations in structure and range in existing sensory transducers. We predict that these individuals will (1) have structural variations in a sensory transducer, for example, as seen in tetra- and pentachromats, and (2) they will be the outliers (greater than $\pm 2\,\sigma$ from the norm) in the range of sensory input processed. In essence, the focus is on individual data and not on averaged normative data.

Determining the variations observed in PC-abled individuals permits screening the general population for similar variations and testing them to see the degree to which they possess PC ability.

Stage 2. Hypothesis of cortical hyperassociative mechanism. While this stage too is an exploratory one, it has scope for greater predictability. The key issue for this stage, as in the previous one, is mapping the cortical structure of individuals with known PC ability—a relatively straightforward task. Further, we have hypothesized that the nature of the RC signal and stage 1 considerations may require a cross-modal connectivity to process the signal. For this, we have proposed a hyperassociative mechanism as seen in synesthetes. This gives rise to two predictions: (1) PC-abled persons will have some form of synesthesia—the nature and type being a secondary line of investigation—as observed in appropriate diagnostic technologies and as determined by standard synesthesia inventories. (2) Known synesthetes will have precognition ability as measured by standard precognition tests. (See May, Marwaha, & Chaganti, 2014/2011 for protocol details.)

As stated, stage 3, cognition, is not instrumental to the *process* of acquiring information, although it does influence when, how, and in what form the information is manifested. As this stage is amenable to a wide variety of considerations—from neuropsychological to personality—we discuss just a few predictions:

1. The MMPC predicts that distinct CNS correlates in functional technologies such as EEGs and fMRIs will not be observed during the process of PC tasking because: (a) Currently, we do not know what kind of signal to look for and hence what the concomitant EEG would look like. (b) Due to the very nature of precognition, in principle, we cannot determine when/where the RC signal was acquired. For example, as mentioned, the RC signal might be acquired by the participant *before* he arrives at the laboratory. (c) Once the signal has been acquired, it may be processed in the same way as normal cognitions, thus making it difficult to determine whether a visual image is arising out of an RC signal, or it is information acquired through other sensory channels, or stored information that is being expressed in a visual or verbal form.

2. While the literature indicates that extraversion correlates with PC ability (Honorton, Ferrari, & Bem, 1998), the MMPC predicts that there can be no fundamental personality correlates for PC ability, that is, there may be no specific PC personality type that can be identified using standard psychological inventories. The extraversion correlates seen in the ganzfeld may be an artifact of the test situation, in that extraverts will be more naturally responsive in the ganzfeld test environment. Fundamentally, the existence of the hypothesized PC transducers, the synesthetic ability, and the possible multisensorial processing are independent of personality type. However, the possibility of a similar biology may contribute to a similar psychology; however, considering personality is also shaped by experience, there may be too many confounding factors to permit a "precognitive-personality type."

3. This model predicts that training for acquiring a PC ability would be ineffective, although training to use the ability effectively, as in response style, identifying and ignoring cognitive overlays, and so on may be possible; this is similar to learning how to use an instrument when one has inherent musical ability. The MMPC model considers the internal processes more analogous to acuity in the visual system, that is, certain aspects of visual perception can be trained, but acuity cannot be improved by training.

4. The MMPC predicts that individuals with PC ability may exhibit a high score on vividness of visual imagery (Marks, 1973), reflecting their ability to translate a pure RC signal into comprehensible cognitive content. Informal assessments of three of our top PC ability participants fall into this category. However, this may not be instrumental for the *process* of precognition, as much as a consequence of the underlying structures.

5. Finally, since there is an obvious variation among individuals in converting implicit information into cognitive awareness, secondarily, the MMPC would predict that individuals who are inherently better

at the process would also be better at precognition. Since there is independent measure of implicit learning, it renders this as a testable element of an aspect of the MMPC model.

The ND premise opens the door for genetic evaluation of PC-abled persons. The search is for the genetic basis of the underlying variations, rather than a gene for precognition per se.

MMPC and Other Psi Phenomena

The basic assumption of the information-centric MMPC is that psi exists, and the only form of psi is precognition.

In analyzing psi phenomena such as PK, survival of bodily death, and mediums using the MMPC, we find that these phenomena can be understood as information acquisition/transfers from future to present. However, for any AC experiment that uses statistical inference to come to some conclusion, there can be two competing explanations. The first of these, say in a PK test, is that "mind" changed the physical target system. An alternative explanation can be that the participant used his or her PC ability to gain information to make decisions that *appear* as if the mind has influenced a change in a physical system. Thus, the hypothesis of PK can be addressed by PC. This provides a different AC mechanism rather than the cherished hypothesis of influence. In some respects, the analogy is that experiment participants can "peek" into some future answer book and mimic just about anything.

Evidence for PK as information rather than force emanating from the brain has been well established by the decision augmentation theory (see Chapter 10, this book). The "super-psi" or "super-ESP" hypothesis—the retrieval of veridical information that is extensive and highly specific acquired via a generalized psychic information channel—has been discussed with reference to survival and mediumship research, and researchers are unable to determine whether it is a "super-psi" or that there is evidence of postmortem survival (e.g., Beischel & Schwartz, 2007; Braude, 1992; Tart, 2009). However, in our analysis, "super-psi" is a redundant concept, as precognition is sufficient to address the observables. As stated earlier, we do not know when and where AC has happened; nor is it implausible within the theoretical framework of the MMPC that information can be accumulated over a period of time—stage 3 of the neuroscience domain—and put to use when required. Thus, it is not essential for retrocausal information to have a high bit rate.

In conclusion:

1. The MMPC enables the reduction of a variety of psi phenomenon into a single phenomenon—precognition—making it a simpler problem to contend with.

2. The person-centric experience of precognition is a manifestation of the fundamental problem of information-centric retrocausal signals, addressing the nature of causality and the arrow of time.
3. Based on the multiphasic model of precognition, *precognition is defined as an atypical perceptual ability that allows the acquisition of non-inferential information arising from a future point in spacetime.*

REFERENCES

Andrews, T. J., Halpern, S. D., & Purves, D. (1997). Correlated size variations in human visual cortex, lateral geniculate nucleus, and optic tract. *Journal of Neuroscience, 17*(8), 2859–2868.

Ashwin, E., Ashwin, C., Rhydderch, D., Howells, J., & Baron-Cohen, S. (2009). Eagle-eyed visual acuity: An experimental investigation of enhanced perception in autism. *Biological Psychiatry, 65*(1), 17–21.

Beischel, J., & Schwartz, G. E. (2007). Anomalous information reception by research mediums demonstrated using a novel triple-blind protocol. *Explore: The Journal of Science and Healing, 3*(1), 23–27.

Bermudez, P., & Zatorre, R. J. (2009). A distribution of absolute pitch ability as revealed by computerized testing. *Music Perception, 27*(2), 89–101.

Blackmore, S. J. (1980). Correlations between ESP and memory. *European Journal of Parapsychology, 3*, 127–147.

Blackmore, S. J. (1981). Errors and confusions in ESP. *European Journal of Parapsychology, 4*, 49–70.

Block, J. (1961). *The Q-sort method in personality assessment and psychiatric research.* Springfield, Ill: Thomas.

Braude, S. E. (1992). Survival or super-psi? *Journal of Scientific Exploration, 6*(2), 127–144.

Broughton, R. S. (2006). Memory, emotion, and the receptive psi process. *Journal of Parapsychology, 70*(2), 255.

Carroll, J., McMahon, C., Neitz, M., & Neitz, J. (2000). Flicker-photometric electro-retinogram estimates of L:M cone photoreceptor ratio in men with photo-pigment spectra derived from genetics. *Journal of the Optical Society of America: A, Optics, Image Science, and Vision, 17*(3), 499–509.

Chen, F., & Loizou, P. C. (2012). Contributions of cochlea-scaled entropy and consonant-vowel boundaries to prediction of speech intelligibility in noise. *Journal of the Acoustical Society of America, 131*(5), 4104–4113.

Delaigle, J. F., Devleeschouwer, C., Macq, B., & Langendijk, L. (2002). Human visual system features enabling watermarking. In *Multimedia and Expo, 2002. ICME'02. Proceedings. 2002 IEEE International Conference* (Vol. 2, pp. 489–492). IEEE.

Eagleman, D. M. (2012). Synaesthesia in its protean guises. *British Journal of Psychology 103*(1), 16–19.

Elmer, S., Rogenmoser, L., Kuhnis, J., & Jancke, L. (2015). Bridging the gap between perceptual and cognitive perspectives on absolute pitch. *Journal of Neuroscience, 35*(1), 366. DOI: 10.1523/JNEUROSCI.3009-14.2015

Farina, M. (2013). Neither touch nor vision: Sensory substitution as artificial synaesthesia? *Biology & Philosophy, 28*(4), 639–655.

Foxe, J. J., Wylie, G. R., Martinez, A., Schroeder, C. E., Javitt, D. C., Guilfoyle, D., Ritter, W., . . . Murray, M. M. (2002). Auditory-somatosensory multisensory processing in auditory association cortex: An fMRI study. *Journal of Neurophysiology, 88*(1), 540–543.

Fu, K. M., Johnston, T. A., Shah, A. S., Arnold, L., Smiley, J., Hackett, T. A., Garraghty, P. E., . . . Schroeder, C. E. (2003). Auditory cortical neurons respond to somatosensory stimulation. *Journal of Neuroscience, 23*(20), 7510–7515.

Gerhard, H. E., Wichmann, F. A., & Bethge, M. (2013). How sensitive is the human visual system to the local statistics of natural images? *PLoS Computational Biology, 9*(1), e1002873. doi: 10.1371/journal.pcbi.1002873

Halpern, S. D., Andrews, T. J., & Purves, D. (1999). Interindividual variation in human visual performance. *Journal of Cognitive Neuroscience, 11*(5), 521–534.

Hansen, N. C., & Pearce, M. T. (2012). Shannon entropy predicts perceptual uncertainty in the generation of melodic pitch expectations. In Cambouropoulos, E. Tsougras, C. Mavromatis, & Pastidis, K. (Eds.), *Proceedings of the 12th International Conference on Music Perception and Cognition and the 8th Triennial Conference of the European Society for the Cognition Sciences of Music,* July 23–28, 2012, Thessaloniki, Greece.

Hofer, H., Carroll, J., Neitz, J., Neitz, M., & Williams, D. R. (2005). Organization of the human trichromatic cone mosaic. *Journal of Neuroscience, 25*(42), 9669–9679.

Honorton, C., & Ferrari, D. C. (1989). "Future telling": A meta-analysis of forced-choice precognition experiments, 1935–1987. *Journal of Parapsychology, 53* (28), 281–308.

Honorton, C., Ferrari, D. C., & Bem, D. J. (1998). Extraversion and ESP performance: A meta-analysis and new confirmation. *Journal of Parapsychology, 62,* 255–276.

Irwin, H. J. (1979). *Psi and the mind.* Metuchen: NJ: Scarecrow.

Irwin, H. J. (1994). *An introduction to parapsychology* (2nd Ed.). Jefferson, NC: McFarland.

Kayser, C., Petkov, C. I., Augath, M., & Logothetis, N. K. (2005). Integration of touch and sound in auditory cortex. *Neuron, 48,* 2, 373–84.

Kee, C., Koo, H., Ji, Y., & Kim, S. (1997). Effect of optic disc size or age on evaluation of optic disc variables. *British Journal of Ophthalmology, 81*(12), 1046.

Krauskopf, C. J., & Saunders, D. R. (1994). *Personality and ability: The personality assessment system.* Lanham, MD: University Press of America.

Lewicki, P., Hill, T., & Czyzewska, M. (1992). Nonconscious acquisition of information. *American Psychologist, 47*(6), 796–801.

Loui, P., Li, H. C., Hohmann, A., & Schlaug, G. (2011). Enhanced cortical connectivity in absolute pitch musicians: A model for local hyperconnectivity. *Journal of Cognitive Neuroscience, 23*(4), 1015–1026.

Macaluso, E. (2006). Multisensory processing in sensory-specific cortical areas. *Neuroscientist, 12*(4), 327–338.

Marks, D. F. (1973). Visual imagery in the recall of pictures. *British Journal of Psychology, 64,* 17–24.

Martino, G., & Marks, L. E. (2001). Synesthesia: Strong and weak. *Current Directions in Psychological Science, 10*(2), 61–65.

Marwaha, S. B., & May, E. C. (2015a). A refutation of the dualist perspective in psi research. *Journal of Consciousness Studies* (accepted for publication).

Marwaha, S. B., & May, E. C. (2015b). Rethinking ESP: Towards a multiphasic model of precognition. *SAGE Open*, January-March 2015, 1–17. DOI: 10.1177/2158244015576056.

Marwaha, S. B., & May, E. C. (under review). Precognition: The only form of ESP?

May, E. C. (2007). Advances in anomalous cognition analysis: A judge-free and accurate confidence-calling technique. *Paper presented at the Parapsychological Association, Winchester, UK.*

May, E. C., Hawley, L., & Marwaha, S. B. (in-process). Entropy experiment.

May, E. C., & Hecker, M. H. L. (1982). *Audiolinguistic correlations with the quality of remote viewing sessions.* April 1982 Final Report MDA903-81-C-0292. Menlo Park, CA: SRI International.

May, E. C., & Lantz, N. D. (2014/2010). Anomalous cognition technical trials: Inspiration for the target entropy concept. In E. C. May & S. B. Marwaha (Eds.), *Anomalous cognition: Remote viewing research and theory,* pp. 280–298. Jefferson, NC: McFarland.

May, E. C., Marwaha, S. B., & Chaganti, V. (2014/2011). Anomalous cognition: Two protocols for data collection and analyses. In E. C. May & S. B. Marwaha (Eds.), *Anomalous cognition: Remote viewing research and theory,* pp. 18–37. Jefferson, NC: McFarland Pub.

May, E. C., & Marwaha, S. B. (in-preparation). *The Star Gate Archives.* Jefferson, NC: McFarland.

May, E. C., & Spottiswoode, S. J. P. (2014/1994). Shannon entropy: A possible intrinsic target property. In E. C. May & S. B. Marwaha (Eds.), *Anomalous cognition: Remote viewing research and theory,* pp. 299–313. Jefferson, NC: McFarland.

May, E. C., Spottiswoode, S. J. P., & Faith, L. V. (2000). Correlation of the gradient of Shannon entropy and anomalous cognition: Toward an AC sensory system. *Journal of Scientific Exploration, 14*(1), 53–72.

McMoneagle, J. W., & May, E. C. (2014/2004). The possible role of intention, attention and expectation in remote viewing. In E. C. May & S. B. Marwaha (Eds.), *Anomalous cognition: Remote viewing research and theory,* pp. 368–376. Jefferson, NC: McFarland.

Moulton, S. T., & Kosslyn, S. M. (2009). Using neuroimaging to resolve the psi debate. *Journal of Cognitive Neuroscience, 20*(1), 182–192.

Neitz, J., Carroll, J., Yamauchi, Y., Neitz, M., & Williams, D. R. (2002). Color perception is mediated by a plastic neural mechanism that is adjustable in adults. *Neuron, 35*(4), 783–792.

Neitz, J., Neitz, M., & Jacobs, G. H. (1993). More than three different cone pigments among people with normal color vision. *Vision Research, 33*(1), 117–122.

Norwich, K. H. (2005). Physical entropy and the senses. *Acta Biotheoretica, 53*(3), 167–180.

Plaga, R. (1997). On a possibility to find experimental evidence for the many-worlds interpretation of quantum mechanics. *Foundations of Physics, 27*(4), 559–577.

Proulx, M. J. (2010). Synthetic synaesthesia and sensory substitution. *Consciousness and Cognition, 19*(1), 501–503.

Quigley, H. A., Brown, A. E., Morrison, J. D., & Drance, S. M. (1990). The size and shape of the optic disc in normal human eyes. *Archives of Ophthalmology, 108*(1), 51–57.

Ramachandran, V. S., & Hubbard, E. M. (2001). Synaesthesia: A window into perception, thought and language. *Journal of Consciousness Studies, 8*(12), 3–34.

Rao, K. R. (2011). *Cognitive anomalies, consciousness, and Yoga.* New Delhi: Centre for Studies in Civilizations for the Project of History of Indian Science, Philosophy and Culture and Matrix Publishers.

Rhine, J. B. (1950). *New frontiers of the mind.* Harmondsworth: Penguin.

Roll, W. G. (1966). ESP and memory. *International Journal of Neuropsychiatry, 2*(5), 505–521.

Roorda, A., & Williams, D. R. (1999). The arrangement of the three cone classes in the living human eye. *Nature, 397*(6719), 520–522.

Rouw, R., & Scholte, H. S. (2007). Increased structural connectivity in grapheme-color synesthesia. *Nature Neuroscience, 10*(6), 792–797.

Sagiv, N., Ilbeigi, A., & Ben-Tal, O. (2011). Reflections on synaesthesia, perception, and cognition. *Intellectica, 55*, 81–94.

Sheehan, D. P. (2006a). Retrocausation and the thermodynamic arrow of time: Frontiers of time. Retrocausation; Experiment and theory. *AIP Conference Proceedings, 863*, 89–104.

Sheehan, D. P. (2006b). *Frontiers of time: Retrocausation. Experiment and theory, San Diego, California, 20–22 June 2006.* Melville, NY: American Institute of Physics.

Sheehan, D. P. (2011). *Quantum retrocausation: Theory and experiment, San Diego, California, USA, 13–14 June 2011.* Melville, NY: American Institute of Physics.

Simner, J. (2012). Defining synaesthesia: A response to two excellent commentaries. *British Journal of Psychology, 103*(1), 24–27.

Simner, J., & Hubbard, E. M. (2013). *The Oxford handbook of synesthesia.* New York: Oxford University Press.

Stephens, G. J., Mora, T., Tkačik, G., & Bialek, W. (2013). Statistical thermodynamics of natural images. *Physical Review Letters, 110*(1), 018701. DOI: 10.1103/PhysRevLett.110.018701

Stilp, C. E., Kiefte, M., Alexander, J. M., & Kluender, K. R. (2010). Cochlea-scaled spectral entropy predicts rate-invariant intelligibility of temporally distorted sentences. *Journal of the Acoustical Society of America, 128*, 2112.

Tahmasebi, A. M., Davis, M. H., Wild, C. J., Rodd, J. M., Hakyemez, H., Abolmaesumi, P., & Johnsrude, I. S. (2012). Is the link between anatomical structure and function equally strong at all cognitive levels of processing? *Cerebral Cortex, 22*(7), 1593–1603.

Targ, R., May, E. C., Puthoff, H. E., Galin, D., & Ornstein, R. (1976). *Sensing of remote EM sources (psychological correlates),* Final Report, Project 4540. Menlo Park, CA: SRI International.

Tart, C. T. (2009). *The end of materialism: How evidence of the paranormal is bringing science and spirit together.* Oakland, CA: Noetic Books, Institute of Noetic Sciences.

Thomson, E. E., Carra, R., & Nicolelis, M. A. (2013). Perceiving invisible light through a somatosensory cortical prosthesis. *Nature Communications, 4*, 1482.

Tyrrell, G. M. (1947). The modus operandi of paranormal cognition. *Paper presented at the Proceedings of the Society for Psychical Research.*

University of Zurich. (2015, January 7). Two brain regions join forces for absolute pitch. *ScienceDaily.* Retrieved January 9, 2015 from www.sciencedaily.com/releases/2015/01/150107081703.htm

VanRullen, R., & Koch, C. (2003). Is perception discrete or continuous? *Trends in Cognitive Sciences, 7*(5), 207–213.

Varma, R., Tielsch, J. M., Quigley, H. A., Hilton, S. C., Katz, J., Spaeth, G. L., & Sommer. A. (1994). Race-, age-, gender-, and refractive error–related differences in the normal optic disc. *Archives of Ophthalmology, 112*(8), 1068–1076.

Wallace, G. L., Happe, F., & Giedd, J. N. (2009). A case study of a multiply talented savant with an autism spectrum disorder: Neuropsychological functioning and brain morphometry. *Philosophical Transactions of the Royal Society B: Biological Sciences, 364*(1522), 1425–1432.

Ward, J., & Wright, T. (2014). Sensory substitution as an artificially acquired synaesthesia. *Neuroscience and Biobehavioral Reviews, 41*, 26–35.

Wesner, M. F., Pokorny, J., Shevell, S. K., & Smith, V. C. (1991). Foveal cone detection statistics in color-normals and dichromats. *Vision Research, 31*(6), 1021–1037.

Whitaker, K. J., Kang, X., Herron, T. J., Woods, D. L., Robertson, L. C., & Alvarez, B. D. (2014). White matter microstructure throughout the brain correlates with visual imagery in grapheme-color synesthesia. *Neuroimage, 90*, 52–59.

Williams, B. J., & Roll, W. G. (2008). Neuropsychological correlates of psi phenomena. *Proceedings of the 51st Annual Convention of the Parapsychological Association and the 32nd Annual Convention of the Incorporated Society for Psychical Research*, August 13–17, 2008, Winchester, England, pp. 264–187.

Zadeh, L. A. (1965). Fuzzy sets. *Information and control, 8*(3), 338–353.

Chapter 8

Consciousness-Induced Restoration of Time Symmetry

Dick J. Bierman

PARAPSYCHOLOGY, PARABIOLOGY, OR PARAPHYSICS?

Are paranormal phenomena in conflict with psychology? The name "parapsychology" suggests that the phenomena do not fit the core of psychology; however, that is not true. Traditionally, psychology assumes the biological findings that humans possess five sensory modalities: sight, hearing, touch, temperature, and taste/smell. These modalities are assumed to provide the human organism with information. Without explicitly stating so, biology assumes there are no more modalities that could provide information, and psychology just conforms to that position. However, current understanding of the senses has extended their number from these traditional five to include time, rhythm, and echolocation. These may be just the few additional senses that cognitive neuroscientists are now beginning to recognize as independent senses (Burdick, Strickland, & Rosenblum, 2011). However, if biology were able to establish another (extra) sensory modality, then psychology might be able to deal with paranormal phenomena. Thus, under the assumption that an extra "sensory organ" is required, these phenomena should be called para-biological.

However, as we will see later in this chapter, the idea that an extra sensory organ is required—an assumption rather explicit in the label ESP—is extremely improbable and actually might have misguided the field of scientific parapsychology for over 60 years.

The major conflict between paranormal phenomena and mainstream science is the role of "time." Precognition and presentiment challenge the concept of traditional causality that causes always precede effects. This may be considered a violation of physics; however, this inference seems to be on weak grounds. Retrocausality is a concept heavily discussed in relativistic physics when considering time travel (as well in quantum physics, e.g., in the context of delayed choice experiments). Hence, para-physics seems not to be a good name for the field either. As the *consciousness induced restoration of time symmetry* CIRTS model (Bierman, 2010) discussed in this chapter asserts, nothing has to be added to the science we know already. The basic ingredient, time symmetry, is already there.

Since psi phenomena are labeled anomalous because they *appear* to be in conflict with our present-day physical worldview, any fundamental psi theory should be an extension or a modification of physics. Extension and modification of physical theories have been proposed by Walker (1975), Millar and Hartwell (1979), Houtkooper (1983), Kornwachs and Lucadou (1985) Josephson and Pallikari (1991), May, Utts, and Spottiswoode (1995), and most notably for the present proposal, Donald and Martin's (1976) framework based upon time symmetric thermodynamics.

The observational theories (Walker, 1975) assume that the act of observation "injects" information into the observed system, independent of time and space. This approach showed that it was possible to unify all psi phenomena in one theoretical framework. The correlations found in telepathy, clairvoyance, precognition, and PK experiments were all supposed to be produced via the observation of the correlation, that is, upon feedback. The observational theories (OTs) are based upon an especially unpopular solution of the measurement problem in quantum physics, called the "radical subjective solution," a position that gave special status to an observer. Thus, these theories are intrinsically dualistic.

In this chapter, I discuss the theory consciousness induced restoration of time symmetry (CIRTS), which focuses upon "time" rather than "information," although the two are related through the second law of thermodynamics. "Consciousness," as used in this model, is defined as "awareness."

CONSCIOUSNESS-INDUCED RESTORATION OF TIME SYMMETRY (CIRTS)

Based upon converging evidence from many different experimental paradigms, most notably presentiment, I propose to take seriously the fact that most physical formalisms—for instance, electromagnetic theories—are inherently time symmetric. Although in practical physical systems time symmetry has not been observed, I propose that conscious observation does remove part of the constraints that prohibit time symmetry to occur. Additionally, CIRTS seeks to integrate the physical and neuro-psychological aspects of paranormal phenomena. This framework results in straightforward hypotheses that can easily be tested.

CIRTS unifies the phenomena that are known under the labels of telepathy, clairvoyance, presentiment, and precognition; it also suggests how, possibly, psychokinesis could be integrated too. Further, the theory gives an account for the difficulty of replication of experimental results and for the decline effects often observed in psi research (Bierman, 2006). Based upon this analysis, ways to overcome these replication and decline problems are suggested. The theory also has well-defined limits. Although it describes how future information may become present as part of the neurological processes, it does not describe how this information is filtered and processed before it becomes conscious. Therefore, it does not deal with any psychodynamic aspects that could be relevant for the eventual manifestation of the precognized information. Moreover, some observed psi phenomena apparently contradict the theory, or the theory cannot easily account for them.

CIRTS: The Fundamental Speculation

The fundamental assumption of CIRTS is that the brain, when it sustains consciousness, is a special system that partially restores time symmetry and therefore allows "advanced" waves to occur.

It should be emphasized that this fundamental assumption does *not* violate any physics, as we currently know it. The only thing it does is to speculate that solutions allowed by the formalisms but never observed might be observed under special conditions involving consciousness. Further, it is not the brain per se that is supposed to be a time symmetry–restoring condition, but only the brain that sustains consciousness. One of the big mysteries in consciousness research has always been that different brain regions process different aspects of an object, such as color, form, and movement. Nonetheless, the conscious percept is an inseparable whole. Global and *coherent* synchrony in firing has been proposed as a means to bind these different aspects again into a whole. Therefore, I propose that coherence is a crucial moderating variable.

The basic assumption can further be specified by assuming that the restoration of time symmetry is proportional to some global coherence measure that also incorporates the brain volume involved in this coherence (Singer, 1999).

Thus, if we present a stimulus to a subject, then the "normal" solution of the physics that eventually results, for instance, in a skin conductance measure, might yield a signal $S = f(t)$. However, if the stimulus is observed consciously, time symmetry will kick in and:

$$S = f(t) + A \times f(-t)$$

$$A = \frac{\text{Relative coherence} \times \text{Brain volume}}{\text{Total brain volume}}.$$

To arrive at predictions that are more precise, we therefore add that the supposed time symmetry is not around the moment of exposure but around the moment of conscious experience. This is according to Libet's famous experiments about 400 milliseconds later (Libet, 1979). The symmetry formula becomes: $S(t + 400) = S(-t + 400)$. The part of the original signal that is not experienced consciously ($0 < t < 400$) will not be reflected in time.

This set of formulae reflects the fundamental assumption, which results in a time-symmetric term in Equation 1, which is the physical part; and Equation 2 offers a link for psychological considerations. For simplicity, we assume that A is not very dynamic and does not change a lot over time. This is, of course, an oversimplification; most notably, the effect of the stimulus might be a reduction in this coherence measure immediately upon the exposure of the stimulus to the subject. Coherence measures can be derived objectively from EEG measures, while the brain volume involved can be assessed using fMRI. Thus, this simple approach allows us to calculate the expected signal over time using objective measures. This generates a simple principle: *What happens after, happens before.*

In general, I argue that the dynamic characteristics of the "advanced" part will mimic those of the "retarded." If we deal with a "slow" signal that peaks, for instance, 4 seconds after a conscious event, we might expect the advanced part to peak about 4 seconds before the conscious event. If the "retarded" signal lasts a week, we might expect the "advanced" signal to start a week before the (consciously experienced) event so that it allows us to make precise predictions, which will be discussed later.

The "Advanced Waves" as a Metaphor

Physical formalisms are mostly time symmetric. For instance, the field of electromagnetism (light being a specific instance) is governed by a number of equations that have to be solved to predict the behavior of a physical system. These equations are solved by entering initial conditions and contextual constraints, for instance, in mirrors (Griffiths, 2008).

There are always two solutions for these equations, which can be described as a "retarded solution"–a wave that develops *with* time—and an "advanced solution"–a wave that develops *backward* in time. This wave is thought to be already present before the initial setup.

Physicists have never reported empirical observation of these "advanced" waves in practical physical systems. Therefore, many experimental physicists consider the "advanced wave" solution to be an artifact of the mathematics. Nevertheless, some theoretical physicists have tried to find an explanation for the nonobservation of something that has theoretically been predicted, assuming that mathematics is sacred (Wheeler & Feynman, 1945).

In the 1970s, Donald and Martin (1976) proposed that advanced waves could be a "carrier" of information used by the organism and that this proposition would give a theoretical underpinning for paranormal phenomena, which they called "memory of future events." Thus, CIRTS is not an entirely new concept, although many implications—especially those that follow from the potential to create time loop paradoxes—were not considered at the time. Nor did Donald and Martin relate their proposal to neuropsychological processes.

The theoretical explanation for why these advanced waves are not observed in physical systems given by Wheeler and Feynman is that there are contextual constraints that prevent advanced waves to become actualized—or better, why they are interfered with in such a way that they annihilate.

A "liberal" way to describe these contextual constraints is that there is an asymmetry in the cosmos with regard to many particle physical systems that *emit* EM radiation in a coherent manner, like lasers do, while there appear to be a much smaller quantity of multiparticle systems that *absorb* EM radiation in a coherent fashion, like Bose-Einstein condensates might do. (Bose-Einstein condensates are multiparticle systems in which the individual particles have lost their identity, like a dancer in a *corps de ballet*. The condensate acts as one entity.)

CIRTS has therefore made the bold step of suggesting that the brain is a similar multiparticle coherent absorber. So, if a normal retarded wave carrying causal information, like light reflecting from the pages of a journal is "absorbed" by the eyes and subsequently by the brain, there will be a causal sequence of brain events that have a retrocausal (time symmetric) counterpart. However, CIRTS claims that this is not always the case. The brain system *has* to be "coherent," and it is assumed the required "coherence" is present only when the brain produces consciousness (awareness). Indeed, in consciousness research, one of the major problems is to explain the "binding" of different aspects of a single percept that are processed in different parts of the brain, and some form of coherence seems to be required. Hence, this theory is called *consciousness induced restoration of time symmetry.* However, a more accurate name would be "brain-supporting-consciousness-induced restoration of time symmetry" as it is a special state of the brain as a physical system that is responsible for the restoration of time symmetry—an idea that is generally lost in physics. At this point, I emphasize that this bold step is metaphorical, and a precise definition of the required "coherence" is currently lacking.

In spite of this explicit vagueness, this formulation allows us to bring in a neurological aspect to account for individual differences and a link with neuropsychology and hence psychology, and is possibly capable of explaining individual differences (Bierman, 2008). For instance, based upon this formulation, it was predicted that subjects that had a global information processing style would perform better in a retroactive psi task than subjects that lacked this trait. This was confirmed in a pre-registered experiment on retroactive training effects (Bierman & Bijl, 2014). The apparent stronger psi in meditators can also been interpreted in terms of coherent brain processing (Roney-Dougal, Solfvin, & Fox, 2008).

Time Symmetry in Physics

Almost all formalisms in physics are time symmetric. Given specific initial conditions, solving the equations generally results in two solutions that are identical but reflected in time: $s(t) = s(-t)$. This holds for classical particle mechanics, electromagnetic theory, and depending on the type of formulation/interpretation, for quantum physics also. In the transactional formulation of quantum physics (QP), this is most obvious. Formulations of QP that interpret the projection postulate as a collapse of the wave function possibly introduce a break of time symmetry at the point of collapse. It should be noted at this point that several authors (Bierman, 1988; Costa de Beauregard, 1998) have already argued that, due to this fundamental time symmetry, paranormal phenomena are natural and *should* be expected as a part of physics.

Thermodynamics, or more generally, formalisms that deal with ensembles such as statistical mechanics, seem to be the only exception, although several authors have argued that this is only due to boundary conditions (Price, 1996). In thermodynamics, it is postulated that closed dynamic systems always develop with time in such a way that the structure in the system becomes smaller.

Thus, a film of the trajectory of a (frictionless) billiard ball can be played forward and backward without anyone being able to discriminate between the two. This certainly does not hold for desolving a sugar cube in hot tea. Actually, *if* time would run backward in a thermodynamic system, one would observe this as an increment in structure. For instance, one could observe a sugar cube arising from a sweet solution by just stirring that solution.

EM Theory, Wheeler, and Feynman

Most physicists assume that the solution S(–t) of the physical formalisms is in some way forbidden. In spite of the fact that this solution apparently has never been observed in physical systems, some theoretical physicists, most notably Wheeler and Feynman (1945), have tried to find a reason why this solution seems to be forbidden rather than impose the restriction ad hoc.

Wheeler and Feynman focused on classical electromagnetic theory because thermodynamic effects related to temperature are irrelevant there. So, the question they tried to answer was: why do we observe a (retarded) wave going from an electromagnetic transmitter outward in space and forward in time, while we don't observe a collapsing (advanced) wave coming from afar to the transmitter (acting then as an absorber) going backward in time?

After a thorough analysis, they suggested that this asymmetry is due to the cosmos being far out of equilibrium. More specifically, they postulated that there was an extreme imbalance between the number of multiple particle coherent (quantum) transmitters, like lasers, and the equivalent multiple particle coherent absorbers (of EM radiation). Possibly a substrate known as Bose-Einstein condensate could be called a multiple particle coherent absorber. It should be noted that Price (1996) argues that the Wheeler-Feynman treatment of time symmetry was circular because by using the concepts of transmitter and absorber, they subtly introduced some "preferred" time direction to begin with. Price also deconstructs suggestions in which the boundary condition of the Big Bang has been used to explain the fact that retarded solutions are totally dominant. The conclusion that this must be the reason for the breaking of time symmetry is still a controversial issue. However, the reason that serious efforts have been made in theoretical physics to "explain" which conditions do result in this asymmetry suggests that there are also conditions under which the symmetry might partially be restored.

Presentiment

Until the last part of the previous century, the major causality challenging psi phenomenon was precognition: somebody having knowledge about a future event while this event could not be deduced from rational reasoning. In experimental research, this future event was decided randomly and hence was fundamentally unpredictable. However, in case reports, people often communicated dark feelings without specifics before a major dreadful event would occur. The experiencer had no cognition about a specific event but only experienced some emotion associated with it. This phenomenon was labeled "presentiment" and allowed for experimental research that was identical to standard emotion research in

psychology. In these studies, pictures of either neutral or emotional contents were presented, and the physiology of the percipient of these pictures was measured. While in standard emotion research the dependent
variable would be the physiological response to these pictures, in presentiment research, the dependent variable would be the physiological anticipation before the pictures were presented. Crucial for the interpretation,
of course, was that the stimuli would be selected randomly so that there
was no way that the percipient could infer what picture was going to be
presented. This paradigm soon turned out to be a very successful one
(Bierman & Radin, 1997, 1998) and was the origin of a host of experiments
in which effects were measured of future manipulations as, for instance,
in Bem's retrocausal experiments (Bem, 2011).

An Anecdote That Suggests That Almost Everybody Might Have Presentiment

In 2012, I received an email from a mainstream neuroscientist who had
obtained very unusual results and was clearly informed that he had to
ignore his findings. For reasons that will become obvious in a moment, I
cannot give his name (yet), but let us call him BN. BN's job was to investigate emotional processes in the brain. He was working in an institution
that did brain surgery on people with epilepsy who are untreatable with
medication. Since these patients already had depth electrodes implanted
in them, BN sought their consent for participating in his research. In one
of the patients, patient X, BN found incredibly strong physiological effects
for the emotional stimuli 300 to 500 milliseconds *before* exposure, instead
of after. His principal investigator (PI) told him this was impossible and
said that there must have been a problem with the method or instrumentation that he used. The procedure was checked and rechecked, and nothing improper could be found. The PI hence called it a statistical anomaly.
He made it clear to BN though, and in a rather blunt way, that he did
not want BN to spend any more time on it. For the sake of not compromis-
ing their working relationship, BN honored his request.

Although, of course, his results might still have been due to some artifact, to me, it suggested another rather interesting option. To understand
this suggestion, one must know that patients with temporal lobe epilepsy
often report very frequent déjà vu experiences, and patient X was even
exceptional in this respect. While a large majority of the healthy population does report déjà vu experiences, the only difference with patients
with temporal lobe epilepsy is the frequency and the intensity of these
experiences. Although déjà vu experiences differ from person to person,
the best way to describe most of them is that there is a feeling of having
been at the place where this experience has occurred sometime in the past,
even though one has never been there before, with a sense of familiarity
and a sense of knowing what will happen next. Could it be that déjà vu

is time symmetry in action, and almost everybody has experienced this a few times in his or her life?

Of course, there are alternative neuropsychological and causal explanations for déjà vu. Most of these come down to some unspecified neural mishap for which there are hardly objective data (see, e.g., Spatt, 2002). It is a tantalizing thought that maybe déjà vu—there is no debate concerning the reality of the phenomenon—is due to the same physical process that we measure in presentiment research.

Time Symmetry in Mainstream Data

As has been noted, the presentiment paradigm is identical to most mainstream stimulus-response experiments with psychophysiological variables, for instance, in emotion research. Thus, it should be easy to locate similar effects in mainstream data. However, randomization in the mainstream is mostly "randomization without replacement" to keep some counterbalancing and have all cells in a design equally populated. This prevents strong conclusions when analyzing the data because "randomization with replacement" is required for strong conclusions. Subjects generally pick up quickly on the distribution of trials over the conditions and start to guess what the condition of the forthcoming trial will be. One could say they fall into the trap of the gambler's fallacy, but alas, in the case of the generally used "randomization without replacement," this is no trap; rather, it gives the subject an above chance possibility of guessing the next stimulus condition. Nonetheless, two data sets of mainstream research could be analyzed, and in both, indicators of presentiment, cautiously called anomalous baselines, could be assessed, with the caveat that they could possibly be explained by weak randomization (Bechara, Damasio, Tranel, & Damasio, 1997; Bierman, 2000; Globisch, Hamm, Estevez, & Ehman, 1999). Recently, mainstream neuroscientists themselves point out that the brain behavior preceding stimuli or events seems to correlate with the type of event that will follow later. Although causal explanations are not totally excluded, these phenomena do puzzle these researchers, and one of them even "confessed" that time symmetry looked like a more natural explanation of his data (Lamme, 2008, personal communication). It concerns phenomena as diverse as monkey brains indicating what the movement of an ambiguous stimulus will be (about 3 seconds before stimulus onset; Naotsugu, 2008), subjects executing a voluntary choice between two alternatives (about 10 seconds before decision; Soon, Brass, Heinze, & Haynes, 2008), transcranial magnetic stimulation (TMS)–induced percept doubling where the illusory percept seems to act as a prime (Joly & Lamme, 2010). Other TMS-induced apparent retrocausal effects are in a Libet paradigm (Lau, Rogers, & Passingham, 2008) and pupil dilation (Einhauser, Stout, Koch, & Carter, 2008).

Symmetry, Causality, and Time Loop Paradoxes: Why Replication Fails

Time symmetry does not imply that one can "change the past." Rather, it implies that at any moment, a signal has determinants that are from past as well as from future boundary conditions. Once the signal is there, one cannot use it to decide to change future boundary conditions. Conceptually, this looks very much like the transactional interpretation of quantum physics in which the present is determined by a kind of handshake between advanced and retarded waves (Cramer, 1986).

Suppose you have a (precognitive?) dream about a fire in your attic caused by a fallen candle, and from the dream, it is clear this is going to happen the following day. What would you do in the morning? You would remove all candles from the attic. But now we have a problem akin to the grandfather paradox in time travel. You have removed the event that apparently triggered your dream, just like the time traveler could kill his grandfather (before he had children), thereby removing the source of the time traveler's own existence.

In the time travel literature, the solution is that one does not forbid time travel per se, but there are restrictions that essentially lead to the idea that one can never create a so-called time loop paradox (Novikov, 1992).

The equivalent for the precognitive dream would be that it is possible to dream about future events, but only if one cannot use this information, that is, for removing the candles. Note that the potential to use the information would already be preventing the information to "run backward in time."

A laboratory psi effect comes generally as a correlation. For example, correlation between intention and a material state (PK), correlation between a bodily state and a future condition (presentiment).

Due to the limiting principle that it is "forbidden" to even have the potential to create time loop paradoxes, psi correlations can occur *only* if the correlation can indeed not be used to create such a paradox. Replication of an experiment, in principle, is building up knowledge about how one could use the anomalous correlations better and better approaching the level that they can be used in the "forbidden" way. Therefore, sequential replication would be problematic in psi lab research. Possibly, parallel replication or retrospective replication are options that can be explored because they seem not to create a direct option to create a paradox. After all, replication is seen as the hallmark of objective science.

It is interesting to note that other theories like the model of pragmatic information (MPI; Lucadou, 1995) and generalized quantum theory (GQT; Atmanspacher et al., 2002) have the same argument about the use of psi correlations, although this argument is a consequence of the no-signaling theorem of QP, not of reflections on time loop paradoxes.

(While this no-signaling theorem has been challenged by a few physicists, mainstream physicists believe that violation of the theorem would imply velocities larger than the speed of light—which would be a major problem for relativistic theories.)

UNIFICATION OF PSI PHENOMENA: NO MORE NEED FOR AN OMNIPOTENT SCANNING MECHANISM

CIRTS gives a unified account for most psi phenomena. Telepathy, for instance, is accounted for in exactly the same way as are precognition and clairvoyance, including presentiment.

Rather than having a "receiver" and a "sender" in a card-guessing experiment, only the person who makes the guesses matters. First, "the receiver" tries to call a target that the other person ("sender") thinks about. Then in most lab experiments, the "receiver" gets feedback. According to the traditional hand waving "extra sensory" theories of psi, the call of the "receiver" is triggered by some mysterious process that amounts to scanning the environment (in this case, the brain of the "sender") for relevant information. According to CIRTS, nothing is scanned; processing the feedback results in a series of physical processes (responses) in the brain, and these processes may also "run backward" just like an advanced wave. In some articles on presentiment, the phenomenon has also been called "presponse," which is a funny but appropriate label because it emphasizes the symmetry.

According to CIRTS, precognition and clairvoyance work in the same way. There is evidence that neither spatial nor temporal distance between "receiver" and "sender" have any impact on the psi effects. So, this mysterious extra sensory scanning mechanism—that has been implicitly assumed in much of the parapsychical research for the past 100 years—would have to be able to transcend time and space, and basically scan everything that ever was and ever will be and out of all this information, the brain should be able to select what is relevant. Although nobody knows the limits of the information processing capacity of the brain, this task seems to me very impossible.

CIRTS, however, restricts the psi process to the brain of the "receiver," and hence we have no need to assume such an omnipotent scanning mechanism that not only transcends time and space but also the limits in brain processing capacity as far as we know them.

In presentiment—where subjects' physiology responds before a random stimulus is presented, we have exactly the same model, although the wording is slightly different. Here the advanced wave is a result of the observation of the stimulus. Presentiment is the time symmetrical counterpart of the normal physiological response.

Psychokinesis

The major physical "law" preventing full time symmetry at the level of material processes is called the second law of thermodynamics: the natural development over time of a system is toward less structure (i.e., maximum entropy), the reason being that these less-structured systems have a larger probability to occur.

It can be argued that in the "advanced world," the second law would reverse, and the natural development would be that systems become more structured (less random). For the observer, this would be like a miracle. Your cup of tea with a dissolved sugar cube would develop into tea with the sugar returning to the cube form.

In the lab environment, PK is generally measured using random number generators (RNGs). These systems have a maximum entropy. A development toward less entropy, as described earlier in this discussion, would result in the RNG becoming less random. Although we can thus account for the occurrence of spontaneous PK cases as well as for the occurrences of RNGs that behave less randomly, the extension to the traditional PK-RNG experiments fails because we are unable to explain the correlations of this "miracle" with the intentions of the subject. Why would time at the RNG "run backward" if the subject has a specific intention? To account for PK, further assumptions have to be made. However, the idea of time symmetry has potential value here too.

CIRTS Predictions

Semiquantitative Predictions

Crucial for each theory is that the theory can be tested, rejected, or improved due to measurements. CIRTS has at least two testable predictions. First, the symmetry aspect. According to CIRTS, in the case of presentiment, when a response (retarded wave) is large, the presponse, or psi anticipation (advanced wave), should also be large. This should be seen as a relative prediction. So if response A is larger than response B, then this would also be the case for the presponses. Thus, emotional pictures would have a larger presponse because people do respond more strongly to emotional pictures. It is not an intrinsic property of the psi process that it has to be emotional. It is a property of the symmetry that the physics predicts. It is possible to consider increasingly sophisticated tests, such as stimulating people with two consecutive pictures; when the response has a double character, so should the presponse have a double bump.

The second way to test the theory becomes gradually possible when we develop a more precise measure for the coherence of the brain. This is a research program in itself. The prediction is that subjects who show a larger brain coherence would exhibit stronger psi effects.

How about the nonusable nature of psi correlations? Here we have two flavors. One is that no use can ever be made of these correlations. The second flavor is that in principle, use could be made of this information, but never should the system allow the potential for use to create a time loop paradox, as in the grandfather paradox in time travel, as discussed earlier. The latter is the prediction that CIRTS would support. There are paradigms that have hardly a potential to create a time loop paradox. Based on this, we would predict that an associative remote viewing (ARV) experiment in which a random set of the trials is bilked would show no psi correlations. While parallel replication might be possible here, we predict that attempts to replicate such a joint effort would decline more rapidly than the general decline of isolated experiments.

An Experiment with Unusable Dependent Variable

As noted earlier, there are two other distinct theoretical frameworks that claim anomalous psi correlations cannot be produced by classical signal transfer. This claim is similar to the inference within CIRTS that the potential to create a time loop paradox using the signals and knowledge from previous experimental outcomes is at the heart of the replication problem. Therefore, the experimental solution that was suggested by von Lucadou (Lucadou, Römer, & Walach, 2007) to circumvent this problem is also applicable in the case of CIRTS.

Lucadou et al. (2007, p. 60) suggested the following general strategies for improving the visibility of synchronistic events:

- One should take care that the organizational closure of the system and its preparation in an entangled state are not destroyed by the observations.

- One should concentrate one's search on conspicuous correlations between different parts of the system rather than on (isolated) causal influences.

- To reduce the decline effect, one should make positive use of the evasion phenomenon. This can be done by simultaneous registration of as many different correlations as possible. Psi effects will then show up as transitory, jumping unexpected and statistically unlikely patterns in the correlation matrix.

Additionally, they suggest two ways by which to avoid replication problems: (1) the experimental setting is designed in such a way that only correlations could be measured, which cannot be (mis-)used for any signal transfer, such as in the EPR-case and (2) the experimental setting allows the effect to "displace" in an unpredictable way (Lucadou et al., 2007, pp. 61–62).

Rather than focusing on a single well-defined correlation, for instance, a correlation between intention and the deviation from chance of a random number generator (RNG), Lucadou proposed using a complete correlation matrix as a dependent variable in an experiment. He measured several physical variables pertaining to the behavior of the RNG, such as maximum deviation and variance. He measured several psychological variables, as he called them, pertaining to the behavior of the subject. These are variables such as number of button presses. Then he calculated the correlation matrix of all these variables. It turns out that the total amount of correlation in these matrices is more than one can expect by chance. (The chance distribution was obtained through control runs with simulated button presses.) Lucadou ran five such experiments, and all but one produced significant results with an effect size of around 0.15. Of course, the significant cells within the matrix varied from experiment to experiment, but every time, there was too much "connectedness". This general knowledge of "too much connectedness" is too limited to be used to code a signal with as in the MPI and GQT framework; it is also too limited to infer how to create a time loop paradox as in the CIRTS framework. Recently, another German group replicated this experiment (Walach, 2014).

Shortcomings of the Observational Theories and CIRTS

CIRTS fails to explain subject-centered psi phenomena in which a subject does not get any feedback. There are some instances in the literature of nonfeedback anomalous correlations, and the only escape for CIRTS is to interpret these as an experimenter-psi-induced PK effect.

This is especially problematic because CIRTS, can hardly handle PK. Either a fundamental extension is required, or we need a second theoretical framework for PK. In all fairness, CIRTS fails especially because observational theories have addressed this adequately.

Observational theories (Walker, 1975) arose out of the measurement problem in quantum physics (Walker, 1972). This class of theories posits that the question of what constitutes a measurement should be answered by *"only a conscious observation is a measurement."* This position is known as the "radical subjective solution of the measurement problem" (Shimony, 1992). Although one can argue that it is tricky to explain one mysterious phenomenon such as psi with some other mysterious set of phenomena such as those in quantum systems, the measurement problem is not settled; however, quantum physics is in itself legitimate to use for the psi problem. Whereas CIRTS does not rely on quantum physics nor extend the physics as we know it, OTs do extend the physics because they posit that the measurement is not a passive process and that information can flow into the observed system, thereby accounting for psychokinesis (PK). The original OT, as proposed by E. H. Walker (1975), also predicted a hitherto unobserved phenomenon called retro-PK. According to the theory, one could pre-record random numbers (say, 1 and 0) and store them for any period before a target was chosen (say, 1). If one then asked a subject to observe the data with the intention of increasing the target number, this should work as well as real-time psychokinesis. As it turned out, that worked a bit better (Bierman, 1996). This was the first time in the history of parapsychology that a theory predicted a new phenomenon. And what is more, none of the current theories, including CIRTS and DAT (May et al., 1995), seem able to elegantly explain retroactive psychokinesis. However, the phenomenon of retroactive psychokinesis, including PK as a whole, is declared nonexistent by some of the authors of DAT.

Experimenter Effects

It is generally acknowledged, although there has not been much formal research, that the experimenter is an important part of the processes that appear to be responsible for psi correlations to occur. This is very naturally explained by the OTs because in all experiments, the experimenter observes the data, often as the first observer. The experimenter often analyzes the data and is the first to consciously realize the outcome of the experiment. In experiments in which the role of experimenter and analyzer are split, there are strong indications that the analyzer is actually the crucial person, that is, someone who is doing something long after the experiment in a traditional interpretation of an experiment is finished is relevant for the outcome.

Some argue that apart from work with special subjects, all experimental psi research actually boils down to experimenter psi (Parker, 2013).

Again, apart from some hand waving arguments that were given before to account for PK, CIRTS fails utterly to explain experimenter and analyzer effects.

Considering the complexity of phenomena, theories cannot be dismissed out of hand for failing to account for all phenomena. Therefore, CIRTS should still be considered together with other theoretical frameworks when doing theoretically relevant process-oriented research.

REFERENCES

Atmanspacher, H., Romer, H., & Walach, H. (2002) Weak quantum theory: Complementarity and entanglement in physics and beyond. *Foundations of Physics*, 32, 379–406.

Bechara, A., Damasio, H., Tranel, D., & Damasio, A. R. (1997). Deciding advantageously before knowing the advantageous strategy. *Science, 275*, 1293–1295.

Bem, D. J. (2011). Feeling the future: Experimental evidence for anomalous retroactive influences on cognition and affect. *Journal of Personality and Social Psychology, 100*(3), 407.

Bierman, D. J. (1988). A world with retrocausation. *Systematica, 6*, 45–54.

Bierman, D. J. (1996). Mind, machines and paranormal phenomena: A rejoinder to Beloff's radical dualist perspective. *Journal of Consciousness Studies, 3*, 515–516.

Bierman, D. J. (2000). Anomalous baseline effects in mainstream emotion research using psychophysiological variables. *Proceedings of Presented Papers. The Parapsychological Association 43rd Annual Convention*, 34–47.

Bierman, D. J. (2006). Empirical research on the radical subjective solution of the measurement problem: Does time get its direction through conscious observation? In D. Sheehan (Ed.), *Frontiers of time, retrocausation: Experiment and theory. AIP Conference Proceedings*, 238–259.

Bierman, D. J. (2008). fMRI-meditation study of presentiment: The role of "coherence" in retrocausal processes. *Paper presented at the symposium of the Bial Foundation*, Porto, Portugal.

Bierman, D. J. (2010). Consciousness induced restoration of time symmetry (CIRTS): A psychophysical theoretical perspective. *Journal of Parapsychology, 24*, 273–300.

Bierman, D. J. & Bijl, A. (2014). Anomalous "retrocausal" effects on performance in a Go/NoGo task. *Journal for Scientific Exploration*. In press.

Bierman, D. J., & Radin, D. I. (1997). Anomalous anticipatory response on randomized future conditions. *Perceptual and Motor Skills, 84*, 689–690.

Bierman, D. J., & Radin, D. I. (1998). Anomalous unconscious emotional responses: Evidence for a reversal of the arrow of time. In S. Hameroff, A. Kaszniak, and D. Chalmers (Eds.), *Toward a science of consciousness III*, pp. 367–386. Cambridge, MA: MIT Press.

Burdick, A., Strickland, F., & Rosenblum, L., D. (2011). The brain. *Discover Magazine*.

Costa de Beauregard, O. (1998). The paranormal is not excluded from physics. *Journal of Scientific Exploration, 12*, 315–320.

Cramer, J. G. (1986). The transactional interpretation of quantum mechanics. *Reviews of Modern Physics, 58*, 647–688.

Donald, J. A., & Martin, B. (1976). Time-symmetric thermodynamics and causality violation. *European Journal of Parapsychology, 3*, 17–37.

Einhauser, W., Stout, J., Koch, C., & Carter, O. (2008). Pupil dilation reflects perceptual selection and predicts subsequent stability in perceptual rivalry. *Proceedings of the National Academy of Sciences USA, 105*, 1704–1709.

Globisch, J., Hamm, A. O., Estevez, F., & Ehman, A. (1999). Fear appears fast: Temporal course of startle reflex potentiation in animal fearful subjects. *Psychophysiology, 36*, 66–75.

Griffiths, D. J. (2008). *Introduction to electrodynamics IE* (3rd ed.). San Francisco: Pearson Education.

Houtkooper, J. M. (1983). *Observational theory: A research programme for paranormal phenomena*. Lisse, the Netherlands: Swets & Zeitlinger.

Joly, J., & Lamme, V. A. F. (2010). Transcranial magnetic stimulation-induced "visual echoes" are generated in early visual cortex. *Neuroscience Letters, 484*, 178–181.

Josephson, B. D., & Pallikari-Viras, F. (1991). Limits to the universality of quantum mechanics. *Foundations of Physics, 21*, 197–207.

Kornwachs, K., & Lucadou, W. von (1985). Pragmatic information as a nonclassical concept to describe cognitive processes. *Cognitive Systems, 1*, 79–94.

Lau, H. C., Rogers, R. D., & Passingham, R. E. (2007). Manipulating the experienced onset of intention after action execution. *Journal of Cognitive Neuroscience, 19*, 81–90.

Libet, B., Wright, E. W., Feinstein, B., & Pearl, D. K. (1979). Subjective referral of the timing for a conscious sensory experience: A functional role for the somatosensory specific projection system in man. *Brain, 102*, 193.

Lucadou, W. von (1995). The model of pragmatic information (MPI). *European Journal of Parapsychology, 11*, 58–75.

Lucadou, W. von, Römer, H., & Walach, H. (2007). Synchronistic phenomena as entanglement correlations in generalized quantum theory. *Journal of Consciousness Studies, 14*(4), 50–74.

May, E. C., Utts, J. M., & Spottiswoode, S. J. P. (2014/1995). Decision augmentation theory: Toward a model for anomalous mental phenomena. In E. C. May & S. B. Marwaha (Eds.), *Anomalous cognition: Remote viewing research and theory*, pp. 222–243. Jefferson, NC: McFarland.

Millar, B., & Hartwell, J. (1979). Dealing with divergence [Abstract]. In W. C. Roll (Ed.), *Research in Parapsychology, 1978*, pp. 91–93. Metuchen, NJ: Scarecrow.

Naotsugu, T. (2008). Initial non-conscious spike activity and later neuronal correlates of consciousness in monkey area MT. *Paper presented at Towards a Science of Consciousness 2008, Center for Consciousness Studies, University of Arizona*, Tucson, AZ.

Novikov, I. D. (1992). Time machine and self-consistent evolution in problems with self-interaction. *Physical Review D, 45*(6), 1989.

Parker, A. (2013, June). Parapsychology's secret, best kept a secret? Responding to the Millar Challenge. *Journal of Nonlocality, 2*(1).

Price, H. (1996). *Time's arrow and Archimedes' point: New directions for the physics of time*. Oxford: Oxford University Press.

Roney-Dougal, S. M., Solfvin, J., & Fox, J. (2008). An exploration of degree of meditation attainment in relation to psychic awareness with Tibetan Buddhists. *Journal of Scientific Exploration, 22*(2), 161–178.

Shimony, A. (1992). Conceptual foundations of quantum mechanics. *New Physics*, 373.

Singer, W. (1999). Neuronal synchrony: A versatile code for the definition of relations? *Neuron, 24*, 49–65.

Soon, C. S., Brass, M., Heinze, H. J., & Haynes, J. D. (2008). Unconscious determinants of free decisions in the human brain. *Nature Neuroscience, 11*, 543–545.

Spatt, J. (2002). Déjà vu: Possible parahippocampal mechanisms. *Journal of Neuropsychiatry and Clinical Neurosciences, 14*(1), 6–10.

Walach, H. (2014). Mind-matter interactions: On the rollercoaster from data to theory and back again. *Proceedings of the 10th Bial symposium* (in press).

Walker, E. H. (1972). Consciousness in the quantum theory of measurement, Parts I and II. *Journal for the Study of Consciousness, 5*, 46–63, 257–276.

Walker, E. H. (1975). Foundations of paraphysical and parapsychological phenomena. In L. Oteri (Ed.), *Quantum physics and parapsychology*, pp. 1–53. New York: Parapsychology Foundation.

Wheeler J. A., & Feynman, R. P. (1945). Interaction with the absorber as the mechanism of radiation. *Reviews of Modern Physics, 17*, 157.

Chapter 9

Activational Model of ESP

Zoltán Vassy

If the mechanism of ESP operation is analogous to normal perception, that is, the percipient senses the target by ESP in some trials but produces only chance guesses in others, then the theory of probability predicts a marked asymmetry between the results of positive-aim and negative-aim sessions in forced-choice ESP experiments. It is a mystery that asymmetry was never found experimentally. A model of ESP operation is presented here in which chance guessing and ESP are combined in the same way in each trial, predicting results in accord with empirical data. The model can be generalized to free-response experiments and spontaneous ESP experiences as well.

Conceptually, the activational model of ESP is straightforward and is based upon results from neuroscience with regard to decision making in choosing one option from a few competing options. Usher and McClelland (2001) show that there are accumulators in the brain, one each for each option, and they compete with each other by their levels of activation. As shown in this chapter, it is possible to insert into a computer-based simulation of these accumulators a bit of ESP as one of the free parameters and then test the results against ESP experiments with Zener cards. The data shown in this chapter have an output metric with a value of 1.05, whereas the same output metric from the neuroscience-based computation is 1.034. This appears to provide a neurological basis for the mysterious lack of predicted asymmetry in the observed data.

NEGATIVE-AIM FORCED-CHOICE ESP EXPERIMENTS: AN EXPECTED ASYMMETRY WITH THE CORRESPONDING POSITIVE-AIM CASE

An ESP experiment is called *forced choice* if there is a finite set of possible, known target symbols and the task in any trial is to choose that symbol that has been selected by some random process. The best-known example is the use of Zener cards, where the symbols are circle, star, waves, cross, and square. A negative-aim forced-choice experiment is similar, with the only difference being that the task is to *avoid* the selected symbol rather than to choose it.

As it was noted long ago by Thouless (1972, pp. 105–106), a subject who can consistently produce a certain rate of excess hits in a usual (that is, positive-aim) Zener card experiment is expected to produce a much smaller rate of excess "successful avoidances" in a corresponding negative-aim experiment. Let us use a simple numerical example to show this.

Suppose that the number of trials in a run is 100, the chance probability of hitting in any trial is 1/5, and the actual number of hits, which a talented subject can do, is 28 per run on the average. These 28 hits come partly from chance, partly from ESP. It can easily be calculated that if the number of ESP hits is 10 in a typical run, then the number of expected chance hits will be $(100 - 10)/5 = 18$; the sum of this number of ESP hits and the $100/5 = 20$ chance hits will then be just 28. From this, we can conclude that our subject is capable of "sensing" the identity of the actual target in 10 trials per run. What will happen in corresponding negative-aim runs with the same subject and the same conditions? The subject again senses 10 targets correctly on average and will successfully avoid them. From the remaining 90 trials, she avoids the target by chance in $90 \times 4/5 = 72$ trials on the average. Therefore, her average number of successful avoidances will be $10 + 72 = 82$. The expected number of successful avoidances by pure chance is 80, so the excess number is 2, only one-fourth of the excess hits in the corresponding positive-aim case.

In general, let us assume that the ESP percipient successfully identifies the target in some trials, while in all other trials, the result is determined only by chance. Therefore, we can define three types of events: hit by perception, hit by chance, and miss by chance. Both chance events are independent of the event "hit by ESP perception" because any chance event, by definition, is insensitive to what other events occur. The event "hit by ESP perception" and the event "hit by chance" are not mutually exclusive because the occurrence of the former does not rule out that the latter also occurs, again because a chance event occurs independently of anything else.

Therefore, we can define the probability of a chance hit, denoted by p_0, the probability of a hit by perception, denoted by p_{perc}, and the actual probability of a hit, which will be denoted by p in the experiment.

For example, $p_0 = 1/5$ in the most typical forced-choice experiments with Zener cards. Since the event "hit by ESP perception" and the event "hit by chance" are not mutually exclusive, we cannot express p as the sum of p_{perc} and p_0. However, we can determine p by noticing that the event of a miss can occur only if neither the event "hit by ESP perception" nor the event "hit by chance" occurs. The probability of the joint occurrence of two statistically independent events is equal to the product of the probabilities of the constituting events. The probability $1 - p$ of an actual miss will then be the product of the probability $1 - p_{perc}$ of the lack of hit by ESP perception, and the probability $1 - p_0$ of a chance miss:

$$1 - p = (1 - p_{perc})(1 - p_0)$$

From this equation we immediately get

$$p = p_{perc} + p_0 - p_0 p_{perc}$$

From Equation 2, the excess hit probability $p - p_0$ is

$$p - p_0 = p_{perc} (1 - p_0).$$

In the positive-aim sessions with Zener cards, $1 - p_0$ is equal to .8, so the excess hit probability is $.8 p_{perc}$. In the corresponding negative-aim sessions with the same subject and the same circumstances, p_{perc} is expected to be the same, $1 - p_0$ is equal to .2, so the excess hit probability is $.2 p_{perc}$. The expected ratio between the excess hit rate in the positive-aim sections and that in the negative-aim sections is $.8 p_{perc} / .2 p_{perc} = 4$. Here is the asymmetry in general that could be seen in the numerical example.

It may be worthwhile to make more explicit the conditions of the asymmetry between the results of the positive-aim and the negative-aim sessions. The laws of probability that were applied in the foregoing derivation are valid if we can define separate events for a hit by ESP perception and for a hit by chance. More generally, *if there are trials in which only chance events occur, and there are others when something else than chance occurs*, then all steps of the derivation are valid and the expected ratio between the positive-aim and the negative-aim excess hit rates will be 4. This conclusion does not depend on the specific (still unknown) mechanism of ESP operation, whatever it may be.

Data from Negative-Aim Experiments

Ratte (1961), Schmidt (1969a,b), and Thouless (1972) published data on forced-choice ESP experiments containing both positive-aim and negative-aim sessions. These studies used the same subjects, targets, and procedures in both kinds of sessions. Seven of these experiments, which

Table 9.1
Trials, Hits, and Excess Hit Rate Ratios in Nine Experiments with Both Positive-Aim and Negative-Aim Parts

Positive aim	Positive aim	Negative aim	Negative aim	Ratio of excess hit rates	Chance hit rate	Reference
Trials	Hits	Trials	Hits	(pos.) / (neg.)		
2500	547	2500	464	1.31	.2	Ratte
2500	524	2500	467	0.73	.2	Ratte
2500	554	2500	472	1.93	.2	Ratte
2144	590	2702	626	1.37	.25	Schmidt a
5672	1541	4328	956	0.75	.25	Schmidt b
1300	316	1300	182	0.72	.2	Thouless

Note: Mean of ratio of excess hit rates = 1.05.

gave significant results, are included here. There were two nonsignificant experiments also, but their results are not relevant to the present analysis because if only chance operates, then the excess hit ratios are expected to be the same anyway.

The results are shown in Table 9.1. The term "excess hit rate" refers to the difference between the measured hit rate and the chance hit rate for both negative- and positive-aim in the appropriate direction.

The ratios between the excess hit rates in positive-aim and corresponding negative-aim sessions were clustered around 1. It is quite obvious that the deviations from mean chance expectation tend to be the same in the two kinds of sessions. This result contradicts the asymmetry that was derived in the previous section: when the chance hit probability was .25, the expected ratio (pos.)/(neg.) should have been 3, and when the chance hit probability was .20, that ratio should have been 4.

It can be noted also that if the positive-aim Zener card experiments tended to give many more deviations from chance expectation than corresponding negative-aim experiments, then the asymmetry between them should have been manifested in the asymmetry between the strengths of psi hitting and psi missing in general. (The term "psi missing" is used for the situation in which an experiment produces significant negative deviation from chance expectation.) The simple reason is that psi missing is equivalent to the tendency of unintended avoidance of the actual target, so its mathematical properties are the same as the mathematical properties of deliberate avoidance. To my knowledge, no researcher ever observed such a marked asymmetry between psi hitting and psi missing in Zener card experiments that would have hinted at a ratio equal to 4 between the deviations from chance in the two cases.

Let us remember the condition of the mathematically derived asymmetry between the results of positive-aim and negative-aim experiments. There are trials in which only chance events occur, and there are others when something other than chance occurs. Since this asymmetry does not show up in the actual experiments, this condition is not fulfilled: We should not assume that the percipient correctly identifies the target symbol in some trials by ESP and in other trials by chance. What happens in her brain is always the same, and still she hits more often than what can be expected by chance. Therefore, we should look for a mechanism of ESP that works in the same way in all trials.

The Activational Model

What seems to be certain in any forced-choice ESP experiment is that a competition takes place between the brain representations of the possible symbols in the brain of the percipient. The winner of that competition becomes the chosen symbol. In psychology, there is a widely accepted model of choice from several options, the so-called *stochastic, leaky, competing integrator model,* or *stochastic leaky integrator model with lateral inhibition* by Usher and McClelland (2001), which is in accord with all empirical findings as well as with known characteristics of brain anatomy and physiology. If ESP is included in that model, provided that there is no difference between the trials in a forced choice ESP experiment, then we can hope that the theoretical predications of the model will also conform to the experimental data.

The basic characteristics of the Usher-McClelland model are as follows:

a. An accumulator belongs to each option, collecting its score in the competition. At the decision point, the winner will be that option whose accumulator has the highest score. In neural terms, the score is represented by the activation level of a given accumulator.

b. All accumulators get some external input. Let us denote them by I_i, where the index i refers to the ith option. In a completely unbiased competition, the external inputs have the same magnitude; this case corresponds to the task of choosing from the options in a completely random way, and the external inputs then represent a uniform drive to choose.

c. The accumulators also receive an additional, randomly fluctuating input denoted by ξ. (This makes the competition possible because otherwise, all options would have always the same score.) The amplitude of this random input is assumed to have normal distribution, characterized by its mean and variance. This type of distribution is intelligible because its stochastic input probably comes from several sources.

d. The activation level of each accumulator tends to decrease in time spontaneously, the rate of decrease being proportional to its actual activation level. The term "leaky" refers to this feature in the name of the model.

e. All accumulators receive a recurrent excitation from themselves, partly compensating for spontaneous leaking. The rate of increase resulting from that excitation is proportional to the actual activation level, just as is the rate of decrease for leakage. Therefore, a "net leakage constant" is defined, which comprises both leaking and recurrent excitation, because these two terms behave mathematically the same way. The net leakage constant is denoted by k and is assumed to be the same for all accumulators.

f. Each accumulator inhibits all others. The rate of this lateral inhibition is proportional to the actual activation level of the accumulator, which sends the inhibition. The inhibition constant is assumed to be the same for all accumulator pairs and is denoted by β.

g. The activation level of any accumulator cannot decrease below zero. This possibility follows from the presence of inhibitions, but it is obvious that no activation level of any neural structure can be negative.

Now, ESP can be included in the model in a quite straightforward way: Let us assume that *ESP helps the actual target symbol of winning the competition* described earlier in this discussion. It means that the accumulator of that symbol receives a small excess input. Mathematically, this help to the mth option can be represented by an increased level of I_m. Since the input to the accumulators is assumed to be in the form of neural activation, the ESP help means an excess activation to the representation of the actual target. Hence the name "activational model."

In this model, the outcome of any trial will be determined by the interplay between chance and ESP. Sometimes, the ESP help is not needed for a hit because the neural representation of the actual target wins anyway by chance. Sometimes, the ESP help is enough to push the representation of the actual target to a winning position at the moment of the decision. Sometimes one or more representations other than that of the actual target are so much ahead that the help of ESP is not enough. In the first two cases, there will be a hit, while in the third case there will be a miss. The important point is that there are no distinguishable "chance hits" and "ESP hits"; all trials are equivalent, and the effect of ESP is only that the probability of a hit increases *in the same way* at all trials. Although the basic mystery of how ESP accomplishes its help is not solved in this model, the paradox of the positive-aim/negative-aim symmetry is solved, as can be seen in the next section.

THE RELATIONSHIP BETWEEN THE EXCESS HIT RATES IN POSITIVE-AIM AND NEGATIVE-AIM EXPERIMENTS: NUMERICAL SIMULATIONS BASED ON THE ACTIVATION MODEL OF ESP

In the simulations, an approximation was introduced to make the computation much simpler without biasing the results. The distribution of the random input was assumed to be uniform, instead of normal. The simulations involved several dozen steps at least, during which the contributions of the random inputs added up, and because of the well known central limit theorem, the value of a random variable resulting from many additive steps becomes normally distributed even if the distribution of the individual terms is different from normal.

Based on the assumptions introduced in points a–g in the previous section, if we denote the activation level of accumulator i at the jth step of the simulation by $a_i(j)$, then its level at the next step can be computed according to the following expression:

$$a_i(j+1) = a_i(j) + I_i - ka_i(j) - \beta \sum_{k \neq i} a_k(j) + \xi.$$

where the various symbol definition can be found in items a–g above, and if $a_i(j+1)$ is less than zero, then from Equation 4 above, then $a_i(j+1)$ must be set to zero because no activation levels can be negative according to step g above in the Usher-McClelland model. Or:

$$a_i(j+1) = 0.$$

In the summation of Equation 4, the index k goes through all indices that are different from i.

The additional effect of ESP in positive-aim sessions is modeled by a small additional input to the activation of the accumulator belonging to the actual target symbol. Let us call it *positive bias*. In negative-aim sessions, a corresponding amount, called *negative bias,* was subtracted from the activation of that accumulator.

As part of a simulation, both biases were administered at each step of the accumulation process and were defined in percent of the common driving input. The computations were carried out for 10 levels of bias, from .1 to 1%, in steps of .1%. The coefficients for (net) leakage and lateral inhibition were also defined in percent of the common driving input. The value of the leakage coefficient was 0.25, and the value of the lateral inhibition coefficient was 0.05. The random component of the input had uniform distribution with zero mean; its range extended from minus to plus for the amount of the driving input. Several other combinations of these parameters were tried, with the condition of producing realistic hit rates for a typical positive-aim ESP experiment; the ratios between excess hit rates for positive-aim and negative-aim runs were practically the same in all combinations, so the results shown in Tables 9.2 through 4 are characteristic for any combination of parameters.

The simulated experiments consisted of N = 10,000 trials per run. The chance hit probability was .2. All individual trials were simulated by Equations 4 and 5. The winner symbol was chosen after a variable number of accumulation steps between 20 and 160; this number of accumulation steps is called *decision time*. The output variable was the run score, that is, the number of hits in each run, denoted by h. From that, the excess hit rate denoted by x was computed, that is, $x_+ = h/N - 0.2$ for positive-aim runs, and $x_- = 0.2 - h/N$ for negative-aim runs. Table 9.2 shows the computed values of x_+ as a function of decision time, measured in accumulation steps, and also as a function of bias, measured in thousandths of the common driving input. Table 9.3 shows the computed values of x_- in the same way.

Table 9.4 shows the ratios between positive-aim excess hit rates and their corresponding negative-aim excess hit rates at the same level of bias, averaged for the values of decision time.

The mean ratio is 1.05. This is in accord with the population value of 1 and is not in accord with the population value of 4. In other words, the simulation has given symmetric results between positive-aim and negative-aim runs, just like the experimental data of 0.996 shown in Table 9.1.

DISCUSSION

Memory as a vehicle of making ESP-originated information conscious was suggested earlier by René Warcollier, William Roll, and Harvey Irwin (summarized in Broughton, 2006). Warcollier, after analyzing his own experiments on picture telepathy, explicitly stated, "there is no carrying of the visual impression from the agent to the percipient" (Warcollier, 1939, p. 133). This conclusion is the same as what follows from the results of negative-aim forced-choice experiments. Roll contrasted the mental process associated with normal sensory perception with that associated with extrasensory perception and stated that the latter involved only memory contents of the percipient (Roll, 1966; Broughton, 2006). Irwin analyzed both spontaneous cases and experimental results, and found that a process analogous with normal sensory perception was not likely (Irwin, 1999; Broughton 2006). The activational model presented here has several antecedents in the literature of parapsychology, converging to the same conclusion from different angles. We still do not know how ESP operates in the brain, but if these converging conclusions are correct, then at least we know better what to look for in search of its mechanism.

Table 9.2
Excess Hit Rates x_+ in Positive-Aim Runs

Bias	Decision time in steps								Mean
	20	40	60	80	100	120	140	160	
1	0.0001	0.004	0.0095	−0.001	0.0055	0.0081	0.0012	0.003	0.0038
2	0.0001	0.0049	0.0065	0.0054	0.0046	0.0044	0.0084	0.0091	0.0054
3	0.0072	0.0125	0.0028	0.01	0.0078	0.0145	0.0095	0.0173	0.0102
4	0.0065	0.0085	0.0071	0.0179	0.0088	0.0118	0.0101	0.0145	0.0107
5	0.0101	0.0143	0.013	0.011	0.0167	0.0232	0.0191	0.0144	0.0152
6	0.008	0.0211	0.0217	0.0152	0.0198	0.029	0.0181	0.0231	0.0195
7	0.0126	0.0143	0.016	0.0162	0.0212	0.0277	0.0286	0.0243	0.0201
8	0.0135	0.0194	0.0277	0.0233	0.0265	0.0223	0.0288	0.0268	0.0235
9	0.0097	0.0189	0.0262	0.0325	0.0296	0.0357	0.0342	0.0372	0.0280
10	0.0142	0.0221	0.0274	0.0351	0.035	0.0344	0.0394	0.0441	0.0315

Table 9.3
Excess Hit Rates x_ In Negative-Aim Runs

Bias	Decision time in steps							Mean
	20	40	60	80	100	120	140	160	
1	0.005	−0.001	0.0031	0.0015	0.0064	0.0018	0.0091	−0.0003	0.0032
2	0.004	0.0028	0.0056	0.0105	0.0114	0.0107	0.0063	0.0038	0.0069
3	0.0112	0.0029	0.0092	0.0109	0.0071	0.0025	0.0052	0.01	0.0074
4	0.0051	0.0071	0.0128	0.02	0.0161	0.0113	0.0141	0.0125	0.0124
5	0.0039	0.0155	0.0127	0.0188	0.0245	0.0146	0.0233	0.0202	0.0167
6	0.0182	0.0201	0.0184	0.0138	0.0262	0.0194	0.023	0.01	0.0186
7	0.0156	0.018	0.0171	0.023	0.0225	0.0255	0.0161	0.0271	0.0206
8	0.011	0.0137	0.0243	0.0255	0.0268	0.0312	0.0246	0.0339	0.0239
9	0.01	0.0272	0.0272	0.0231	0.0307	0.0319	0.0274	0.0291	0.0258
10	0.0159	0.0156	0.03	0.0247	0.0311	0.0342	0.036	0.036	0.0279

Table 9.4
Ratios between x_+ and x_-

Bias	1	2	3	4	5	6	7	8	9	10
Ratio	1.18	0.788	1.383	0.861	0.912	1.046	0.976	0.986	1.0840	1.126

The symmetry between the results of positive-aim and negative-aim ESP experiments is probably one of the most reliable facts in scientific parapsychology. Several other findings are considered suspicious because of the possible psychological and/or even parapsychological influence of the experimenter, favoring her hypothesis. However, negative-aim experiments were never done with the purpose of comparing them to their positive-aim counterparts, and their actual experimenters did not seem to notice anything unusual about the symmetry they found. Therefore, it is highly unlikely that an inherently 4:1 or 3:1 ratio between the excess hit rates of positive-aim and negative-aim runs would have been changed to the ratio of 1:1 by an unconscious experimenter effect.

The activational model outlined here can apply to forced-choice and free-response experiments as well. When a remote viewing subject, for example, wants to obtain impressions of a place where an agent is located, a wide set of representations of visual elements are competing in her brain for becoming conscious. That situation is very similar to the competition of representations of ESP cards or other forced-choice targets, with the only difference that the competitors are not restricted to members of a predetermined group. The Usher-McClelland model seems to be just as adequate.

In the case of spontaneous ESP experiences, the experiencer usually does not want to choose anything; an impression just pops up in her mind. In terms of the Usher-McClelland model, there is no universal drive input in that case to the accumulators corresponding to the various options. That is, the term I_i is missing from Equation (4). However, this does not prevent the model from being applicable. The excitation level of an accumulator can reach the threshold of making its represented mental content conscious even without a universal drive input, provided that there is enough input from other sources. It apparently happens quite often: people do have spontaneous impressions (parapsychological or otherwise) when a mental representation becomes conscious without any intent.

The activational model does not necessarily imply that there is no brain representation of the psi-originated information, for example, the actual target symbol in ESP card experiments. It is possible that there is a representation, but it behaves differently from the behavior of perceptional representations: it does not become itself conscious but only helps the brain representation that corresponds to the same symbol as itself. Since all trials are as equivalent here as in the representation-free activational model, the same symmetry holds between positive-aim and negative-aim excess hit rates.

There is, however, a general argument against the existence of such brain representations. Consider a case when the same event is perceived by a person several times, an event that has some emotional significance for him or her. This event can be as trivial as hearing a mosquito buzz around the bed in the night, or catching the sight of an attractive person of the favored sex on the street. We know from the literature that precognition exists, and more specifically, that precognition of events happening in the immediate future can elicit an emotional response a few seconds prior to its occurrence (Bierman & Radin, 1997; Spottiswoode & May, 2014/2003), although the situation may be more complicated, as is argued in May, Paulinyi, and Vassy (2014/2005). Now suppose that the brain mechanism of that precognitive response involves the formation of a specific neural representation of the coming event. That representation will then precede the perception of the real event repeatedly, which is the typical situation of the well-known classical (Pavlovian) conditioning: the representation of the precognitive impression gets associated with the perception of the event. The result will be the gradual strengthening of the precognitive response. Needless to say, this does not happen in reality; if it did, precognition would be a normal fact in psychology and in everyday life, instead of being considered "paranormal." In addition, in an experiment (Vassy, 2005) where a Pavlovian conditioned reflex was intended to develop between telepathic messages and electric shocks, the conditioned response (measured by monitoring skin electric conductance) did not stabilize after the initial buildup. Psychological investigations has shown that in the human brain, any conditioned stimulus becomes easily associated with any unconditioned stimulus (Schwartz, 1989). Therefore, if it does not happen with precognitive conditioned stimuli, it means that precognitive stimuli probably do not get represented in the brain. This again corroborates the activational model as opposed to the classical concept of ESP, which addresses it in analogy with normal perception.

Acknowledgment. I am indebted to Dr. Jiri Wackermann, who directed my attention to the literature of decision behavior, and Dr. Edwin C. May, who suggested useful corrections for making the chapter more readable.

REFERENCES

Bierman, D. J., & Radin, D. I. (1997). Anomalous anticipatory response on randomized future conditions. *Perceptual and Motor Skills, 84,* 689–690.

Broughton, R. S. (2006). Memory, emotion, and the receptive psi process. *Journal of Parapsychology, 70*, 255–274.

Irwin, H. J. (1999). *An introduction to parapsychology* (3rd ed.). Jefferson, NC: McFarland.

May, E. C., Paulinyi, T., & Vassy, Z. (2014/2005). Anomalous anticipatory skin response to acoustic stimuli: Experimental results and speculation about a mechanism. In E. C. May & S. B. Marwaha (Eds.), *Anomalous cognition: Remote viewing research and theory*, pp. 158–171. Jefferson, NC: McFarland.

Ratte, R. J. (1960). Three exploratory studies of ESP in a game situation. *Journal of Parapsychology, 25*, 175–184.

Roll, W. G. (1966). ESP and memory. *International Journal of Neuropsychiatry, 2*, 505–521.

Schmidt, H. (1969a). Clairvoyance tests with a machine. *Journal of Parapsychology, 33*, 300–306.

Schmidt, H. (1969b). Precognition of a quantum process. *Journal of Parapsychology, 33*, 99–108.

Schwartz, B. (1989). *Psychology of learning and behavior.* New York and London: W. W. Norton and Company.

Spottiswoode, S. J. P., & May, E. C. (2014/2003). Skin conductance prestimulus response: Analyses, artifacts and a pilot study. In E. C. May & S. B. Marwaha (Eds.), *Anomalous cognition: Remote viewing research and theory*, pp. 131–151. Jefferson, NC: McFarland.

Thouless, R. H. (1972). *From anecdote to experiment in psychical research.* London: Routledge and Kegan Paul.

Usher, M., & McClelland, J. L. (2001). The time course of perceptual choice: The leaky, competing accumulator model. *Psychological Review, 108*, 550–592.

Vassy, Z. (2004). A study of telepathy by classical conditioning. *Journal of Parapsychology, 68*, 323–350.

Warcollier, R. (1939). *Experiments in telepathy.* London: George Allen & Unwin.

Chapter 10

Experimenter Psi: A View of Decision Augmentation Theory

Edwin C. May

The issue of whose psi is it in experiments has plagued researchers since the 1970s (Broughton, Millar, Beloff, & Wilson, 1977; Broughton, 1978; Kennedy & Taddonio, 1976; Kennedy & Haight, 1978; Stanford, Zenhausern, Taylor, & Dwyer, 1975). The idea is as straightforward as it is troubling. Suppose a complex experiment protocol calls for a physiological measurement when, unlike traditional studies, the stimulus is presented *after* a response has been measured. The cherished hypothesis here is that the participant's autonomic nervous system responds via psi in advance of the stimulus (Bierman & Radin, 1997; May, Paulinyi, & Vassy, 2014/2005; May, & Spottiswoode, 2003; Radin, 1997). There is, however, a different explanation that could yield the exact same outcome—experimenter psi. To illustrate this point, imagine a fair coin (i.e., the probability of landing heads is exactly 0.5) that is flipped 10,000 times, and each time, someone writes down on a long piece of paper the result for each flip. So the beginning may look something like H T H H T T T T H T .... Suppose the task is to walk along the paper and using one's eyes mark a spot to begin counting flips such that for the next 500 there are statistically too many heads than would be expected by chance alone. By the very nature of true randomness, this would be a simple task, indeed. In this case, there is no psi involved, nor would the real coin flipper be affected in any way. But now, consider an electronic version of a "coin" flipper (a computer) that does the same thing. In a psi experiment with this apparatus, a participant is told to "cause," ostensibly by PK, the electronic coin flipper to have statistically more heads than are expected by chance. The experimenter (or participant) presses a button that starts the device flipping 500 coins. Let us further assume that it appears that the next 500 flips have statistically a significant amount of excess heads. The cherished hypothesis here is that the participant used PK to "force" the coin flipper to produce too many heads. However, the experimenter-psi hypothesis holds that the experimenter (or participant) uses precognition (not PK) to wait to begin counting heads (by pressing the button) until the next 500 flips would be statistically deviant, but the total sequence remains unperturbed and random. This leads to the exact same result as in the aforementioned putative PK case except the coin flipper has not been perturbed in any way, and therefore what looks like PK is just another example of precognition.

Getting back to the physiology experiment in which the cherished hypothesis is that the participant is responding in advance of a future stimulus. An alternative, then, is that that the experimenter uses psi to press the start button optimally to capture unperturbed and random physiological fluctuations in order to mimic the cherished hypothesis. In such a study, May, Paulinyi, and Vassy (2014/2005) were able to demonstrate that experimenter psi drove the result rather than the hypothesis that participants were responding in advance of startle stimuli. We note that when the participant presses the start button, it cannot be experimenter psi by definition, but nonetheless, the more important question is what is the mechanism—is the response due to the cherished hypothesis or psi-mediated button pressing to mimic the cherished hypothesis?

The first attempt to understand experimenter psi quantitatively from a psychological perspective was the psi-mediated instrumental response (PMIR) model (Stanford, 1974a,b, 1976). PMIR proposes that an organism nonintentionally uses psi to scan its environment for need-relevant objects or events or for information crucially related to such events and that when such information is obtained, the organism tends to act in ways that are instrumental in satisfying its needs in relation to the particular object or event in question. While Stanford (1974a) outlines nine experimentally testable assumptions for the "psi-mediated instrumental response model" (PMIR model), a few are repeated here for emphasis—using Stanford's numbering:

1. In the presence of a particular need, the organism uses psi (ESP), as well as sensory means, to scan its environment for objects and events relevant to that need and for information crucially related to such objects or events.

2. Preparation for or production of PMIR often involves such changes as motivational or emotional arousal, attention-focusing responses, and other preparation for response.
3. All else being equal, the strength of the disposition toward PMIR is directly and positively related to: (a) the importance or strength of the need(s) in question, (b) the degree of need-relevance of the need-relevant object or event, and (c) the closeness in time of the potential encounter with the need-relevant object or event.
4. PMIR tends to be accomplished in the most economical way possible.

As Stanford (1974a, p. 43) remarks with regard to the nine PMIR assumptions, "Some of the assumptions already have considerable experimental support; some are untested. All require further investigation."

I will illustrate PMIR with an anecdote involving my own experience. Many years before cell phones, I was teaching physics at City College of San Francisco when I received a phone call from an East Coast colleague who was unexpectedly in town for a conference. He suggested we meet at the curb just outside his hotel at 5 p.m. in downtown San Francisco right in the middle of rush hour. Sitting in my office about five miles away at 4:30 p.m., I really did not want to go at that time to be caught up in the gridlock of traffic, so I procrastinated for an hour doing administrative work to support my teaching job. Finally, knowing my colleague would be upset with me for being an hour late, I drove to the hotel and parked at the curb. Much to my surprise, my colleague rushed out the door, climbed into the car, and was breathlessly full of apologies for *him* being an hour late! Had I showed up at the original time, I would have had a real problem looking for a place to park and would have wondered where my colleague was. This account is precisely what Stanford meant by his PMIR model.

More than psychological or philosophical/psychological musing, Stanford outlined how his PMIR model could also apply to PK (Stanford, 1974b). All through this paper, Stanford acknowledges that applying PMIR to PK is more speculative, in that the model is primarily a psychological one—an organism fulfilling some need. Two examples are of note. The first is from what is called nonrecurrent spontaneous psychokinesis. I quote from Stanford (1974b, p. 323):

A well-known example of such a case is the loud, explosive sound which seemed to come, twice, from a bookcase in the presence of Freud and Jung when they were rather heatedly arguing about the occurrence of psi phenomena (Jung, 1963). In this instance the phenomenon certainly seemed to have need-relevance-at least for Jung, who was advocating the reality of psi phenomena in the face of opposition from Freud.

The second example comes from recurrent spontaneous psychokinesis (RSPK). Again quoting from Stanford:

> Parapsychologists today consider that most RSPK ("poltergeist" phenomena) are unconsciously produced by a living individual and subserve his own needs including, often, a need for the release of pent-up feelings which cannot easily find more open expression. ... Such investigations have repeatedly shown that a "central person," or "agent," is involved, a person whose presence seems required for the occurrence of the phenomena. (1974b, p. 325)

By "poltergeist" phenomena, Stanford means examples of what appears to be macro-PK; that is, objects flying around the room, doors slamming, and the like. To get a feel for what this is like, watch a popularization of such phenomena in the 1982 movie *Poltergeist*, the screenplay for which was written by Spielberg and others.

As Stanford indicates above, even these dramatic events may be mediated by psychological needs of "agents" in the near environment. Often, these people are ostensibly troubled pre- or just post-pubescent teenagers who may feel threatened by the presence of a new infant in the family. For details of cases and circumstances, see Hastings (1978, 2013) and Krippner (2011).

The final point here is that even in remarkably large-scale phenomena, Stanford's PMIR model suggests that people are fulfilling some psychological need—a clear example of what in modern times we might label as experimenter psi.

An Observation of Random Number Generator (RNG) Data

In a typical RNG experiment, the hardware consists of a true (as opposed to a computer algorithm) random number generate that produces a stream of binary bits (i.e., the electronic "coin" flipper in the previous example). A research participant is asked to use PK to enforce more binary 1s than would be expected. A variety of statistical measures are used to assess the degree to which this might have occurred.

The seminal paper that kicked off an ongoing research paradigm was entitled, oddly enough, "Precognition of a Quantum Process" (Schmidt, 1969). Schmidt was suggesting that observed deviations of the RNG data arose not from PK but rather because of precognition—similar to the coin flipping analogies. However, in his very next paper, he reconsidered, and the term "micro-PK" was born (Schmidt, 1970). The idea of micro-PK came about because the putative PK effects influenced the individual binary bits instead of, say, moving the apparatus across the lab by PK—macro-PK. The concept of micro-PK became the hallmark of RNG studies, and that idea has lasted ever since. The one exception to this rule comes from the now closed Princeton Engineering Anomalies Research (PEAR) laboratories wherein their later claim was that the micro-PK happens not at the individual bit level but at the variance of a collection of bits (Nelson, 2006). (I will address this point in detail later in the chapter.) This view represents a change from the individual bit, micro-PK that PEAR and the rest of the community shared since the 1970s. For example, the dean of engineering at Princeton University and head of the former PEAR lab, Robert Jahn, illustrates the general point of view (Jahn, 1982, p.149):

> Over this large data base [PEAR's RNG data], there arises some quantitative statistical regularity in the PK process, epitomized by the mean slopes of the cumulative deviations ... [which can be] traced back to the elemental binary samples, these values imply *directed inversions* [emphasis added] from chance behavior of about one or one and a half bits in every one thousand or, alternatively, of 0.2 or 0.3 bits per trial.

The mean shift of the parent distribution remained deeply embedded in the PEAR zeitgeist. Jahn, Dunne, and Nelson (1987), writing in the first issue of the *Journal of Scientific Exploration*, emphasized in text and in graphics the mean shift in all their RNG work—they call the devices random event generators (REGs).

It is beyond the scope of this chapter to go further into an ongoing debate about the mechanisms for RNG-PK, but the details can be found elsewhere (Bancel, 2011; May & Spottiswoode, 2011a,b; Nelson, 2011).

Nonetheless, for the vast majority of research on perturbation of random number generators, it was assumed that the micro-PK nomenclature meant a PK-mediated force per individual bit. If this is true, it has direct consequence with regard to the data at large.

DECISION AUGMENTATION THEORY

The components of decision augmentation theory (DAT) are as follows:

- *Proposition.* This differs little from that proposed by Stanford (1974a). That is, we add to the complex number of variables with regard to decision making in general an additional, albeit weak, psi component to "bias" the decision process toward more favorable outcomes.

In PK experiments, for example, DAT suggests that rather than mind influencing some target system, an array of precognition-mediated decisions by the experimenter and/or participant are made to mimic PK.

- *Mechanism*. Precognition.
- *Domain*. All models have a domain in which they are apropos. For example, the physics theory of special relatively is a must to consider only for speeds approaching that of the speed of light but can be safely ignored at human-scale speeds. DAT *may* be important in any experimental study in any discipline that uses statistical inference to come to some conclusion.
- *Falsifiable*. Falsifiable in this context means that psi-mediated decisions that may mimic a cherished hypothesis can be shown to be incorrect. As I will show later in this chapter, DAT is unfalsifiable for a single point measure—say, collecting RNG data at only one sequence length. However, the model provides explicit measures to determine which of two competing mechanisms (i.e., PK or precognition) is a better fit to the data by using two or more measures. For example, in an RNG study, DAT requires taking data at two (or more) sequence lengths.
- *Statistical*. In experimental science, especially that involving human participants, there are two distributions to consider: the parent distribution—the way nature *actually* is; and the sampling distribution—the collection of data to estimate what the parameters are for the parent distribution. In psi experiments, there are four possibilities:
  1. Nothing is happening. Mean chance expectation is confirmed.
  2. The parent distribution is perturbed, and the sampling distribution is a fair approximation to it—an interaction is implied.
  3. The parent distribution is unperturbed, but the sampling distribution is biased—DAT.
  4. The parent distribution is perturbed, and the sampling distribution is biased.
- *Testable*. The model provides a number of ways to test its concepts. By using a multipoint measure (e.g., two different RNG sequence lengths resulting from single button presses), then a basic regression analysis easily provides statistical evidence to support or not a mean shift in the parent distribution. As will be shown later in this discussion, additional tests result from manipulating the number of decision points in a study.

Random Number Generator Data

In binary RNG studies, it had been known for years that the z-scores should scale as the square root of the number of binary bits if micro-PK were operating at the individual bit level. The formula for this scaling is given by:

$$Z_2 = \sqrt{\frac{n_2}{n_1}}\, Z_1;$$

that is, accumulate four times as much data to double the z-score. (Set $n_2 = 4 \times n_1$ in the equation above.) The problem we all had was that statistically, the z-scores were independent of the number of binary bits in the RNG sequence. David Saunders of MARS Measurement and Associates in private communication told us that this implies that the PK effect size would have to vary exactly as the inverse of the square root of the number of trials. Or since by definition:

$$Z = \sqrt{n} \times ES,$$

where n is the number of bits resulting from a single button press and ES is the effect size, then

$$ES \sim \frac{1}{\sqrt{n}}, \quad \text{then } Z = \text{constant.}$$

To develop DAT mathematically, we start with the idea that the mean of the parent distribution that initially is μ_0 (i.e., ½ for binary RNG studies) has been shifted by PK to a new value, μ_1. Because the majority of researchers thought micro-PK happened at the individual bit level, we assumed that only the mean has been shifted, and the variance of the parent distribution remains constant (σ_0^2). Then the PK effect size is given as:

$$\varepsilon_{pk} = \frac{(\mu_1 - \mu_0)}{\sigma_0}.$$

Under the assumption that the parent distribution is unperturbed and the sampling distribution is normal but biased, the resulting z-score is given by:

$$z \sim N\left(\mu_z, \sigma_z^2\right),$$

where the formula says that the z-score is normally distributed with a mean of μ_z and a variance of σ_z^2.

Table 10.1
Normal Parent Distribution

Quantity	MCE	Mechanism micro-PK	DAT
$E(z^2)$	1	$1 + n\varepsilon_{pk}^2$	$\mu_z^2 + \sigma_z^2$
$Var(z^2)$	2	$2\left(1 + 2n\varepsilon_{pk}^2\right)$	$2\left(\sigma_z^4 + 2\mu_z^2 + \sigma_z^2\right)$

ε_{pk} is the PK effect size, and μ_z and σ_z are the parameters of the sampling distribution.

The first attempt to cast these ideas into a formal mathematical context came with DAT's first name *psychoenergetic data selection* (May, Humphrey, & Hubbard, 1980). Later, however, the name was changed to *intuitive data sorting* (Utts, May, & Frivold, 1987) in which they examined RNG data to date and tried to fit the effect size with a $1/\sqrt{N}$ dependence. Finally, because neither of these names was appropriate, the name was changed to *decision augmentation theory*, which appeared to be closer to the observable. It is beyond the scope of this chapter to provide the mathematical details, and they can be found in the original paper (May, Utts, & Spottiswoode, 2014/1995); however, I will summarize the major points. Zoltán Vassy suggested in private communication that the DAT analyis should be done as a function of Z^2 rather than Z alone, since that would not only make the algebra simpler but also account for negative z-sores. Table 10.1 shows the results assuming a normal distribution for the parent distribution.

Table 10.2 shows the results of the computations assuming that the parent distribution is Binomial.

For large values of n, the PK mechanism is the same for both types of parent distributions. The important message here is that assuming PK manifests by shifting the mean of the parent distribution, then a test of RNG data becomes clear.

First, produce a scatter plot of RNG studies wherein the y-axis is the square of the z-scores for the study, and the x-axis is the number of binary bits that were accumulated from a single button press. Next, conduct

Table 10.2
Binomial Parent Distribution

Quantity	MCE	Mechanism micro-PK	DAT
$E(z^2)$	1	$1 + (n-1)\varepsilon_{pk}^2$	$\mu_z^2 + \sigma_z^2$
$Var(z^2)$	$2 - \frac{2}{n}$	$2\left(1 + 2n\varepsilon_{pk}^2\right)*$	$2\left(\sigma_z^4 + 2\mu_z^2\sigma_z^2\right)$

*The variance shown assumes $p_0 = .5$, $\sigma_0 = 0.5$, and $n \gg 1$.

a regression analysis of these data, or in physics terms, find the best-fit straight line through the data. Consider the following line:

$$Z^2 = Z_0^2 + b(n - \bar{n}),$$

where $\bar{n}$ is the mean of the various sequence lengths, b is the slope of the best fit line through the data, and z_0^2 is a constant and equal to the value of Z^2 at $n = \bar{n}$. As the first application of DAT, May, Spottiswoode, and Utts (2014/1995) analyzed 128 studies from the literature and found that the slope of the best fit line on this scatter plot was given by $b = (1.73 \pm 3.19) \times 10^{-6}$ ($t = 0.543$, $df = 126$, $p = .295$). (We purposely did not include the huge database from the PEAR labs in this analysis so as not to overwhelm the contributions of many different laboratories, worldwide.) That is, the one standard error in the estimate for the slope easily encompassed zero, and the fit was not significantly different from zero. This means that the data suggest that the PK effect size is zero (i.e., no PK). Yet, the intercept was significantly above mean chance expectation: $z_0^2 = 1.036 \pm 0.004$. The t score for the intercept being different from 1.0 was 9.1, $df = 126$, $ES = 0.63$, $p = 4.8 \ 10^{-20}$. In these 128 studies, two things are clear: there is strong evidence of a psi effect, yet at the same time, there is no evidence of a force / bit leading to the result.

In one RNG study, the evidence against PK was even stronger (May, Spottiswoode, & Utts, 2014/1995, p. 261). In that study, the hardware created random bits at a rate of *1,000* bits per second (i.e., a bit per millisecond). After a byte (eight bits) had been accumulated, it was sent to a computer while a second byte was being accumulated. This is called double buffering. In this way during a run, there was a continuous and uninterrupted stream of data, parsed as bytes, from the generator. Bit number four (starting at zero on the right) in each byte was designated as the PK target bit, and it was the single bit that was used to provide feedback to the participant, and it served as the basis for analysis. Since a byte is eight bits, each bit represented temporal pre- and posthistory surrounding the target bit of four and three milliseconds, respectively. May and colleagues argued that there was no known physiological mechanism that could volitionally be turned on or off in 1 millisecond. That is, all known biological processes in the human body are of the 10 to 250 millisecond time scale, which is much faster than the individual bit or even byte rates in the experiment. Therefore, they expected that the bits neighboring the target bit should be highly correlated or perhaps even 100% correlated under the PK hypothesis. Figure 10.1 shows the $\chi^2(df = 1)$ for all the correlations between bit four (target bit) with its neighbor bit three; bit four with its neighbor bit five; and neighbor bits three and five for all 33 individually significant runs. In this experiment, May and colleagues used sequential

Figure 10.1
Correlations of the target bit with its neighbors. The smooth curve is a nonparameter theoretical χ^2 fit to the observed correlations.

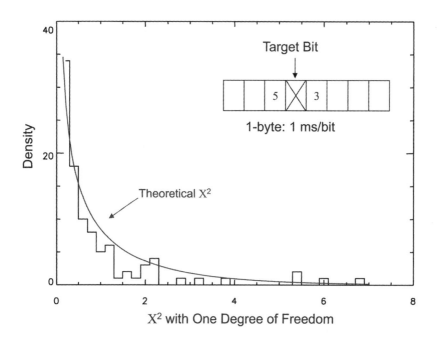

sampling, which enabled a valid way to tell if a given run was individually significant. It is beyond the scope of this chapter to describe the details of this single RNG study, but they can be found elsewhere (May, Humphrey, & Hubbard, 1980).

The histogram shows the χ^2 for the various correlations among the bits. The smooth curve is the no-parameter theoretical expectation under the null hypothesis of no correlations among the bits (Mann–Whitney–Wilcoxon test of the fit: $p = .193$). So, it is likely that no force of any type was applied to the random sources in this experiment.

Stouffer's Z DAT Test

One consequence of DAT is that more decision points in an experiment lead to stronger results because an operator has more opportunity to exercise psi abilities. Here, we derive a test criterion to determine whether a force-like interaction or an informational mechanism is a better description of the data based upon the number of decision points.

Consider two experiments of M decisions at n_1 and N decisions at n_2, respectively. Regardless of the mechanism, the Stouffer's z for the first experiment is given by:

$$z_s^{(1)} = \frac{\sqrt{n_1} \sum\limits_{j=1}^{M} \varepsilon_{1,j}}{\sqrt{M}} = \sqrt{n_1 M} \times \varepsilon_1,$$

where ε_{1j} is the effect size for one decision and where ε_1 is the average effect size over the M decisions. Under the micro-PK assumption that the effect size, ε_1 is constant regardless of n, Stouffer's z in the second experiment is given by:

$$z_s^{(2)} = \sqrt{\frac{n_2 N}{n_1 M}}\, z_s^{(1)}.$$

Under the DAT assumption that the effect size is proportional to $1/\sqrt{n}$, the Stouffer's z in the second experiment becomes:

$$z_s^{(2)} = \sqrt{\frac{N}{M}}\, z_s^{(1)}.$$

As in the other tests of DAT, if data are collected at two values of n, then a test between these Stouffer's z values may yield a difference between the competing mechanisms.

Discussion of the Model

We now address the possible n-dependence of the model parameters. A degenerate case arises if ε_{pk} is proportional to $1/\sqrt{n}$. If that were the case, we could not distinguish between the micro-PK model and DAT by means of tests on the n dependence of results. If it were the case that in the analysis of the data from a variety of experiments, participants, and laboratories, the slope of a Z^2 versus n linear least-squares fit for the slope were zero, then either ε_{pk} is proportional to $1/\sqrt{n}$, the accuracy depending upon the precision of the fit (i.e., errors of the zero slope), or there was no PK in the first place. An attempt might be made to rescue the micro-PK hypothesis by explaining the $1/\sqrt{n}$ dependence of ε_{pk} in the degenerate case as a fatigue or some other time dependence; that is, it might be hypothesized that anomalous perturbation abilities would decline as a function of n; however, it seems improbable that a human-based phenomenon would be so widely distributed and constant and give the $1/\sqrt{n}$ dependency in differing protocols needed to imitate DAT.

We prefer to resolve the degeneracy by wielding Occam's razor: If the only type of anomalous perturbation that fits the data is indistinguishable from precognition, and given that we have ample demonstration of precognition by independent means in the laboratory, then we do not need to invent an additional phenomenon called psychokinesis. Except for this degeneracy, a zero slope for the fit allows us to reject all micro-PK models that suggest a mean shift of the parent distribution, regardless of their n-dependencies.

DAT is not limited to experiments that capture data from a dynamic system. DAT may also be the mechanism in protocols that utilize quasi-static target systems. In a quasi-static target system, a random process occurs only when a run is initiated; a mechanical dice thrower is an example. Yet, in a series of unattended runs of such a device, there is always a statistical variation in the mean of the dependent variable that may be due to a variety of factors, such as Brownian motion, temperature, humidity, and possibly the quantum mechanical uncertainty principle (Walker, 1974). Thus, the results obtained will ultimately depend upon when the run is initiated. It is also possible that a second-order DAT mechanism arises because of protocol selection—how the order in tripolar protocols is determined and who determines them. In second-order DAT, there may be individuals other than the formal subject whose decisions affect the experimental outcome and are modified by precognition. Given the limited possibilities in this case, we might expect less of an impact from DAT.

In surveying the range of anomalous mental phenomena, for the most part, we reject the evidence for experimental macro-PK because of poor artifact control and accept the evidence for precognition and micro-PK because of the large number of studies and the positive results of the meta-analyses. We believe that DAT, therefore, might be a general model for anomalous mental phenomena in that it reduces mechanisms for laboratory phenomena to only one—the anomalous transtemporal acquisition of information.

APPLICATION OF DECISION AUGMENTATION THEORY

The domain in which DAT may operate is in any circumstance in which statistical inference is used to determine the statistical relevance of an experiment or drug trial. Many possible retrospective applications, however, cannot be addressed quantitatively because, as we have noted earlier in the chapter, DAT requires more than a single point measure (e.g., two sequence lengths in an RNG study, two differing numbers of decisions in a study), and most studies are content with only a single point measure—the efficacy of a drug in a drug trial, for example.

DAT Analysis on a Single Biological PK Study

During the Star Gate era,[1] the SRI International team contracted the Mind Science Foundation (MSF) to conduct a prospective test of DAT (Hubbard, Utts, & Braud, 1987). The MSF conducted a formal investigation to determine whether a relatively large number of unselected participants would be able to exert a distant mental influence upon the rate of hemolysis of human red blood cells. When red blood cells are placed in a saline solution, the process of osmosis causes the cell to rupture. This process is called hemolysis.

For each of 32 participants, red blood cells in 20 tubes were submitted to osmotic stress (hypotonic saline). The subjects attempted to protect the cells in 10 of the tubes, using visualization and intention strategies; the remaining 10 tubes served as noninfluence controls. For each tube, rate of hemolysis was measured photometrically over a 1-minute trial period. Participants and an experimenter were "blind" regarding critical aspects of the procedure, and participants and tubes were located in separate rooms to eliminate conventional influences. Results indicated that a significantly greater number of participants than would be expected on the basis of chance alone showed independently significant differences between their "protect" and "control" tubes ($p = 1.91 \times 10^{-5}$). Overall, blood *source* (i.e., whether the influenced cells were the participant's own cells or those of another person) did not significantly influence the outcome. Additional analyses of the results were performed by SRI International researchers to determine whether the data were better described by remote action (causal) or by intuitive data sorting (informational) predictions. In the published account, Braud (1990) indicates that the preliminary DAT analysis conducted by the SRI team was inconclusive; however, a later analysis showed a strong tendency toward the PK hypothesis.

In the DAT part of the experiment, a participant attempted to delay the hemolysis of the blood (i.e., protect it) and was blind to whether there were two test tubes or eight test tubes in the infrared measuring system—a two-point measure required by DAT. The hemolysis rate was averaged separately over each set of tubes (i.e., two or eight). A PK effect would predict that the resulting z-score would be twice as much for the eight tubes than for the two tubes. This, of course, is a direct result of one of the DAT–PK assumptions; that is, the PK effect size remains constant regardless of the number of tubes. The SRI team computed that the Z^2 for eight test tubes was 5.25 ± 1.17. By the equation show in Table 10.1, this implies a PK effect size squared of 0.521. Then we

---

[1]Star Gate is the last nickname for the U.S. government's $20 million use of and research into extrasensory perception and psychokinesis during the Cold War from 1972 to 1995.

compute the value for Z^2 for two test tubes using this value for $1/\sqrt{n}$ to find it to be 2.06. The Z^2 data at n = two test tubes is 2.5 ± 0.6. Thus, the PK prediction lies within the one standard error of the data. So, in this single case of biological PK, the cherished hypothesis of a PK interaction is confirmed.

A DAT Analysis of the Global Consciousness Project

As stated earlier, it is well beyond the scope of this chapter to review the decades-long debate between the developers of the Global Consciousness Project (GCP) and many researchers outside. May and Spottiswoode (2011a) looked at the published data online at http://noosphere.princeton.edu for the project as of August 2009. At that time, there were 65 RNGs—called EGGS by their project—which were scattered worldwide in what we consider as an engineering tour de force in that on a second-by-second basis, each EGG uses its own true random number generator to generate 200 binary bits. The number of binary 1s, then, is uploaded to a central server in Princeton, New Jersey, each second from each EGG worldwide. The date and time stamp along with the data are available at no charge from http://noosphere.princeton.edu. In their paper, May and Spottiswoode (2011a) stipulate to the null hypothesis that the network of EGG met the usual definitions of being total random in the absence of "events." In addition to the raw data, the GCP site has a growing list of events that have been included in their formal analysis.

The most succinct statement of the hypothesis to date can be found in Bancel and Nelson (2008): "Periods of collective emotional or attentional behavior in widely distributed populations will correlate with deviations from expectation in a global network of RNGs."

At the time of the writing, May and Spottiswoode (2011a) analyzed the published 300 events and independently arrived at the same overall statistic as published—a combined z-score of 5.81, which is consistent with the value 5.78 that appeared on the site. From a DAT (or experimenter psi) perspective, the question before us is this: Is this the cherished hypothesis that the EGGs deviate from chance because of collective emotional or attentional behavior in widely distributed populations, or is this an example of experimenter psi? There were two ways May and Spottiswoode (2011a) attempted to answer this question. As it turns out, the first method was similar to the one described earlier in this chapter for the general RNG database. That is, square each of the published z-scores and use the number of EGGS that were used to compute that z-score. As it turns out, that was an error (Bancel, 2011). The problem with regard to that analysis will be considered later in this discussion.

However, they addressed the question of experimenter psi at the protocol level. The GCP group is to be commended once again for publishing all the details for each of the formal events that went into the analysis. In addition to the statistics associated with the event and the number of EGGS for each event, the event portion of the GCP site also lists the individual who brought each event to the attention of the GCP.

Of the 300 formal events, we found that Nelson, the founder and arguably the driving force of the GCP, either singularly or among others brought 234 events to the project; all others totaled 66 only. The Stouffer's Z for the "Nelson" events was 5.91 and for the others, the Stouffer's Z was 1.26. The z-score for the difference is 3.29 ($p = 4.97 \times 10^{-4}$). Thus, there appears to be something "special" about the events that were brought to the attention of the GCP by Nelson.

There are at least two possibilities for this outcome, but we hasten to emphasize that we are not accusing Nelson of any kind of fraud. We are, however, "accusing" him of using his own psi to mimic the cherished hypothesis, since the statistics suggest virtually all the significant GCP events were brought by Nelson ($Z = 5.91$) compared to the overall statistics of $Z = 5.81$. This is strongly suggestive of experimenter psi. The second possibility is that it could be argued that Nelson had some special insight into the type of events that would affect the network of EGGs. This alternative is, of course, testable. If Nelson were to publish a category list of events that are the most likely to affect the network and then retire from bringing any individual event, then the cherished hypothesis would be confirmed if the overall statistics remained the same. If not, then Nelson's own psi is responsible for the GCP data.

THE FUTURE OF DAT AND EXPERIMENTER PSI

Because unconscious psi may impinge upon any study that uses statistical inference to come to some conclusion, it is my belief that many years from now, this aspect of psi may be among the few findings of psi research that will survive the test of time. It may be, perhaps, the only psi finding that does so in that it has such a broad base of applications.

One major weakness of the current formulation is that it is assumed that the parent distribution remains normal and that the variance remains constant under the PK hypothesis. The next step would be to modify the formalism such that under PK, the variance could also change and may be a function of the PK effect size. For example, start with a parent distribution as:

$$N(\mu_0, \sigma_0^2) \rightarrow N(\mu_0, \sigma_1^2),$$

where μ_0 and $1/\sqrt{n}$ are the mean and variance of the unperturbed parent distribution, and N signifies a normal distribution. Under PK influence, the parent distribution remains normal with no mean shift, but now the variance is $1/\sqrt{n}$. Future DAT research should begin here to develop the expectation value of Z^2 under this variance shift of the parent distribution and extend it later to a general arbitrary distribution for a final influenced parent distribution.

We must keep in mind, however, that DAT was originally formulated to answer this simple question in random number generator experiments: is there a micro-PK force per bit? The answer to that is clearly "no."

REFERENCES

Bancel, P., & Nelson, R. D. (2008). The GCP event experiment: Design, analytical methods, results. *Journal of Scientific Exploration, 22*(3), 259–269.

Bancel, P. A. (2011). Reply to May and Spottiswoode's "The Global Consciousness Project: Identifying the source of psi." *Journal of Scientific Exploration, 25,* 690–694.

Bierman, D. J., & Radin, D. (1997). Anomalous anticipatory response on randomized future conditions. *Perceptual and Motor Skills, 84,* 689–690.

Braud, W. G. (1990). Distant mental influence of rate of hemolysis of human red blood cells. *Journal of the American Society for Psychical Research, 84,* 1–24.

Broughton, R., Millar, B., Beloff, J., & Wilson, K. (1977). PK investigation of the experimenter effect and its psi-based component. *Research in parapsychology,* 41–48.

Broughton, R. (1978). Repeatability and experimenter effect: Are subjects really necessary? *Parapsychology Review, 10*(1), 11–14.

Hubbard, G., Scott, Utts, J., & Braud, W. (1987). *Experiment protocol for heyolysis: Confirmation experiment,* Final Report, Objective E, Task 2. Menlo Park, CA: SRI International.

Jahn, R. G. (1982). The persistent paradox of psychic phenomena: An engineering perspective. *Proceedings of the IEEE, 70*(2), 35.

Jahn, R. G., Dunne, B. J., & Nelson, R. D. (1987). Engineering anomalies research. *Journal of Scientific Exploration, 1*(1), 21.

Jung, C. G. (1963). *Memories, dreams, reflections.* New York: Pantheon.

Kennedy, J., & Taddonio, J. L. (1976). Experimenter effects in parapsychological research. *Journal of Parapsychology, 40*(1), 33.

Kennedy, J. E., & Haight, J. (1978). Are psychological tests nonintentional psi tasks? *Journal of Parapsychology, 42,* 33–50.

May, E. C., Humphrey, B. S., & Hubbard, S. G. (1980). *Electronic system perturbation techniques,* Final Report Project 8585, Menlo Park, CA: SRI International.

May, E. C., Paulinyi, T., & Vassy, Z. (2014/2005). Anomalous anticipatory skin conductance response to acoustic stimuli: Experimental results and speculation upon a mechanism. In E. C. May & S. B. Marwaha (Eds.), *Anomalous cognition: Remote viewing research and theory,* pp. 158–171. Jefferson, NC: McFarland.

May, E. C., & Spottiswoode, S. J. P. (2003). Skin conductance response to future audio stratle stimuli. Paper presented at the *The Parapsychological Association 46th Annual Convention, Vancouver, Canada.*

May, E. C., & Spottiswoode, S. J. P. (2014/2011a). The Global Consciousness project: Identifying the source of psi. In E. C. May & S. B. Marwaha (Eds.),

Anomalous cognition: Remote viewing research and theory, pp. 268–277. Jefferson, NC: McFarland.

May, E. C., & Spottiswoode, S. J. P. (2011b). The Global Consciousness project: Identifying the source of psi: A response to Nelson and Bancel. *Journal of Scientific Exploration, 25*(4), 695.

May, E. C., Spottiswoode, S. J. P. & Utts, J. (2014/1995). Applications of decision augmentation theory. In E. C. May & S. B. Marwaha (Eds.), *Anomalous cognition: Remote viewing research and theory*, pp. 244–267. Jefferson, NC: McFarland.

May, E. C., Utts, J., & Spottiswoode, S. J. P. (2014/1995). Decision augmentation theory: Toward a model for anomalous mental phenomena. In E. C. May & S. B. Marwaha (Eds.), *Anomalous cognition: Remote viewing research and theory*, pp. 222–243. Jefferson, NC: McFarland.

Nelson, R. (2006). The Global Consciousness project. *Explore: The Journal of Science and Healing, 2*(4), 342–351.

Nelson, R. (2011). Reply to May and Spottiswoode on experimenter effect as the explanation for GCP Results. *Journal of Scientific Exploration, 25*(4), 683.

Radin, D. (1997). Unconscious perception of future emotions: An experiment in presentiment. *Journal of Scientific Exploration, 11*(2), 163–180.

Schmidt, H. (1969). Precognition of a quantum process. *Journal of Parapsychology, 33*(2), 10.

Schmidt, H. (1970). PK test with electronic equipment. *Journal of Parapsychology, 34*(3), 7.

Stanford, R. G. (1974a). An experimentally testable model for spontaneous events: I. Extrasensory events. *Journal of the American Society for Psychical Research, 68*, 34–57.

Stanford, R. G. (1974b). An experimentally testable model for spontaneous psi events: II. Psychokinetic events. *Journal of the American Society for Psychical Research, 68*, 321–356.

Stanford, R. G. (1976). A study of motivational arousal and self-concept in psi-mediated instrumental response. *Journal of the American Society for Psychical Research.*

Stanford, R. G., Zenhausern, R., Taylor, A., & Dwyer, M. A. (1975). Psychokinesis as psi-mediated instrumental response. *Journal of American Society for Psychical Research, 69*, 127–133.

Utts, J., May, E. C., & Frivold, T. J. (1987). *Intuitive data sorting*, Final Report. Menlo Park, CA: SRI International.

Walker, E. H. (1974). Foundations of paraphysical and parapsychological phenomena. In E. Oteri (Ed.), *Proceedings of an international conference: Quantum physics and parapsychology*, pp.1–53. New York: Parapsychology Foundation.

Chapter 11

The Model of Pragmatic Information

Walter von Lucadou

From its beginning, parapsychology never suffered from a lack of theoretical models, but most of them did not allow for quantitative predictions; they were more general in nature and could thus mainly be considered as philosophical approaches. Since the Geneva conference titled "Quantum Physics and Parapsychology" in 1974 (Oteri, 1975), a new era of theoretical parapsychology has developed. Several scientists contributed to the development of the different approaches for the observational theories (OTs) of psi, which share a common starting point and which can be compared in relation to different experimental predictions.

The basic starting point of the observational theories can be seen in an apparent similarity between the structure of quantum phenomena and psi phenomena. This similarity is mainly seen in the nonlocality of the wave function and the seeming independence of spacetime in psi phenomena. Another aspect of this isomorphism is the role of measurement in quantum theory and the role of an observer in psi events.

The model of pragmatic information (MPI) was first proposed by Lucadou (1987) and over the years has been applied primarily to the analysis of various types of psychokinetic (PK) events, including both macro- and micro-PK. The basic difference between the MPI and other observational theories (OTs) is that it does *not* start at the level of quantum theory; rather, it starts on a very general level of systems theory, which studies events, behaviors, and experiences in complex systems. The advantage of systems theory is that it can be applied to psychological as well as physical problems, as it does not say anything about the underlying structures but deals only with the structure of our descriptive language and the way we are representing and mapping information that we can get from experiments based on this description. Thus, while it does not say anything about the source of the psi events, it operationalizes the process and interprets our description of our interaction with the external physical world (Kornwachs & Lucadou, 1985).

The model of pragmatic information (MPI) represents a paradigm shift from the implicit model of the Rhinean paradigm (Lucadou, 2002). The Rhinean paradigm can be summarized as follows:

1. Rhine considered PK as an "influence"; that is, a kind of energy or power that emanates from a person, is transferred to a physical process, and changes the process. An additional "PK signal" is imprinted on the physical process. It will therefore leave a "trace" that is unequivocally distinguishable from "normal" physical processes. In the first instance, this assumption about PK appears so self-evident that we can hardly think of an alternative.

2. The virtue of the statistical method lies in the fact that it enables the accumulation of small effects. Processes are conceivable, however, with which this does not happen. For example, emotions such as surprise cannot be "amplified" through statistical summation.

3. Especially with regard to experiments, it is generally assumed that the outcome should be independent of time and place. Only the physical and psychological conditions of the actual situation should be relevant for this outcome. In physics, it is easy to conceive of processes that do directly (explicitly) depend on time and that are therefore usually termed "not ergodic." One might hypothesize that PK is determined by the age of the world.

4. In his experiments, Rhine took as an additional starting point the assumption that, in principle, a psi effect can be separated from the meaning of its contents. This is to say the meaning the display has for the subject is irrelevant for the PK effect. The experimenter could just as easily use a visual display as an acoustic one. Rhine, of course, does not deny that the subject's psychological response may vary with the type of display. He was confident, however, that these psychological factors can, in principle, be distinguished from "pure" psychokinesis. This is in stark contrast to the MPI, where the meaning represents an inseparable part of the phenomenon.

MODEL OF PRAGMATIC INFORMATION (MPI) AND
GENERALIZED QUANTUM THEORY (GQT)

The MPI is a general model of psi phenomena that includes both ESP and micro- and macro-PK. The model draws from synchronicity theory initiated by C. G. Jung and W. Pauli, and interprets psi phenomena not as a result of any causal influence of mind on matter or other minds. Rather, it employs "meaningful coincidences" as correlations not produced by causal interaction of the kind physicists know and apply successfully, but mediated by correspondences of sense and meaning. The MPI starts from a system-theoretic viewpoint and uses concepts drawn from generalized quantum theory (GQT), which had its origin in what was called weak quantum theory (Atmanspacher, Römer, & Walach, 2002) that relaxed many of the underlying requirements imposed by quantum mechanics in order to sharpen the often vague and metaphoric usage of originally quantum theoretical terms such as "complementarity" and "entanglement" in fields of knowledge differing from physics.

BASIC ASSUMPTIONS OF MPI

There are two basic assumptions of the MPI: first, any description of nature must have a structure, which is similar to the axiomatic structure of quantum theory (QT), and second, there must be an exchange of a minimal amount of pragmatic information or interaction with another system to enable informational exchange and a measurement of it. This is simply another formulation of the inevitable interaction in a measurement.

There are several arguments for these basic assumptions, the simplest of which is that QT is the most successful basic descriptive language of natural systems and, so far, there are no indications that the axioms of QT have failed. The axioms of QT describe, in a very general way, how information can be obtained from any system when the interaction of the "measurement process" cannot be neglected. However, this does not necessarily imply that we can transpose without further assumptions the detailed structure of a special quantum physical system to another field as it is done in the observational theories of psi and in some reductionist models (Walker, 1975, 1979; Hameroff, 1994). The MPI and the GQT are two theoretical models that start from this very fundamental level and that can also be applied in normal psychology. These models are not completely independent of each other and can describe somewhat different aspects of the problem.

The initial idea of GQT was described in 1972 (Lucadou, 1974, 1991a,b, 1998), and a mathematical formulation of GQT was given by Römer, Atmanspacher, and Walach (Walach & Römer, 2000; Atmanspacher, Römer, & Walach 2002; Filk & Römer, 2010). This formulation is so general that it covers both QT as well as psychology, thus showing that the concepts of complementarity and entanglement can be applied beyond physics.

In GQT, the fundamental notions of *systems, states,* and *observables* are appropriated from ordinary quantum theory:

- A *system* is any part of reality in the most general sense, which can, at least in principle, be isolated from the rest of the world and be the object of an investigation.

- A system is assumed to have the capacity to reside in different *states.* The notion of state also has an epistemic side, reflecting the degree of knowledge an observer has about the system. Unlike in ordinary quantum mechanics, the set of states is not necessarily assumed to have an underlying linear Hilbert space structure.

- An *observable* of a system is any feature of a system that can be investigated in a more or less meaningful way.

The details of the mathematical representation of the MPI are beyond the scope of this chapter; however, they may be found in Lucadou (1995).

The most important aspect of the MPI (Lucadou, 1984, 1987, 1995, 1998, 2001, 2002; Kornwachs & Lucadou, 1985) is the so-called "non-transmission-axiom" (Lucadou, Römer, & Walach, 2007). It assumes that the origin of psi phenomena are not signals, but entanglement correlations, which are created by the "meaning" (pragmatic information) of the situation. MPI and GQT assume that these entanglement correlations cannot be used as signal transfers or causal influences. This axiom leads to a naturalistic explanation of the decline-effect and the displacement effect (Lucadou, 1983, 1989, 2000, 2001) and to the temporal development of recurrent spontaneous psychokinesis (RSPK) phenomena (Lucadou & Zahradnik, 2004). Lucadou et al. (2007) consider the MPI as a subclass of the GQT. In agreement with GQT, the MPI assumes that the structure and function of a system are complementary observables. Entanglement correlations are pattern matches within organizationally closed systems measured from outside of the system that are created by the relevant pragmatic information.

The Endo-/Exo- Perspective

Similar to the concepts of structure and behavior of a system, the endo-/exo- distinction represents two complementary categories for the description of systems. The exoperspective refers to the usual view from "outside," where the observer and the observed are separated (Primas, 1992). The endoperspective takes into account that (at least in nonclassical systems) the observer is part of the system (Lucadou, 2002).

The terms endosystems and exosystems are defined in the following way: "A strictly closed physical system without any concept of an observer is called an endo-system. If the endo-system is divided into an observer and an observing part, we speak of an exo-physical description. The world of the observers with their communication tools is called an exo-system" (Primas, 1992).

Key Concepts of the MPI

The key concepts in the MPI are: pragmatic information, novelty, confirmation, autonomy, reliability, temporal dimensionality, and minimum action.

- *Pragmatic information (I).* The meaning of given information measured by its action on a system.
- *Novelty (E).* Aspect of pragmatic information that is completely new for the receiving system.
- *Confirmation (B).* Aspect of pragmatic information that is already known by the receiving system.
- *Autonomy (A).* Behavior of a system that cannot be predicted.
- *Reliability (R).* Behavior of a system that is expected.
- *Temporal dimensionality (D).* Measure of the interrelationship of temporal events that belong to a history.
- *Minimum action (i).* Smallest amount of action on a system that cannot be avoided during a measurement or observation.

The concept of pragmatic information has been developed to quantify the meaning of given information. It is assumed that the potential action that the meaningful information exerts on a system can be used for such quantification. Weizsäcker (1974) proposed that pragmatic information could be written as a product of two observables that he called *Erstmaligkeit* (novelty) (E) and *Bestätigung* (confirmation) (B). This approach takes into account that to produce a change (ΔC) in the receiving system, each piece of meaningful information must contain two elements: (1) a certain prestructure, for example, one's native language, to be understood by the receiving system, and (2) a new element. The changes in the system are measured in terms of changes of complexity $\Delta C / \Delta t$ of the system (Kornwachs & Lucadou, 1975). For example, a joke in one's native language (the presence of a prestructure) will elicit laughter (change), and the repetition of the joke (absence of novelty) will not bring on a response. This implies that pragmatic information is a dynamic process.

PK events are considered to be exceptional or novel in MPI terms. This is especially the case in spontaneous cases in which psi events occur unexpectedly. We can also say the pragmatic information that describes the entanglement correlation is mainly represented by novelty. Implicitly, this means that there is not much confirmation present. Since pragmatic information is the product of novelty (E) and confirmation (B), the same amount of pragmatic information can be expressed either as more novelty and less confirmatory or vice versa. However, if the total amount of pragmatic information is limited, then novel spontaneous events (E) cannot occur very often, which would imply a confirmation (B).

The most important difference between a psi experiment and an experiment in other fields of science is that in psi experiments, the normal causal links between subject and target have to be ruled out, whereas in other fields, the structure of such normal causal links is investigated. While this definition is problematic, researchers in the field are beginning to share a common minimum consensus that psi effects could positively be defined as "meaningful nonlocal entanglement correlations" between a living system and other (causally) separated systems (Lucadou, 1984, 1991b). Thus, one could redefine parapsychology as the investigation of "nonlocal effects in entangled living systems." The term "nonlocal," however, is not just a new word for "psi," as it has a definite meaning in the context of the axiomatic structure of GQT. It is important to note that "nonlocality" is, in principle, not different from other types of physical interactions. The term "nonlocality/nonlocal," in this context, means that an observable does not explicitly depend on time and distance (e.g., the importance of a personal relationship). To isolate nonlocality for investigations, causal interactions have to be ruled out. In physics, entanglement can be considered as a more or less well-established fact; however, most researchers doubt that it may play a role in living systems.

Laws of MPI

In general, the model can be formulated in two main laws:

1. *Psi phenomena are nonlocal entanglement correlations in socio-psycho-physical, self-organizing, organizationally closed systems, which are induced by the pragmatic information, which creates the system.*

Assuming psi is a time-independent effect (as in precognition or backward causation) and it can lead to real physical effects, we could test this by building an "oracle" that could be used to create an intervention paradox. The oracle would be a significant deviation of a random sequence from the null hypothesis in a psi experiment that operationalizes backward causation. For example, in an experiment, if a subject is supposed to respond to a random sequence, but we do not use it, it creates a paradoxical situation in that the subject will not be able to exert an influence on the sequence, although that was the reason for its selection.

The MPI makes the assumption that nature does not allow for intervention paradoxes. Known as the grandfather paradox, it says that a time traveler cannot travel back in time and kill his grandfather before he is married so that his father is not born and thus he cannot be born. However, if he is not born, then he cannot travel back in time and kill his grandfather, thus ensuring that he is born. However, in GQT, this condition is more stringent, in that situations in which the time traveler could *potentially* kill his grandfather do not occur.

2. *Any attempt to use a nonlocal correlation as a signal transfer makes the nonlocal correlation vanish or change the effect in an unpredictable way (e.g., the effect may show up in a different variable, which was not in consideration beforehand, known as displacement effect).*

This limiting principle is a result of the nontransmission axiom (Lucadou et al., 2007). In QT, entanglement correlations cannot be used for any signal transfer or causal link. This has to be accepted as an axiom for general systems. We may conclude that natural systems themselves may produce larger fluctuations if they are not observed. In quantum physics, this is known as quantum zeno effect, which states that an unstable particle when observed continuously will never decay. In other words, a watched pot never boils (Atmanspacher et al., 2004). It is a fundamental assumption of the model of pragmatic information that observation and negative-result observation (Renninger, 1960) are different aspects of the system.

MPI AND PK RESEARCH

Qualitatively, evidence suggests that spontaneous PK experiences seem to be much more elaborate and larger than the very small, but highly significant, deviations seen in laboratory experiments (Lucadou, 2000, 2001). Starting from this idea, a measure for the "historical meaning" of events was developed. It is called dimensionality of temporal events or temporal dimensionality (D). Mathematically, it is defined as a Hausdorff dimension of a fractal structure in time. Similar to the geometrical case, the Hausdorff dimension for temporal events tells us how many temporal subelements are needed to create a new "enlarged" unity, which creates a history.

A possible interpretation of the definition of temporal dimensionality (D) is that every singular event is not an independent event that counts for its own value but is only a "partial" event. For a normal binary random sequence $D = 1$, and each "singular event" is independent. Thus, one could also say that a singular event in a sequence with D > 1 is only "a fractal part (namely 1/D) of an event." If such a sequence is the target of a psi effect, obviously such "partial events" do not fully contribute to the limitations that are induced by the second law. Thus, for the simplest case, this can be expressed as:

$$ H = \frac{c\sqrt{D}}{\sqrt{n}}; \quad D = D(n). $$

If D is large enough, quite large effect sizes may occur. In principle, this can be applied for experiments. However, it does not seem useful to work with "ideal" random event generators (REGs) anymore. One could speculate whether the decline effect observed in meta-analysis may partly be a result of using increasingly "better" REGs. Of course, one has to avoid statistical artifacts. A possible solution to this problem could be the use of Markov REGs. A further experimental requirement from our consideration is that very long runs are not really helpful because due to the limiting relations, the psi effect would be blurred out. Thus, according to the MPI, very long runs are not really helpful, as the limiting relations will blur the PK effect. This could also contribute to the observed decline, especially in PK research, where the run length has become abundantly large during the past decade (*see* Lucadou, 2001).

If we have a normal binary random sequence, the psi effect has no "working-surface"—in computer terms, no "user surface." In contrast to PK experiments, homoeopathic treatments, for instance, have a large working surface or an effective user surface. The "therapeutic ritual" has a high dimensionality (D), at least as far as it is not "blinded out" by double blind conditions.

One could also say that dependent singular events are better targets for nonlocal effects. Further it is to be expected that the first singular event shows the highest effect size. This could give a natural explanation for the fact that spontaneous psi events (SPE) and recurrent spontaneous PK (RSPK) seem to have a much higher effect size than experimental events. Everyday life events, and especially SPE and RSPK, are normally dependent events, which are part of long, complicated, and interwoven (personal) histories such that "psi" has "enough possibilities to link with." Further, the limiting law (the second law of MPI) does not apply because the events are either spontaneous, of short duration, or of poor documentation quality and mainly elusive (see Lucadou, 1983, 1989, 2000).

Recurrent Spontaneous Psychokinesis (RSPK)

"RSPK" is the term used to denote unexplained events that repeatedly occur in the vicinity of an individual or "agent." The MPI can be used to analyze RSPK. To do so, we have to start with the system from an exoperspective (i.e., when the observer and observed are separated); the anomalous RSPK phenomena contain mainly novelty (E) and little confirmation (B). From an endoperspective (i.e., the observer is part of the system), the system is described by the complementary concepts of autonomy (A) and reliability (R). The dynamics of RSPK are described as the dynamics of pragmatic information within a hierarchically nested system, which is created by the persons inside the system (focus person, naïve observers) and the reaction of critical observers and the society that describe the system from "outside," as shown in Figure 11.1.

When the RSPK phenomena are observed from "inside" or from "outside" of a certain systemic description level, the gestalt change that occurs in RSPK cases is described as follows: pragmatic information = reliability × autonomy = confirmation × novelty, which governs the dynamics of RSPK cases.

The hierarchical model of the MPI can be applied in quite different situations and contexts because it deals only with the flow and exchange of pragmatic information and its dynamic development. It could be applied in a general way for all types of psi events and to the dynamics of scientific evidence (Lucadou, 2001).

Figure 11.1
Hierarchical RSPK model.

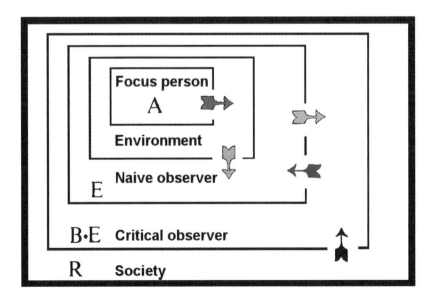

RSPK phenomena are considered as a kind of "externalized psychosomatic" reaction, expressing a hidden problem that cannot be recognized by the persons concerned. One could primarily consider the focus person and his or her environment (the "focus system") as an organizational closure, but interactions with the family, other "observers," and finally with the whole social environment are so strong that the boundary of the organizational closure is always changing. A PK phenomenon can be understood as a mark of the autonomy (A) of the focus system. The recurrence of the phenomenon is a mark of the reliability (R) of the focus system. Any interaction of this system with other "observers" must be described as an exchange of pragmatic information (I). However, not only is the focus system delivering pragmatic information, the observers are also "producing" pragmatic information that manipulates the focus system by, for instance, their expectations. For instance, if these "observers" would "expect" more confirmation (B) of the focus system for a specific "surprising" phenomenon x, such that the product $E(x) \times B(x)$ would exceed the product $I = A \times R$, the phenomenon may produce a displacement in such a way that something unexpected x' happens for which $E(x') \times B(x') = A \times R$ holds.

MPI Predictions for RSPK Phenomena

The MPI leads to several predictions concerning RSPK phenomena. The first prediction is that RSPK phenomena show two clusters of phenomena, which can be considered as structural and functional anomalous RSPK phenomena. In a cluster analysis of 54 RSPK cases, Huesmann and Schriever (1989) corroborated this prediction.

The second prediction is that the development of RSPK cases contains four phases: surprise phase, displacement phase, decline phase, and suppression phase. In the surprise phase, the RSPK activity starts rapidly with strong effects, but they are not attributed to the focus person. This happens in the displacement phase, when the phenomena usually change in an unpredictable way. In the decline phase, the message is understood and the phenomena are expected; therefore, the phenomena disappear. The final suppression phase can be understood as a kind of reaction of the society.

The third prediction is that observers can control the RSPK activity by their observation or documentation. This is the result of a kind of "uncertainty relation" of the MPI, which says that the effect size of the phenomena is limited by the quality of their documentation. This also holds for so-called sitter-group experiments.

The fourth prediction is that we have to expect two types of RSPK cases: active and passive (Lucadou & Zahradnik, 2004). These concepts describe how persons involved cope with the RSPK phenomena.

Of course, the coping strategies of the persons include "system control." System control describes how an organizationally closed system controls itself by interaction with the environment. In the active case, the focus person serves as the "master" part of the control cycle and the environment as a "slave." In the passive case, it is just the other way round. The focus person is not able to control anything and is not able any more to stabilize his or her world. The active focus person, in contrast, is even overcontrolling his or her environment, which leads to macroscopic random fluctuations, that is, RSPK phenomena.

Here is an illustrative example. We assume here that everybody under normal circumstances subconsciously controls his or her environment to stabilize it. This means that random fluctuations that are too large are suppressed. This can be seen, for instance, in the sitter-group experiments and in many PK experiments with subjects who do not get deviations from chance but instead a smaller variance.

From this point of view, it could be assumed that in a case of depression, the person steadily loses control over the organizational closed environment, which shows up in fluctuations within this environment. This means that the integrative power that keeps the whole system together cannot suppress individual fluctuations within the system, which may destroy the system. In this case, it is expected that this will occur only in a certain period before the whole system dies out. In such cases, we have no real displacement phase but only a decline phase, and even the suppression phase is not necessary. The decline phase is not driven by the attempt to produce the phenomena but simply by exhaustion.

Correlation Experiments

It may seem that the MPI predicts that repeatable psi experiments are not possible at all because they violate the second law in any case. On the contrary, on the basis of the MPI, an experimental method has been developed, where the decline effect is at least partially avoided by circumventing the nontransmission axiom due to a correlationmatrix technique. In these experiments (Lucadou, 1986, 1993, 1994, 2006; Radin, 1993), psychological variables were correlated with outcome in PK experiments, with feedback and without (control). Only the number of significant correlations between psychological variables and physical variables of a PK experiment are counted and compared with controls (runs without feedback or runs without subjects).

In these studies, the psychological variables were measured before the PK experiment by standard personality questionnaires. In studies 5 and 6 (Lucadou, 2006) in Table 11.1, the psychological variables were behavioral (pressing of buttons). The physical variables were several statistical test values describing properties (such as mean value, variance,

Table 11.1
Result of All Correlation Studies

Study	$N_{sigcorr}$	N_{subj}	PsVar	PhVar	#corr	Z	ES
1. Lucadou 1986	75	299	24	23	552	5.13	0.218
2. Lucadou 1993	23	307	16	8	128	3.10	0.274
3. Radin 1993	32	1	16	23	368	2.63	0.137
4. Lucadou 2006	39	336	27	18	216	6.22	0.423
5. Lucadou 2006	11	336	27	18	216	0.04	0.003
6. Lucadou 2006	21	220	27	18	216	2.25	0.153

$N_{sigcorr}$ = number of significant correlations, N_{subj} = number of subjects, PsVar = number of psychological variables, PhVar = number of physical variables, #corr = number of correlations, Z = z-value, ES = effect size

autocorrelation) of a binary random sequence (Markov chain) produced by a quantum physical random event generator (REG). The physical REG was carefully shielded against any putative physical influence by the subjects.

The results in all the studies indicate that the overall distribution of the physical variables showed no deviation from the theoretical expectation values for both experimental and control conditions. Several techniques were applied to find a PK signal (tracer) within the experimental random sequences, but none was found. This is a strong argument for the assumption that indeed, no signal transfer between the observing subject and the random event generator was involved. Nevertheless, the number of (significant) correlations between the psychological and physical variables is significantly increased for the experimental runs compared with the number of correlations of the control runs. The deviation is given in Table 11.1 by z values.

In these experiments, the effect size is computed as:

$$ES = \frac{Z}{\sqrt{n}},$$

where n = the number of correlations. This effect size depends primarily on the organizational closure of the system. This can mainly be seen in studies 5 and 6 in Table 11.1. Both studies had an identical design and were carried out in parallel. Study 5, which was not significant, was performed by unselected subjects with low motivation (during an exhibition), whereas all significant studies (studies 1–4) were performed by highly motivated subjects who came to the lab because they were interested in taking part in a psi experiment. A more detailed analysis shows, however, that the unselected subjects in study 5 were not completely unsuccessful.

A subgroup (study 5), who showed more "innovative behavior" showed an increase of correlations. Finally, it could be demonstrated in the study that the structure of the correlation matrix is not stable if the experiment is repeated, but the number of correlations remains roughly the same (for details, see Lucadou, 2006).

Although no "PK signal" could be found in individual random sequences, the robust and repeatable correlations in Table 11.1 seem to constitute a "signal." However, this argument is only true if and only if the individual correlations between a given psychological and a given physical variable would be stable if the experiment is repeated. But this is obviously not the case, as only the number of correlations is conserved, and not the precise position of correlated variables. The "signal" is only a pseudo-signal, as discussed later. This fact, however, does not exclude the possibility that certain pairs of psychological and physical variables show stronger correlations that occur more frequently with replications. This implies that certain regions in the correlation matrix may show a somewhat predominant structure indicating certain characteristics of the psycho-physical system in question, but it does not imply that a signal is hidden in the matrix.

The study of Dean Radin (1993) is the only independent experiment in the literature that used the correlation technique. In this case, however, there was only one subject, and the psychological variables also contained environmental variables; therefore, the study is not completely comparable.

The examples provided here showing decline and displacement could easily be augmented by several others, and it would be an interesting research task to implement the presented ideas in future meta-analyses of experiments including nonlocal effects.

Decline Effects

As stated earlier, the partitioning of pragmatic information into novelty and confirmation depends on the measurement we apply to get the information from the system. Thus, the experimental conditions mainly determine whether we get mainly novelty or confirmation or both from our organizationally closed system. Assuming we could perform two PK experiments in which all conditions except the run length could be kept equal, (practically this would, of course, be very difficult) and assuming further that the z-score of our PK experiments is a good measure for the PK correlation, then we could conclude that the hit rate ES depends on the run length (n) in the following way (May, Utts, & Spottiswoode, 2014/1995):

$$ES(n) = \frac{c}{\sqrt{n}}.$$

This means that the accumulated deviation from the statistical expectation of the run must decline with the run length. Here we have made the assumption that the z-score is a meaningful measure for the psi effect, which means that it is used as criterion for the subject to signal the success of fulfilling the experimental condition. Criteria other than the z-score would, of course, yield different functional dependences.

The most impressive example of decline effect is the replication study of the Princeton (PEAR) PK studies (Jahn, 1981; Jahn et al., 2000). A consortium of research groups at Freiburg, Giessen, and Princeton using identical protocols collaborated to attempt a replication of prior PEAR experiments that had demonstrated anomalous deviations of the outputs of electronic random event generators in correlation with pre-stated intentions of human operators. Table 11.2 shows the results of this collaboration.

It is evident that effect size declines continuously with each replication. However, the "psi effect" does not disappear completely; it shows up in other variables in the post hoc evaluation. The authors state: "Various portions of the data displayed a substantial number of interior structural anomalies in such features as a reduction in trial level standard deviations; irregular series position patterns; and differential dependencies on various secondary parameters, such as feedback type or experimental run length, to a composite extent well beyond chance expectation" (Jahn et al., 2000, p. 499). It should be mentioned here that on the basis of the MPI, a clear-cut prediction about the outcome of the replication study was made in advance. It was kept in the minutes before the final evaluation began, but, unfortunately, it is not mentioned in the final research report.

Pseudo-Signals

The impression of many observers and operators in PK experiments that PK is a "real force" that should not be laid aside as a mere illusion. From the point of view of the observer (i.e., from the endoperspective), the observer is "influencing" the observed random sequence according

Table 11.2
Effect Size of the PEAR Experiments and Its Replications (the numbers are taken from the figures in the references)

Study	Computation (Hi-Lo)	ES
First PEAR (1981) report	6000/13050	0.46
All PEAR studies before replication	35000/834000	0.042
Replication (2000) study	7070/750000	0.0094

The effect size is given by: $\dfrac{(hits_{Hi} - hits_{Lo})}{\text{total number of trials}}$

to the instructions. Since this leads to many typical misunderstandings with respect to a proper distinction of endo- and exodescriptions of a system, it is useful to introduce the specific notion of a pseudo-signal in order to characterize nonlocal correlations as they seem to emerge from within the system. From the subject's point of view, pseudo-signals appear to be deterministic "signals." However, from the exoperspective they are nothing but nonlocal correlations.

As stated earlier, Primas (1992) introduced the distinction of the endo- and exoperspective with respect to physical systems. The exoperspective is the perspective of the experimenter or the critical observer in relation to the "object" that has to be observed or measured. The endosystem is, in contrast, the "real nature" in its ontic existence. Concerning the psychology of the observer, it becomes obvious that the description of such inaccessible ontic states is not meaningless, since the "impression" (of signals) of the observer is necessary to create (in the endosystem) the pragmatic information, which produces the organizational closure of the psychophysical system as a whole and thus the entanglement correlations and PK effects. Without these "illusionary impressions," psychophysical entanglement correlations could not emerge. Thus, metaphorically speaking, as long as we are in this world, we are a part of the universal laws of nature and thus interconnected with everybody and everything that has "meaning" for us.

It is an illusion to believe that these pseudo-signals can be used to transfer information from mind to matter. Information transfer requires a real measurement, which is not possible inside the endosystem; an "impression" is not operationalization. It is also impossible to transfer information by pseudo-signals into the external system, where "impressions" might be operationalized (e.g., by measuring actions). In the exosystem, *a pseudo-signal is not a signal; rather, it is just a nonlocal correlation.* In metaphorical language: If the subject leaves the "paradise of unintentional, holistic interconnectivity" and enters the "hell of observer experiments," the subject is no longer able to use the nonlocal correlations in a definite way because he or she is cut off by the separation of the observer and the observed in the external system. There may remain "patterns" as a vague "memory of the paradise," but in most cases, these patterns have lost their meaning. If we detect by normal signal transfer that such a pattern fits with a pattern in the external world, we call this a "hit" or "clairvoyance."

In psychological systems, however, one might think of a conversion from a given exo-system into an endosystem, for instance, by introducing a meta-description in such a way that the meta-level becomes a new exosystem and hence the original level can be regarded as corresponding endosystem (Figure 11.1, above, represents such a hierarchically nested system). In experiments, this can be done, for instance, by measuring the motivation, absorption, creativity, the awareness of impressions, or the awareness of emotions of the subjects (see Lucadou, 2006). In this case, the "awareness of impressions" and so on can be regarded as an exosystem and the system of impressions as an endosystem. It is important to realize that the concept of "awareness of impressions" cannot be applied to the level of "impressions" themselves, but often such different levels of description are not clearly distinguished.

In general, it is not always easy to avoid the illusion that PK is a kind of influence of the "mind over matter." It seems plausible that this misunderstanding is one of the reasons (in terms of sociology of science) observer effect—experimenter psi—has been overlooked for such a long time both in physics and in psychology.

A NEW EXPERIMENTAL PARADIGM

The present status of scientific evidence in parapsychology and our theoretical considerations does not mean that psi phenomena cannot be investigated by scientific methods anymore or that scientific evidence for psi has died out, but the resulting experimental paradigm may appear counterintuitive to a conventional parapsychologist.

The basic implication of the MPI is that *psi is not a classical signal originating from the mind; rather, it is merely a (nonlocal) entanglement correlation, and neither the signal nor the evidence of its existence can be accumulated.* This means that we have to give up Henry Sidgwick's (1882) optimistic program of accumulating evidence for psychokinesis. Thus, our first recommendation is: *Do not treat PK as a signal!*

Eleven requirements, described in detail here, are more or less consequences of this principle of the MPI: (1) no accumulation of data; use short runs; (2) close to the physical process, fluctuations, many channels; (3) correlations with physiological and psychological variables; (4) complete recording of the processes (no data reduction); (5) no independent events (Markov chains); (6) simple display (instruction unequivocally, no quirks); (7) triple-blindness; (8) organized closure of the experiment (spatially and temporally); (9) evaluation with "distance" (let it ripen!); (10) conceptual replications (identical is not possible); and (11) nonorthogonal variables. It should be mentioned that these 11 requirement are not independent of each other.

The idea that short runs may do better than long runs (point 1) is not new, and the reason that is given for it is mainly psychological. It is assumed that long runs are boring. However, we consider short runs to be better because long runs can be used to code a signal if the expected effect size is large enough.

Also, the second requirement (point 2) has to do with the idea that psi is not a signal emerging from the mind. Most micro-PK experimental procedures use random event generators (REG), and it is assumed that the physics behind them are irrelevant for the psi process. This means that the deviation from a given expectation value is an indication of a PK signal. However, if PK is considered to be a correlation in an entangled psychophysical system, it is important to get as much as possible information about the "interface" between the psychological and the physical description of the system. According to the MPI, the PK correlation needs as many channels as possible to establish itself, as described in Brunswick's lens model (1956) (point 3), in which the psychophysical correlation is established in a network of many possible channels. If, due to experimental conditions, one of the channels is blocked (e.g., by a violation of our fundamental rule), the system seeks to use another channel that is not expected to show a "PK effect." Thus, the psychophysical system is permanently continuously changing its internal structure to maintain psychophysical entanglement. This does not mean that predictions are no longer possible; one could, for instance, predict the number and strength of the sum of all correlations but not of a single one.

On the physical side, the correlations are linked with statistically possible fluctuations of the system. The information about the correlations should not be given away by data reduction of the REG process, as occurred in the PEAR experiment due to sampling and/or output switching (point 4). Reconstructing this information afterward requires sophisticated techniques, as the analysis of subsets of the FAMMI data (Atmanspacher & Scheingraber, 2000; Pallikari & Boller, 1999) shows.

Moreover, one of the most important results of the MPI is that pure random sequences are not good at all as random sources, at least in PK experiments. Instead, one should use random sequences that show internal dependencies (correlations), which have their own "history." They are called Markov chains (point 5).

Point 2 holds, of course, also for the psychological and physiological part of the psychophysical system (point 3). At present, this is generally accepted among parapsychologists as a psychological requirement and need not be discussed further. For the same reason, many experiments use fancy displays. Again, the motivation is to avoid boredom. However, this conflicts sometimes with the requirement of the MPI, which maintains that it is important to establish an organizational closure of the psychophysical system. The crucial point is "pragmatic information of the display." It means that the subject must attribute a clearcut meaning to the display taken from the context of her instruction. This has been shown in one of the PK experiments mentioned earlier (Lucadou, 1986). From this point of view, it seems useful to keep everything that is presented to the subject as simple and unambiguous as possible (point 6). This also includes avoiding misinforming the subject. It seems plausible that such strategies give rise to suspicion and prevent entanglement in the psychophysical system.

Keeping things simple and unambiguous (point 6) does not mean that the subject must be informed about each and every detail of the experimental setting; on the contrary, both the experimenter *and* the subject should be blind in relation to the experimental hypotheses (i.e., double blindness). But double blindness is not sufficient in light of the MPI, since the operational knowledge of previous experiments has a real influence on any future experiment; thus, the experimenter and the subject have also to be blind in relation to the operational results of previous experiments. We have called this "triple blindness" (Lucadou, 1990, 1991a). This is difficult to realize because, again, it has nothing to do with the subjective knowledge of experimenter and/or subject. This is one of the reasons why identical replications are not possible (point 10).

One possible way to obtain triple blindness is to delay the evaluation of an experiment as long as possible (point 9) and to perform parallel replication studies in the meantime. In this case, knowledge of the first experiment cannot potentially be "used" in other studies. But a delayed evaluation has also another advantage—it keeps the organizational closure between the experimenter and the psychophysical system as small as possible, whereas the organizational closure between subject and experimental setting is preserved (point 8).

Fulfilling the experimental requirements of the MPI implies that many traditional experimental methods have to be modified. Many of the new requirements have been used earlier, mainly with a more intuitive substantiation, and they were often very successful. They did not contain long series, reliable randomization, reduction of data, or fancy displays, and they did not allow identical replication or accumulation of effects. In those experiments, no considerations were made to check whether the dependent or independent variables of the experiments were orthogonal (statistically independent) (point 11). In "modern" experiments, however, one strives to use only factorized (orthogonal) variables to minimize the variance of the investigated correlations, which does not hold for entanglement correlations. Here it is advantageous to use "superposition" of variables (nonorthogonal variables) because only in this case can a difference between a local and a nonlocal correlation be measured. In other words, the Bell inequality shows only differences from the classical case for nonorthogonal situations.

It is true that from the viewpoint of classical models these quantitative experiments showed considerable methodological flaws, and, of course, they were not convincing for the scientific community in general.

But now, we may be able to understand that they were not "successful" due to flaws or artifacts but possibly because the investigators had some intuitive insight into the structure of psychophysical systems, long before the MPI revealed it. But the MPI is also able to describe the process of evidence of psi phenomenon within the scientific community (Lucadou, 2001).

The MPI concept can be stated as pragmatic information = reliability × autonomy = confirmation × novelty on a system. Any piece of pragmatic information (I) of PK data or models and of prevailing scientific paradigms interacts with the whole system and therefore produces more pragmatic information, but with a new partitioning of novelty (E) and confirmation (B) that can be interpreted as the "reaction" of the sub- or supersystem, as shown in Figure 11.1. Thus, an interesting future question is whether human society, as the upper system, is willing to accept the existence of nonlocal entanglement correlations in socio-psychophysical, self-organizing, organizationally closed systems that are induced by the pragmatic information that creates the system as a matter of fact.

In conclusion, from the model of pragmatic information viewpoint, there seems to be no hope that a post-Cartesian science (Primas, 1990) could ever enable us to heal the Cartesian cut by consciously sending real signals from "mind to matter." The "reunification of the world" or a "re-entry into the paradise" can occur only on a subconscious (dreamlike) level. For this kind of "perception," the term "entanglement perception" seems to be appropriate. It can be considered as the "forgotten" category in the sense of the German philosopher Immanuel Kant, who described the perception of space, time, and causality as fundamental categories of human perception. But in spite of the impossibility of a conscious operationalization, psi effects demonstrate that the Cartesian separation between mind (*res cogitans*) and matter (*res extensa*) is less fundamental than we have been taught to believe.

REFERENCES

Atmanspacher, H., & Scheingraber, H. (2000). Investigating deviations from dynamical randomness with scaling indices. *Journal of Scientific Exploration*, *14*, 1–18.

Atmanspacher, H., Filk, Th., & Römer, H. (2004). Quantum zeno features of bistable perception. *Biological Cybernetics*, *90*, 33–40, http://arxiv.org/abs/physics/0302005

Atmanspacher, H., Römer, H., & Walach, H. (2002). Weak quantum theory: Complementarity and entanglement in physics and beyond. *Foundations of Physics*, *32*, 379-406. http://arxiv.org/abs/quant-ph/0104109

Brunswick, E. (1956). *Perception and the representative design of psychological experiments*. Berkeley: University of California Press.

Filk, T., & Römer, H. (2010). Generalised quantum theory: Overview and latest developments. *Axiomathes, 21.* doi:10.1007/s10516-010-9138-4

Hameroff, S. R. (1994). Quantum coherence in microtubules: A neural basis for emergent consciousness. *Journal of Consciousness Studies, 1*(1), 91–118.

Huesmann, M., & Schriever, F. (1989). Steckbrief des Spuks. Darstellung und Diskussion einer Sammlung von 54 RSPK-Berichten des Freiburger Instituts für Grenzgebiete der Psychologie und Psychohygiene aus den Jahren 1947–1986. *Zeitschrift für Parapsychologie und Grenzgebiete der Psychologie, 31,* 52–107.

Jahn, R. G. (1981). The persistent paradox of psychic phenomena: An engineering perspective. *Proceedings of the IEEE, 70*(2), 136–170.

Jahn, R. G., Dunne, B., Bradish, C., Dobyns, Y., Lettieri, A., Nelson, R., Mischo, J., Boller, E., Bösch, H., Vaitl, D., Houtkooper, J., & Walter, B. (2000). Mind/machine interaction consortium: PortREG replication experiments. *Journal of Scientific Exploration, 14*(4), 499–555.

Kornwachs, K., & Lucadou, W. v. (1975). Beitrag zum begriff der komplexität. *Grundlagenstudien aus Kybernetik und Geisteswissenschaft, 16,* 51–60.

Kornwachs, K., & Lucadou, W. v. (1985). Pragmatic information as a nonclassical concept to describe cognitive processes. *Cognitive Systems, 1*(1), 79–94.

Lucadou, W. v. (1974). Zum parapsychologischen experiment - Eine methodologische Skizze [To the parapsychological experiment: Methodological outlines]. *Zeitschrift für Parapsychologie und Grenzgebiete der Psychologie, 16,* 57–62.

Lucadou, W. v. (1983). Der flüchtige spuk [The elusive spook]. In E. Bauer & W.v. Lucadou (Eds.), *Spektrum der parapsychologie,* pp. 150–166). Freiburg i.Br.: Aurum Verlag.

Lucadou, W. v. (1984). What is wrong with the definition of psi? *European Journal of Parapsychology, 5,* 261–283.

Lucadou, W. v. (1986). *Experimentelle untersuchungen zur beeinflußbarkeit von stochastischen quantenphysikalischen. Systemen durch den Beobachter.* Frankfurt: H.-A. Herchen Verlag.

Lucadou, W. v. (1987). The model of pragmatic information (MPI). In: R. L. Morris (Ed.), *The Parapsychological Association 30th Annual Convention, Proceedings of Presented Papers.* pp. 236–254.

Lucadou, W. v. (1989). Vom abgrund der systeme [From the abyss of the systems]. *Zeitschrift für Parapsychologie und Grenzgebiete der Psychologie, 31,* 108–121.

Lucadou, W. v. (1990). Was man nicht wiederholen kann - zum Problem der Replizierbarkeit bei Experimenten mit komplexen Systemen. *Zeitschrift für Parapsychologie und Grenzgebiete der Psychologie, 32,* 212–230.

Lucadou, W. v. (1991a). Some remarks on the problem of repeatability of experiments dealing with complex systems. In H. Atmanspacher & H. Scheingraber (Eds.), *Information Dynamics,* pp. 143–151. NATO ASI Series, Series B: Physics Vol. 256. New York & London: Plenum.

Lucadou, W. v. (1991b). Makroskopische nichtlokalität [Macroscopic nonlocality]. In K.W. Kratky (Hrsg.), *Systemische Perspektiven: Interdisziplinäre Beiträge zu Theorie und Praxis,* pp. 45–63. Heidelberg: Carl Auer.

Lucadou, W. v. (1993). Lassen sich 'PK-impulse' lokalisieren? - Korrelationen zwischen persönlichkeitsmerkmalen von beobachtern und quantenphysikalischen fluktuationen. *Zeitschrift für Parapsychologie und Grenzgebiete der Psychologie, 35,* 41–70.

Lucadou, W. v. (1994). Locating psi-bursts: Correlations between psychological characteristics of observers and observed quantum physical fluctuations. In E. W. Cook & L. D. Delanoy (Eds.), *Research in Parapsychology, 1991,* pp. 39–43. Metuchen, NJ: Scarecrow.

Lucadou, W. v. (1995). The model of pragmatic information (MPI). *European Journal of Parapsychology, 11,* 58–75.

Lucadou, W. v. (1998). The exo-endo-perspective of non-locality in psychophysical systems. *International Journal of Computing Anticipatory Systems, 2,* 169–185.

Lucadou, W. v. (2000). Spuk [RSPK]. In S. M. Schomburg-Scherff & B. Heintze (Eds.), *Die offenen Grenzen der Ethnologie,* pp. 219–230. Frankfurt a.M.: Lembeck.

Lucadou, W. v. (2001). Hans in luck: The currency of evidence in parapsychology. *Journal of Parapsychology, 65,* 3–16.

Lucadou, W. v. (2002). Theoretical contributions to psi: Does parapsychology go mainstream? In V. Gowri Rammohan (Ed.), *New Frontiers of Human Science,* pp. 79–94. Jefferson, NC: McFarland.

Lucadou, W. v. (2006). Self-organization of temporal structures: A possible solution for the intervention problem. In D. P. Sheehan (Ed.), *Frontiers of time: Retrocausation. Experiment and theory,* pp. 293–315, AIP Conference Proceedings, AIP, Melville, NY.

Lucadou, W. v., Römer, H., & Walach, H. (2007). Synchronistic phenomena as entanglement correlations in generalized quantum theory. *Journal of Consciousness Studies, 14*(4), 50–74.

Lucadou, W. v., & Zahradnik, F. (2004). Predictions of the MPI about RSPK. In S. Schmidt (Ed.), *Proceedings of the 47th Annual Convention of the Parapsychological Association,* pp. 99–112.

May, E. C., Utts, J. M., & Spottiswoode, S. J. P. (1995). Decision augmentation theory: Toward a model for anomalous mental phenomena. *Journal of Parapsychology, 59,* 195–220.

Oteri, L. (Ed.) 1975. *Quantum physics and parapsychology.* New York: Parapsychology Foundation.

Pallikari, F., & Boller, E. (1999). A rescale range analysis of random events. *Journal of Scientific Exploration, 13,* 25–40.

Primas, H. (1990). Mathematical and philosophical questions in the theory of open and macroscopic quantum systems. In A. I. Miller (Ed.), *Sixty-two years of uncertainty,* pp. 233–257. New York: Plenum.

Primas, H. (1992). Time-asymmetric phenomena in biology complementary exophysical descriptions arising from deterministic quantum endophysics. *Open Systems & Information Dynamics, 1*(1), 3–34.

Radin, D. (1993). Environmental modulation and statistical equilibrium in mind-matter interaction. *Subtle Energies and Energy Medicine 4,* 1–29.

Renninger, M. (1960). Messungen ohne Störungen des Messobjekts. *Zeitschrift für Physik, 158,* 417–421.

Sidgwick, H. (1882). Presidential address. *Proceedings of the society for psychical research*: I. 1882–83, 7–12.

Walach, H., & Römer, H. (2000). Complementarity is a useful concept for consciousness studies: A reminder. *Neuroendocrinology Letters*, *21*, 221–232.

Walker, E. H. (1979). The quantum theory of psi phenomena. *Psychoenergetic Systems*, *3*, 259–299.

Weizsäcker, E. v. (1974). Erstmaligkeit und bestätigung als komponenten der pragmatischen information [Novelty and confirmation as components of pragmatic information]. In E. v. Weizsäcker (Hrsg.), *Offene Systeme I*, pp. 83–113. Stuttgart: Klett.

Chapter 12

First Sight: A Way of Thinking about the Mind, and a Theory of Psi

James Carpenter

Parapsychology has a theory. Often, this field has been thought of as a disciplined collection of anomalies. Not just any anomalies, to be sure, but still a motley array of anomalies, all of which somehow seem to suggest that minds respond to minds, and matter responds to minds, in ways that go beyond the ordinary boundaries of our bodies and our present moment. Many carefully done research reports have been rejected by editors who said something like this: "Your findings seem to be significant, but they make no sense. We have no way of understanding how something like this could work, and we cannot publish reports of mere anomalies."

The author may try to object, "But we have a primitive theory to the effect that minds can reach minds and matter in unusual ways."

To which our editor responds (if he or she bothers), "This is not a theory, this is a circular restatement of your results. You have no theory. Go away."

As this volume indicates, parapsychology actually has several theories. The one I know best is the one I constructed, called first sight. I offer an overview of the theory here (Carpenter, 2012a).

First sight is a psychological theory, not a physical one, although there is no reason it should not prove to be compatible with physical and physiological theories like those discussed in this volume.

As a psychological theory, it attempts to account for what psi means, how it works, and how it fits in with all the rest of what we currently know about our psychological functioning. It suggests what psi is "for" in everyday life. It offers guidance for a comprehensive and integrative program of research.

FIRST SIGHT THEORY

The name of the theory is a play on the colloquial term "second sight," which implies that psi experiences are extra and mysterious, vaguely mystical events that lie outside of ordinary perception and behavior and occasionally supplement them. To say that psi is *first sight* is intended to convey the opposite—that psi is a process that is ordinary, common, and crucially important, in fact, that it is something we use all the time in a way that precedes our every thought and action. It comes first.

Two Basic Premises

The first sight theory (FST) is embedded in an unusual model of the mind. I start with two assumptions that seem to be necessary if we are to make any sense of psi. Although perhaps not directly testable, these premises are useful inasmuch as they provide a framework within which many testable ideas can be understood. The first premise proposes a virtually unlimited unconscious mind. The second says that unconscious cognitive processing stands behind and produces all experience and behavior, and that this processing includes an extrasomatic reference to a wide world apprehended by what we call psi.

1. *Organisms are psychologically unbounded. They transact with reality in an unconscious way beyond their physical boundaries.*

   a) They are unconsciously engaged psychologically with an extended universe of meaning of indefinite extent in space and time. This engagement is continuously ongoing and is referred to as psi. The efferent (expressive) aspect of these engagements is referred to as psychokinesis (PK). The afferent (receptive) aspect of the engagements is referred to as extrasensory perception (ESP). These two aspects of psi are always intimately conjoined in their unconscious functioning.

   b) If the afferent engagement refers to some event in the future, it is called precognition, and if it refers to another person's experience, it is called telepathy. Direct access to the meanings of future events is necessarily prior to our potential access to those events in the present, and direct engagement with extrasomatic information necessarily precedes that information being able to reach the senses. For these reasons, psi may be referred to as first sight—hence the name given to the model and theory.

2. *All experience and all behavior are constituted out of unconscious psycho-logical processes carried out purposefully on multiple sources of informa-tion, including psi information, as mediated by unconscious intention and contextual appraisal.*

   a) These processes are automatic in the sense that they are not voli-tionally conscious (we are not aware of choosing to do them), but they are not impersonal or mechanical. Inasmuch as it is capable of thinking at all, an organism thinks (makes discrimina-tions and carries out cognitive/affective actions) unconsciously as well as consciously.

   b) Unconscious thought considers several sources of information, including nonlocal information (psi), sensation, memory, imagi-nation, goals, and values. Consideration of the various sources of information occurs rapidly, holistically, and efficiently toward the end of bringing to consciousness the most useful thing for con-sciousness to consider at each moment.

   c) Unconscious intention is the primary guide that is used by uncon-scious thought in constructing experience and action. As certain strands of potential meaning become more pertinent to intention, other strands are assessed in relation to them and may be expressed or excluded from the ultimate products of experience and action.

   d) These unconscious bits of potential meaning are not thought of as *perceptions,* since that implies a conscious experience. Yet, they are engagements with reality—with sensory stimulations, extrasen-sory events, remembered events, and so on. FST calls these acts of engagement *prehensions,* a term borrowed from the philosopher Alfred North Whitehead. The term means, at root, to get hold, to grasp. Unconscious prehensions grasp things unconsciously, and psi prehensions grasp things that are beyond the ordinary boun-daries of the body. Just like the phrase "to grasp," prehension is intended to have connotations that are both active (to take hold of) and receptive (to come to know about). The ESP aspect of psi receives something; the PK aspect physically acts upon it.

   e) While unconscious psychological processes are not directly avail-able to awareness, their activity is often expressed implicitly and inadvertently by various physiological, behavioral, and experien-tial responses. These implicit activities often achieve other person-ally desirable ends through behaviors that are adaptive to the situation but that may never result in an act of consciousness, such as making a certain consumer choice based partly upon an implicit memory. These activities also facilitate adaptive behaviors through physiological, emotional, and cognitive kinds of arousal that implicitly prepare the organism for an effective response to its situation. For example, subliminal information about something prior to awareness acts to prepare a person for a correct recognition of that thing a split second later as a conscious perception has time to form and the perception can be construed as the thing that it is. Similarly, an extrasensory evocation of a mood or state of physical arousal helps to prepare a person for a quickly effective response to a danger as soon as that can be accurately perceived.

f) These implicitly adaptive responses are the means by which the existence and activity of unconscious psychological processes can be discerned. Since unconscious cognitive processes (including psi) are never available as such to consciousness, they can be detected only by virtue of experiences and behaviors that imply them and express them inadvertently. When a conscious perception and/or action is completed, these implicit aspects of response are generally unnoticed and uninterpreted by the person who is perceiving and acting. If perceptions and actions are frustrated and not completed, the implicit aspects may be more available to awareness.

Twelve Corollaries of First Sight Theory

There are 12 corollaries that expand the two basic premises and define their testable implications. These corollaries comprise the gist of the theory. Together, they provide a picture of how psi "works" and what patterns its functioning should be expected to follow. In the context of personal experience, they inform us when psi (ESP and PK) experiences should or should not occur. In the context of the laboratory, they aid in predicting when significant PK or ESP scoring should occur; and when it does occur, whether it will be in a positive or negative direction. A brief description of each corollary is presented here, details of which can be found in Carpenter (2012a).

1. *Personalness corollary.* Unconscious cognitive processes, including the mind's use of psi information, is essentially a personal business because it is always implicitly guided by an individual's personal constellation of intentions, needs, memories, and concerns. It will never be adequately reduced to an impersonal account in terms of general physical processes, biochemical reactions, or neural activities. The physical level of analysis will be useful in understanding how psi works, but it will never fully account for it. As J. B. Rhine once said, "psi is a psychological process."

2. *Ubiquity corollary.* Unconscious processing of psi information is always going on. It is implicitly present in every scrap of thought and flicker of experience. Psi is often thought of as rare; for first sight, it is the most common thing imaginable.

3. *Integration corollary.* Experiences and behaviors do not just bloom forth all by themselves. They are constructed unconsciously by our minds. This construction process is holistic and rapid, and takes account of a vast amount of information, which the mind swiftly integrates. A simple visual perception, for example, seeing an apple, is constructed out of sensations that impinge upon the retina, including subliminal ones that occur so briefly that they never become conscious. Additionally, the mind also consults other matters, including unconscious long-term memories, general concerns and values, momentary states, and the purposes guiding the moment. For example, if you are looking for fruit in your orchard, you will spot an apple more quickly than if you are watching for migratory birds. Extrasomatic information (a.k.a., psi) is also consulted and added into the constructive mix. Some is known, but much is to be learned about the principles that govern this unconscious process of construction. FST posits the working assumption that the processing of these different strands of preconscious information (memories, subliminal stimuli, extrasensory information, goals, momentary states, concerns) will tend to follow similar patterns. This is called the *hypothesis of functional equivalence.*

To emphasize here, the primary function of FST *is to provide a framework for developing our scientific understanding of the principles governing unconscious processing and integration—including the processing of psi information.* Its reach is broader than psi.

4. *Anticipation corollary.* The mind seeks to anticipate events. We all wish to move into the future adaptively, moment by moment. Unconscious cognitive processes seek to understand reality as it develops in time, predict its outcomes, and behaviorally respond consciously and unconsciously in optimal ways. Psi information is part of what the mind uses for this. FST shows its teleological cast here, saying that this forward-pressing construction is the primary thing that psi is "for."

5. *Weighting and signing corollary.* Although the processes of unconsciously integrating and constructing experience and behavior are so rapid and complex that we can scarcely imagine them, we can say that each bit of information—sensory, extrasensory, remembered, or felt—must somehow be subjected to two basic acts. First, it must be assessed for its importance in the moment. FST calls this *weighting.* Then if it is sensed to be important at all, an unconscious

dichotomous choice must be made as to how to utilize it. The mind elects either to incorporate the bit by making reference to it in the developing act/experience, or to exclude it from any implication in action or experience. FST assumes that all unconscious cognition functions in this binary way: approach or avoid, include or exclude. FST calls this the act of *signing*.

Weighting and *signing* are the basic constructs we will use to try to understand when, in everyday life, an expression of psi will be strong enough to be noticeable. In the laboratory, we want to understand when a measurable expression of psi (a "score") will be extreme enough to be clearly extrachance and if it is extreme enough, whether it will be in a positive or negative direction of expression.

6. *Summation corollary.* Each bit of experience and behavior is thus based upon a summation of a very quick and complex, holistic, unconscious process of weighting and signing. The beginning point of this summing process is extrasomatic (psi is "first sight"), but in the case of sensory perception, reference to psi is followed quickly by the use of subliminal sensations, and this is followed by full-blown conscious, sensory experience. Each stage of this very rapid process poses tentative questions or proposes orienting stances toward later information. For example, an extrasensory prehension, if weighted heavily, orients the unconscious mind toward a range of potential meanings, which guide unconscious attention to subliminal stimuli. As these stimuli appear to confirm some possible meanings more than others, conscious attention is sharpened still more toward a narrow subset of the original possibilities and poses narrower questions for experience to answer. Then a full conscious experience is generated, and it is construed in the way sensed to be most optimal. This construction then feeds back to the unconscious processes, orienting both extrasensory and subliminal-sensory attention to "look out for" further information that is particularly pertinent to the content that has been constructed. Further unconscious information is then processed in this light, and the next experience or behavior is shaped accordingly.

As an example, consider an extrasomatic and unconscious arousal of neurological activity that might imply a sense that something important and dangerous might be about to unfold—what parapsychologists call a *presentiment*. Along with the physiological arousal, a certain area of the visual field is sensed to be important, and classes of things that might be involved are suggested. Guided by all of this, unconscious attention is then instantly drawn to vague, subliminal movements approaching quickly from that direction. Then immediately, preconscious attention is sharpened still more, and one becomes aware of being approached by a cloud of small things. Then conscious attention, sharpened further, concludes that a swarm of angry bees has risen up and is on the attack. This construction (bees attacking!) then feeds back to extrasomatic and subliminal levels of processing, requiring them only to contribute further orienting information pertinent to the issue of escaping bees and excluding anything else.

Thus, the organism develops its experience and behavior quickly over time. For FST, a whole lot goes into each lived moment, almost all of it is unconscious, and psi plays a continuously important but mostly invisible part.

7. *Bidirectionality corollary.* This corollary elaborates the intrinsically bidirectional nature of unconscious cognitive processes. Inclusion of information is called *assimilation,* and the exclusion of information is called *contrast-formation.* The excluding process of contrast does not mean that a bit of information is simply ignored—it is positively excluded and avoided. Thus, if the meaning of "apple" is subjected to contrast, the idea or perception of *apple* will be found to occur in the flow of ideas and perceptions *significantly less often than it ordinarily would by chance.* This sort of negative effect has been observed in many research contexts. In the literature on subliminal perception, this is called negative priming. In memory literature, such avoidant negation appears to be involved in various phenomena, including "false memory," blocked memory, amnesia, and simple forgetting. In parapsychology, this kind of active avoidance of certain content is called psi missing.

8. *Intentionality corollary.* What guides the unconscious decisions of weighting and signing, assimilation and exclusion, and the consequent construction of experience and action? In less teleological, more reductionist theories, this might be held to be some property of the stimulus, such as its intensity; or it might be some physiological process, such as neurochemical thresholds and events. In FST, however, it is held to be *unconscious intention.* If an element of apprehended meaning (either intrasomatic or extrasomatic) is sensed to be useful and desirable in the context of the individual's situation in the moment, then it will be weighted heavily and assimilated positively. Thus, to sum up the postulated action of unconscious cognition, it consists essentially in unconscious *choices* (not physical processes) being carried out on sensed potential *meanings* (not physical stimuli) guided by unconscious *intentions* (not impersonal, mechanical processes). Since FST assumes that consciousness is determined by unconscious psychological processes, it can be said to operate within the meta-theoretical framework called *psychological determinism.* This

framework was also used by Sigmund Freud in his theory of psycho-analysis (Freud, 1958; Rapaport & Gill, 1959).

Since unconscious intention is, by its nature, unavailable to introspection, one can assess it only by its implicit expression in experience and behavior. Its action is assumed to be systematic and predictable, and the scientific task is to uncover the principles governing it. Some of the principles assumed to govern unconscious intention are outlined later in this chapter.

9. *Switching corollary.* At a given moment, unconscious intention may choose to sign a particular element of potential meaning either positively or negatively. It may hold this decision unequivocally or somewhat ambivalently; and it may hold it consistently over time, or it may change to the other direction. This act of changing sign is called a *switch.* A switch in direction will act to cancel out the previous decision, since a tendency to assimilate the meaning will be replaced by a tendency to exclude it, or vice versa.

Just as signing is determined by unconscious intention, the rate of switching is determined by the consistency of unconscious intention. If intention is mixed or shifts, the sign switches.

10. *Extremity corollary.* An expression of psi will not only be in a positive (assimilative) or negative (exclusionary) direction, it will also occur to some degree of extremity. A more extreme expression may draw conscious attention in natural situations or may earn statistical significance in a laboratory experiment. A less extreme expression will not do those things. The concept of switching helps us understand this degree of extremity.

Switching must always occur sooner or later, more quickly or more slowly, as events and their salience flow on in time. In general, slow switching will produce stronger (more extreme) expressions of psi, and rapid switching will lead to weaker expressions. If switching is very slow, references in the same direction to a given potential meaning will be able to accumulate long enough to produce a strong experience or a significant score. If switching is rapid enough, scores in an ESP or PK test will show an odd effect: *They will hover so closely to chance expectation that they will not be reasonably attributable to chance.* In fact, this extrachance chance-level scoring has been observed sometimes and appears to be meaningful.

Both slow switching and rapid switching are useful in everyday functioning. Slow switching makes it highly likely that a given meaning will either be accessed or avoided in experience. Rapid switching is useful for rendering some potential meaning irrelevant to ongoing experience, averting any distracting influence that might otherwise arise from it. Rapid switching is presumably adopted unconsciously to ensure that the information involved plays no part at all in the formation of experience and action.

11. *Inadvertency and frustration corollary.* This corollary identifies how and when we are most likely to be able to see psi at work. The mind's unconscious commerce with extrasomatic meanings (psi) are intrinsically unconscious. They are never available to an individual's conscious experience. Thus, FST considers it a misleading misnomer to speak of an "ESP experience" or a "PK experience." Then how do we ever know that an extrasomatic, psi interaction has occurred? By virtue of the implicit expressions that arise in consciousness and behavior.

While never conscious, psi events do contribute continually to the *formation* of conscious experience, and they do this by arousing networks of ideas and feelings (if heavily weighted and positively signed) that are useful in suggesting what the content of consciousness may prove to be. They help guide the formation of consciousness by alerting subliminal and then supraliminal attention about certain possibilities to focus upon, while excluding others. Because of this arousal, psi engagements can be glimpsed by noticing the apparently causeless "margins" of experience. When we are in relaxed and unfocused states, we can see this flow, the flotsam and jetsam of experience and behavior—the unbidden sequence of impulses, ideas, memories, and feelings—the things in the environment that grab one's attention for no apparent reason, the shifts in mood that arise out of nowhere. These things are all *inadvertencies* from the point of view of consciousness. They constitute the allusory language of psi and of all unconscious cognitive processing.

One other thing is necessary if we are to notice such inadvertent allusions to psi engagements. The successful development of experience must be somehow frustrated. We must not yet be clearly perceiving, not yet making a decision, not yet able to remember, not yet able to act. This is because when experience and behavior are forming fully and smoothly, the preconscious allusions contributed by unconscious processing flow immediately into perception or memory or action, too quickly to ever be seen as such. They vanish obediently and never trouble awareness and the clear focus it has just achieved. When cognitive closure and behavioral action are *frustrated* for some reason, we may glimpse the implicit promptings of unconscious thought in their own right by the inadvertent bits of thought and feeling and action that they provoke.

12. *Liminality corollary.* Inadvertent and implicitly allusory bits of experience and behavior "pop up" at the line at which unconscious cognitive processing takes form in experiences and behaviors that are available to awareness. We may call this the *limen* between unconscious and

conscious processes, and these marginal phenomena may be referred to as *liminal*. Such liminal phenomena include dreams, moods, impulses, psychoneurotic symptoms, "flashbacks" (in the context of PTSD), errors, imagery, felt preferences or aversions, acts of forgetting, hunches, and vague impressions. In such events, we see motivated prehensions uncoupled from conscious understanding.

People differ in terms of how interested they are in such liminal phenomena, and in how instructive they are seen to be; and some states of mind are more productive of liminal material than others. More liminal states of mind and more liminally oriented people are expected to express more psi phenomena and to show more implicit signs of all unconscious cognitive processes in general.

This is related to the issue of *cognitive closure*. People differ in how much they typically attain and prefer clear cognitive closure, as opposed to a greater tolerance for and interest in ill-defined possibilities. This is the trait of *openness*. More open people are more likely to assimilate a broader range of unconscious information than more closed people, since they unconsciously will tend to consider that information to have greater potential value. In fact, this long-standing value is assumed, in FST, to be the basis of their openness. For FST, *liminality* and *openness* are overlapping constructs.

Two Guiding Questions

The development of this model of the mind and theory of psi was aided by two analogies that can be expressed as questions:

- Is ESP like subliminal perception?
- Is psychokinesis like unconsciously expressive behavior?

These analogies suggest some of the purposes that psi might serve and point the way to possibilities about how they might function. For simplicity, we focus this discussion on ESP.

What If ESP Is Like Subliminal Perception?

Subliminal perception is popularly thought of as a weird and possibly threatening way of manipulating people into doing things they might not ordinarily choose to do. However, psychologists have come to understand that subliminal perception is going on continually as we engage the world with our senses. There is a preconscious level of sensory stimulation that is too brief or too faint or too unattended to be consciously perceived. Yet, these unconscious bits of stimulation effect our experiences and behavior. A subliminal stimulus acts as a *prime*. Such primes have several effects:

- They evoke physiological responses. For instance, a threatening subliminal stimulus (e.g., an angry face) exposed too briefly to consciously perceive will tend to arouse heightened autonomic activity.

- They alter perceptions. Suppose a research participant is being asked to identify as quickly as possible the content of pictures that appear on a screen. If an emerging picture has been preceded by a subliminal prime that represents a congruent category (e.g., a smiling face is preceded by the prime of the word *happy*), the perception will be quicker than if the picture had been preceded by a conflicting category (e.g., the word *sad*).

- They affect the probability of different kinds of behaviors. One study exposed participants to a subliminal prime that was either emotionally neutral or had aggressive content and then placed them in a waiting room situation with someone behaving in an annoying manner. Those who had been exposed to the unconscious aggressive prime behaved in either a more quarrelsome or avoidant manner than those who had been exposed to the neutral prime.

- If ESP is like subliminal perception, then extrasensory engagements will be expected to evoke similar kinds of perceptions and responses.

Subliminal perception is a continuously active part of the history of every perception. Look around you now. Each thing you see, each conscious visual perception, is actually preceded by a host of subliminal impressions that impinge upon your retina and are processed by your unconscious mind. Psychologists have understood for a long time that every single perception has an unconscious developmental history to which many subliminal impressions contribute.

These subliminal impressions act to guide the construction of each thing we perceive. They orient consciousness to focus on certain things as opposed to others and come to understand what they are in certain ways.

All of the subliminal impressions, and all the processing that the mind does with them, is unconscious. It is a misnomer to speak of subliminal "perceptions," since they are never consciously perceived. Their function is invisible. We know for sure that they are going on only because psychologists have designed experiments in which the full development of a conscious experience is prevented (as by stopping a visual exposure too quickly to be consciously perceived). The thing that was exposed is never seen, but implicit signs of its orienting activity can be noticed by attending to physiological responses or changes in perceptual readiness, mood, or spontaneous behaviors that follow the exposure.

While this activity is unconscious, it is incorrect to think of it as mechanical or impersonal, consisting only of neurochemical actions, somehow blindly triggered by physical stimuli. Below consciousness, we assume (and we are taught) lie mechanical chemical processes. This might be sensible, except for the fact that subliminal perceptions are about *meanings, not meaningless stimulations*. No one has yet been able to explain how chemical processes can appreciate meanings or be guided by intentions. The processing that leads to consciousness is guided implicitly by the individual's personal intentions and unconscious assessments. Research on subliminal perception has demonstrated this in hundreds of ways. Different individuals with different intentions will process the same subliminal information differently, in accord with their personal needs (e.g. Milyavski, Hassin & Schul, 2012; Veltkamp, Aarts & Custers, 2008). Subliminal perception does not just *happen to us*. It is something we *personally do for our own purposes*, but it is something we do unconsciously.

If ESP is like subliminal perception, then it also is part of the history of every perception. It also serves to orient the development of consciousness in particular ways. It also functions unconsciously and is never available to conscious awareness as such. It also functions automatically but not impersonally, as it, too, is guided by the individual's personal needs and intentions and developing assessments.

Psi Is the Initial Step in the Formation of Experience

Every bit of experience and behavior has a rapidly unfolding history. This history of development is ordinarily unconscious, but psychologists have been ingenious at devising experiments that allow us to know of its existence and tease out some knowledge about how it works.

What most psychologists have not known, and what parapsychologists add to the picture, is that this rapid prehistory of experience begins a step earlier with psi—with unconscious engagements with reality that take place beyond the ordinary boundaries of the organism.

This is the basic, every-moment, function of psi. We might say that it is what psi is *for*. It reaches beyond us and before us, and implicitly helps guide the construction of each piece of what we experience and what we choose to do.

This is why psi is not *second sight*. Psi is *first sight*. It involves the prehensions of potential meanings that are beyond the sensory system and prehensions of events that are still in the future and have yet to occur. It comes first.

If Psi Is Real, Where Is It Hiding?

The findings of parapsychologists appear to tell of almost magical human powers that are belied by everyday experience. We cannot see the future, read others' minds, or move objects about by sheer intention. If psi is real, why do we not see it?

The answer is that psi is intrinsically unconscious, always at work, but always out of sight. FST also asserts a more nuanced idea of what psi is not. ESP is not knowledge. Knowledge is something we consciously experience, and we can never experience ESP as such. ESP is part of the unconscious processing that develops acts of knowing, a part that reflects extrasomatic prehensions. FST also asserts that psychokinesis is not action, inasmuch as we normally reserve that term for behaviors that are consciously and deliberately carried out. Psychokinesis contributes to the development of acts of behavior, primarily by serving as the link between the mental realm of unconscious intention and the physical realm of the person's own nervous system. Psi is the link, long debated and long sought, between mind and body. By its nature, however, psychokinesis is not limited to the boundaries of the body, and under certain circumstances, unconscious intention may be expressed implicitly by events in the external physical world—including within the nervous systems of other people.

So while no one *knows* anything by way of ESP, and no one *does* anything via PK, both of these unconscious processes can sometimes be noticed at work by virtue of the bits of experience, behavior, and physical events that have been aroused by them and that implicitly express their guiding activity.

So psi is hiding in the most ubiquitously present way imaginable. Psi is implicitly present in every thought.

Changes in Perspective Implied by First Sight Theory

I will list several things that most people commonly believe about psi and discuss the different idea proposed by first sight theory.

There Is a Good Chance That Psi Is Not Real at All

The apparent expressions of psi are so equivocal, and their occurrence is so erratic and uncommon, that most people think that there is some possibility that they may not represent anything real at all. Even people inclined to be "believers" admit to some degree of uncertainty about this.

Probably the most compelling reason to have some doubt about the reality of psi is the apparent absence of such phenomena in the everyday lives of most people.

For FST, the apparent absence of psi is a consequence of its unconscious nature and is a useful economy in the business of living effectively. Psi is a real dimension of our engagement with our worlds, but it functions smoothly in the background, just as we breathe and digest effectively without being conscious of the nerve impulses that trigger the diaphragm or the enzyme actions that disassemble a steak.

Psi Is Unpredictable and Unreliable

Psi is our engagement with our worlds beyond our bodies and beyond the present moment in time, and according to FST, it is utterly reliable in its everyday use, which is to help construct optimally effective experiences and behaviors. It is our ability to predict the expressions of psi that is currently rather unreliable. And while the rather erratic signs of psi at work are too unreliable to be a major guide in life decisions, at an unconscious level, where psi does its major work, it appears to function very reliably.

Psi Is an Ability That Is Limited to a Few Special People and Unusual Circumstances

According to FST, psi is a level of unconscious engagement that is going on all the time for everyone. "Psychics," who are better at consciously using psi to gain new information or effect new actions in the world, are persons who are relatively prone to generating psi-expressive inadvertencies and who have developed the skill of interpreting them. This is presumably possible for anyone, although like any cultivation of experience and skill, not everyone develops it equally.

From this perspective, psi is not an ability at all. It is an intrinsic aspect of our unconscious being-in-the-world. It is more like the way we interact with gravity, as material beings, or the way we are connected to other people, as social beings. We all have an unconscious commerce with reality that extends beyond our bodies. The consciously useful *expression of psi* is a skill that varies among people, but the psi itself—the extended engagement—is alien to no one.

It is true that certain kinds of situations, especially situations of danger to oneself or important others, are especially likely to occasion apparent psi-expressing experiences. But this is because psi, like all preconscious processing, is guided by our most pressing unconscious intentions. These events are the sort that are most likely to be heavily weighted and consistently signed in a positive direction and hence are likely to arouse many implicit allusions that are more likely to be noticed and interpreted.

TWO MAJOR CHANGES IN RESEARCH ORIENTATION

This different conception of psi suggests that research should be conducted differently in at least a couple of major ways, in terms of the kinds of procedures we employ and the kinds of questions we ask.

Studies Will Not Try to Capture Psi, They Will Attempt to Reveal It

Most parapsychological research has attempted to measure the expression of psi by challenging participants to somehow consciously produce evidence of a psi "ability." In an ESP experiment, they might be asked to guess the contents of some distant or hidden thing. In a PK experiment, they might try to consciously affect some physical process, such as the output of random number generators. But for FST, ESP is not any form of knowledge, and PK is not any form of action. Psi is an intrinsically unconscious process that helps to anticipate knowledge and action, and its allusory expression tends to be suppressed in the context of conscious work. Therefore, such consciously oriented procedures are not optimal. We assume that psi is a perpetually ongoing, unconscious process that expresses itself implicitly only when the ordinary outcomes of experience and behavior are somehow frustrated, so it should be better for the experimenter to devise situations in which such ongoing participation can be revealed in its natural functioning.

Studies in the unconscious, spontaneous expression of psi have already become more common for parapsychologists in recent years. I will discuss a few of them, since they illustrate the kind of research that should be most productive.

John Palmer (2006) carried out a series of studies that tested the idea that people could make implicit reference to future events as well as contemporaneous ones. He asked people to observe strings of random numbers while misleading them to believe that there was some sort of order in the numbers, which they should try to identify. Then he asked them to try to test the order theory they were developing by correctly guessing the next number that was to appear in the string. He found that they did impute imaginary orders and test them out, as bright and compliant research participants should do. This unordered list was followed by another list that did in fact have a hidden order, and they repeated the task. The interesting point is that in the first part of the experiment when numbers were random, the order theory people tested out tended to conform to the actual hidden pattern that they were about to receive in the next list. With no actual pattern to find, participants unwittingly made reference to a future order (precognition). A second study confirmed the pattern.

A group of friends and I (Carpenter, 2012b) met weekly for hour-long unstructured sessions. In most of the sessions, all members were psycho-therapists, so all were comfortable with fairly intense and emotionally genuine interactions. While meetings were taking place, a computer in another town selected a random number that would identify a picture tar-get that we hoped might be expressed in the conduct of our meeting—the things that we happened to dwell upon, the significant events that occurred, the mood of the session, and so on. No one knew the identity of this target. After the session was over, the target and three decoy pic-tures were presented to the group and were ranked for their relevance to the day's session. The group met for 386 sessions and was able to identify the correct picture to a strongly significant degree without any normal means to do so. As a few examples, in one session, a picture of devastating hurricane damage accompanied a meeting with much gloomy talk of death. A picture of two children happily holding hands and walking away together was the target on a day when a long-standing conflict between two members was resolved joyfully. A picture of a reckless bull in a china shop was given on a day when one member behaved with unusual aban-don and spontaneity. Each day, we spontaneously developed our interac-tion as any group of friends and therapists might do, but without being conscious of it, we also expressed implications of the unknown pictures that were our targets.

Dean Radin (1997, 2004) and others (Mossbridge, Tressoldi, & Utts, 2012) have carried out a number of studies on what has been called the *presentiment effect*. All these studies ask research participants to be still and do nothing but pay attention while they are exposed to a series of stimuli, while aspects of their psychophysiological arousal are being monitored. Pictures are generally used, but other kinds of stimuli such as sounds have been used as well (May, Paulinyi, & Vassy, 2014/2005). Some of the stimuli are unpleasant and emotionally arousing (pictures of gruesome surgical procedures, harsh noises), while others are pleas-ant or neutral. Which type of stimuli occur when is determined ran-domly by a computer, and no one knows what is to come next in any trial. It is well known that a host of subtle physiological changes occur when people are exposed to shocking and unpleasant stimuli. Skin per-spires more, peripheral blood vessels shrink, heart rate and blood pres-sure change, and so on. These participants showed the normal responses to the stimuli when they flashed before them. But Radin and others also looked at the period *just before* the stimuli were presented. What they found is that the same sort of stress responses that would fol-low the stimuli also *preceded them* a few seconds before the computer made the random decision and displayed the stimulus. The responses before the stimulus were less pronounced, and were probably never strong enough to rise to conscious awareness, but they were strongly

significant across many studies. These people physiologically anticipated the emotional response they were about to be called upon to produce by a currently unknown event.

Daryl Bem (2011) reported a series of nine experiments, all of which
demonstrated, in different ways, that people will tend to express the
implications of future events not by their physiological response but in
their behaviors and choices—and do so completely unconsciously. In one
example, participants were asked to make a choice between two pictures
of blank screens on a computer monitor. Immediately after the choice
was punched, the computer made a random decision such that one of
the screens would lead to a pleasant erotic picture, while the other
would not. Participants unwittingly picked the rewarding screen significantly more often than the alternative. In another example, Bem time-
reversed a familiar priming effect. In the normal paradigm, people are
asked to say whether a picture that appears before them is positive or negative. Just before the picture appears, a word that is either positive or negative is flashed on the screen subliminally. It is well known that
participants will tend to make the correct identification more quickly
when the subliminal prime is congruent in emotional quality (both prime
and target word are positive, or both are negative) than they will if they
have opposite qualities. Bem time-reversed this paradigm by showing
the picture first and then, after the participant identified the quality,
flashed the positive or negative prime. Participants made their identifica-
tions more quickly when the *prime that was to come* was emotionally congruent than when it was emotionally incongruent. Since Bem's paper
appeared, 81 more studies have been conducted on the general premise
of time-reversed effects, most of which were exact replications of Bem's
studies, and a meta-analysis of the whole body of work of work has been
compiled that shows a very strongly significant rate of replication. This
paper is awaiting publication.

Elmar Gruber (1980) took advantage of devices that captured the time it
took for cars to pass through a tunnel in central Vienna, Austria. Only one
car could pass through this tunnel at a time, and sensors recorded the
moment each car entered and exited. Gruber focused his study on rush
hour periods. His "agents" employed their intention in an attempt to
speed up the trip for cars passing through during certain randomly
chosen blocks of time. Other blocks served as control periods. He found
a significant effect. Cars moved more quickly through the tunnel during
periods in which a "speed up" intention was "sent" to them.

Note that in these studies, none of the participants whose behavior is
being examined is being asked to know anything by way of using ESP,
or affect anything using PK. They are doing thoroughly ordinary and nonparanormal things. Palmer's participants are trying to discern patterns in
an uncertain situation, my group members were shaping an interpersonal

interaction, Radin's were whiling away their time and viewing pictures as they popped up, not unlike random surfers on the Internet. Those involved in Bem's studies were making minor choices, or trying to assess how good or bad something was, and Gruber's drivers were simply moving along as usual on a daily commute. These are familiar behaviors that almost everyone engages in every day with nothing extraordinary or "paranormal" going on at all. Yet, in each of these cases, the experimenters devised the situation in such a way that a completely unconscious, inadvertent psi effect can be seen at work. Such studies reveal an unconscious psi element in everyday life. This is the sort of research that FST most encourages.

Studies Will Relate Psi to Other Unconscious Processes

It is a basic tenet of FST that psi is employed by the unconscious mind in similar ways to that used with other strands of preconscious meaning, including subliminal perception, and long-term or procedural memory (the *hypothesis of functional equivalence*). This implies that the expression of psi should be seen inadvertently in the same sorts of activities that most display other kinds of unconscious cognitive processing, such as dreams, creative work, shifts in mood, mind-wandering, and spontaneous behavioral impulses (what FST calls *liminal* phenomena).

Psi should be studied in designs that allow us to hold it up against subliminal perception and memory and assess the similarities and differences in the patterns governing their expression. We should also focus primarily upon liminal kinds of behaviors and experiences because it is there that we most expect to be able to see psi at work. If some interesting pattern of unconscious functioning has been found in the blessedly well-funded and socially sanctioned world of mainstream psychology, parapsychologists are perfectly free to snatch it up and test out its applicability to extra-somatic responses.

We Want to Know More about Two Main Things

First, we want to know when the unconscious mind will tend to incorporate information and when it will exclude it. When will information be *assimilated,* and when will it be subjected to *contrast-formation* and avoided in behavior and experience? In a test of psi, we want to know when scoring will be positive (above chance) and when it will be negative (below chance). FST refers to this as the *direction of signing,* and it is the first thing we want to understand and be able to predict.

Second, we want to know how strong and clear an expression of psi will be. Will scores in an experiment be weak, or will they be strongly different from chance? In ordinary life experience, will an indication of psi be vivid enough to notice or so weak that it never attracts attention. FST calls this *extremity*.

Unconscious Intention

As stated in the earlier discussion of the intentionality corollary, unconscious intention is the basic determiner of the direction of signing. If an item of information is sensed to be "most relevant" to the dominant intentions of the moment, the information will tend to be assimilated. If it is not relevant, it will tend to be excluded and avoided. Various aspects of the information are thought to enter into that sensed intention, and all of these comprise testable hypotheses.

The consistency of unconscious intention, both in the moment and across time, determines the extremity of an expression of psi. Mixed or shifting intentions lead to weak or no discernable expression of extrasomatic material. Highly consistent and internally integrated intention leads to strong, extreme expressions.

Several hypotheses can be stated about these principles, and others await elucidation. Most of those listed here are drawn from research in cognitive, social, and personality psychology, as well as parapsychology, and some from FST itself. The ones listed here have to do with considerations the unconscious mind uses to determine the direction of signing. They all involve various qualities of the information in question.

The Perceived Reliability of the Information Affects Intention

This implies at least two relationships:

1. Sensory information should usually be responded to more affirmatively than extrasensory information. This is because the content of sensory information is quickly accessible to consciousness and discernment. It is more nearly able to be construed, validated, and understood. Extrasensory information, even when implied by inadvertent behavior, lacks sensory validation, is innately hypothetical, and can never be interpreted with certainty. Understanding this, the mind will tend to give preference to sensory experiences over extrasensory information, if the sensory experiences are available.

   With regard to the expressive, psychokinetic side of psi, preference will likewise be given to actions that the body can reliably perform, and the action of unconscious intention upon matter will be contained within that arena that is understood to be most controllable—one's own physical action; that is, unconscious intention will seek expression through affecting the individual's own nervous system and consequent behavior. If such action is not possible in the situation, the less reliable arena of expression outside the body will be consulted and possibly employed.

2. The perceived source of unconscious information may be understood to be more or less reliable. Given this, the unconscious mind will tend to prefer to get its guidance from the intimations coming from the source thought to be more reliable. For example, in terms of subliminal priming, it has been found (Weinberger & Westen, 2008) that people respond differently to subliminal cues associated with different political candidates, depending upon their own political affiliations and those of the candidates. Similarly, parapsychologists have found that people respond positively or negatively to extrasensory targets, depending upon whether they believe that ESP is impossible (the "sheep-goat effect," Schmeidler & McConnell, 1958).

The Pertinence of the Information in Terms of Goals and Values Affects Intention

Several aspects of this can be important.

1. The task of the moment guides unconscious intention. If one is intent on solving a problem, subliminal and extrasensory information that is pertinent to the problem would be more likely to be assimilated than information that is not pertinent. If one is looking for fruit in an orchard, unconscious cues relevant to fruit will be assimilated more readily than other kinds of potential information.

2. Long-term values and general goals determine pertinence. For example, a highly extraverted person is likely to have a general concern with obtaining social approval, especially in groups (Lucas et al., 2000). For such a person, information that is associated with a greater likelihood of achieving this goal is more likely to be assimilated into experience and behavior than information that does not carry this relevance. A test might involve a choice between two doors, one of which will lead to a friendly group and the other to an empty room. This is a pertinent issue for most extraverts, so it is likely to lead to greater correctness (positive assimilation) in the choice. As another example, physical danger is something that almost all people are concerned with avoiding whenever they can. If an unconscious apprehension arouses a sense that danger could be imminent, this will often tend to lead to some kind of assimilation into experience or behavior, even if the conscious task-of-the-moment is something different. Such assimilation may be more likely to be behavioral (arousal and exiting a situation) than an act of consciousness.

3. Success at the psi task may itself be more or less goal-pertinent. For example, an extravert performing on a stage may be expected to do relatively well at an ESP test, regardless of the content of the targets, since successful performance in itself will lead to social approval. Performing anonymously in an empty room would not offer this potential reward so would not be as likely to lead to successful assimilation. In other cases, the pertinence of success for goal attainment might itself be outside of awareness and available only unconsciously. For example, one experiment (Stanford & Rust, 1977) showed that persons performed better on an ESP test when their good score led to another person having a rewarding experience, even though neither party knew of the contingency.

4. When information belongs to a domain of experience that has been associated with rewarding and valuable experiences in an individual's past, it is likely to be assimilated, while information associated in the past with frustrating or painful experiences is likely to be subject to contrast-formation and suppressed.

The Degree of Congruence between the Information and an Interpretation Already Formed or Nearly Formed Affect Unconscious Intention

There are several aspects to this.

1. When a preponderance of information (particularly sensory and subliminal sensory information) that is consulted in a given moment points in a certain direction of interpretation, extrasensory and other subliminal-sensory information that is congruent with that interpretation is likely to be assimilated, whereas information that is contrary is likely to be avoided.

2. When a construction of an experience has already been clearly formed (cognitive closure), unconscious cues that lie outside of the context defined by that meaning will tend to be avoided in further experience and behavior. Information that lies within that domain and that promises greater discrimination will tend to be assimilated. In other words, the degree of cognitive closure determines the range of potential inclusion. In subliminal priming research, this has been called the principle of exclusion (Schwartz & Bless, 1992).

3. Congruence can have to do with emotional state more than with cognitive content. A person in a cheerful mood will be more likely to assimilate unconscious information with happy connotations than information that is sad or depressing. A frightened person will be especially likely to assimilate information pertinent to the mood of fear, as opposed to information with other qualities.

States of Mind Affect Intention

This may take several different forms.

1. The quality of mood matters. More positive moods tend to evoke a wider range of unconscious sampling of potential information, including psi. Positive moods have also been found to increase the expression of subliminal primes.
2. The amount of cognitive work going on determines the direction of intention. Conscious cognitive processing narrows the band within which the mind draws upon unconscious sources of information. Whatever is being focused upon defines a strict zone of relevance and requires unconscious thought to find almost everything not immediately pertinent to the task to be excluded from reference.
3. Anxiety may affect intention strongly. Fear tightens the zone of sensed relevance for unconscious processing. More anxious states of mind tend to lead to negative expressions of psi (and other pre-conscious) material, unless the information is highly pertinent to the fearful concern.
4. Degree of motivation is reflected in unconscious intention. Caring strongly about the task, about the information to be expressed, or about the consequences of expressing it correctly are all expected to directly affect unconscious intention and lead to positive expression of unconscious information. This is a bit tricky, since when people are highly motivated, they also tend to work hard (cognitive work), so the two tendencies can cancel each other out. The most psi-propitious state is one in which motivation is high but there is little cognitive work. For many people, this seems paradoxical.
5. Being either focused or open influences intention. Everyone has times in which they are relatively unfocused and open, in which a wide range of thoughts and feelings may drift through awareness without much need to bear down hard upon anything in particular. Such states of mind permit unconscious intention to sample far and wide among bits of potential meaning, and these states are likely to permit positive expression of unconscious material. More intently focused states tend to the opposite, since the focus defines a narrow zone of sensed relevance.

All of these states can be more or less repetitively characteristic of an individual. Some are prone to engage in cognitive work in most situations, some are frequently anxious, some usually open, and so on. People who have such marked stylistic tendencies frequently will tend to express psi information, or not, accordingly.

Various Things Are Expected to Affect the Consistency of Unconscious Intention—and Therefore Affect the Extremity of Expression

1. *How important the situation and the relevant information is.* Something sensed to be highly pertinent to some concern that is very pressing is apt to galvanize unconscious intention. If a bit of preconscious meaning is sensed to be relevant in such a case, it should be extremely and positively expressed. If it is sensed to be irrelevant, it will tend to be extremely expressed by distinct avoidance.
2. *How imminent an issue is.* If subliminal material is about to enter into awareness, or if precognitive information is close at hand in terms of time, unconscious intention is apt to regard it as especially relevant and maintain a positive or negative sign with enough consistency to permit extreme expression.
3. *How dangerous something is.* Danger may mean physical danger, or it may mean that some possibility represents potential humiliation or loss of love or security or status. Whatever the sort of danger, such an impending meaning will tend to be met with a relatively consistent intention to either approach or avoid, which will be expressed extremely.
4. *How stable and integrated a person's intentions are.* There are times when one's intentions (conscious and unconscious) are relatively integrated and consistent. These tend to be times in which the expression of any pertinent unconscious information will be extreme. On the other hand, everyone has times in which intention is scattered, ambivalent, and self-contradictory. Such times will produce weak and nonreferential expressions—sometimes even scores that are so close to chance that this is statistically significant! Individuals also differ in terms of how ambivalent, scattered, or single-minded they tend to be, and this will generally affect their expression of psi.

The Kinds of Questions FST Research Will Tend to Ask

What questions a researcher thinks are scientifically interesting are determined largely by the theoretical context in which the work is being done—even if the theory is unarticulated and mainly implicit. Someone who thinks that psi phenomena express the actions of discarnate spirits may want studies to find out when spirits are more or less disposed to become involved. A scientist who thinks of psi in neurobiological terms may wonder what sorts of neurotransmitter activity accompanies psi experience. First sight is a psychological theory that is highly person centered, so its questions are nominated accordingly.

1. What most arrests our attention? We will want to know when something is of interest to the individual, when it matters, when it draws attention. This should tell us something about the action of unconscious intention, and hence the expression of psi.
2. What do different sorts of people find especially important? People differ in terms of their characteristic concerns. Sometimes, individuals can be usefully sorted by personality tests, although a researcher guided by FST will usually prefer some more implicit form of assessment, since tests that require self-conscious self-reports tend to lack validity with regard to spontaneous behavior, including psi behavior.
3. How do we access implicit meanings differently depending upon different situations or states of mind?
4. What factors influence the expression of other forms of unconscious information, such as subliminal perception or procedural memory, or the employment of long-term goals? What sort of influence do these factors have? We will look for clues in patterns that have been found in other areas of research that may apply to the expression of psi. This sort of theft is perfectly legal and, by virtue of the hypothesis of functional equivalence, will often be useful.
5. What affects the direction of psi expression as distinct from what affects the extremity of expression? FST guided research will always examine these two parameters of performance separately, whereas they have often been confounded in the past.

THE APPLICATION OF THEORY TO EXISTING BODIES OF WORK

While theory should guide research moving forward, it may also be tested by examining existing research to see how well findings conform to the expectations of theory. It may also help resolve problems and inconsistencies that have been noted.

Parapsychology is a small discipline, but it has accumulated decently large bodies of data on several psychological questions. The main ones are the relationships between psi and fear or anxiety, memory, extraversion, creativity, subliminal perception, and attitudes about psi. In my book (Carpenter, 2012a), I examine several hundred studies in both parapsychology and mainstream psychology to examine how well FST accounts for patterns that are reported. It seems to me that the fit is remarkably good. Space in this chapter does not allow discussion of all of this, but I will suggest the flavor by mentioning a few summary points in a couple of areas.

Fear and Psi

Does fear or anxiety play a role in the expression of psi? Hundreds of studies have been carried out that bear on the question, but the results are mixed. The most general finding is that people who tend to be anxious tend to do poorly on tests of psi, generally scoring below chance. However, other lines of research report that it is the more fearful people who show the strongest effects, and spontaneous reports of psi suggest that dangerous, fearsome events are the most likely ones to be reflected in psi experiences. FST resolves this by saying that fearful events are indeed likely to be heavily weighted and hence expressed in consciousness and behavior, but that the *sign* of expression will vary depending upon other factors. We must distinguish between consciousness and behavior (including unconscious physiological behavior) in this case, and pose different hypotheses for them. FST predicts that an unconscious behavioral response to a fearsome event will generally be in accord with the person's intentions and should often be observed, strongly and positively expressed. When we examine research on the physiological response to disturbing stimuli (presentiment and contemporaneous psi response to alarming things), this is exactly what we see. An awareness of danger "registers" unconsciously and seems to prepare the person for a response. On the other hand, FST predicts that in most cases, a conscious awareness of danger would be a poor response inasmuch as debilitating anxiety could result, which might impede effective action. Also, since it is known that an anxious state of mind shrinks the window of unconscious material that is consciously accessed, most psi events would be excluded. Research on psi and anxiety often has asked participants for some conscious access to extrasensory information (a guess). FST would predict that such conscious productions would tend to be wrong more often than right when the person is anxious and/or the information is fear evoking. This is what has been found with strong consistency.

I examined mainstream research on unconscious processing of subliminal sensory information, in hopes of confirming the hypothesis of functional equivalence. In this literature, it is quite clear that measures identifying the sheer placement of unconscious attention (as by the orientation of visual focus) show that fearful material facilitates quick response. However, when a conscious identification is asked of the participant, fearful material impedes response, making it slower and less accurate (Bar-Haim et al., 2007). In both the parapsychological and mainstream studies, the cases in which more fearful people are tested with more anxiety-arousing material are the ones in which such unconscious effects are the strongest, as FST predicts.

Are Memory and Psi Related?

This is another area of work in which a relatively large number of studies have accumulated. Most assessed both memory and ESP performance
in the same individuals and looked for correlations between them. This
work started with an observation of a positive relationship, and that is
what has most often been reported. However, many studies also found
either no relationship or negative relationships, so the question has foun-
dered in uncertainty. We must note that much of this work was rather
unsophisticated about mainstream research on memory, which is extensive and complex. Different measures of memory were used in ESP
studies without regard for what memory function they were assessing.
Long-term memory (which is involved when you remember details of some
early birthday party, for instance), like ESP, is facilitated by an open state
of mind, unimpeded by cognitive work (Navon & Miller, 1987). Another
class of memory is *working memory*. You use that when you hold numbers
in mind long enough to carry out arithmetical calculations upon them.
This is cognitive work for sure (Barrouillet et al., 2004). FST asserts that
positive access to extrasensory information is facilitated by a free-
floating openness to liminal material, while not engaging in cognitive
work and without clear cognitive closure. On the other hand, cognitive
work defines and sharpens what is of interest to the unconscious mind
and will tend to exclude extrasensory information (driving scores in a
negative direction). FST therefore predicts that when someone is engaged
in a working memory task, he is unlikely to do the sort of free-ranging
sampling of unconscious material that is required for a positive ESP score.
On the other hand, sampling long-term memory is much like drawing
upon extrasensory information. They are compatible tasks, requiring similar conditions. So, when memory and ESP are tested together, we should
find a negative relationship with tests involving working memory and a
positive one when long-term memory is involved. In fact, the results
reported do fall into this pattern with good consistency, resolving the apparent contradiction in findings.

First Sight as a Direction for Parapsychology

Parapsychology is a very diverse discipline. People with many different kinds of scientific training have engaged in it, and they have studied
many different kinds of questions. Physicists, engineers, biologists, neu-
rologists, physicians, and sociologists have all applied their points of view
to the questions of how mind interacts with mind and with matter beyond
the bounds of the body. I think most observers will agree, however, that it
is in the psychological research that we see the most robust regularities for
this irregular field. FST is a psychological theory that proposes a structure

for organizing and understanding what we have already found, and it gives guidance for what sorts of questions are likely to be most fruitful in the future. As I have looked at our body of findings, and as I have carried out my own research using the lenses of FST, I have had the satisfying experience of seeing a degree of order, predictability, *and meaning* that always eluded me before. I believe the same will be true of anyone who understands the theory and applies it in their research.

One consequence of this is that it is becoming clearer how smoothly psi functions among all our other unconscious cognitive processes. Whether general psychology knows it or not, or wishes it or not, one of its domains is parapsychology. It represents a part of how we tick. Including it in our general study of psychology will greatly broaden and deepen our understanding. Daryl Bem said it perfectly in a review he wrote of *First Sight*: "Psi is not a psychological anomaly."

REFERENCES

Bar-Haim, Y., Lamy, D., Pergamin, L., Bakermans-Kranenburg, M. J., & van Ijzendoorn, M. H. (2007). Threat-related attentional bias in anxious and nonanxious individuals: A meta-analytic study. *Psychological Bulletin, 133*, 1–24.

Barrouillet, P., Bernardin, S., & Camos, V. (2004). Time constraints and resource sharing in adults' working memory spans. *Journal of Experimental Psychology: General, 133*, 83–100.

Bem, D. J. (2011). Feeling the future: Experimental evidence for anomalous retroactive influences on cognition and affect. *Journal of Personality and Social Psychology, 100*, 407–425.

Carpenter, J. C. (2012a). *First sight: ESP and parapsychology in everyday life.* Lanham, MD: Rowman & Littlefield.

Carpenter, J. C. (2012b). Spontaneous social behavior can implicitly express ESP information. *Paper presented at the annual conference of the Parapsychological Association*, Durham, NC.

Freud, S. (1958). The psychopathology of everyday life. In J. Strachey (Ed. and Trans.), *The standard edition of the complete psychological works of Sigmund Freud* (Vol. 7). London: Hogarth Press. Original work published 1912.

Gruber, E. (1980). PK effects on prerecorded group behavior of living systems. *European Journal of Parapsychology, 3*, 174–182.

Lucas, R. E., Diener, E., Grob, A., Suh, E. M., & Shao, L. (2000). Cross-cultural evidence for the fundamental features of extraversion. *Journal of Personality and Social Psychology, 79*, 452–468.

May, E. C., Paulinyi, T., & Vassy, Z. (2014/2005). Anomalous anticipatory skin conductance response to acoustic stimuli: Experimental results and speculation upon a mechanism. In E. C. May & S. B. Marwaha (Eds.), *Anomalous cognition: Remote viewing research and theory*, pp. 158–171. Jefferson, NC: McFarland.

Milyavsky, M., Hassin, R., & Schul, Y. (2012). Guess what? Implicit motivation boosts the influence of subliminal information on choice. *Consciousness and Cognition: An International Journal, 21*, 1232–1241.

Mossbridge, J., Tressoldi, P., & Utts, J. (2012). Predictive physiological anticipation preceding seemingly unpredictable stimuli: A meta-analysis. *Frontiers in Psychology, 3*, 390. doi: 10.3389/fpsyg.2012.00390

Navon, D., & Miller, J. (1987). Role of outcome conflict in dual-task interference. *Journal of Experimental Psychology: Human Perception and Performance, 13*, 435–448.

Palmer, J. (2006). Anomalous anticipation of target biases in a computer guessing task. *Proceedings of the Parapsychological Association, 49*, 127–140.

Radin, D. (1997). Unconscious perception of future emotions: An experiment in presentiment. *Journal of Scientific Exploration, 11*, 163–180.

Radin, D. (2004). Electrodermal presentiments of future emotions. *Journal of Scientific Exploration, 18*, 253–273.

Rapaport, D., & Gill, M. M. (1959). *The points of view and assumptions of metapsychology: The collected papers of David Rapaport* (M. M. Gill, ed.). New York: Basic Books.

Schmeidler, G. S., & McConnell, R. A. (1958). *ESP and personality patterns.* New Haven, CT: Yale University Press.

Schwartz, N., & Bless, H. (1992). Constructing reality and its alternatives: An inclusion/exclusion model of assimilation and contrast effects in social judgments. In L. L. Martin & A. Tesser (Eds.), *The construction of social judgments*, pp. 217–245. Hillsdale, NJ: Lawrence Erlbaum Associates.

Stanford, R. G., & Rust, P. (1977). Psi-mediated helping behavior: Experimental paradigm and initial results [Abstract]. In J. D. Morris, W. G. Roll, & R. L. Morris (Eds.), *Research in Parapsychology, 1976*, pp. 109–110. Metuchen, NJ: Scarecrow.

Veltkamp, M., Aarts, H., & Custers, R. (2008). Perception in the service of goal pursuit: Motivation to attain goals enhances the perceived size of goal-instrumental objects. *Social Cognition, 26*, 720–736.

Weinberger, J., & Westen, D. (2008). Rats, we should have used Clinton: Subliminal priming in political campaigns. *Political Psychology, 29*, 631–651.

Chapter 13

Anomalous Cognition and the Case for Mind-Body Dualism

David Rousseau

Mind-body dualism, the view that minds and brains represent two distinct orders of existence in Nature, is an unpopular but persistent view in philosophy and in science. Ever since it was formulated as an exact hypothesis by René Descartes in the seventeenth century (Descartes, Cottingham, Stoothoff, & Murdoch, 1985/1641), philosophers and scientists have argued about the logical and scientific challenges that face such a view. Many kinds of dualism have been proposed over the years, and dualism is a thriving minority interest in contemporary philosophy (see, e.g., Antonietti, Corradini, & Lowe, 2008), although almost no one has been a *Cartesian* dualist in the past two centuries.

One reason dualism persists as a philosophical view is that it seems, at least at first, to provide a plausible route toward accommodating the fact that mental states have characteristics such as subjectivity and intentionality[1] that appear to be irreducible to the properties of physical matter, which are objective and reflexive. However, dualism faces significant challenges from a scientific point of view. There are many, but three stand out in particular. First, there is the challenge of how to account for the apparent interaction between the mind and the body if they are fundamentally different kinds of things. Second, dualistic interaction would apparently violate important scientific principles such as conservation of energy and causal closure of the physical world. Third, there appears to be no scientific evidence for the existence of some kind of "mental matter" in Nature, from which an objectively existing mind could be constituted. For these and other reasons, it appears that philosophical and scientific considerations rule out the possibility of dualism.

Philosophers have frequently suggested that anomalous phenomena of the kind studied in psychical research and parapsychology would, if proved real, supply scientific evidence that would weaken science's presumptive case against the truth of dualism (e.g. Armstrong, 1993, pp. 53, 361–362). A significant subclass of such phenomena is "anomalous cognition" (AC). This refers to the gaining of noninferential knowledge under conditions that appear to exclude the involvement of the known sensory channels, for example, knowledge of phenomena isolated from the subject by physical, spatial, or temporal barriers. This chapter will take a critical look at the hypothesis that evidence for AC provides support for mind-body dualism.

BACKGROUND

Origins of Anomalous Cognition Research

Anomalous cognition (AC) has been investigated scientifically for more than a century under names such as telepathy, clairvoyance, extrasensory perception (ESP), remote viewing, psi gamma, and precognition. There is a significant body of high-quality evidence for the existence of AC (Gurney, Myers, & Podmore, 1886; Kelly et al., 2007; May & Marwaha, 2014), but this evidence is not widely known among philosophers and scientists, and its significance remains controversial.

A common initial response, from both philosophers and scientists, to claims that such cognitions occur is to contend that if this were true, it would imply that persons are more than just physical systems and that this would imply the truth of mind-body dualism and the falsity of materialism (see, e.g., Price, 1967, pp. 36–38). In fact, *scientific* investigation of AC and other "supernormal" phenomena began in the late nineteenth century on the basis of such speculations by the moral philosophers Henry Sidgwick[2] and Frederic Myers. In their time, scientific advances had triggered a crisis in religious belief and, as Alan Gauld reports, they "feared that the ultimate victory of materialism would have disastrous social effects" (Gauld, 1968, p. 142). They reasonably concluded that if ethics were to have a compelling basis, it would have to be established scientifically, rather than by appeals to religious authorities. They also thought that this would require providing scientific evidence for the existence of a spiritual realm in which humans would have an afterlife governed by God, ensuring appropriate ultimate consequences for moral or immoral behavior in this life. As Myers put it, they hoped that from the study of such phenomena as AC, "science might in our age make sufficient progress to open the spiritual gateway which she had been thought to close; – to penetrate by her own slow patience into the vestibule of an Unseen World" (Myers, 1901, p. 455; see also Gauld, 2010).

The idea that a compelling ethics would require some kind of "moral government" by a theistic God can be critiqued but the potential relevance of "supernormal" phenomena to moral philosophy and naturalism cannot (Rousseau, 2014d), and the subject has attracted substantial attention from many significant moral philosophers, including William James, C. D. Broad, and H. H. Price.[3]

Interestingly, the founders of psychical research (and most of their successors) did *not* think that evidence for a morally significant supernormal reality would support supernaturalism. Myers defined and commented on the early descriptive term of their subject area in the following way:

> *Supernormal.*—Of a faculty or phenomenon which goes beyond the level of ordinary experience, in the direction of evolution, or as pertaining to a transcendental world. The word *supernatural* is open to grave objections; it assumes that there is something outside nature, and it has become associated with arbitrary interference with law. Now there is no reason to suppose that the psychical phenomena with which we deal are less a part of nature, or less subject to fixed and definite law, than any other phenomena. Some of them appear to indicate a higher evolutionary level than the mass of men have yet attained, and some of them appear to be governed by laws of such a kind that they may hold good in a transcendental world as fully as in the world of sense. In either case they are above the norm of man rather than outside his nature. (Myers, 1903, 1:xxii).

Whether one can coherently conceive of Nature as going beyond materialism without embracing supernaturalism, and hold that AC implies mind-body dualism within such a framework, will be the central focus of this chapter.

Strategy for Assessing the Significance of AC

Although speculation that proof of AC would support dualism and falsify materialism (and perhaps even support supernaturalism) continues to attract supporters, these connections cannot easily be made in a principled way. The situation is much more complicated than initial impressions might suggest. Whether people have souls was a central dispute between the Pharisees and the Sadducees 2,000 years ago, but the conceptual and scientific context for evaluating such questions has been transformed since then, especially in the past 100 years, and very complex nuances need to be considered now. As will be discussed later in this chapter, materialism and physicalism are not the same view any more; there are at least 15 kinds of naturalism, 14 philosophically significant kinds of mind-body models, seven philosophically significant kinds of dualism (some of which qualify as naturalistic), and dozens of philosophically significant kinds of supernaturalism.

For those people not steeped in the several relevant disciplines, it is easy to underestimate the subtlety and variety of options available in contemporary philosophy, science, and engineering, and hence to overestimate the explanatory challenges presented by the claimed characteristics of AC. Such misestimates can easily lead one to misjudge the significance of AC.

To assess the relevance of AC to a case for dualism, and the consequential implications for materialism and naturalism, it is necessary briefly to review the options that exist for kinds of mind-body model and the options that exist for kinds of materialism and naturalism.

Armed with these understandings, it will then be possible to consider what is known about the nature of AC and assess the degree to which it might lend weight to the case for dualism. I will argue that AC *does* provide important support for dualism, but not in the way usually supposed, and not for the kind of dualism usually anticipated.

PERSPECTIVES ON NATURALISM AND DUALISM

Recent developments in philosophy have brought into focus historical ambiguities in the use of the terms *naturalism*, *materialism*, *physicalism*, *supernaturalism*, and *mind-body dualism*, and provide a basis for us to now make clearer distinctions between their meanings and also to consider important variants on the central concepts they each represent. The terminology has not yet completely stabilized, but the conceptual terrain is well delineated and so one can, for the sake and duration of a particular discussion, settle on a "discourse domain" that specifies distinct usages that are widely accepted in contemporary academic practice. However, one must then be careful in reading more widely, especially the historical material, because the same term may have a different referent in this wider literature and in ordinary use. However, once one is sensitive to the nuances, keeping track of the meanings despite homophony in the terminology is not a serious problem.

PERSPECTIVES ON THE NATURE OF *NATURE*

To enumerate coherent options for models about the nature of Nature, we have to first formulate an adequate discourse domain. In what follows,

I draw extensively on my previous treatments (Rousseau, in preparation c, 2011a, 2013a,b, 2014b), which in turn draw extensively on Bunge (1977, 1979, 2000, 2010), De Caro and Macarthur (2008), Goetz and Taliaferro (2008), and Heil (2003).

The terms in the discourse domain enable us to be clear and consistent in how we formulate three important theoretical positions, namely:

1. An "ontology," which is our model of what exists "ultimately" or "most fundamentally"; ontological terms represent "particulars," that is, irreducible subjects of predication, and thus provide the basic conceptual building blocks for constructing theories about the nature of the world (e.g., physical particles, spirits, and wave functions)
2. A "metaphysics," which is our fundamental view about the nature of the world and describes how things can behave (naturalism and supernaturalism are examples of metaphysical views)
3. An "epistemology," which is our theory about how we can come to have knowledge of what exists and how things can behave (e.g., science and mystical revelation)

The key to defining such a set of terms is to define each one relative to the meanings of the others so that one can see how each aspect of concern is addressed somewhere in the network of terms (Rousseau, in preparation c). In the following, I will briefly describe such a schema, which is summarized in Figure 13.1.

This schema is built on the supposition that the fundamental constituents of the world are *things*, rather than, for example, processes, events, information, percepts, or measurements. These other categories are derivative: events are changes in things or the locations of things, processes are causally connected series of events, information requires a substantive carrier, percepts must be abstracted from observations of things, and measurements are interactions that reveal the properties or states of things. Therefore, none of these other kinds of particulars could be the fundamental existents (Bunge, 1977, p. 152).

Existence, Thinghood, and Realness

I start with the definition that some particular "exists" if it is a bearer of properties, and it is a "thing" if it exists as a complete unit all at the same time, that is, "things" are not inherently extended over time periods the way events and processes are.[4] Something is "real" if it has *inherent* properties, that is, if it is what it is independently of the sense we might make of it. Quantum objects qualify as real under this description because they inherently have such properties that they would, upon being measured,

Figure 13.1
Ontological terminology conventions for "things"

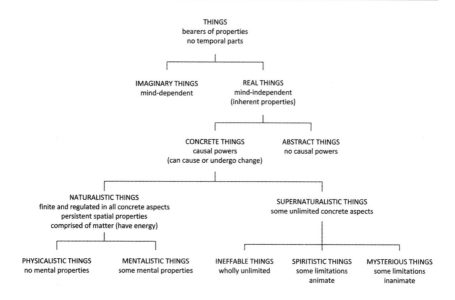

Note: In this figure, things inherit the properties of their parent classes, so qualifications such as "only" or "some" in the definitions should be understood as "only" or "some" in addition to what is already present by inheritance.

exhibit the behaviors predicted by the quantum formalism. They are like this irrespective of whether we have any knowledge of quantum mechanics or whether we think about them or try to measure them.

Concrete Things

A real thing is "concrete" if it has causal powers, that is, it can cause and undergo change. Causal powers are properties that *make* interactions with things that turn out a certain way. An important consequence of this definition is that things that can interact with each other must necessarily have a property in common (the one involved in the interaction).

Naturalistic Things, Naturalism, and Scientism

A concrete thing is "naturalistic" if all the changes it can cause or undergo are constrained and proportional to other changes taking place. For such things, there is always a sufficient reason for any change that has occurred. "Naturalism" is the *metaphysical* view that all particulars that exist in a concrete way are naturalistic.[5] Naturalistic properties make science possible, in that laws and control mechanisms can be discovered by tracing these proportionate causal transactions along spacetime tracks. Science is therefore the *epistemological* counterpart of naturalism. Note that for science to be able to trace causal transactions, naturalistic things necessarily have to be continuously located in spacetime while they exist—if not, it would be scientifically impossible to distinguish between similar things existing at the same time, associate the same thing with itself existing at a later time, and show that correlated changes reflect causal relations rather than just coincidences.

Note that the proportionality of natural changes, and the causal connectedness of the natural world, is mirrored in the logicality and coherence of the explanatory mechanisms postulated in scientific theories. Incoherence, irrationality, and magical connections are sure signs of deviation from naturalism.

If naturalism is true, then, in principle, science can comprehensively reveal the nature and extent of what ultimately exists. The view that this is the case can (nonpejoratively) be called "scientism."

Supernaturalistic Things and Supernaturalism

Given these definitions, "supernaturalism" can then be construed as the view that particulars exist that can produce unconstrained and/or disproportionate change in the world. If such causal processes existed, they would subvert the investigative and predictive potential of science and falsify naturalism and scientism.

Energy and Conservation Laws

An important but widely misunderstood element in these considerations is the scientific notion of "energy," which is well explained by Mario Bunge (2000). Simply put, having energy[6] is having the property that makes something naturalistic, that is, something has energy if it can change, but only in proportionate ways. The *kinds* of change a naturalistic thing can undergo are then qualified as the kinds of energy it has, and the *amount* of change it can undergo is then quantified as the amount of energy it has. Note that energy is a kind of property and not a kind of stuff, and hence the conventional references to "transfers of energy" or "flows of energy" during causal interactions are metaphorical and are not, strictly speaking, correct.

Given that naturalistic change is always proportionate, it can be seen that the "principle" according to which energy is conserved in naturalistic interactions is actually a *law*, in that it follows from the definitions of "naturalistic" and "energy," and hence if conservation of energy fails in practice, then naturalism would be falsified. It can also now be seen that all the "laws of nature" are special cases of the energy conservation law.

Matter, Material Things, Materialism

To have concrete properties, things have to be constituted of something that grounds their properties (a "substrate" or "stuff"). As Bunge explains (2000), stuff that has energy is called "matter," so "matter" is a special case of "stuff." Something that can change in disproportionate ways might still be comprised of stuff, but this would not be *matter*.

Naturalistic things are therefore *material* things, and "materialism" is the view that everything that exists in a concrete way is a material thing, that is, it is constituted of a stuff that can only change proportionately. Materialism is therefore the *ontological* component of naturalism. Note that "being material" does not equate with "having mass" but only with having energy. Mass is only one possible way in which having energy can manifest. Photons, for example, are material objects (they have energy), but they have no rest mass.

Immaterial Things

In this light, supernatural things would (if they exist) be *immaterial* things and hence not subject to conservation laws. In such a scenario, science would be limited in capacity, and naturalism, scientism, and materialism would all be falsified. In this case, the possibility of having knowledge would depend significantly or wholly on *revelation*, rather than scientific investigation.

Material Things That Are Nonphysical

An important issue for contemporary metaphysics is the distinction between *materialism* and *physicalism*. The notion of "physical" is a slippery one in philosophy, and the term is usually defined relatively or negatively, for example:

> A property is physical if and only if: it either is the sort of property required by a complete account of the intrinsic nature of paradigmatic physical objects and their constituents or else is a property which metaphysically (or logically) supervenes on the sort of property required by a complete account of the intrinsic nature of paradigmatic physical objects and their constituents. (Stoljar, 2009)

In my analysis, suggested by the schema given in Figure 13.1, "physical" properties are reflexive properties other than energetic or spatial ones, for example, mass, charge, hardness, reflectance.

In principle, the aforementioned definition of materialism allows for the logical possibility of the existence of "nonphysical" kinds of matter, that is, matter that has concrete properties in addition to, or instead of, physical ones. This is a coherent possibility, for so long as what exists ultimately can only change in constrained and proportionate ways, it would count as being naturalistic and scientifically investigable, even if it involved properties other than physical ones. The main reason for thinking that "nonphysical" kinds of matter might exist is to provide for a naturalistic way of grounding mental properties in a nonreductive way.[7]

"Physicalism" is a restricted version of materialism, according to which the only kind of matter that exists is physical matter, and hence every material thing is a physical thing.[8] Physicalism is thus the ontological component of a restricted version of naturalism called strict naturalism (Bunge, 1979, p. 251; 2010, p. 103). In the light of how this conceptual terrain has evolved, "physicalism" now stands for the meaning that used to be referred to by "materialism," and "materialism" has a wider meaning that opens up naturalistic possibilities between physicalism and supernaturalism. This is an important distinction because it means that if "nonphysical" kinds of matter exist, then physicalism would fail, but materialism (and naturalism) would be preserved, and the world would remain accessible to scientific inquiry.

Although these distinctions have been established for at least 40 years, it is still common for researchers and philosophers to conflate some of these important distinctions and, for example, say "materialism" when they mean "physicalism." In particular, it is common to talk of *challenges to materialism* when, in fact, all that is being argued for are *challenges to physicalism* (e.g., Koons & Bealer, 2010; Tart, 2009). As Michael Scriven put it, these are merely challenges to *"yesterday's* materialism" (1976, p. 183) and do not put materialism or naturalism at risk. Caution is needed in reading such arguments to ensure one does not mistake just what they really aim at.

Broad, Standard and Strict Naturalism

A metaphysical position that affirms the existence of nonphysical matter is called "broad naturalism". There are many broad naturalisms, differing from each other in how they propose to extend, replace, or supplement physical matter so as to provide for concrete mental properties (De Caro & Macarthur, 2008; Goetz & Taliaferro, 2008; Koons & Bealer, 2010). The materialism of broad naturalism is called "broad materialism."

Given these variants, "ordinary" naturalism is sometimes referred to as "standard naturalism" and its materialism as "standard materialism." The key characteristics of standard naturalism are that it denies the existence of immaterial substances and affirms the existence of material ones. However, it is uncommitted about which kinds of matter exist.

The different metaphysical positions so far are summarized in Table 13.1.

Table 13.1
Basic Metaphysical Models

			Ontological substrates		
Metaphysical model	Epistemological model	Ontological model	Physical matter	Mental matter	Immaterial substances
Strict naturalism	Science	Physicalism	✓	✗	✗
Standard naturalism	Science	Standard materialism	◇*	◇*	✗
Broad naturalism	Science	Broad materialism	◇	✓	✗
Supernaturalism	Revelation	Immaterialism	◇	◇	✓

Key: ✓ It exists; ✗ It does not exist; ◇ It possibly exists; * At least one of these should be a tick, but Standard Naturalism (SN) is uncommitted about which way it will go. Once a commitment is made, SN resolves into one of the other Naturalisms.

The ways in which the options indicated by diamonds in Table 13.1 might be taken up multiply the number of positions one can select between, both for kinds of naturalism and for kinds of supernaturalism.

From Three to 15 Kinds of Naturalism

In Table 13.1, the label "mental matter" is only meant to indicate matter that supports concrete mental properties. This leaves open several naturalistic options, for example, this matter could have both physical and mental properties ("dual aspect" matter), have neither physical nor mental properties in an essential way ("neutral" matter), or have mentalistic properties but no physical properties ("ideal" matter). These three options each provide a naturalistic alternative to physical matter. It is unclear, at the outset, which of these four kinds of matter, or which combinations of them, exist empirically. There are 15 possible selections. These would all represent naturalistic ontologies.[9] An ontology consisting of one kind of stuff is called a "hylic monism," of two kinds a "hylic dualism" and more than two kinds a "hylic pluralism."

From One to 105 Kinds of Supernaturalism

Supernaturalism as denoted in Table 13.1 is not a monolithic position either. For example, it need not entail the existence of spiritistic things (animate things with some unlimited aspects)[10] but only the existence of inanimate things with unconstrained aspects (the collapse of entangled quantum states might form a basis for such a model, since the outcome is insensitive to the separation distance between the entangled states). Such an inanimate kind of supernaturalism is called "mysterianism."

The most radical supernaturalistic option includes entities that are wholly unlimited and that would be ineffable from a scientific perspective. A supernaturalist can include in his or her model of reality any selection of the three supernaturalistic things just enumerated and, optionally, any selection of the four naturalistic kinds of matter enumerated earlier in this discussion, giving 105 options.

Discourse Domains and Coherent Claims

It is clear from this available variety of views that one cannot meaningfully make claims about the implications of AC for naturalism, materialism, or physicalism if one has not first gained a clear understanding of the conceptual landscape in which a position is being picked out nor made disciplined use of the terms available to refer to the relevant concepts. This is equally true for the implications that AC might have for mind-body models, where there is also a surprisingly wide variety of options.

Perspectives on the Mind-Body Relationship

The Question and the Criteria

The quest for mind-body philosophy is to identify a metaphysical scheme that would enable us to give an explanation of the basis of consciousness that is understandable, logically consistent, logically connected, and consistent with scientific knowledge. Failure to meet these criteria would render the model supernaturalistic, in the sense that it would embed irreducible mysteries or depend on divine interventions to bridge the gaps in the explanation. Invoking mysteries as explanatory maneuvers is unprincipled because, as William James put it, "it makes a luxury of intellectual defeat" (1890, pp. 178–179). Interestingly, the resistance to invoking divine interventions to fill gaps in explanations of everyday happenings holds for both atheists and theists because for the latter, it seems an insult to God to argue that anything in His creation works only because of His constant maintenance. As Leibniz famously put it in 1715, "I hold that when God works miracles, he does it not to meet the needs of nature but to meet the needs of grace. Anyone who thinks differently must have a very mean notion of the wisdom and power of God" (quoted in Bennett, 2007, p. 1).

The Structure of Mind-Body Models

It was Descartes who first framed a mind-body model in a way that made it susceptible to scientific and philosophical critiques of this sort. Unfortunately, pretty much everything that can go wrong has gone wrong in Descartes's model. However, fixing these shortcomings is not so easy.

The whole history of mind-body philosophy can be viewed as a series of attempts to expose and repair these shortcomings, and the project is far from concluding. There is a great variety of models on offer today; however, none solve all the Cartesian problems, and they all have challenges of their own. To understand this conceptual landscape, we need to consider four factors involved in formulating a mind-body model:

1. The proposed mind-body architecture. Here there are two main positions, namely "structural dualism," under which view the mind and body are distinct things, and "structural monism," under which view mind and body are different aspects or functions of a single thing.
2. The kinds of stuff that might be involved in realizing either architecture. Here there are six main positions. There are four "hylic monisms," according to which the ultimate stuff is either "ideal" (it has no physical properties), "physical" (has no mental properties), "dual aspect" (has both physical and mentalistic properties), or "neutral" (is only contingently physicalistic and/or mentalistic). There are two "hylic dualisms": according to the one, both material and immaterial kinds of stuff exist, and according to the other, things are comprised of matter and causally active "forms."
3. Ways of providing for the "ordinary facts" about conscious beings such as (apparently) having mentalistic properties, experiencing mind-body interaction, being distinct from other individuals, and being identifiable as the same individual at different times.
4. Consistency with scientific fundamentals such as conservation of energy, causal continuity and causal closure of the physical world, and the apparent absence of scientific evidence for the existence of mental matter and spirits.

It is notable that in this arena, everyone wants to be a naturalist, and in general, theorists with religious convictions will still strive to construct naturalistic mind-body models even though they have to find ways of making their model of persons consistent with the metaphysical aspects of their religious model (some examples are given later in this chapter). However, staying within naturalism has proven to be difficult to do, even for secular philosophers, and most of those who claim to be proposing naturalistic models in fact do not, as I explain later on.

The Variety of Mind-Body Models

The first two factors mentioned in the previous section can be used to show that there is logical room for 12 possible categories, as I do in Figure 13.2. I have populated this figure to indicate some of the

Figure 13.2
The spectrum of contemporary mind-body philosophers

			Kinds of Mind-Body Structure	
			Structural Monism	**Structural Dualism**
Kinds of Stuff	**Hylic Monism**	**Ideal**	1[†] Leibniz[†] *Hegel* Robinson[†] Foster	7 Berkeley[†]
		Physical	2 Democritus Davidson Putnam Stitch Bunge[◊] Crane[◊] Zimmerman[◊*†] Baker[†] van Inwagen[†] Hudson[†] Corcoran Merricks	8 Bahm[◊] *Potts*[*†] Taliaferro[◊] *Hasker*[◊] Plantinga[◊] Searle[◊] *Meixner*[◊] Popper[◊]
		Dual Aspect	3 Spinoza Chalmers Rosenberg *Edge Braude*[†]	9 Anaxagoras *Griffin*[†] *Laszlo*[‡]
		Neutral	4 Russell Silberstein	10 Heraclitus Tertullian[†] *Woodhouse*[†] Hart Thompson *Rousseau*[†]
	Hylic Dualism	**Material & Immaterial**	5 Sadducees [Zimmerman[◊*†] Hudson[†] Baker[†] van Inwagen[†]]	11 Pharicees[†] Plato[†] Descartes[†] *Beloff, Dilley*[†] *Lund*[†] H.D. Lewis[†] *Badham*[†] *Habermas*[†] Swinburne
		Matter & Forms	6	12 Aristotle Aquinas[†] Oderburg[†] Leftow

Notes:
* marks philosophers who are physicalists <u>about human persons</u> but hylic dualists 'overall' (i.e. they hold that immaterial substances exist e.g. God and angels)
[†] marks philosophers who hold that personal consciousness can survive bodily death
[‡] marks philosophers who hold that consciousness endures in a non-personal way
[◊] marks philosophers who are Emergentists
philosophers in bold italics accept the reality of anomalous cognition

contemporary philosophers who support each view. As the annotations show, there are diverse views per category, providing opportunities for some further division. To give some historical perspective, I have also included some iconic or originating representatives of the views depicted.

As Figure 13.2 shows, nine categories have contemporary support. Category 7 is extinct, 6 has never had any support, and 5 overlaps with a subcategory of 2. However, there are four significant subcategories in category 2, and two each in categories 9 and 10, so in effect, we have 14 models with contemporary support.

Figure 13.2 is by no means exhaustive in terms of allocating philosophers and may not be wholly accurate, largely because it is easier to find out what philosophers are against than what they are for, and their views are in any case neither immutable nor unconditional. My apologies to anyone I left out, assigned wrongly, or did not caveat properly.

Core Challenges and Offered Solutions

Cartesian Dualism

Cartesian dualism fits in category 11 of Figure 13.2. For Descartes, the mind is a distinct thing and has no properties in common with the body; unlike the body, the mind is not located in space and hence has no location, size, or shape; also, it has no internal structure, is indivisible, and is immortal. However, mind and body interact. This model is clearly supernaturalistic and not scientific, since it postulates interactions between things having no properties in common and unique causal interactions between things located in space and things not so located, and it violates the causal closure and energy conservation requirements.

Many proposals have been offered for addressing these issues, but they typically generate new problems of equal severity. Very few philosophers have been Cartesian dualists in the past century, but notably John Beloff, a past president of the SPR and for many years the editor of its journal, was one. Cartesian dualists typically accept the existence of AC.

Idealisms

One possibility is to deny the objective existence of the physical world, reducing it to a hallucination (categories 1 and 2). Such a model would easily accommodate AC, and some idealists have embraced it (e.g., Hegel). However, idealism has been shown to be logically circular (Searle, 1995, Chapters 7, 8; Stove, 1991, Chapters 5, 6). This creates a significant hurdle for modern theorists who try to construct models that make consciousness the fundamental reality (e.g., Goswami).

Physicalism

Another possibility is to deny the existence of subjective states or mentalistic stuff altogether. Interestingly, physicalistic models are not automatically naturalistic, structurally monist, or incompatible with AC (or even atheistic). There are structural monists here (category 2) who deny causally active mental states (e.g., Davidson, Putnum), and ones who affirm them as emergent properties of physical complexity (e.g., Crane, Zimmerman). Some of these structural monists believe in an immaterial God, and therefore they do not reject the existence of immaterial substances but only deny the involvement of such stuff in the constitution of human persons (this position overlaps with 5). Some of these structural monists believe that personal consciousness can survive bodily death, in that God can create a replica physical body with the identical "pattern" in heaven (e.g., Hudson), or "spirit away" the original earthly body and replace it with a replica on earth (e.g., van Inwagen). Some physicalists are structural dualists and argue that something distinct "emerges" from complex physical stuff that has independent causal powers, rather like how radio antennas can generate fields that carry information and have causal powers (e.g., Taliaferro, Searle). Some of these believe that this extra component can survive the death of the body, analogously to how radio waves depend on antennas for their creation but not their continued existence (e.g., Potts), but some deny survival, believing that this extra element will degrade when the body does (as a magnetic field does when the magnet is damaged or destroyed) (e.g., Bahm). Some of these philosophers accept the reality of AC (e.g., Potts, Hasker) but see nothing in it that opposes physicalism about human persons.

The physicalistic models face significant challenges, since some versions deny some of the relevant facts (e.g., the causal powers of minds), mangle the concept of emergence (by claiming emergence can produce a categorical shift in properties from reflexive to intentional ones), or misconstrue the nature of fields (by claiming physical fields can have volitional properties and can independently change their structure once generated).

Dual Aspect Monism

Ascribing both mentalistic and physical properties to the fundamental stuff appears to make room for mental properties and mind-body interactionism in a naturalistic way (#3 and #9). Some do this in terms of structural monism (e.g., Chalmers) and some in terms of structural dualism (e.g., Laszlo). AC is accepted both by some monists (e.g., Edge) and some structural dualists (e.g., Griffin). Some of the structural monists who take AC seriously deny survival of consciousness (e.g., Edge), but some support it (e.g., Braude), as do some of the structural dualists (e.g., Griffin). Laszlo proposes survival in a nonpersonal way, via reabsorption of the person's "mind" into a kind of global consciousness field after the death of the body. These models seem to open the door for AC and survival, and moreover, Laszlo's model attempts to account for mystical unitive experiences as well.

However, significant challenges remain. The claim that everything is comprised of dual-aspect stuff is inherently problematic, since by that token, paradigmatically physical things such as rocks and telephones are claimed to have mentalistic properties. Moreover, in the case of structural dualism, it is mysterious why science cannot detect this "mind," since it does have physical aspects.

Neutral Monism

The first of these problems can be avoided if the ultimate stuff has neither mentalistic nor physical properties but can be configured or unfolded in some way to have either or both these kinds of properties (4 and 10). Some neutral monists are structural monists (e.g., Silberstein), and some are structural dualists (e.g., Woodhouse). For structural dualists, the mind can be construed as having spatial but not physical properties (e.g., Hart) or as having both physical and mental properties (e.g., Rousseau). Some structural monists reject AC and survival (e.g., Russell), but some of the structural dualists accept both (e.g., Rousseau).

These kinds of models satisfy more criteria than any of the others, but in versions such as Hart's, the mechanism of mind-body interaction is still radically unclear, and in versions such as Rousseau's, there is still the question of why science cannot detect the mind as a distinctly existing thing.

Hylemorphic Dualism

Finally, for completeness, I mention the view that persons are comprised of "prime matter" configured by a substantial "form," the interaction between the two producing the person (12, e.g., Oderburg). This model has the advantage of giving the body an essential role in the establishment of human personality. However, it is impossible to explain how immaterial "forms" can interact with matter in a naturalistic way.

The Potential Value of AC to Mind-Body Philosophy

This survey shows that the conceptual landscape regarding the mind-body relationship is very complex. As shown, physicalism does not entail structural monism nor preclude the survival of consciousness after bodily death, and it does not guarantee that the model is naturalistic. On the other hand, structural dualism does not entail supernaturalism or even the survival of consciousness.

To date, knowledge of the reality of AC has not made much difference in this debate, and among the philosophers who take AC seriously, there are atheists and theists, naturalists and supernaturalists, survivalists and nonsurvivalists, and both structural monists and dualists. My impression is that on the whole, philosophers do not take account of AC when selecting their basic model; rather, they use knowledge of AC only to suggest support or caveats for a mind-model they had already chosen on other grounds. For example, the Christian philosopher Gary Habermas defends veridical out-of-body experiences (OBEs) as providing evidence for the existence of a soul, but despite believing in survival, he rejects apparitions as due to demonic subterfuges because his religious model excludes communication between the living and the dead.

That said, the variety of mind-body models advocated in contemporary philosophy suggests that mind-body philosophers typically do not know enough relevant science to make their models compelling or testable and that scientists studying supernormal phenomena typically do not know enough relevant philosophy to interpret and promote relevant data appropriately. Perhaps it is for this reason that even though most contemporary philosophers of mind claim to be naturalists, all the models outlined above, except perhaps the neutral monisms, fail to be naturalistic in practice because they are logically circular, incoherent, make claims inconsistent with the empirical evidence, or invoke mysterious qualities via brute claims.

However, I think that in the light of the scientific and philosophical understandings sketched out thus far in this discussion, a closer look at the implications of AC can take the debate forward to a significant degree.

DOES THE NATURE OF AC SUGGEST DUALISM AND/OR SUPERNATURALISM?

The existence of AC is well established, even if not widely recognized. Substantial meta-analyses of experimental data on AC indicate that the effect is real with a high degree of confidence (Bem & Honorton, 1994; Storm, Tressoldi, & Di Risio, 2010; Utts, 1991). Much is now known about the nature of AC, perhaps enough to be able to meaningfully address the question of whether it implies that people have senses other than bodily, physical, or naturalistic ones.

To evaluate this issue, we have to take, as our baseline, what we know about how *ordinary* noninferential cognition works and assess whether in terms of such models AC deviates from being physical, naturalistic, or bodily. We have much information to draw on for this from the positions of cognitive psychology, medical science, biology, engineering, communication theory, physics, and the philosophy of science.

Ordinary noninferential cognition involves a number of elements, namely:

1. *Source or target.* The state of affairs that will become known via noninferential cognition.
2. *Signal generation.* The production of a signal that encodes, in its nature and structure, information about the source/target situation. This can be active (e.g., generating a sound wave by speaking) or passive (e.g., light reflecting off a colored surface).

3. *Signal transmission.* The travel of the signal from the generator to the observer.
4. *Sensing.* The capture of the signal, by sensors of the observer, in such a way that the nature and structure of the signal is extracted and recorded.
5. *Data processing.* Analysis of the sensor output to extract data relevant to conditions at the source situation.
6. *Evaluation.* The assessment of the extracted data to produce knowledge of the source situation. This is not part of the communication system as such but part of the general meaning-making capacity of the mind.

For present purposes, we can focus particularly on elements 1–5 and at the outset ask the following questions:

a. Assuming signals are involved, do they behave like naturalistic ones?
b. Assuming sensors are involved, do they behave like naturalistic ones?
c. Assuming there is data processing, does this subsystem behave naturalistically?

In such a model, for the present, we do not know what these signals might be, how they travel from source to sensor, where and what the sensors might be, and where and how the data processing takes place. However, we can assess the questions we have raised indirectly because we have the end result (the information produced in the evaluation stage), and we know something about the source situation and the conditions under which the cognition occurred.

Nevertheless, some caution is needed not to make inferences as though we can clearly separate the contributions of the intermediate stages to the final outcome. For example, a sophisticated data processing system can mitigate for shortcomings in the sensory system and for noise in the transmission channel, so the signal transmission and sensory aspects of an AC model cannot be assessed independently of the data processing aspect. All this is a large subject worthy of detailed analysis, but for brevity, I will discuss only a few key issues to show the drift of how such an analysis is likely to go.

Sensory Aspects

Much is known about the principles involved in how biological sensors work. Sensors are not merely detectors of the presence of signals but are also the first stage of signal processing, extracting, and recording data that represent the nature and structure of the signal. The structure of a signal can be represented by a measure called Shannon entropy (Shannon, 1948). Biological sensors work by reacting to changes in the structure of the incoming signal, that is, the gradient of the Shannon entropy.

In a series of groundbreaking studies, Edwin May and colleagues showed that success in AC tasks scales with the gradient of the Shannon entropy of ordinary signals the targets would produce. This suggests that the AC system utilizes a sensory mechanism that works in a similar way to the biological sensors we know, matched to a signal that is generated in similar ways to how physical ones are (May, Spottiswoode, & Faith, 2000). This suggests that AC is naturalistic, and though it does not indicate whether these sensors and signals involve physicalistic or mentalistic materials, it perhaps creates a bias in favor of a physicalistic model. However, because in a dualistic model minds could have physical as well as mental properties (as per types 9 and 10 above), this finding does not have any implications for the structural dualism/monism debate.

Environmental Aspects

The suggestion from the entropy study that AC involves a naturalistic mechanism opens up the way for further analysis. Several issues might be considered here. Physical signals are carried by fields, and these typically weaken with distance traveled because they spread out in space, and they can be blocked or distorted by environmental factors. Moreover, the performance of physical sensory and data processing systems can be affected by environmental factors.

Signal Distortion

Taking environmental factors first, there is substantial data suggesting that the success of AC, and the prevalence of spontaneous cases of AC, varies with local environmental conditions in a systematic way. In particular, AC appears to be enhanced when there is a reduction in the volatility of changes in specific frequency bands of the local geomagnetic field. Such reductions may correlate with variations in solar activity (e.g., solar flares and sunspot activity), solar time (orientation relative to the sun), sidereal time (orientation relative to the stars), and seasons (distance from the sun) (Ryan, 2008; Spottiswoode, 1990, 1997), although the relative significance of each remains unclear (Ryan & Spottiswoode, Volume 1, Chapter 14), and there are complex differences regarding gender responses and types of AC (Ryan, in press). These geomagnetic variations are local to the observer, and this means it is unlikely that these variations in AC performance are due to interference with the "AC signal"; rather, they are more likely to be due to impacts on the perceiver, *either* by interfering with the AC elements involving sensor, data processing and evaluation stages (which would imply that at least one of these has physical aspects) *or* merely due to interference with the ordinary workings of the brain. Because the brain is involved in normal cognitive functioning, and multiple cognitive activities are normally ongoing simultaneously in the mind-brain system, we are not presently able to distinguish where the geomagnetic effects come into play, and hence we cannot infer anything about the mechanism of AC from these geomagnetic effects. The balancing effect with either conditions in the environment or conditions in the brain suggests that it works in a naturalistic way, but this does not allow us to say anything about the extent to which AC involves physicalistic as opposed to mentalistic aspects, and it does not have any implications for the structural dualism/monism debate.

Signal Shielding

AC is not blocked by normal physical isolation such as conditions of sensory deprivation and screening from electromagnetic radiation by Faraday cages of the observer (Tart, 1988a,b). In fact, AC seems to be *enhanced* under such conditions. Placing targets to be observed in AC experiments in locked safes or under deep seawater similarly does not block AC (Edwin May, personal communication about the Star Gate program). The enhancing effect of observer isolation is probably due to the greater attention paid to low-key cognitive inputs when mental demands are low. However, it is a puzzle how the "AC signal" might reach the observer under these conditions. There are three naturalistic possibilities that can be suggested.

One, the AC signal might be a nonphysical but nevertheless material one. This is not very likely because to date, science has not identified any nonphysical force fields.

Two, the AC signal might involve a kind of physical force field unknown to present science. This is plausible, since we have discovered at least three new force fields since the 1950s (the weak and strong nuclear forces and "dark energy").

Three, AC might involve signal propagation via a pathway outside normal space—see Chapter 2 in the volume. In this case, the physical barriers would not work even if the signal involves a known type of force. This option is no longer as radical as it once seemed because we now have models in mainstream physics suggesting that our world is a kind of three-dimensional "membrane" embedded in a higher order space (Randall & Sundrum, 1999), and it has recently been argued that correlations between quantum states may be due to causal linkages mediated via such hyperspatial pathways (Christian, 2012).

Given these options we cannot, based on present knowledge, adjudicate between these possibilities or between them and supernaturalistic options and therefore, this aspect of AC has no special relevance for either the naturalism debate or the structural monism/dualism debate. However, the slight enhancement of AC under certain isolating conditions, suggesting some kind of balancing relationship, and the possibility of the naturalistic solutions outlined earlier in this chapter, creates a slight bias in favor of naturalism.

Signal Decay

AC is often reported to be independent of the distance between the observer and the target (Palmer, 1978). If AC really is insensitive to distance, this might present an interesting challenge to naturalism, although not inevitably a devastating one. At the very least, there is still the possibility that the signal travels via a hyperspace and hence the distance being referred to is not the relevant one. However, I want to suggest a less exotic alternative, one that is opened up by the idea that AC involves a communication system. Sophisticated communication systems contain sophisticated data processing subsystems, and the impact of this on system performance can be considerable.

To see how this might work, consider the workings of a radar system. The target here is an aircraft at varying distances from the radar system, and the radar system displays an illuminated dot on a screen when it detects an aircraft, giving its position on a map overlying the screen. Electromagnetic waves bouncing off the aircraft travel toward the radar antenna, decaying with distance in the normal manner and picking up distortions along the way due to other environmental factors. After the signal is received by the radar antenna, it is processed to work out if there is data about an aircraft encoded in its structure. If the processing unit "decides" there is an aircraft there, it sends an appropriate signal to the display unit to produce a dot in the appropriate location. In this scenario, the intensity of the display dot is unaffected by the distance to the target and the strength of the signal, since the display dot is merely generated to report a yes/no decision about the presence of an aircraft at that location. The data processing unit can sometimes get it wrong, not reporting an aircraft when there is one (perhaps because the signal was distorted by contingent factors) or reporting an aircraft when there is not one (perhaps because contingent factors produced a spurious artifact in the signal), but for true detections, it always displays a dot of equal intensity irrespective of the distance to the aircraft.

The complexity of the data processing system matches the complexity of the signal and the environment, and the observer of the radar display is typically oblivious to the very real effect distance and environment have on the signal. Likewise, in an AC system, data processing could mask declines or distortions in the AC signal from the observer, who either reports the target or not, irrespective of the separation (subject to erroneous reports from time to time). In such a scenario, the apparent distance insensitivity of AC would not be due to supernaturalistic processes, nor would it involve exotic mechanisms such as hyperspaces; rather, it would merely reflect the competence of the human data processing system.[11]

Assessment

As these brief analyses show, the situation, and the nature of AC, is complex, but there appear to be good reasons for thinking that AC is naturalistic, despite the fact that we know very little about the mechanisms involved. However, there appears to be nothing in what is known about the *nature* of AC to suggest the need for a nonphysicalistic ontology, and there is certainly no suggestion or support for a dualistic mind-body model. In fact, consideration *of only the nature of AC* strengthens a presumption in favor of physicalism because insofar as we can make judgments, AC seems to work in similar ways to physical systems and is impacted by physical conditions. From this, we might well presume that the AC mechanism is part of the physical bodily capacities. That, however, is an unsafe assumption, as I will argue next.

IS AC A CAPACITY OF THE PHYSICAL BODY?

If AC is a capacity of the physical body, then AC performance should be closely dependent on bodily conditions, just as "ordinary" cognition is. If AC is due to a separate system, then it might be able to function relatively well even under conditions where normal cognition is not physically supported. If such evidence exists, then the *context* under which the AC occurs would suggest some kind of structural mind-body dualism even though the *nature* of AC does not.

In what follows, I will argue that we have such data from cases of veridical out-of-body experiences (OBEs) under conditions of cardiac and prolonged pulmonary arrest. This is a special subclass of near-death experiences (NDEs). However, the situation is complicated by the possibility that the AC involved is not synchronous with the arrest but due to precognitive or retrocognitive experiences that occur immediately before or immediately after the arrest period. This complication is a special case of the "super-ESP" hypothesis. I will argue later that for NDE cases, the super-ESP hypothesis can be discounted and hence that we can interpret reports of veridical OBEs under cardiac arrest as involving synchronous AC.

The Credibility of Reports of AC under Conditions of Cardiac Arrest

NDEs are profoundly moving events that are thusly called because people typically experience them during life-threatening situations. NDEs are phenomenologically rich, and all the types of AC have been reported in the context of NDEs (Zingrone & Alvarado, 2009). NDEs have been a subject of extensive academic study since 1975 (for a review, see Holden, Greyson, & James, 2009), but many aspects of these experiences remain medically and philosophically puzzling (Greyson, 2013).

In about 60% of NDE cases, people report an OBE in which they experience themselves as being outside their bodies and observing the material world from an elevated perspective.

Interestingly, about 10 to 20% of the people who survive cardiac arrest report having had such experiences during their arrest (Greyson, 2003).

According to mainstream medical and philosophical paradigms, such experiences cannot happen. Cardiac arrest leads within 10 to 20 seconds to a state called clinical death, with no heartbeat, no breathing, no detectable electrical activity in the brain, and no brain-stem reflexes (Fenwick & Fenwick, 2008, p. 206; Greyson, 2010). If people really can remain conscious under such conditions, then this would strongly support a case for structural mind-body dualism.

More than a hundred cases of OBEs reported during cardiac arrest have been published in the scholarly literature (Kelly et al., 2007, p. 418), and their credibility is strongly reinforced by their high accuracy. In a recent review, Janice Holden found that 90% of OBE reports of perceptual experiences under physically challenging conditions such as cardiac arrest or prolonged respiratory arrest contained no errors (2009, p. 196). Around 35% of these reports had been independently corroborated (Holden, 2009, p. 196).[12]

Very importantly, in nearly 20% of the published cardiac arrest cases, the OBErs reported observing very unusual or surprising incidents that occurred during the crisis, and that were subsequently verified, including both local and remote events (Cook, Greyson, & Stevenson, 1998; Rousseau, 2011b).[13] These cases strengthen the credibility of these OBE reports and also reinforce the claim that they represent cognition of the contemporaneous situation.

If we could be confident that these cognitions occur synchronously with the arrest, then this would strongly suggest that some kind of structural mind-body dualism is true and that both consciousness and AC are due to structures "beyond the body." This would drastically narrow the "option space" for mind-body philosophy. However, that "if" represents a significant caveat and must be addressed before we can further analyze the implications of these OBE cases.

Discounting the Super-ESP Hypothesis

The significance of these cardiac arrest OBEs for structural mind-body dualism could be challenged with the notion that reports of OBEs under cardiac arrest are not due to *synchronous* AC but to precognitive or retrocognitive experiences that occur immediately before or immediately after the arrest period. In such a case, the person would actually be unconscious during the period of his or her cardiac arrest but have a memory of what happened during the arrest. To them, it would seem that they were conscious *during* the arrest, but this would be a mistaken inference. This is a variant of the so-called super-psi or super-ESP hypothesis. The super-ESP hypothesis has been a long-standing and serious challenge to the "survival hypothesis," which asserts, on the basis of evidence from veridical mental mediumship, veridical memories of previous lives, and veridical apparitions, that personal identity survives death of the physical body (Sudduth, 2009). If the super-ESP hypothesis could be applied here, the significance of these NDE cases for structural dualism would be radically diminished. However, I have shown elsewhere that super-ESP theories have no bite against NDEs and that this result can be used to break the general impasse between the super-ESP hypothesis and the survival hypothesis (Rousseau, 2012).

The argument is extensive, but briefly, and too simply, it goes as follows. The super-ESP hypothesis is grounded in an assumption that the use and focus of AC faculties is, just like any other faculty, determined by the agent's needs and interests. In the present context, the idea is then that in relation to crisis events, factors such as innate fear of death might provide the motivation for activating powerful psychic functioning, to gather veridical information that is then incorporated in a hallucinatory episode that provides the agent with the reassurance he or she needs. This hallucination might then include experiences of the local scenario (to show that she is not dying, despite the condition of her physical body) and encounters with the spirits of deceased relatives (to show that if her body did die, she would survive as a spirit being). The OBE is then an example of a psychological coping mechanism, perhaps only unusual for the fact that it involves psychic functioning.

As I have shown elsewhere there is a range of NDE cases in which the super-ESP hypothesis simply does not fit the facts (Rousseau, 2012). Examples include cases in which:

1. The requisite motivations for activating super-ESP are not in place (e.g., certain cases involving very young children and highly committed atheistic physicalists).
2. The outcomes are actually contrary to the super-psi hypothesis's expectations (e.g., people are traumatized rather than reassured by the experience).

3. The outcomes are not due to the mechanisms proposed by the super-ESP hypothesis (e.g., there is a strong rise in belief in an after-life [typically from around 30% to approximately 100%], but the incidence of encounters with long-dead relatives is very low [about 10%]).

In my chapter, I further compare the super-ESP hypothesis with the survival hypothesis on a range of "theoretical virtues," which are qualities "good" scientific theories have, such as simplicity, explanatory power, predictive power, falsifiability, coherency, limited ad hocness, empirical adequacy, and consistency with well-established theories. In recent philosophy of science, more than two dozen such criteria have been identified, and they facilitate trade-offs between theories with different underlying assumptions that explain the data equally well (Chibeni & Moreira-Almeida, 2007; Matthewson & Weisberg, 2009; Maxwell, 2004). These criteria enable C. S. Pierce's "inference to the best explanation" to be generalized to become "inference to the best theory." In historical terms, theories that have more of the theoretical virtues have the best performance in terms of requiring no or only slight modification in the light of new evidence, for forming the bases of even more competent theories, and for outlasting competing theories.

In my comparison, I could identify nine virtues held by either hypothesis. My final analysis, incorporating the results from my NDE-based arguments, showed that the survival hypothesis has all nine virtues, while the super-ESP hypothesis has only two, and in both cases, the survival hypothesis has stronger versions of those virtues.

In light of this analysis, it is highly unlikely that the AC associated with OBEs under conditions of cardiac or prolonged pulmonary arrest is due to asynchronous super-ESP. In this light, the evidence strongly suggests that both consciousness and AC are due to structures "beyond the body" and hence that some kind of structural mind-body dualism is true. This raises a prospect and a question. The prospect is that if AC is not a bodily capacity, then it will not be understood unless it is studied in the context of a framework of structural mind-body dualism. However, as discussed earlier in this chapter, there are many possibilities for how such a dualism could be construed, and there is then the question of what kind of dualism suits the empirical facts and whether this model remains within the bounds of naturalism or transcends it.

TOWARD A DUALISTIC FRAMEWORK FOR AC RESEARCH

I will now briefly outline how one might go about delineating a suitable dualistic framework in a principled way. This is a large subject, though, and therefore, only some brief remarks will be presented here about how such a framework can be developed and what it might look like. For fuller treatments see Rousseau (in preparation a, 2011a)

First, note that the term "mind" in expressions such as "mind-body system" should now be understood very broadly. This "mind" clearly has more kinds of properties than just the iconic mental ones such as consciousness, rationality, and will, having additionally inherent perceptual capacities (which enable what we know as AC) and also properties that enable it to exist as a distinct thing in addition to the body.

Second, it is an open question whether this dualistic framework can be developed in a naturalistic way. The nature of iconic mental qualities, and the nature of AC, does not per se suggest supernaturalism, so at the outset, the situation favors naturalism. If one *assumes* that the framework will be naturalistic, then one can, by applying the conditions pertaining to naturalistic things as described earlier in the section on the perspectives on the nature of Nature, generate a range of hypotheses that could then form the basis for further investigations.

For example, for something to be naturalistic, it must be material, so here some kind of broad materialism must be postulated so that naturalistic minds are comprised of a kind of mentalistic matter that possesses energy. Furthermore, for naturalistic things to be unique individuals and participate in causal interactions, they must each be located in a specific and finite region of space. If the mind has material and spatial properties, and sensors to facilitate AC, then it must have a complex internal structure, so it cannot be point-like but must be spatially extended and hence have a shape and a boundary. Causal powers are properties, and therefore, naturalistic mind-body interaction requires that the mind has properties in common with the body. Since the body is a physical thing, this implies that to interact naturalistically with the body, the mind must have physical properties in addition to its mental and spatial ones. Collectively, these implications of assuming naturalism postulate that the mind is something like a "material soul," having energetic, spatial, physical, and mental properties, rather like the model proposed by the ancient Christian writer Tertullian (160–220 CE), which was recently revisited by philosophers Michael Potts and Amy Devanno in the *Journal of the Society for Psychical Research* (2013).

Postulating such requirements raises several questions that can be empirically investigated. Some of these have already been raised in relation to mind-body models discussed earlier in this chapter.

First, what is the relationship between the mentalistic matter proposed here and physical matter? Are they each ontologically fundamental (suggesting a kind of interactive hylic pluralism), or is each derived from some kind of neutral substance? Colleagues and I have argued elsewhere that the existence of a suitable naturalistic neutral substance is logically plausible and has some support in empirical evidence we already have

(Rousseau & Rousseau, 2012; Rousseau, in preparation b, 2011a). This model needs further development and buttressing, but it shows that a case can be made for a naturalistic mind-body model grounded in neutral monism, with the mind-stuff being empirically "dual-aspect" while the body is empirically physical.

Second, as per the main objection raised relative to such a model earlier in this discussion, if the mind has physical properties and is located in space, why have such structures not been detected by physical instruments? One answer that can be suggested is that the mind is not in ordinary three-dimensional space but is actually located in a proximate hyperspatial region. This is a radical proposal, but there is significant evidence for such a possibility. We have many reports from NDErs in which they describe the world as if from a hyperspatial perspective. Just as an ordinary person can normally see everything laid out on a two-dimensional surface, so these NDErs report being able to see things in the three-dimensional world from all angles simultaneously, see through things, and so on. Here is a typical example:

> I was hovering over a stretcher in one of the emergency rooms at the hospital. I glanced down at the stretcher, knew the body wrapped in blankets was mine, and really didn't care. The room was much more interesting than my body. And what a neat perspective. I could see everything. And I do mean everything! I could see the top of the light on the ceiling, and the underside of the stretcher. I could see the tiles on the ceiling and the tiles on the floor, simultaneously. Three hundred sixty degree spherical vision. And not just spherical. Detailed! I could see every single hair and the follicle out of which it grew on the head of the nurse standing beside the stretcher. (Ring & Cooper, 1999, p. 107)

Many more cases are reported and discussed in the literature (Audain, 1999; Brumblay, 2003; Greene, 1999, 2003; Jourdan, 2000, 2001, 2006, 2011). Studies show that around 70% of NDE OBE reports contain such features (Jourdan, 2011).

The idea that the "ordinary" physical world is a sort of three-dimensional "membrane" embedded in an extensive hyperspatial "bulk" is not orthodoxy, but it is a credible view in current physics circles and is supported by contemporary physicists (e.g., Kaku, 1995; Randall, 2006), cosmologists (Carr, 2007), and philosophers (e.g., Hudson, 2008). Although the models we have so far do not fully support interactions of the sort described earlier in this discussion, the present situation is much more promising than in earlier eras in which researchers claimed that hyperspatial geometries could account for supernormal phenomena, but there were no credible theories grounded in physics to lend support to their views (e.g., Zollner, 1880). Indeed, some contemporary cosmologists (e.g., Carr, 2008) and philosophers (e.g., Hudson, 2008, pp. 193–204) have begun to explore the possibility of such interactions to account for super-normal phenomena in general.

If the mind is located in a proximate hyperspace, this would not only explain why it has not been detected by ordinary physical instruments but also why physical barriers around the body do not block AC.

This brief discussion is sufficient to show that if we have a good grasp of what would be required for something to be naturalistic, and what sort of conceptual problems are raised by various kinds of mind-body models, then it is possible to rapidly develop and investigate hypotheses about the nature of the mind and the world, and thereby develop a suitable onto-logical and metaphysical framework for studying the nature of AC in a productive and scientific way. I have elsewhere described in more detail such possibilities and opportunities (in preparation a, 2011a,b,c, 2012), but much more work needs to be done in this area. However, as the afore-mentioned examples illustrate, and my wider work also suggests, it is likely that naturalism will be upheld in the development of these insights and models.

CONCLUSION

In this chapter, I have argued that the *nature* of AC does not threaten physicalism and/or naturalism, nor does it provide support for mind-body dualism, as has often been claimed. However, I showed that the *context* in which AC sometimes occurs does suggest structural mind-body dualism and indicates that AC is a capacity of the mind existing as a con-crete thing in addition to the physical body. I have argued that this infer-ence cannot be undermined by appeals to the super-ESP hypothesis.

I proposed that in this light, AC will be understood only if it is studied from the perspective of a complex naturalistic framework that is dualistic about the mind-body structure but could be monistic about kinds of mat-ter. I have given some suggestions of how the development of such a framework might proceed and some reasons for holding that this frame-work will be a naturalistic one. Given these outcomes, it is likely that the scientific study of AC will be important for our understanding of the nature of persons and of the world.

Notes

1. "Intentionality" (also called "aboutness") is the property of being *directed at* or *about* something else—for example, a wish is *for* something, anger is *about* some-thing, belief is *that* something is the case. It is the intentionality of ideas that give them the capability of being true or false about the nature of the world.

2. Sidgwick was Knightbridge Professor of Moral Philosophy at Cambridge University from 1883 to 1900. Sidgwick's *Methods in Ethics* (1873) stood as the most significant work on moral theory for the next 130 years and was only surpassed in 2011 by Derek Parfits's *On What Matters* (Singer, 2011). Sidgwick was a co-founder of the Society for Psychical Research (SPR) and its president in eight of its first 11 years (1882–1884 and 1888–1892).

3. In the 132 years of the SPR's existence, philosophers have presided in more years than any other discipline (32, 14 by moral philosophers), but none have so served since 1976. Physicists have led in 29 years (8 since 1976) and psychologists in 30 years (21 since 1976).

4. For ontological purposes, this view regards the notion of spacetime, in which time is treated as a kind of spatial dimension, as a mathematical convenience rather than an ontological hypothesis. For a defense of ontological "four-dimensionalism," see Sider (2001); for criticism see Baker (2009) and Hawthorne (2007).

5. Note that "naturalistic" is not coextensive with "natural." The opposite of "natural" is *artificial* or *contrived* or *manufactured*, whereas the opposite of "naturalistic" is *supernaturalistic*.

6. "Energy" is a property something has if it has the inherent ability to change but only in proportionate ways. The kinds of change something can undergo signifies the kinds of energy it has, and the amount of change it can undergo signifies the amount of energy it has.

7. For simplicity, I will use the term "mental" to refer to all the properties relating to *psyche*, for example, consciousness, rationality, the subconscious, emotions. "Psychical" is the standard term for this, but in the present context, that might be confused with "psychic," which typically now refers to supernormal capacities such as telepathy and clairvoyance.

8. For brevity, I am here including concrete spaces in the category "physical thing," even though, strictly speaking, they are not physical things but spatial ones. This is innocuous in the present context, since physicalists do not deny the existence of concrete spatial things (e.g., the quantum vacuum), and the two are often conflated in practice, as when physicists talk of "physical space" when they really mean "concrete space." When they say "physical space," they are, of course, trying to make clear that they are not referring to *metrical* space (which is abstract and has no causal powers) but to *substantial* space (which *does* have causal powers, e.g., the Casimir effect produced by the quantum vacuum).

9. For brevity, I earlier bundled spatial things in with physical things. Technically, they are distinct kinds, and if accordingly we postulate that a kind of "spatial" matter exists (having energetic and spatial but no physical or mental properties), then the number of combinations go up to 31.

10. This usage of the term "spiritistic" should be carefully distinguished from terms such as "spiritual" and "spirituality." In contemporary parlance, the terms "spiritual" and "spirituality" refer to the beliefs that life has meaning, value, and purpose, and the quest to live up to these and have no essential linkage to notions about the existence of supernatural entities (Rousseau, 2014a). As I have argued elsewhere, there is good reason to assume that the grounding of *spirituality* is naturalistic (Rousseau, 2014c, d). It would be fair to say that Sidgwick's and Myers's motivation in founding the SPR was a spiritual but not a spiritistic one.

11. This supposition might be tested by investigating correlates of AC *failures*. In the case of radar systems, false detections (either positive or negative) can be due to static or dynamic characteristics of the environment and target. If AC failures show similar dependencies, this would suggest that AC's apparent distance insensitivity is due to sophisticated signal-processing rather than non-naturalistic signals.

12. In contrast, in Penny Sartori's prospective hospital study she found that cardiac arrest survivors who did not report OBEs were unable to make accurate guesses as to what happened during their resuscitation (2008).

13. For example, in one case, the patient had an out-of-hospital acute massive heart attack and was brought in unconscious and cyanotic. An attending (male) nurse removed the patient's dentures before attaching the ventilation mask. After he recovered, the patient asked for his dentures, but no one knew what had become of them. The patient reported that he had observed what happened from his OBE state. He recognized the nurse in question and said that he had placed the dentures on a shelf on the crash cart, where they were then found (Smit, 2008; Van Lommel, van Wees, Meyers, & Elfferich, 2001).

REFERENCES

Antonietti, A., Corradini, A., & Lowe, E. J. (Eds.). (2008). *Psycho-physical dualism today*. New York: Lexington.

Armstrong, D. M. (1993). *A materialist theory of the mind* (rev. ed.). London and New York: Routledge.

Audain, L. (1999). Near-death experiences and the theory of the extraneuronal hyperspace. *Journal of Near-Death Studies, 18*(2), 103–115.

Baker, L. R. (2009). Identity across time: A defense of three-dimensionalism. In B. Schick (Ed.), *Unity and time in metaphysics*, pp. 1–14. Berlin: Walter de Gruyter.

Bem, D. J., & Honorton, C. (1994). Does psi exist? Replicable evidence for an anomalous process of information transfer. *Psychological Bulletin, 115*(1), 4–18.

Bennett, J. (2007). Exchange of papers between Leibniz and Clarke. http://www.earlymoderntexts.com/pdfs/leibniz1715.pdf

Brumblay, R. J. (2003). Hyperdimensional perspectives in out-of-body and near-death experiences. *Journal of Near-Death Studies, 21*(4), 201–221.

Bunge, M. (1977). *Ontology I: The furniture of the world*. Boston: Reidel.

Bunge, M. (1979). *Ontology II: A World of Systems*. Dordrecht, The Netherlands: Reidel.

Bunge, M. (2000). Energy: Between physics and metaphysics. *Science & Education, 9*(5), 459–463.

Bunge, M. (2010). *Matter and mind: A philosophical inquiry*. New York: Springer.

Carr, B. (2007). *Universe or multiverse?* Cambridge: Cambridge University Press.

Carr, B. (2008). Worlds apart? Can psychical research bridge the gulf between matter and mind? *Proceedings of the Society for Psychical Research, 59*(221), 1–96.

Chibeni, S. S., & Moreira-Almeida, A. (2007). Remarks on the scientific exploration of "anomalous" psychiatric phenomena. *Revista de Psiquiatria Clínica, 34* (Suppl. 1), 8–15.

Christian, J. (2012). *Disproof of Bell's theorem: Illuminating the illusion of entanglement.* Boca Raton, FL: BrownWalker.

Cook, E. W., Greyson, B., & Stevenson, I. (1998). Do any near-death experiences provide evidence for the survival of human personality after death? Relevant features and illustrative case reports. *Journal of Scientific Exploration, 12*(3), 337–406.

De Caro, M., & Macarthur, D. (2008). *Naturalism in question.* Cambridge, MA: Harvard University Press.

Descartes, R., Cottingham, J., Stoothoff, R., & Murdoch, D. (1985/1641). *The philosophical writings of Descartes* (Vol. 2 of 3). Cambridge: Cambridge University Press.

Fenwick, P., & Fenwick, E. (2008). *The art of dying: A journey to elsewhere.* London: Continuum.

Gauld, A. (1968). *The founders of psychical research.* New York: Schocken.

Gauld, A. (2010). Henry Sidgwick, theism and psychical research. In *Ethics, Psychics and Politics: Proceedings of the 2nd International Congress on the philosophy of Henry Sidgwick, 2009–2010.* University of Catania. http://www.henrysidgwick.com/4th-paper.1st.congress.cat.eng.html

Goetz, S., & Taliaferro, C. (2008). *Naturalism.* Cambridge: Eerdmans.

Greene, F. G. (1999). A projective geometry for separation experiences. *Journal of Near-Death Studies, 17*(3), 151–191.

Greene, F. G. (2003). At the edge of eternity's shadows: Scaling the fractal continuum from lower into higher space. *Journal of Near-Death Studies, 21*(4), 223–240.

Greyson, B. (2003). Incidence and correlates of near-death experiences in a cardiac care unit. *General Hospital Psychiatry, 25*(4), 269–276.

Greyson, B. (2010). Implications of near-death experiences for a postmaterialist psychology. *Psychology of Religion and Spirituality, 2*(1), 37–45.

Greyson, B. (2013). Near-death experiences. In E. Cardeña, S. Krippner, & S. Lynn (Eds.), *Varieties of anomalous experience: Examining the scientific evidence* (2nd ed.), pp. 333–367. Washington, DC: American Psychological Association.

Gurney, E., Myers, F. W. H., & Podmore, F. (1886). *Phantasms of the living* (Vols. 1–2). London: Trubner and Co.

Hawthorne, J. (2007). Three-dimensionalism vs. four-dimensionalism. In T. Sider, J. Hawthorne, & D. W. Zimmerman (Eds.), *Contemporary debates in metaphysics,* pp. 263–282. Malden, MA: Wiley-Blackwell.

Heil, J. (2003). *From an ontological point of view.* Oxford: Oxford University Press.

Holden, J. M. (2009). Veridical perception in near-death experiences. In J. M. Holden, B. Greyson, & D. James (Eds.), *The handbook of near-death experiences: Thirty years of investigation,* pp. 185–211. Santa Barbara, CA: Praeger/ABC-CLIO.

Holden, J. M., Greyson, B., & James, D. (Eds.). (2009). *The handbook of near-death experiences: Thirty years of investigation.* Santa Barbara, CA: Praeger/ABC-CLIO.

Hudson, H. (2008). *The metaphysics of hyperspace.* Oxford: Oxford University Press.

James, W. (1890). *The principles of psychology: In two volumes* (Vol. 1). New York: Henry Holt & Co.

Jourdan, J.-P. (2000). Juste une dimension de plus... (English translation by author available on-line at http://iands-france.org.pagesperso-orange.fr/SRC/PDF/justextra.pdf). *Les Cahiers de IANDSFrance,* Occasional Scientific Issue

No.   1.   http://iands-france.org.pagesperso-orange.fr/SRC/PDF/
justextra.pdf

Jourdan, J.-P. (2001). Les dimensions de la conscience. *Cahiers de IANDS-France,* Occasional Scientific Issue No. 2.

Jourdan, J.-P. (2006). *Deadline: Dernière limite.* Paris: Les 3 Orangers.

Jourdan, J.-P. (2011). Near death experiences and the 5th dimensional spatio-temporal perspective. *Journal of Cosmology, 14.* http://journalofcosmology.com/Consciousness152.html

Kaku, M. (1995). *Hyperspace: A scientific odyssey through parallel universes, time warps, and the tenth dimension.* New York: Oxford Paperbacks.

Kelly, E. F., Kelly, E. W., Crabtree, A., Gauld, A., Grosso, M., & Greyson, B. (2007). *Irreducible mind: Toward a psychology for the 21st century.* Lanham MD: Rowman & Littlefield.

Koons, R. C., & Bealer, G. (Eds.). (2010). *The waning of materialism.* Oxford: Oxford University Press.

Matthewson, J., & Weisberg, M. (2009). The structure of tradeoffs in model building. *Synthese, 170*(1), 169–190.

Maxwell, N. (2004). Non-empirical requirements scientific theories must satisfy: Simplicity, unification, explanation, beauty. In J. Earman & J. Norton (Eds.), *PhilSci Archive.* Pentire Press. http://philsci-archive.pitt.edu/1759/

May, E. C., & Marwaha, S. B. (2014). *Anomalous cognition: Remote viewing research and theory.* Jefferson, NC: McFarland.

May, E. C., Spottiswoode, S. J. P., & Faith, L. V. (2000). The correlation of the gradient of Shannon entropy and anomalous cognition: Toward an AC sensory system. *Journal of Scientific Exploration, 14*(1), 53–72.

Myers, F. W. H. (1901). In memory of Henry Sidgwick. *Proceedings of the Society for Psychical Research, 15,* 452–464.

Myers, F. W. H. (1903). *Human personality and its survival of bodily death* (Vols. 1–2). London. Longmans Green.

Palmer, J. (1978). Extrasensory perception: Research findings. In S. Krippner, M. L. Carlson, M. Ullman, & R. O. Becker (Eds.), *Advances in parapsychological research,* pp. 59–243. Boston, MA: Springer.

Potts, M., & Devanno, A. (2013). Tertullian's theory of the soul and contemporary psychical research. *Journal of the Society for Psychical Research, 77*(4), 209–219.

Price, H. H. (1967). Psychical research and human personality. In J. R. Smythies (Ed.), *Science and ESP,* pp. 33–46. London: Routledge.

Randall, L. (2006). *Warped passages: Unravelling the universe's hidden dimensions.* London: Penguin.

Randall, L., & Sundrum, R. (1999). An alternative to compactification. *Physical Review Letters, 83*(23), 4690–4693.

Ring, K., & Cooper, S. (1999). *Mindsight: Near-death and out-of-body experiences in the blind.* Palo Alto CA.: William James Center for Consciousness Studies.

Rousseau, D. (in preparation, a). *Minds, souls and nature* [Monograph].

Rousseau, D. (in preparation, b). Naturalistic neutral monism.

Rousseau, D. (in preparation, c). Systemic semantics: Framework for a transdisciplinary discourse domain.

Rousseau, D. (2011a). *Minds, souls and nature: A systems-philosophical analysis of the mind-body relationship in the light of near-death experiences.* PhD Thesis, University of Wales Trinity Saint David, Lampeter, Wales, UK.

Rousseau, D. (2011b). Near-death experiences and the mind-body relationship: A systems-theoretical perspective. *Journal of Near-Death Studies, 29*(3), 399–435.

Rousseau, D. (2011c). Understanding spiritual awareness in terms of anomalous information access. *Open Information Systems Journal, Special Issue: Information and Spirituality, 3*(1), 40–53.

Rousseau, D. (2012). The implications of near-death experiences for research into the survival of consciousness. *Journal of Scientific Exploration, 26*(1), 43–80.

Rousseau, D. (2013a). Philosophical conditions for sustainable outcomes to complex systemic interventions. Presented at the ISSS Conference on Curating the Conditions for a Thrivable Planet: Systemic Leverage Points for Emerging a Global Eco-Civilization held in Hai Phong City, Hai Phong, Vietnam, July 14–19, 2013. In *Proceedings of the 57th World Conference of the International Society for the Systems Sciences.*

Rousseau, D. (2013b). Reflections on the meaning and significance of general system theory. Seminar presented to the Centre for Systems Studies, University of Hull, Kingston upon Hull, East Yorkshire, UK, October 30, 2013.

Rousseau, D. (2014a). A systems model of spirituality. *Zygon: Journal of Religion and Science, 49*(2), 476–508.

Rousseau, D. (2014b). Foundations and a framework for future waves of systemic inquiry. *Proceedings of the 22nd European Meeting on Cybernetics and Systems Research (EMCSR 2014), 2014, Vienna, Austria.*

Rousseau, D. (2014c). Reconciling spirituality with the concrete sciences: A systems-philosophical perspective. *Presented at the Third International Conference of the British Association for the Study of Spirituality*, May 19–21, 2014, Ashridge House, Berkhamsted, Hertfordshire, UK.

Rousseau, D. (2014d). Reconciling spirituality with the naturalistic sciences: A systems-philosophical perspective. *Journal for the Study of Spirituality. 4*(2), 174–189.

Rousseau, D., & Rousseau, J. (2012). Is there "ultimate stuff" and are there "ultimate reasons"? In *The Foundational Questions Institute's 2012 Essay Competition: Questioning the Foundations (Finalist).* http://fqxi.org/community/forum/topic/1539; http://www.systemsphilosophy.org/publications/ROUSSEAU_Ultimate_Stuff_and_Ultimate_Reasons.pdf

Ryan, A. (in press). Physical correlates of psi. In E. Cardeña, J. Palmer, & D. Marcusson-Clavertz (Eds.), *Parapsychology: A handbook for the 21st century.* Jefferson, NC: McFarland.

Ryan, A. (2008). New insights into the links between ESP and geomagnetic activity. *Journal of Scientific Exploration, 22*(3), 335–358.

Sartori, P. (2008). *The near-death experiences of hospitalized intensive care patients: A five-year clinical study.* Lampeter: Edwin Mellen.

Scriven, M. (1976). Explanations of the supernatural. In S. C. Thakur (Ed.), *Philosophy and psychical research*, pp. 181–210. London: Allen & Unwin.

Searle, J. R. (1995). *The construction of social reality.* London: Allen Lane.

Shannon, C. E. (1948). A mathematical theory of communication. *Bell System Technical Journal, 27*(Part 1), 379–423.

Sider, T. (2001). *Four-dimensionalism.* New York: Oxford University Press.

Singer, P. (2011, May 20). One mountain. *Times Literary Supplement*, pp. 3–4.

Smit, R. H. (2008). Corroboration of the dentures anecdote involving veridical perception in a NDE. *Journal of Near-Death Studies*, *27*(1), 47–61.

Spottiswoode, S. J. P. (1990). Geomagnetic activity and anomalous cognition: A preliminary report of new evidence. *Subtle Energies*, *1*(1), 91–102.

Spottiswoode, S. J. P. (1997). Apparent association between effect size in free response anomalous cognition experiments and local sidereal time. *Journal of Scientific Exploration*, *11*(2), 1–17.

Stoljar, D. (2009, Fall). Physicalism. In E. N. Zalta (Ed.), *The Stanford encyclopedia of philosophy*. http://plato.stanford.edu/archives/fall2009/entries/physicalism/

Storm, L., Tressoldi, P. E., & Di Risio, L. (2010). Meta-analysis of free-response studies, 1992–2008: Assessing the noise reduction model in parapsychology. *Psychological Bulletin*, *136*(4), 471–485.

Stove, D. (1991). *The Plato cult and other philosophical follies*. Oxford: Blackwell.

Sudduth, M. (2009). Super-psi and the survivalist interpretation of mediumship. *Journal of Scientific Exploration*, *23*(2), 167–193.

Tart, C. T. (1988a). Effects of electrical shielding on GESP performance. *Journal of the American Society for Psychical Research*, *82*(2), 129–146.

Tart, C. T. (1988b). Geomagnetic effects on GESP: Two studies. *Journal of the American Society for Psychical Research*, *82*(3), 193–216.

Tart, C. T. (2009). *The end of materialism*. Oakland, CA: New Harbinger.

Utts, J. (1991). Replication and meta-analysis in parapsychology. *Statistical Science*, 363–378.

Van Lommel, P., van Wees, R., Meyers, V., & Elfferich, I. (2001). Near-death experiences in survivors of cardiac arrest: A prospective study in the Netherlands. *The Lancet*, *358*(9298), 2039–2045.

Zingrone, N. L., & Alvarado, C. S. (2009). Pleasurable Western adult near-death experiences: Features, circumstances, and incidence. In J. M. Holden, B. Greyson, & D. James (Eds.), *The handbook of near-death experiences: Thirty years of investigation*. Santa Barbara, CA: Praeger/ABC-CLIO.

Zollner, J. (1880). *Transcendental physics*. London: W. Harrison.

Part II

The Future
of Psi Research

Chapter 14

Has Science Developed the Competence to Confront the Paranormal?

Charles Honorton

Editor's Note: The following is a reproduction of the presidential address for the Parapsychological Association annual meeting in Santa Barbara 1975, given by the late Charles Honorton (1946–1992). His observations are as valid today as they were 40 years ago. While psi research has made substantial advances in its methods, areas of study, use of statistics, and theoretical understanding, as these volumes indicate, the "establishment science"—as Chuck calls it—is still mired in perceptions about psi that they held 40 years ago when psi research was a nascent modern science. We appreciate that the Parapsychological Association granted us permission to reproduce Chuck's presidential address in this volume.

Explaining their decision to publish a preliminary report on "remote perception" experiments performed at Stanford Research Institute in the fall of 1974, the editors of *Nature* openly posed the issue whether science has yet developed the competence to confront claims of the paranormal. The editors of *Nature* deserve a great deal of credit for having the courage to raise this question, and in order to explore the issue further, I think it will be helpful to examine both "establishment" science and "paranormal" science.

Charles Honorton in his research laboratory at Maimonides Medical, Brooklyn, New York (Edwin C. May)

ESTABLISHMENT SCIENCE

It is appropriate to begin with establishment science, the scientific orthodoxy, or "mainstream," since this is what defines and limits the scope of factual knowledge. Through its publication practices, establishment science controls the dissemination of research findings. Through the top-level policies of its executive councils, establishment science controls the disposition of research funds. And through our educational institutions, establishment science teaches what is currently known and/or believed about the nature of reality. Has establishment science developed the competence to confront claims of the paranormal?

Before pursuing this question further, I think it is important to recognize that despite the impressive accomplishments of modern science and its applied technologies, science has yet to come to grips with some of the fundamental problems underlying much of what it currently regards as normal. Among the still unanswered questions of normal science are these: What is the source of power of the atomic nucleus? How is biochemistry translated into consciousness? Where is memory? These and similar questions tend to be ignored, but are kept alive by our truly great scientists, men like Eddington, Eccles, Wigner, and Wheeler.

Those of you who are familiar with the history of paranormal research will, I think, agree that establishment science competently confronted claims of the paranormal during the period we now call the "ESP Controversy" of the 1930's. During the five-year period following publication of J. B. Rhine's *Extra-Sensory Perception* in 1934, the scientific community responded as it should to any claim of new discovery, by disseminating both positive and negative research findings, by careful scrutiny of the experimental and evaluative techniques, and by encouraging fresh replication efforts.

During this period, there were approximately 60 critical articles by 40 authors, published primarily in the American psychological literature. Fifty experimental studies were reported during this period, two-thirds of which represented independent replication efforts by other laboratories of the Duke University work. The critical issues raised during this period were, for the most part, legitimate ones, and the experimentalists were quick to modify their procedures to accommodate valid criticism.

By 1940 there was, if not a general consensus on the reality of ESP, at least a general consensus on what constituted a good ESP experiment. Yet despite the adequacy of many of the experimental studies, conceded even by the leading critics of the period, and despite the continued accumulation of new experimental confirmations, the active confrontation between establishment science and claims of the paranormal went into hibernation for a decade and a half. Between 1940 and the mid-1950's, very little discussion of paranormal claims appeared outside the parapsychological specialty journals. Virtually no funding was available for research and graduate students who wanted their degrees were strongly discouraged from pursuing parapsychological topics. Aside from occasional textbook and lecture references to obsolete criticisms of the early Duke work, establishment science, during this period, sought to ignore rather than to confront claims of the paranormal.

In the 1950's, the two leading interdisciplinary journals of science published speculative attacks on paranormal research. *Nature* carried what in itself was a "paranormal" claim, in the form of Spencer Brown's attack on probability theory (Brown, 1953). *Science* gave special prominence to George Price's article on *Science and the Supernatural* (Price, 1955). Price's confrontation with the paranormal began with the assumption that ESP and other paranormal claims are impossible. While conceding the methodological and statistical adequacy of many of the experiments purporting to demonstrate ESP, Price argued that since ESP is impossible, experimental evidence that cannot otherwise be explained away should be regarded instead as evidence of experimenter incompetence or dishonesty. Seventeen years later, in a cryptic *Apology to Rhine and Soal*, Price (1972) retracted these allegations.

Our current situation shows definite signs that establishment science is once again attempting to actively confront claims of the paranormal. There are numerous indications of this, but I will discuss just two. While federal grant support for parapsychological research is still virtually non-existent in comparison with more conventional research on, say, military frisbee design, a beginning has been made in the support of a few projects. There is at least now some inclination on the part of funding agencies to consider individual proposals on the basis of merit, past accomplishment, and the likelihood of continued success.

Aside from providing financial support for new research, the greatest contribution establishment science can make toward the resolution of controversy over *any* new claim, I believe, is to allow the dissemination of research findings, both positive and negative. In this regard, the current confrontation between establishment science and claims of the paranormal must be considered to be highly ambivalent.

On the positive side, symposia on parapsychological methods and research findings are becoming a regular feature on the annual programs of a number of scientific societies, including the American Psychological Association and the American Association for the Advancement of Science. The affiliation of the Parapsychological Association with the AAAS in 1969 has provided an important new forum for the dissemination and discussion of parapsychological findings, primarily through symposia at AAAS annual meetings.

Yet while the AAAS encourages us to sponsor symposia at its annual meetings, its journal, *Science*, continues to suppress the interdisciplinary dissemination of our research findings. Even since our admission into the AAAS, *Science* has published only reports of negative findings. Since *Science* is a highly selective journal, accepting only about 20 percent of the reports submitted to it for consideration, the publication of negative findings indicates that the editors of *Science* regard the problem-area to be one of some importance. If this is so, why has *Science* consistently rejected competent experimental reports with positive findings?

There is no more effective means through which to answer *Nature's* editorial challenge than to allow interdisciplinary consideration of both positive and negative findings in this area. This would allow the interdisciplinary scientific community to know just exactly what is being claimed about the paranormal; to assess for itself the degree of competence and the level of development; and to stimulate new independent replication efforts.

Yet, despite encouraging indications to the contrary, the current status of the situation is still, I think, subject to the constraints imposed, in a well-known quote from the physicist, Max Planck, by what I shall call

"Planck's Second Constant": "A new scientific truth does not triumph by convincing its opponents and making them see the light, but rather because its opponents eventually die and a new generation grows up that is familiar with it" (Planck, 1949). For the moment, I think we must conclude that while *Nature* has developed the competence to confront claims of the paranormal, *Science* hasn't.

PARANORMAL SCIENCE

Has parapsychology developed the competence to confront claims of the paranormal? Not as much as we would all like, but much more than anyone has a right to expect given the level of support, the degree of irrational prejudice, and the small number of competent investigators who have been able to sustain themselves in this field. In fact, I suggest to you that some of our paranormal claims have much more support behind them than many of the more widely accepted claims of normal science.

Let us examine the replication status of findings in parapsychology and other areas of behavioral research. Almost all of the discussion of this important topic has occurred without the necessary bookkeeping. First, let us return to the card-guessing experiments of the 1930's and examine the replicability of that work. The central claim upon which ESP was based during this period was formulated as follows: "Is it possible repeatedly to obtain results that are statistically significant when subjects are tested for knowledge of (or reaction to) external stimuli (unknown and uninferable to the subject) under conditions that safely exclude the recognized sensory processes?" (Rhine et al., 1940, p. 15).

Even among parapsychologists there is a rather widespread belief that most of the independent replications of the early Duke work were nonconfirmatory and I suspect this may be especially true among those of us who were not around in the 1930's (which, incidentally, accounts for about three-fourths of the participants at this convention). In fact, I was surprised myself to find that this wasn't so when I undertook a review of all of the English-language ESP experiments reported during the period between 1934 and 1939 (Honorton, 1975a). The results of this survey, in terms of replication, are shown in Table 14.1.

This work involved a database of approximately 3.3 million individual trials. As Table 14.1 indicates, 61 percent of the independent replications of the Duke work were statistically significant. This is 60 times the proportion of significant studies we would expect if the significant results were due to chance error. Of course, there is also experimental error and some of these studies left much to be desired in terms of methodology. Yet on the basis of my own study of this literature, I concluded that at least 33 of these 50 studies were methodologically adequate on the basis of the experimental reports.

Table 14.1
All English-language ESP Experiments Involving Statistical Assessment
of Data, 1934–1939 inclusive*

	Number of experiments	No. reporting statistical significance ($p \leq .01$)	Percent significant
Duke group	17	15	61
All other laboratories	33	20	61
Total	50	35	70

*Chi square (Duke vs. Other × Significant vs. Nonsignificant) = 1.70 (df = 1; nonsignificant)

The next question, then, is this: Were all of these laboratories suppressing mountains of nonsignificant data?

I think this is very unlikely, judging from the temper of the times, but it is not necessary to rest our case on this. It is legitimate to ask what volume of research data could realistically have been generated during this period. It is important to recall, in considering this question, that in the 1930's there were only two funded research laboratories in parapsychology, one at Duke University and the other at Stanford University. (I believe the Stanford endowment still exists, although the Stanford officials have consistently allowed it to be used for other purposes.) It is also important to bear in mind that the volume of *reported* work during this period was 3.3 million individual trials and that it takes time to shuffle ESP cards and to record subjects' guesses.

About six months ago, my friend and colleague, Edwin May, opened a suitcase, which he had carried all around India. Inside was an electronic random number generator. Just to illustrate what a little technology will do for an impoverished research area, this instrument is the third or fourth generation version of an instrument that was introduced in parapsychology only five years ago by Helmut Schmidt. It looked to me more like something one would find at Mission Control in Houston than in a parapsychological research laboratory in deepest Brooklyn. Ed explained the myriad of controls that decorate the front panel. "These knobs," he said, "allow us to ask "physics-type" questions about PK. This one allows us to adjust the trial rate from one trial every ten seconds to a million trials in ten seconds. . . . in millisecond increments, of course," he added with a smile.

Eager to play, we decided to run a control series of random checks. Several minutes and millions of trials later, I suddenly realized that we had just collected more trials in those few minutes than had been reported during the entire 60-year period between 1880 and 1939.

Even if we assume a position of extreme conservatism and allow for the possibility that for each published study between 1934 and 1939 there were five studies that were not reported and were nonconfirmatory (that is, 250 unpublished studies with 16.5 million nonsignificant trials), the rate of replication of the ESP hypothesis would still be highly significant.

REPLICATION IN PARAPSYCHOLOGY AND OTHER AREAS

It has become clear to me that the replication status of parapsychological findings must be viewed within the larger perspective of replication in other areas of research. Last year at Maimonides we completed a two-year dream research project, which was supported by the National Institute of Mental Health (Honorton & Ullman, 1975). This project was designed to replicate and extend our earlier telepathic dream work as well as to replicate certain nonparapsychological findings by another investigator. This investigator, while still analyzing data from a project begun six years earlier, had published several preliminary accounts of findings based on general impressions of his data. His tentative conclusions had gained fairly widespread acceptance, despite the exploratory character of his initial reports. To make a long story short, we not only failed to replicate our own telepathic dream findings, we also failed to replicate three of the four nonparanormal claims of this other investigator.

Recently, a number of us have begun exploring the possible role of mental imagery as a mediator of psi (i.e., paranormal information flow). Six reports have appeared thus far relating ESP performance to one very popular scale, which purports to measure the vividness of imagery. While three of these studies showed some relationship between psi and imagery, as defined by this scale, the direction of the relationship has shown a disconcerting tendency to vary from study to study. We might be tempted to ascribe such lack of consistency to that perennial scapegoat, the "elusiveness of psi," were it not for the fact that similar reversals between this scale and a variety of nonparanormal performance measures seem to be more the rule than the exception (Honorton, 1975b).

I could go on, but I know that many of you can provide similar instances of how the findings of more established–nonparanormal–fields cannot be relied upon. My point is simply this: the problem of replication did not begin and does not end with parapsychology. In fact, parapsychology may actually be in a better position vis-à-vis replication than many other areas of behavioral research.

Let us take a brief look at the publication practices of the American Psychological Association, for example. A number of studies have been reported of APA publication practices. I will summarize just two. Sterling (1959) sampled 362 research reports published in three of the leading APA journals. He found that while 97 percent of the studies basing conclusions on significance tests reported rejection of the null or specific hypothesis, *none* of the research reports was of a replication of previously reported findings. Similarly, Bozarth & Roberts (1972) sampled 1344 research reports published in four additional journals. They found that while 94 percent reported findings based on the rejection of the null or specific hypothesis, *less than one percent* were of replications of previous findings. I do not see how we can avoid the conclusion that it is impossible to assess the validity of findings and degree of replication in many areas of psychology.

Now let us return to our own situation and examine the replication status of research findings in contemporary parapsychology. Let us begin by examining what is being reported right here at this meeting and then step back and see how well or poorly some of our findings are holding up relative to similar earlier work.

Two dozen research laboratories are represented on the program of this year's convention. There are 48 experimental reports with findings based at least in part on significance tests. Rejection of the null or specific hypothesis is reported in 63 percent of these studies and by 17 different laboratories. Moreover, 73 percent of the studies reported at this convention are of attempted replications of previously reported findings. Of these, 43 percent report significant confirmation of earlier findings.

I will now examine in somewhat greater depth two areas that have sustained systematic research efforts over a period of years. My selection is somewhat arbitrary and reflects my own research interests. There are other areas that could serve equally well.

INTERNAL ATTENTION STATES

The first area involves the use of internally-deployed attention states, brought about by a variety of means, to detect and register paranormal information flow. We can formulate the central claim or finding in this area as follows: psi information flow is more easily detected and recognized when the receiver is in a state of sensory relaxation and is minimally influenced by ordinary perception and proprioception.

A good case can be made for this claim on analytical grounds alone and the empirical support for it pervades nearly every aspect of our literature, from our studies of cultural practices and spontaneous experiences to our clinical case histories and experimental reports.

Let us first examine some of the analytical considerations. For these we are indebted to the late Cambridge philosopher, C. D. Broad, whose theoretical contributions to parapsychology have not yet received the attention and recognition they clearly deserve. Broad was among the first to suggest that if paranormal phenomena occur at all, they are probably much more pervasive in our everyday lives than has traditionally been recognized.

Drawing an analogy with the discovery of magnetic fields, for example, he wrote:

> Had it not been for the two very contingent facts that there are lodestones and that the one element, iron, which is strongly susceptible to magnetic influences, is fairly common on earth, the existence of magnetism might have remained unsuspected to this day. Even so, it was regarded as. . . .[an] anomaly until its connection with electricity was discovered, and we gained the power to produce strong magnetic fields at will. Yet all this, while magnetic fields had existed and had been producing effects whenever and wherever electric currents were passing. Is it not possible that natural mediums might be comparable to lodestones, that paranormal influences are as pervasive as magnetism, and that we fail to recognize this only because our knowledge and control of them are at about the same level as were men's knowledge and control of magnetism when Gilbert wrote his treatise on the magnet? (Broad, 1953)

Broad pointed out that psi interactions need not involve conscious experience at all, that those that do are merely the tip of an iceberg, and that below the surface, psi interactions may occur as totally unconscious influences on our moods, our dispositions, our thought processes, and so on. As we have already seen at this convention and in the literature over the last several years, experimental support for this far-out notion has begun to emerge through the work of Stanford and his associates (Stanford, 1974; Stanford et al., 1975).

As for the relative rarity of *recognized* psi interactions (i.e., psi experiences), Broad's analysis of the conditions necessary for the recognition of paranormal input makes it clear that these conditions are normally seldom fulfilled. This analysis also makes it clear why psi experiences are so often associated with internal attention states.

Suppose, recasting Broad's analysis in the communications terminology proposed by Morris (1975), that the output of an information source served as an influence on a sensorially-remote receiver. In order for the receiver influence to be detected and identified with its source, all of the following conditions are necessary and must be fulfilled:

- The receiver influence must be detected. With human receivers, this means that the influence must take the form of overt behavior or conscious experience, which the receiver can and does attend to.
- The experience must be sufficiently prominent, or carry sufficient impact, to allow the receiver to distinguish it from among the many other, nonparanormal inputs, which are concurrently influencing

him. In this context, normal perceptual, somatic, and cognitive influences on the receiver may constitute sources of noise.

- The experience must be stored and reported prior to receiver-source contact through normal channels, otherwise it cannot be considered evidential.
- There must be subsequent confirmation of a meaningful correspondence between the source and the receiver.

This correspondence must be sufficiently unusual or consistent over repeated efforts to eliminate chance coincidence as a reasonable explanation.

These detection criteria can account for some of the most prominent features of spontaneous paranormal experiences. The high incidence of spontaneous psi experiences occurring in dreams and other internal attention states would be expected, inasmuch as such states are associated with deafferentation–sensorisomatic noise-reduction–and deployment of attention inward, toward mentation processes such as thoughts and images, which may serve to carry psi information, thus increasing the likelihood of detection. The utilization of imagery and other forms of mentation in the processing of environmental information has been demonstrated in studies of subliminal stimulation–which, incidentally, is also facilitated by internal attention states (Dixon, 1971).

The high incidence of paranormal experiences occurring between friends and relatives and the low incidence of occurrence between remote acquaintances and strangers would also be expected, since there is naturally a greater likelihood of *confirmation* in the former case. Unless the source and receiver know each other and are in relatively frequent contact with one another, the likelihood of confirmation is very low. Furthermore, unless the relationship between the two permits some degree of intimacy, it is unlikely that either would be sufficiently uninhibited to share unusual personal experiences.

Similarly, the high incidence of crisis cases involving situations of sudden, unexpected emotional significance would be expected, since such experiences carry more impact and are more likely to be remembered and recalled than relatively trivial mundane experiences.

The association between paranormal information acquisition and internal attention states can be traced back at least as far as the Vedic period of India and the reports of *siddhis* or paranormal powers manifest in yogic meditation. Then there are the claims of the powers of entranced medicine men and the shaman of the nontechnological societies; the "higher phenomena of hypnotism" reported by the early Mesmerists; the phenomenological descriptions of cognitive strategies employed by gifted individuals, such as Mary Craig Sinclair; and finally, the cross-cultural validation of dreaming as the state-of-choice in spontaneous psi experiences and psychotherapeutic case reports.

Now let us look at the status of controlled laboratory experimentation in this area. I have been able to find 89 experimental studies spanning a 30-year period and involving controlled investigations of psi retrieval in internal attention states brought about by dreaming, guided imagery and hypnosis, meditation, perceptual isolation, and progressive muscular relaxation (Honorton, 1977). At least two different laboratories have reported work with each of these five procedures and this work was contributed by a total of 26 different laboratories or investigator teams. For present purposes, I will examine these studies primarily from the standpoint of replicability. The question is this: How many of the studies with each procedure and overall have reported clear-cut evidence that paranormal processes were operating within the design of the experiment, and how does this number compare with what we would expect purely on the basis of chance error? For the purpose of this analysis, I am defining as "significant" only those studies in which, on the basis of overall psi scores or clearly stated prediction, the investigators rejected the null or specific hypothesis at the .05 level or lower. These results are summarized in Table 14.2.

The replication rate with each of these five procedures is statistically highly significant ($p \leq 10^{-5}$). Overall, of the 89 experiments, 50 reported

Table 14.2
Replication Status of Experimental Studies Involving Psi Retrieval during Internally Deployed Attention State, 1945–1975

Procedure	No. of experiments	No. of experiments significant at $p \leq .05$	No. of significant experiments expected by chance	Binomial p less than*	No. of labs	No. of labs confirming
Dreaming	18	10	0.90	1×10^{-5}	4	2
Hypnosis-guided imagery	39	19	1.95	1×10^{-5}	19	8
Meditation	11	8	0.55	1×10^{-5}	4	3
Perceptual isolation	15	8	0.75	1×10^{-5}	7	2
Progressive relaxation	5	5	0.25	1×10^{-5}	2	2
Totals	89	50	4.45	1×10^{-10}	26	17

*Exact binomial probabilities calculated on the basis of the number of studies significant at $p \leq .05$ out of the total number of studies for each procedure.

rejection of the null or specific hypothesis. This is 10 times the number we would expect on the basis of chance error. Significant findings were reported by 17 of the 26 laboratories; that is, by two-thirds of the laboratories involved.

Over 60 percent of these studies involved free-response ESP designs, which, as you know, are much more time-consuming than shuffling ESP cards. Nevertheless, let us assume for the sake of extreme conservatism that for each published study there are five that were not reported and were not statistically significant. This would require 445 unreported, nonsignificant studies. I cannot imagine how anyone who is familiar with the amount of time these studies require and with the level of support and research output of this field, could really believe that there are anywhere near this number of unreported studies; but let us assume that there are. The rate of replication in this area would still be highly significant.

Now let us compare these data with the new work being reported here at this conference. This year there are 11 experimental reports involving psi and internal attention states, contributed by five different laboratories. Six of these experiments report rejection of the null or specific hypothesis. This gives a replication rate of 55 percent compared to the 56 percent rate for the earlier work. These significant confirmations are reported by four of the five reporting laboratories and this year's crop is 10 times greater in proportion than we would expect on the basis of chance error. This harvest would still be significant if we were to posit five nonsignificant and unreported studies for each one reported at this conference.

I cannot take time now to describe some of the more interesting secondary findings related to this area. Elsewhere I have shown that the information rate for psi studies combining free-response designs with internal attention states is several orders of magnitude larger than for forced-choice guessing designs (Honorton, 1975c).

Nor have I discussed the quality of methodology in these studies. These experiments all utilized standard procedures for eliminating sensory contact between source and receiver, for randomizing targets, and so on. It is doubtful that any of them would live up to the reputation for super-control enjoyed, for a time, by Soal's work with Shackleton and Stewart. But this is not necessary. Each of these studies asked a question and provided a tentative yes-no answer, which, in turn, led to another study, in-house and by another laboratory. This, after all, is how normal science operates, at least in its better moments. The experimental claim results in another experiment rather than in a posthumous attack on the integrity of an individual investigator. Soal's honesty would not now be the topic of idle speculation (Mundle, 1973; Scott & Haskell, 1973) if he had had a replicable procedure rather than a gifted subject.

The existence of a new or hitherto unrecognized natural phenomenon cannot rest upon unrepeatable experiments by isolated investigators working with unique practitioners. Gifted subjects have much to contribute to our knowledge and understanding of psi, but so far, we have largely wasted their talents.

MICRODYNAMIC PSYCHOKINESIS

The second area I have selected for special attention involves psychokinesis on microphysical systems. The central claim or finding in this area may be formulated as follows: a human observer provided with sensory feedback to an external source of randomness produced by a microphysical process can, by attending to the feedback signal, effect an influence on that microphysical process with the result of decreasing its randomness.

Order out of disorder, as a function of intention, perhaps. The history of PK, even more than that of ESP, is tainted with fraud, malobservation, and uncontrolled events occurring in suspicious circumstances. Despite the apparently good controls employed a century ago by Sir William Crookes in his investigations of D. D. Home, or the Naples sittings with Eusapia Palladino, or even the impressive credentials of certain members of the "Metal Benders' Guild" in contemporary Great Britain, such observations have never carried great conviction outside the small circle of firsthand observers present.

Moving from the macroscopic effects associated with poltergeists, hyperactive tables, and compass-needles, into the arena of controlled experimentation, perhaps the most obvious trend has to do with the shrinking size of the PK target. When J. B. and Louisa Rhine salvaged PK from the darkness of séance rooms and noisy tables, they introduced light, dice, and quarter distributions of the half-set.

Yet despite the "overwhelming" evidence for PK provided by the quarter distribution data, I believe psychokinesis might have died prematurely in the late 1940's had it not been for the work of W. E. Cox. Ed Cox nurtured PK research for nearly two decades. He replaced the dice with, among other things, BB's running down paper straw pathways, and his research provided some of the first really strong evidence, not only for the occurrence of PK, but also for the hypothesis that PK is *goal-directed.*

Helmut Schmidt has replaced Cox's BB's with electrons and has substituted solid-state data paths for Cox's paper straws. His electronic random generators show good randomness when run in unattended control checks and highly significant departures from randomness when human subjects attempt to exert feedback-guided influence. Schmidt has found in a series of highly ingenious experiments that the internal complexity

Table 14.3
Survey of All Microdynamic PK Experiments, 1970–1975

Report	Experiment	p less than
Schmidt (1970)	Preliminary Series	.12
	Main Series	.00087
Schmidt & Pantas (1971)	Preliminary Series	.0124
	Series I	6.3×10^{-5}
	Series II	.0093
Matas & Pantas (1971)		.0143
Andre (1972)	Experiment I	.1067
	Experiment II	.0093
Honorton & Barksdale (1972)	Group Experiment	.034
	Individual Ss Experiment	.826
	Single Subject Experiment	3.4×10^{-6}
Schmidt (1973)	Exploratory Experiment	5.6×10^{-5}
	Confirmatory Experiment	2.1×10^{-8}
Schmidt (1975)	Experiment I	.00084
	Experiment II	.0017
Stanford et al. (1975)		.0069

Total significance: chi square = 202, df = 32; $p < 10^{-10}$

of the instrument does not appear to affect the degree of influence, and he too concludes that PK is goal-directed (Schmidt, 1974).

Since Schmidt introduced this line of research five years ago, 16 microdynamic PK experiments have been reported, primarily by Schmidt and his collaborators. The results are summarized in Table 14.3.

Thirteen of these 16 studies, over 80 percent, yielded statistically significant outcomes. This is 16 times the number of significant studies we would expect on the basis of chance error. However, since data collection is so much faster in this area, let us assume for the sake of extreme conservatism that for each of these reported studies there are 10 which were not reported and which are not statistically significant. That is, let us posit 160 unreported, nonconfirmatory studies. Even if this were so, the replication rate for microdynamic PK would still be highly significant.

Now let us compare this with the new work being reported here at this conference. This year there are seven experimental studies of microdynamic PK, contributed by four different laboratories. Five of these seven studies report significant confirmation of microdynamic PK influence and these positive replications are contributed by three of the four reporting laboratories. This is a 71 percent confirmation rate, is 14 times the number we would expect by chance error, and compares nicely to the 80 percent rate for the earlier studies.

TAKING PARAPSYCHOLOGY SERIOUSLY

It is time we take parapsychology and its phenomena seriously, that we stop being defensive with people who are skeptical but are unfamiliar with the serious literature of this field, its better research, the degree of control, and advances in methodology. I believe that it is time for us to go to the journals such as *Science* and to the funding agencies in Washington and demand that they at least examine our serious literature before they reject our papers and our grant proposals. We can present a strong case for our field and it is time that we do so.

I really wanted to take this occasion to develop some speculative areas, but considering the slender basis of support that is currently sustaining this field, I decided upon the present approach. Most of the participants at this conference are here at great personal expense, do not know whether their research will be supported six months or a year from now (if it is supported now), and cannot publish their research in any journal but those that have a circulation of less than 2500.

We must not continue merely bemoaning the fact that parapsychology is not accepted by establishment science; we ought not to feel that, despite the fact that we know our literature and what we are doing in our laboratories, there must be something wrong with the work since it is not accepted; we should not continue to play the game that eventually, after all, science is objective and our findings will eventually become accepted on their merit. I do not believe this. We have been struggling against irrational prejudice for a long time. Patience goes only so far and I think that if the situation is going to change, we are going to have to change it.

Our findings deserve better than they have received from the scientific establishment. If our work is faulty, it should be criticized, but the criticism must be substantive, not *a priori*. The scientific community has an obligation to assess, without prejudice, the serious research in this area. The only way in which this can be done is through dissemination of research reports to a wide scientific audience. As the *Nature* editors suggested, this would have the effect, not of providing an endorsement of any claims, but rather of stimulating critical discussion and further replication. I can see no basis of justification for the refusal of journals such as *Science* to accept research reports of good quality.

SUBLIMINAL STIMULATION AND BIOFEEDBACK

There are some very provocative parallels between two areas of non-paranormal research and the two areas of paranormal research I have focused on in this address.

These areas of "normal" research are subliminal perception and biofeedback. I do not have time to explore either of these in great detail, but

I would like at least to highlight a few points that I think are of special interest.

I think anyone who is familiar with the internal states work in parapsychology and who has read Norman Dixon's (1971) careful survey of the subliminal perception literature must be struck by the parallels. Both subliminal and psi influences are facilitated by internal attention states, both are subject to subtle experimenter effects and situational factors, and both involve the transformation and mediation of stimulus influence through ongoing mentation processes. Perhaps the similarity is no more than skin deep, but the point I wish to emphasize now is that we can begin to exploit these similarities to advantage in using subliminal versus psi comparisons. Those of us who have been involved in free-response psi research have not had any real basis of comparison in terms of how strong our psi mentation-target correspondences are relative to strength and quality of correspondences in a weak sensory setting. A beginning has been made in this direction (Smith, Tremmel, & Honorton, 1976), and to the extent that the same kinds of stimulus distortions and transformations occur in *both* subliminal and psi tasks, we can have greater confidence in the informational characteristics of our psi findings. In fact, I suggest that this may be a useful prototype for a new methodology for studying psi processes, one that moves us away from a strictly theoretical baseline in assessing the significance of psi results.

The implications of biofeedback for parapsychology have usually been discussed in terms of developing biofeedback shortcuts to psi-conducive states. I agree that this is potentially very important, but I would also suggest that what has been referred to as the *goal-directedness* of psychokinesis is found also in biofeedback in the form of *passive volition*. Robert Thouless (1951) described the mind-set associated with his own success in PK dice experiments in the late 1940's as "effortless intention to succeed." This description would immediately be recognized by contemporary biofeedback researchers as passive volition. Elmer Green (1973-4) has described passive volition with an analogy to farming. He says, "A farmer (a) desires a crop, (b) plants the seed, (c) allows nature to take its course, and (d) reaps."

We are puzzled by the fact that a subject can psychokinetically influence a process, which he knows nothing about solely on the basis of intention to succeed and the guidance of a peripheral feedback display. Yet this is exactly what occurs in biofeedback. Let us take the example of single motor unit control. The motor unit is the functional unit of striated muscle. It consists of the nerve cell body, located in the spinal cord, its axon, terminal branches, and all the muscle fibers supplied by these branches. A single spinal motor neuron may supply anywhere from a half-dozen to several hundred muscle fibers. It is now known, chiefly through the work of John Basmajian (1972) that a human observer can learn to isolate and control single motor units using sensory feedback techniques. This despite the fact that most subjects do not even know what cells look like or where they are located. Here is Basmajian's (1969) summary of his results:

> normal human beings can quickly, in a matter of 15 or 20 minutes, be trained to isolate only one motor unit from the population of perhaps 100 or 200 which are within an area of pick-up of an electrode pair. They can suppress all of the units, fire single units, they can manipulate those units, turn them on and off easily, they can suppress the one they started with, pick up another one, train it, suppress it, turn to a third and then, on command, they can respond with signals from the unit that you choose for them to respond with.

I think it is safe to say that ten years ago the voluntary control of a single cell would almost certainly have been regarded, along with psychokinesis, as a paranormal claim. And perhaps it is. Basmajian and a number of other biofeedback researchers have resurrected the concept of volition as a metaforce to account for this type of control. Is it possible that PK has always been closer to us than we've realized? This is, for the present, farfetched speculation. We now have the methodology and the beginnings of a technology, however, to begin asking such questions on an empirical basis.

NORMALIZATION OF THE PARANORMAL

Has science developed the competence to confront claims of the paranormal? I believe the most satisfactory answer to *Nature's* question is this: we have begun to develop competent approaches to the paranormal. We have developed at least a few approaches that work well enough to allow us to build upon them. The job will not be done until we have succeeded in eliminating the "para-" and have normalized these phenomena. This will require further articulation of the positive attributes and antecedent conditions of psi, as well as the determination of the role of psi in our normal life experience. We are beginning to make progress in this direction, on several fronts, and I have tried to indicate a few of these.

I believe we should give up our "para-" terms, even the one that serves to identify this Association. Psi phenomena are as relevant to physics and, I suspect, to neurophysiology, as they are to psychology. We are studying psychophysical interactions, and I would suggest that the term *psychophysics* more properly identifies the range of activities we have called parapsychological.

My own inclination, which is provisional and subject to modification as a result of new data, is that we are, along with physicists and neurophysiologists, on the threshold of a new scientific enterprise, that we are beginning to do some serious psychophysical reality-testing, perhaps to erect a bridge connecting the perennial dualities of mind and matter, physics and psychology. We are, I believe, dealing on an empirical basis with what Eddington called "mind-stuff" and what we have found thus far supports the notion that mind is a real force in nature. I suggest that in the years ahead it will be useful for us to reconsider the type of theory proposed in various forms by Frederic Myers, Henri Bergson, and Sir John Eccles, that the brain is a *transmitter* of mind rather than its *generator*, and that mind manifests through the brain by psychokinetic influence on neural tissue.

OBSERVATION AND PARTICIPATION IN SCIENCE

In closing, I would like to speak briefly about one other area of psi research, the role of the experimenter. Experimenter effects represent a sort of skeleton in our collective closet. This is a topic we discuss not infrequently in private, but seldom in public. We are concerned with the possibility that we ourselves, as experimenters may, to some extent, be the source of the psi influences we observe in our laboratories.

Of course, there are different kinds of experimenter effects: from experimenter fraud on one end of the scale (as we learned last summer) to experimenter psi on the other end of the scale. I think it is interesting to note that many of the successful experimenters in psi research have also been successful subjects. Both J. B. Rhine and Robert Thouless were able to demonstrate PK effects with dice. The French pioneer in the cognitive study of psi, René Warcollier, was successful as a percipient in telepathy-oriented drawing experiments, and so on. Among our currently active experimenters, William Braud was one of the most successful receivers in the Brauds' work on psi and progressive relaxation. Rex Stanford was successful in an EEG/telepathy-oriented study with Ian Stevenson. Robert Morris showed that it is possible to gain nonrandom entry points in tables of random numbers using a complex psi procedure. (Morris's studies on cognitively complex psi provide further evidence for the goal-directedness of psi.)

My own accomplishments as a subject mainly involve a series of PK experiments that I reported several years ago (Honorton & Barksdale, 1972). Helmut Schmidt lent me a manual random number generator and since I was teaching at the time, I decided to do a group experiment with my students. I formulated the hypothesis, based on Ted Serios, Kulagina, and other macro PKers, that unlike ESP, PK may require a high level of arousal and activation. I had my students alternate PK runs in which they tensed and relaxed. The results were very nice: the muscle tension runs were associated with significant psi-hitting. The overall results were significant and this was due to the contribution of the muscle tension condition. I returned to the laboratory very pleased with myself for having confirmed my hypothesis. I then set Warren Barksdale to the task of replicating this experiment with 20 individual subjects, following the same procedure for relaxation and tension. His experiment yielded only chance results. We then decided to run a third experiment in which I would be the solo subject and Warren would be the experimenter.

I tensed and relaxed, and we alternated which of the two display lights was target for an equal number of runs, and so on. The muscle tension runs were about 3.5 standard deviations above chance and the relaxation runs were about 3.5 standard deviations below chance. Again, my hypothesis had been confirmed. The question that now arose in my mind, however, was who were, or was, the subject in that first successful experiment?

Recently, my very good friend John Stump really threw me a curve. When my study dealing with another type of experimenter effect, involving the demeanor of the experimenter as an influence on subjects' psi performance, appeared (Honorton, Ramsey, & Cabibbo, 1975), John examined the control data. In this study, there were two samples of "control random checks." These were run by me, manually depressing the random generator response buttons and attempting not to exert a psi influence on the instrument. Sample A was collected before the experimental data and Sample B was collected after the experimental data. Taken separately, each sample provided good randomness. What John Stump found, however, was that looking at the difference between the two samples, there was a significant difference for each of the four analyses. Since this was a two-choice generator, we looked for sequence effects: how many times did "red" follow "red"; how many times did "red" follow "green"; "green" follow "green"; "green" follow "red"? In each of these four cases, a nonsignificant positive or negative deviation in Sample A was followed by a nonsignificant deviation in the opposite direction in Sample B. The overall result of this was associated with a probability of 10^{-5}. The experimental hypothesis itself was only confirmed at the .001 level.

John Stump went a step further. He used this post hoc analysis as a pilot study. His confirmation consisted of going back to an earlier study, which I had reported with Malcolm Bessent as subject (Honorton, 1971). Again there were pre- and post-experimental random checks; and again the randomness was good within each sample, but with deviations in opposite directions, so that the difference between pre- and post-test deviations was again significant ($p = .002$).

It appears that John Stump has confirmed Jule Eisenbud's hypothesis about what he has colorfully termed the "individual mind-prints" of the experimenter. I frankly do not know what to do about this problem and I am sure that most of you don't either. But we had better start giving serious consideration to these experimenter psi effects and, to show at least that we are not alone, I will close now with a comment from the distinguished Princeton physicist, John Archibald Wheeler, which I think is pertinent to this:

Insofar as we've learned to understand the quantum principle, it's the small tip of an iceberg that tells us that the momentum and the position of an electron are not qualities that exist independently of us, but depend upon our consciously making a decision to measure the position and the momentum in order to bring these features into evidence. I think that through our own act of consciously choosing and posing questions about the universe we bring about in some measure what we see taking place before us. Therefore, I think the word "observing" is inadequate. A better word is "participation." We are going to come to appreciate that the universe itself in some strange way depends upon our being here for its properties. (Wheeler, 1973, p. 32)

REFERENCES

Andre, E. (1972). Confirmation of PK action on electronic equipment. *Journal of Parapsychology, 36,* 283–293.

Basmajian, J. (1969). EMG Feedback. *Proceedings of the First Annual Meeting of the Biofeedback Research Society, 2,* 4.

Basmajian, J. (1972). Electromyography comes of age. *Science, 176,* 603–609.

Bozarth, J. D., & Roberts, R. R. (1972). Signifying significant significance. *American Psychologist, 27,* 774–775.

Broad, C. D. (1953). *Religion, philosophy and psychical research.* New York: Harcourt-Brace.

Brown, G. S. (1953). Statistical significance in psychical research. *Nature, 172,* 154–156.

Dixon, N. (1971). *Subliminal perception: The nature of a controversy.* New York: McGraw-Hill.

Green, E., & Green, A. (1973–1974). Regulating our mind-body processes. *Fields within Fields, 10,* 16–24.

Honorton, C. (1971). Automated forced-choice precognition tests with a "sensitive." *Journal of the American Society for Psychical Research, 165,* 476–481.

Honorton, C. (1975a). Error some place! *Journal of Communication, 25,* 103–116.

Honorton, C. (1975b). Psi and mental imagery: Keeping score on the Betts scale. *Journal of the American Society for Psychical Research, 69*(4), 327–332.

Honorton, C. (1975c). Receiver-optimization and information rate in ESP. Paper presented in the symposium, "The Application and Misapplication of

Findings in Parapsychology," at the 141st *Annual Meeting of the American Association for the Advancement of Science*, New York City, January 27, 1975.

Honorton, C. (1977). Psi interactions and internal attention states. In B. B. Wolman (Ed.), *Handbook of parapsychology*. New York: Van Nostrand Reinholt Co.

Honorton, C., & Barksdale, W. (1972). PK performance with waking suggestions for muscle tension versus relaxation. *Journal of the American Society for Psychical Research, 66,* 208–214.

Honorton, C., Ramsey, M., & Cabibbo, C. (1975). Experimenter effects in extrasensory perception. *Journal of the American Society for Psychical Research, 69,* 135–150.

Honorton, C., & Ullman, M. (1975). *Comparison of sensory and extrasensory influences on dreams,* Final Report prepared for the U. S. Public Health Service, National Institute of Mental Health (MH-21628).Matas, F., & Pantas, L. (1971). A PK experiment comparing meditating versus nonmeditating subjects. *Proceedings of the Parapsychological Association, 8,* 12–13.

Morris, R. L. (1975). Tacit communication and experimental theology. In Parapsychological Association, *Research in Parapsychology, 1974.* Metuchen, NJ: Scarecrow, 179–198.

Mundle, C. W. K. (1973). The Soal-Goldney experiments. *Nature, 245,* 54.

Planck, M. (1949). *Scientific autobiography and other papers* (F. Gaynor, trans.). New York: Philosophical Library.

Price, G. R. (1955). Science and the supernatural. *Science, 122,* 359–367.

Price, G. R. (1972). Apology to Rhine and Soal. *Science, 175,* 359.

Rhine, J. B., & Pratt, J. G. (1940). *Extrasensory perception after sixty years. A critical appraisal of the research in extra-sensory perception.* New York: Henry Holt.

Schmidt, H. (1970). A PK test with electronic equipment. *Journal of Parapsychology, 34,* 175–181.

Schmidt, H. (1973). PK tests with a high-speed random number generator. *Journal of Parapsychology, 37,* 105–118.

Schmidt, H. (1974). Psychokinesis. In E. D. Mitchell (Ed.), *Psychic exploration: A challenge for science.* New York: Putnam.

Schmidt, H. (1975). Observation of subconscious PK effects with and without time displacement. In Parapsychological Association, *Research in Parapsychology 1974,* pp. 116–121. Metuchen, NJ: Scarecrow.

Schmidt, H., & Pantas, L. (1971). Psi tests with psychologically equivalent conditions and internally different machines. *Proceedings of the Parapsychological Association, 8,* 49–51.

Scott, C., & Haskell, P. (1973). "Normal" explanation of the Soal-Goldney experiments in extrasensory perception. *Nature, 245,* 52–54.

Smith, M., Tremmel, L., & Honorton, C. (1976). A comparison of psi and weak sensory influences on ganzfeld mentation. In Parapsychological Association, *Research in Parapsychology 1975.* Metuchen, NJ: Scarecrow.

Stanford, R. G. (1974). An experimentally testable model for spontaneous psi events: I. Extrasensory events. *Journal of the American Society for Psychical Research, 68,* 34–57.

Stanford, R. G., Zenhausern, R., Taylor, A., & Dwyer, M. (1975). Psychokinesis as psi-mediated instrumental response. *Journal of the American Society for Psychical Research, 69,* 127–134.

Sterling, T. C. (1959). Publication decisions and their possible effects on inferences drawn from tests of significance: Or vice versa. *Journal of the American Statistical Association, 54,* 30–34.

Thouless, R. H. (1951). A report on an experiment in psychokinesis with dice and a discussion on psychological factors favoring success. *Journal of Parapsychology, 15,* 89–102.

Wheeler, J. A. (1973, June). Interview in *Intellectual Digest,* p. 32.

Chapter 15

Next Step: Process-Oriented Research: Guidelines for Experimenters

Edwin C. May and Sonali Bhatt Marwaha

In recent years, the discipline of psi research has seen a number of publications put out by leading researchers in the field. Among others, these include *Parapsychology in the Twenty-First Century: Essays on the Future of Psychical Research* (Thalbourne & Storm, 2005), *Advances in Parapsychological Research* (Krippner, Rock, Beischel et al., 2013), *The Survival Hypothesis* (Rock, 2013), *Anomalous Cognition: Remote Viewing Research and Theory* (May & Marwaha, 2014a), *Evidence of Psi: Thirteen Empirical Research Reports* (Broderick & Goertzel, 2015), and *Parapsychology: A Handbook for the 21st Century* (Cardeña, Palmer, & Marcusson-Clavertz, 2015). Including these two volumes, in addition to the numerous papers in peer-reviewed journals, it becomes evident that psi research is thriving and making slow but steady strides in the development and advancement of the field.

These strides are also reflected in the number of universities offering courses in parapsychology. There are several universities where it is possible to take undergraduate classes on parapsychology in the UK (University of Central Lancashire, University of the West of England [Bristol], Derby University, Goldsmiths–London, University of Greenwich, University of Northampton, University of Edinburgh, Queen Margaret's

University–Edinburgh) and the United States (University of West Georgia offers parapsychology classes as part of the undergraduate degree program). Postgraduate studies are also offered at the University of Northampton, which offers a master's degree in which you can specialize in parapsychology. Doctoral supervision is available at the University of Northampton, University of Hertfordshire, University of Edinburgh, York University, Goldsmiths–London, and the University of Central Lancashire (Simmonds-Moore, personal communication).

As discussed in Chapter I, "The Fundamentals of Psi" (Volume I) and Chapter I, "The Fundamental Issues for Psi Theorists" (Volume II) of this work, the questions with which researchers are faced are indeed complex. Nevertheless, the data are in. ESP, specifically precognition, exists. Considering the fundamental problems are as "boggling" to the researcher as they are to the skeptic, skepticism by researchers has taken a positive turn in their continued endeavors in addressing the question of *how* the apparent violations in nature occur. In the same vein, other areas such as psychokinesis and survival research are under intense scrutiny to determine their validity. Theoretical developments in the field also point toward a greater clarity on the issues under consideration. The existence of multiple theoretical perspectives points to a robust dialogue within the field that has as its goal finding answers to the complex issues that ESP raises.

As a philosopher, Richard Corry has concluded after a reasoned argument in his chapter titled, "ESP, Causation and the Possibility of Precognition" (Volume I), "there is nothing impossible about ESP, nor is it impossible that we could find good empirical reason to believe in ESP." As the physics chapters in this volume indicate, psi does not necessarily violate the known physical laws of causality and spacetime, though it seems a bit of a stretch in some cases. One might state with confidence that the parent discipline of psi research has to be physics and the "hard" sciences, more so because physics permits the freedom for theoretical speculation, since much of the external physical world remains a mystery. This freedom of speculation is not available to the "soft" sciences where the subject matter is ourselves, and we all "know" our selves. Thus, if *I* do not experience something, I can state with extreme confidence that that experience or event does not exist, leaving very little room for speculation for the plausibility of its existence giving rise to a substantial degree of incredulity over the experience of others that do not match our own. Color synesthete Maureen Seaberg (2011, pp. 19–20) has expressed this well:

> I believed this [seeing colors] was normal for the first several years of life, as I learned the alphabet and numbers and how to use a calendar and play the piano. . . . It didn't occur to me at first that other people didn't enjoy their letters the way I did, with all their swirling,

    attendant hues. That's the thing about life: If something's always been your reality, how do you know it's different from other people?

For us as individuals, our understanding of the world is indeed extremely colored by the limitations of our species-specific endowments, our genetic makeup, and our idiosyncratic life experiences.

    Skeptics might state that it is the absence of critical thinking that leads psi researchers to consider a "logically impossible" event as a true representation of reality. However, considering that our academic training, the world over, is extremely narrow and structured within some specialty or superspecialty, it prevents us from the knowledge base that is the mainstay of another discipline. This limits the data we have in hand for critical thought in areas that transcend the boundaries of our specific academic disciplines. Thus, for instance in nuclear physics, because of the extreme specialization, researchers even in subdisciplines, such as the nuclei count of $N = 50$ and $N = 200$, cannot or maybe not have the proper vocabulary to discuss common interests, or common relations between the two sets of problems. Sadly, this fractionalization is common to most disciplines, and psi research is not immune to it.

    In part, this "messy" organization arises because of the academic "publish or perish" phenomenon—that is, entire journals arise as a vehicle for publishing subdisciplines in a field. This negative notion is clearly offset by the positive one of allowing academics to follow their own special interests.

    Thus, our assertion, through these two volumes, is to underscore the multidisciplinary nature of the psi enigma. As a future trend in psi research, we emphatically emphasize the need for a multidisciplinary team arising from within traditional departments of the hard and soft sciences. The research and theories presented in these volumes provide a grounding for the creation of a multidisciplinary team; and there is much more that psi research itself can contribute toward taking the next step forward.

    The history of modern scientific psi research (see Chapter 2, "A Brief History of Psi Research," in Volume I) has shown that it has always comprised of researchers from a variety of disciplines. As a nuclear physicist involved in psi research for 40 years now, it is heartening for May to see many young researchers, emerging from a variety of disciplines, who are intellectually invigorated to approach psi research with the advances of their discipline. In coming over to the "dark side" as such, it is our hope that these volumes provide an impetus for them and many others to view psi research the way it should be, rather than the prejudiced view that is prevalent in many quarters of academia.

    As we have seen, psi research has made substantial progress, despite the criticism and absolute negation of the field as seen in the skeptical onslaught on the Internet and elsewhere by what may be a small community of über-skeptics. It may also surprise many readers that many psi researchers—from its historical past to the present—are also skeptics, as good science would require. Aside from their familiarity with the literature and research data—both significant and nonsignificant—psi researchers are also privy to qualitative data, including that of individual well-performing participants. These data are usually lost in the statistical averaging process. The qualitative data, we believe, is what prompts the researchers to persist in their continuing search for answers to understand the observables. Perhaps a golf metaphor will elucidate this idea. Consider the experience in a round of golf during which the golfer has played terribly and produced a score well above par. On the seventeenth hole (i.e., second last hole), the golfer is ready to sell his/her clubs and quit the game altogether. Then on the eighteenth hole, the golfer gets a birdie (i.e., one under par), which has the effect of negating the terrible experience of the previous 17 holes and keeps the golfer engaged in the sport. We discuss this concept later in the chapter.

Before we proceed, we will take a detour to an overview of the Star Gate program, with which we are most familiar and which has guided our work. We have added this section to give one exemplar of a research program that was successful in its approach. Of course, there are other examples we could have considered as well, such as any number of successful academic approaches that provide a wider area of inquiry. Examples include Edinburgh University and the University of Northampton in the United Kingdom.

THE STAR GATE PROGRAM

The U.S. government's military intelligence community funded anomalous cognition and PK applications and research for over 20 years at a total level of about US $20 million. While small in terms of what is usually budgeted for traditional programs within these organizations, such funding represented the largest support in the history of the field of parapsychology during its time (1972–1995). In 1985, when May became the program director of the contract effort for the Star Gate program, there was a substantial shift from collecting intelligence by using psi to providing research in support of a military in-house psi-spying unit housed at Ft. Meade, Maryland, and assessing the degree to which national adversaries of the day posed a psi threat. Under May's term as director, the effort was tasked to provide operational research in support of Ft. Meade's psi intelligence collection effort and to conduct basic research to determine the underlying mechanisms of psi, for which they were given about US $15 million from 1985 through 1995.

This daunting task was overseen by three long-term committees that were invaluable in assisting in research direction—efficiency, efficacy, and analysis of the effort. The committees were:

- *Scientific Oversight Committee (SOC).* The SOC had three primary tasks: to review and approve the detailed experimental protocol for every experiment to be conducted under the government contracts; to exercise unannounced drop-in privileges to see firsthand what was happening; and to review critically, in writing, the final reports for each of the tasks in the contractual statement of work. For example, in the first year of a US $10 million army contract, there were 38 separate research tasks in the official statement of work, each with their individual reporting requirements.
- *Institutional Review Board (IRB).* The IRB (a.k.a., Human Use Committee) was constituted according to the U.S. Department of Defense's regulations with regard to the use of humans in DoD-sponsored research. This committee had to approve all experimental protocols with regard to the possible risk to the people involved before any experiment could begin.
- *Policy Review Board (PRB).* The PRB consisted of three senior government employees who reported directly to the Office of the Secretary of Defense. Their mission was to assure the DoD that the program was meeting the mission requirements set forth by the intelligence and military communities.

What emerged from all this oversight was a clear set of near- and long-term goals and metrics to determine whether these goals were met, and substantial guidance for future research. The DoD was always concerned about not only the efficacy of the ongoing research but also whether the long-term mission had been strictly adhered to during the life of the program.

Much of what follows in this section arises from the 20 years of government-sponsored psi research and applications. While it is true that the reader should be skeptical of any results from a single laboratory, there were, at its height, 12 full-time researchers from a variety of disciplines, and, as we mentioned earlier, the program enjoyed significant skeptical oversight. Figure 15.1 provides a hint of the extensive work that went on during the Star Gate era.

Of the total number of about 410 documents, which include proposals as well as quarterly and yearly reports, there were approximately 204 final reports to various clients, 152 technical reports, and 54 proposals. By technical reports, we mean draft copies, notes to various government committees, technical reports, and IRB protocols. These exclude interim reports, memos, and presentations to and from contractors as well as administrative and financial records.

Remote viewing (RV) research conducted by the Stanford Research International (SRI)–Science Applications International Corporation

Figure 15.1
This represents the number of reports that were generated during the Star Gate era as a function of year and document type. The gap at 1990 represents the transition time between SRI International and Science Applications International Corporation.

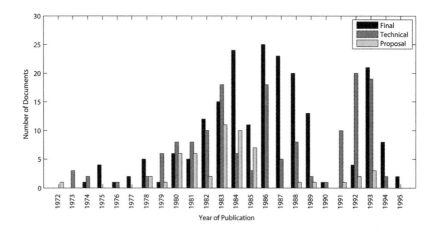

(SAIC) team involved applied research (how to make the output more robust and reliable) and basic research (how psi works). The following is a partial summary of that work.

Research and Applications

Reliable and Calibrated Participants

Research and applications need high-quality remote viewers. Especially during the second half of the program, the application results emboldened the military to ask how to find more psi-talented individuals on the one hand and/or to determine the degree to which any random individual could be trained to be a high-functioning psi practitioner. The problem is identifying psi-talented people within the general population or within specific special populations such as the cadre of intelligence professionals. The Star Gate program used several approaches for determining the profiles of talented viewers. These included medical profiles, psychological/personality profiles, correlations with other phenomena, and behavioral profiles. Although the number of talented viewers was small, it was found that their medical profiles were essentially normal without any discernible predictive (for psi ability) value in them. Some of the psychological/personality measures produced significant results, but it appears that these correlations were likely to be either artifacts of the collection methodology or too small to be predictive of psi performance. Psi ability appears to be statistically stationary within a given individual and, like other human activities, there is considerable variability across individuals.

While extraversion is considered a characteristic of psi believers (Honorton, Ferrari, & Bem, 1998), it has not been an effective criterion for identifying people with psi ability. In a series of studies carried out at SRI in the 1980s, using measures such as the Myers-Briggs Type Indicator (MBTI), Wechsler Adult Intelligence Scale (WAIS), the Personality Assessment System (PAS), and Q-Sort, it was found that identifying talented viewers from the general population was a problematical task. Personality assessment measures have not proved to be effective methods for identifying people with good remote viewing (RV) skills.

Appropriate Targets

It has been known for some time that the results from targets that are symbols, such as simple geometric figures or alphabet letters—called forced choice in that a participant is required to respond only within the symbol set—are an order of magnitude smaller than they are when the targets are photographs or video clips, which are relatively unrestricted with regard to content—called free response in that a participant is not constrained in reporting what she or he is experiencing. We have found, however, that the "noise" (i.e., incorrect elements in responses) increases as the number of potential differentiable cognitive elements increase in the target pool; however, this noise is a trade-off with the forced-choice target stimuli (May & Spottiswoode, 2014/1994). Recent results suggest that the quality of psi is statistically proportional to the gradient of Shannon entropy for photographs or video targets (May & Marwaha, 2014b). We hypothesize that this result would extend to gradients of thermodynamic entropy for physical targets because of the relationship between Shannon and thermodynamic entropy and because of a number of results in the application data set. That is, accelerators, directed energy systems, and explosions appear to be easily sensed (May & Lantz, 2014/2010; May, 1988, 1989).

Optimal Protocols for Data Collection

Although we have not studied all protocol issues systematically, we have evolved to an operating environment that is productive. As guidelines, we believe that for participants, one (preferably) or two anomalous cognition (AC) sessions per day lasting no more than an hour each is near the upper limit. For short periods of time, this pace may be maintained about every other day. Altered states of consciousness such as dreaming or hypnosis appear not to increase AC quality for gifted psi individuals.

Optimum Data Assessment

How to determine, in a statistically valid way, whether an information transfer anomaly (i.e., AC or RV) exists is the basis of the analysis problem, although, simply put, the analysis of AC data in the laboratory is a complex issue. For example, what constitutes a control depends upon the question under study. After seeing an example of AC that has high visual correspondence with the intended target, the natural question is: What is the probability that the participant would respond that way if there were no targets? While compelling, that question is impossible to answer in any specific instance and can be addressed only on the average. In laboratory studies, we ask a different question: Given a response, what is the probability that it matches the randomly chosen intended target? This can be answered with statistical rigor because the random element, which is necessary in a statistical analysis of this type, is the initial target choice rather than the response, which cannot be assumed to be random. In the application environment, the analysis problem is compounded in that often the details of the intended target are not known. For example, how should the analysis proceed when the target is the whereabouts of a crashed commercial jetliner?

Regardless of the analysis technique, an inviolable condition that must be met is that the analyst (an independent researcher or the participant himself) must be held blind to the intended target. The analysis of choice for laboratory experiments is the rank-order method. In this technique, a target pack, from which the target will be randomly selected, is constructed prior to the experiment. Usually great care is exercised to include targets within a pack to be as different from one another as possible and to ensure the random number generator meets all accepted criteria for being random. For a single response, an independent analyst who is blind to the experimental details rank orders the targets within a pack from the one that best matches the given response, which is second best, and so on through the pack. Under the null hypothesis, the average rank after many such trials should be $(N + 1)/2$, where N is the number of targets in the pack. Typically $N = 5$ in our studies, so the expected average rank is 3. Our best participants generally produce average ranks of approximately 2.

We have also explored a variety of other methods, including concept analysis—reducing a response to conceptual elements, rating scales, and an elaborate application of fuzzy set procedures. If a researcher is interested in exploring correlations of psi with external variables such as local sidereal time or MBTI status, using a rank-order method is simply a mistake. A general rule in all experimental science is to reduce sources of *noise* wherever possible before data collection begins rather than using sophisticated statistical techniques such as ANOVA after the fact. Using a rank-order method of analysis violates that principle in that the outcome of a rank-order analysis clearly depends upon how orthogonal (i.e., different) the analysis packet of target stimuli is, whereas a rating method such is done with fuzzy sets is an absolute measure of a response to its intended target stimulus only (May, Utts, Luke et al., 2014/1990; May, 2014/2007).

In the application environment, we have developed a variety of approaches that rely upon historical responses to similar situations or invoke pre- and postsession calibrations where the target material is completely known.

Basic Research

By basic research, we mean the type of research that is primarily aimed at understanding the mechanisms that allow psi to operate. From 1972 to the end of 1985, little in the Star Gate statements of work was concerned with basic research. While there were a few exceptions, the team "hid" what little that could be done under different rubrics such as foreign assessment; that is, if intelligence reports claimed that country X reported that they realized phenomenon Y, then we were allowed to investigate phenomenon Y. For example, reading in the Chinese version of *Nature* scientific magazine, we saw a claim that youngsters trained in the art of qigong could identify Mandarin characters affixed to the front of a photomultiplier—a very sensitive device to measure light down to individual photons. The report further claimed that when the character was correctly identified, there was a 1000:1 signal to noise ration signal from the photomultiplier! In essence, remote viewing a target stimulus causes it to glow in the dark! We were asked to determine the degree to which this claim was correct. We were unable to verify that claim.

Source of Psi

What is the source of the energy/information that is available to psi participants? Clearly, the target stimulus can be anywhere in spacetime. Some in the psi research community believe we are dealing with nonphysical parameters and that traditional science must be significantly modified to account for psi phenomena. The SRI, and subsequently SAIC and the Laboratories for Fundamental Research (LFR), approach is more conservative. The assumption is that psi will eventually be explained by the known laws of nature, or perhaps small modifications to them. As of yet, there is no known transfer of information on which you "can do work," that is, without a concomitant transfer of energy. The Star Gate research team assumed that this must be true for psi as well. Our latest results from LFR suggest that the gradient of Shannon entropy is, or is related to, the source for psi; that is, the larger the entropic gradient of the target stimulus, the better the psi (May, 2014/2011). Considerably more research is required to validate this finding, but to our knowledge, this is the first physical variable that is exclusively related to the target that produces reliable correlations with the quality of psi.

Transmission

How does the information propagate from the source to the participant? What is the carrier for the information? Since there is compelling evidence for precognition (i.e., access to noninferential futures), the transmission is required to be, at a minimum, a four-dimensional space mechanism. Very little has been explored in this domain; thus, it is premature to comment on this other than to say that this is one of the future research challenges.

Detector

What are the physiological mechanisms for the detection of psi information? Early on, the Star Gate team generally proposed that psi is detected by an additional sensorial system. This was based upon the observable that the quality of the psi depended upon the gradient of the entropy and not the entropy itself—completely analogous to all the known sensory systems.

During the 1972–1976 period, the Star Gate team found significant alpha blocking in a few participants that was concomitant with an isolated visual stimulus. Although the experiments were conducted carefully, the results were weak, and the number of participants was small. This line of investigation was abandoned until 1987, at which time a multiyear effort was initiated using magnetoencephalography to measure central nervous system (CNS) magnetic responses to isolated visual stimuli. Early results were especially encouraging, but later replications revealed a subtle statistical artifact that accounted for the earlier results. However, all is not lost; each replication attempt yields suggestions for the next experiment. Later studies posited that since external stimuli, cognitive thought, or conscious attempts at moving a body part all interrupt alpha rhythm (i.e., event-related desynchronization [ERD]), it is reasonable to assume that psi stimuli will also invoke an ERD. In 1993–1994, the SRI team conducted a series of experiments that used matched filters derived from direct stimuli to search for ERDs in the CNS record resulting from psi stimuli.

The results of this study illustrated two major points. In any psychophysiological experiment designed to look for correlations with psi, it is mandatory to have an independent (of the physiology) psi channel to assure that psi happened in the study. In this experiment (May, Spottiswoode, & Faith, 2014/2005), three participants contributed a total of 70 trials. A blind and independent psi assessment showed a significant result of $z = 2.5$ with an associated ES $= 0.3$ (p. 183). Yet, no significant correlation between alpha power changes and psi were observed.

The second major point, and the most difficult, is how do we know when psi happens? In personal communication, our current cadre of experienced participants say they do not have control over when the psi information becomes available. So, perhaps, the participants experienced all the psi while parking their cars in the lot *prior* to the collection of the data, thus rendering the sophisticated protocol moot.

Psychokinesis

Beginning with PK experiments with dice in the 1930s–1950s, it has been claimed in the literature that small statistical effects can result from the mental intention of participants. Helmut Schmidt (1969) used modem technology to address this question when radioactive or electronic noise devices were used as target systems. The Star Gate team carried out nearly 19 studies in bio-PK and micro-PK that were hi-tech in their engineering details, and the results suggest that such effects are possible on a variety of target systems; however, the effects are all small and can be observed only after sophisticated statistical analyses. This research gave rise to decision augmentation theory (DAT; May, Utts, & Spottiswoode, 2014/1995). DAT holds that statistical anomalous perturbation can be considered a form of anomalous cognition. That is, participants in these experiments are "statistical opportunists" who initiate a trial to capture a locally deviant subset from an unperturbed parent population.

Search

In general, search psi is the reverse process of standard anomalous cognition. Rather than specifying a target location and seeking a description, search specifies the description and seeks the location. For example, suppose an enemy submarine is lurking off the U.S. coast. A forward-direction AC task would be to describe the details of the submarine, perhaps the captain and crew as well; however, with remote viewing outside the submarine, all the viewer senses is water. Even if all the psi data were totally accurate, it would not help in locating the submarine. The search approach to this example is to provide a photograph and description of the submarine and ask, "Where is the submarine currently located?" Used properly, *search* can minimally reduce the resources needed by traditional means to locate the lost item.

With computer-generated laboratory tasks and statistical averaging techniques, it appears possible to locate hidden targets. In this technique, a hidden checkerboard, each square is assigned to a future search area, and one of them is assigned to the none-of-the-above category. Then a participant is asked to find the "hot" square using whatever means available.

A real-world example will illustrate the technique. The SRI team was asked to join the Red team during the Carter and Reagan administrations to attempt to nullify the concept of the MX missile racetrack idea. As part of a proof-of-principle exercise, each circle on a computer display was assigned to a specific missile launcher that was located at one of 10 possible locations. The participant sees only 10 circles scattered across the computer screen, and for each of many trials, the circles change positons randomly; yet, how many times each circle is selected by the participant is tracked for each circle regardless of its location on the display screen. One and only one circle corresponds to a given potential launch site, and the participant's task is to find that circle, somehow, on repeated trials.

In the proof-of-principle study, one circle met the predefined threshold for significant psi-mediated selection. That circle indeed did contain the missile launcher. Details of this case, including a letter from a major senator to the secretary of defense giving credit to remote viewing for being able to compromise the multibillion-dollar proposal are available in May, Rubel, and Auerbach (2014, pp. 84–87).

In a potential application if, by using computer-assisted search techniques, expended resources could be reduced by a few percentage points, the technique would contribute significantly to solving many intelligence and industrial problems. Generally speaking, however, what has been called dowsing in the literature is difficult to confirm in the laboratory. Although there are examples in the program office of spectacular hits with search, the rate is generally lower than it is for forward-direction AC. Information models suggests that this may be because of a channel bandwidth limitation, since finding something requires more information than just describing it.

This body of research, along with research from other labs, has informed us as we look for a way forward for future research in anomalous cognition.

PROOF-ORIENTED RESEARCH

Psi research is at a critical juncture. Some of our colleagues agree with us that as a research community, we have done almost all that we can collectively accomplish if our goal is to produce evidence of psi. The data are in. There is evidence for precognition, and the evidence for psychokinesis is questionable. Thus, if you are a serious researcher, *there is no further need for proof-oriented research.* Considering the scarce resource allocations for this field, in our view, there are classes of experiments that we need never conduct again. These classes include the ganzfeld, remote viewing, psychokinesis upon random number generators, and prestimulus response and its variants as methods for proof-oriented research. Here we discuss these briefly.

The Ganzfeld

In this kind of study, a participant is induced into a mild altered state of consciousness. This is accomplished by providing unpatterned stimuli both visual—uniform red light is incident upon translucent eye goggles—and auditory—low intensity white noise. The participant is then asked to free-associate aloud. Meta-analyses (Bem & Honorton, 1994; Parker, 2000; Bem, Palmer, & Broughton, 2001; Storm et al., 2010) show an overall significant effect size for unselected participants; that reported by Storm et al. has a mean effect size of 0.142 ± 0.026 ($z = 5.48$, $p = 2.13 \times 10^{-8}$).

What is needed now for the ganzfeld is to deconstruct the various elements (e.g., color of light, if any, and types of sound as white noise, if any). This may shed light on the inner processes of that type of anomalous cognition.

Remote Viewing (RV)

May and Marwaha (2014c) and May, Hawley, Chaganti, and Ratra (2014) give a number of protocols and procedures for data collection and analyses for this form of anomalous cognition. The research team at SRI International (May, Utts, Trask, Luke, et al., 1989)—the leading team in RV research—found an effect size for unselected participants of 0.164 ± 0.036 ($z = 4.6$, $p = 2.1 \times 10^{-6}$); for consistent and recognized high-performing participants, the effect size was 0.385 ± 0.071 ($z = 5.39$, $p = 3.5 \times 10^{-8}$). One characteristic of these data is that unlike other databases, they do not have a file drawer problem by definition. The file drawer problem as described in the literature is a tendency to publish significant findings only and put the nonsignificant ones in the file drawer. At one time, human science and medical journals would accept only significant studies; fortunately, in modern times, most journals have recognized this error.

Like in the ganzfeld, what we need now in remote viewing research is to parse the problem into logical domains and focus upon them separately (see Chapter 7, "Multiphasic Model of Precognition," in this volume).

Psychokinesis upon Random Number Generators

Is it possible to affect physical/biological objects by mental means alone in such a way that statistical analysis is not required to observe the effects? Examples include stopping the hearts of animals, levitation, and materialization and dematerialization of objects. Based on the SRI studies and on the knowledge of the vast number of ways to mimic large-scale remote perturbations, the claim for such effects on mechanical systems cannot be validated. Additionally, May has had lengthy and continuing conversations with the first deputy of the former KGB back in the days of the Soviet Union. Major General Nickolai Sham, who wrote the foreword for *ESP Wars: East and West* (May, Rubel, & Auerbach, 2014), reports that the KGB funded 40 different institutes to develop and deploy a form of macro-PK device called psychotronic weapons. General Sham also tells (private communication with May) that all the money, time, and institutes with highly motivated researchers could not make any of the macro-PK weapons work—more circumstantial evidence against the existence of macro-PK.

In random number generator (RNG) studies, a source of true random signals such as noise from an electronic diode or the decay of some radioactive material is converted into a sequence of (usually) binary 1's and 0's. A participant is tasked to affect the RNG such that it produces more binary ones than would be expected by chance. There are substantial variations on this theme, but this is the general idea. The effects are referred to in the literature as micro-psychokinesis or μ-PK for short. The first experiment of this genre was conducted by Schmidt (1969). By 1980, Radin, May, and Thompson found 332 RNG studies. It is difficult to report an effect size for these and later studies. One observable from this substantial amount of data is that the z-scores reported were essentially constant regardless of the number of binary bits collected; or viewed from an effect size perspective, it decreases according to $\frac{1}{\sqrt{n}}$. This trend inspired the development of decision augmentation theory (DAT; May, Spottiswoode, & Utts, 2014/1995; see Chapter 10 in this volume). The DAT analysis is quite convincing in that if μ-PK is influencing the RNGs at the bit level, it is not shifting the mean of the statistical parent distribution at all; that means if the fair RNG has an innate probability of producing a binary one on the average of 0.50000, then μ-PK is not changing the number at all. However, if μ-PK operates on other moments of the parent distribution such as the variance or any that are symmetric about the mean would be ignored by the current DAT analysis. Bösch, Steinkamp, and Boller (2006) conducted an extensive meta-analysis of the RNG data to 2006 and found in 380 studies a significant but small effect size.

What is needed in RNG studies is to determine whether there is a causal effect on the various devices or as DAT suggests, an informational form of psi, and to extend DAT to be sensitive to symmetric changes in the parent distribution. As with the other phenomena described in this section, the evidential data are in.

Prestimulus Response (a.k.a., Presentiment)

Study of this phenomena, along with distant mental influence on living systems (DMILS), was an attempt at bypassing one of the major problems with trying to measure psi; that is, individuals are asked first to have a psi experience and then to report it cognitively as best they can. First-person reporting has always been a problem because of the huge variation in accurate reporting of personal experience. Chabris and Simons (2010) estimate that approximately 40% of first-person experience reporting is suspect—the experience is what it is, it is only the reporting of the experience that is suspect. Clearly, this would insert considerable "noise" in psi reporting as well.

There is a general principle in experimental endeavors at work here. Experimenters should try to reduce the noise *before* collecting data rather than afterward with sophisticated statistical techniques such as ANOVA. In this context, relieving people of the burden of self-reporting of their experiences would substantially reduce the noise before data collection.

One way to avoid this reporting problem is to measure psychophysiology instead; that is, let the human autonomic nervous system respond to psi stimuli so that a cognition is not required. One of the first studies of this type was conducted by Vassy in the 1960s but reported on much later (Vassy, 1978). In this experiment, eight of 10 isolated sender/participant pairs showed significant effects in their skin conductance *before* receiving a mild electric stimulus. Later, the stimuli in presentiment experiments were changed to affective photos and startle acoustic stimuli in the prestimulus response work. In one study May and Spottiswoode (2014) used startle stimuli in the form of 1 second of very loud white noise and observed a 5σ effect for more skin conductance activity before a startle stimulus compared to silent controls. A detailed description and meta-analysis of all this research can be found in Mossbridge, Tressoldi, and Utts (2012).

While these kinds of studies can and should be used as teaching aids, to conduct any of them to provide proof of principle is not a good use of precious resources. One caveat to this is that these well-calibrated protocols could be used as screening tools to identify persistent and excellent AC practitioners.

Another consideration related to not conducting more evidential studies is that there is no accepted standard as to how many are enough and what effect size is sufficient. Jessica Utts, in Volume I, Chapter 7 of this series, addresses the issue of what constitutes replication in general and in psi research in particular. In the introduction to this volume—"Fundamental Issues for Psi Theorists"—we outlined a catch-22 situation with regard to data and theory. While on one hand, skeptics will ignore the psi data because, as they see it, there is no underlying theory, on the other hand, theory papers are often rejected by journals because they do not believe the veracity of the data.

With regard to precognition, we agree with the following statement: There is incontrovertible evidence for an information transfer anomaly we currently do not understand. Yet, we have conduced casual surveys of the psi research community in venues from Moscow, various locations in India, many locations in the UK and in the United States. Much to our surprise and, frankly, disappointment, roughly 20% by show of hands agree with that statement with 100% conviction.

So, if we should not conduct evidential studies for the most part, what should we be doing? In the following section, we will outline a number of suggestions from procedural to specifics with regard to determining a sound direction for process-oriented research.

PROCESS-ORIENTED RESEARCH

As stated in the introduction to this volume, a psi theory raises four fundamental issues:

1. *Causality violation.* From a person-centric view, is it possible that something can happen *before* what caused this to happen happens first?
2. *Information transfer from a distant spacetime point.* How can information transfer backward in time, and what is the carrier of such information?
3. *Perception of information emerging from distant spacetime point.* Considering we do not know the nature of the information carrier, we assume it is something that is not part of the normal human repertoire. In which case, what is the mechanism for the perception of this information carrier?
4. *Individual differences.* Can individual differences account for the presence of psi ability in only a small percent of the population?

These issues provide guidelines for process-oriented research in psi, which we will discuss in this section. But first, we provide an example of qualitative data that serves to inform us about psi-obtained information and challenges us to seek answers for the process by which it occurs.

Example of Qualitative Data

To underscore what we mean by a single qualitative example that challenges our thinking, we provide a single trial from an ongoing precognition experiment wherein the target stimuli are natural locations in the San Francisco Bay Area. Figure 15.2 shows the complete response and the

Figure 15.2
The complete annotated response to a single trial. Photograph taken during target selection nine months before the trial (a). In the meantime, no one on the research team knew the construction had been finished. Photograph of the participant taken during the feedback phase (b).

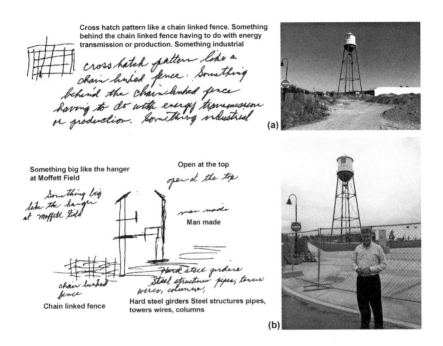

feedback of the target stimulus, which was chosen randomly by an individual who was blind to the response *after* that response had been given and secured.

So far, one of the questions that has loomed over us is whether the remote viewer (RVer) is accessing information from the feedback provided to him of the target stimulus on the computer, or is it the distant target location where he is taken to for feedback following the session. As this example shows us, Figure 15.2(a) is the photograph of the target taken nine months *before* the session, during the phase of developing the target pool and is available in real time in the data collection and computer analysis along with 21 other photographs; none of these is ever displayed to anyone. The adjacent drawing on the left of Figure 15.2 is the transcript and drawing by the RVer that was provided as his response during the session—*before* the stimulus target was randomly generated. If one were to look only at the stimulus picture, the response would have wrong elements in it—the "cross hatch pattern like a chain linked fence." However, on reaching the target site, the researchers were extremely surprised to find the "chain linked" fence that had been constructed around the site since the time of taking the target photo (Figure 15.2(b)). This kind of qualitative data is also seen in the remote viewing transcript of a submarine base in Severodvinsk, Russia (see Chapter 11, "Evidence for Precognition from Applied Remote Viewing," Volume I).

Examples such as these, no doubt the best, seem to make it clear that there is at least an acasual separation between the target and the viewer. The question of *when* the information was received by the RVer—during the session proper or before commencement of the session—still remains open.

Qualitative data such as these are the white crows that falsify the null hypothesis. They provide a major challenge to theorists and experimenters to determine *how* that information was received by the RVer, which is a problem for those addressing the physics domain of the psi problem, and how the information was cognized by the viewer, which is a problem for those addressing the neuroscience domain of the problem. This leads us to consider challenges for the experimenter.

Challenges for the Experimenter

In considering the challenges for the experimenter, the process-oriented structure provided in our multiphasic model of precognition will serve us well. To illustrate:

I) *Physics domain.* Addresses the question of information transfer from a distant spacetime point.

II) *Neuroscience domain.* Addresses the experiential aspect of psi.

1. *Stage 1: Perception of information.* Addresses psychophysical issues related to the perception of psi information.
2. *Stage 2: Cortical processing of information.* Rests entirely in the domain of the neurosciences.
3. *Stage 3: Cognitive processing.* Addresses the psychological aspects of ESP.

Physics Domain

The physics domain (PD) addresses the question of what happens in the external physical world vis-à-vis information, transfer of information, and the question of retrocausation. These three elements serve as problems for experimenters and theorists alike.

What is the form that retrocausal information takes? What is the carrier for this information? Can this carrier emerge from a distant spacetime point, as the experimental evidence indicates?

These fundamental problems lie within the domain of theoretical physics. The news is not all bad in that theoretical debates/discussions are ongoing in the mainstream physics community, and May and Depp (Chapter 6, "Entropy and Precognition: The Physics Domain of the Multiphasic Model of Precognition," this volume) provide detailed discussions on these points and extensive pointers into the physics literature.

Psi data, such as the example shown earlier in this chapter, has to inspire mainstream physicists to examine these data closely, as they are indicators of the transcendence of spacetime by perceptible information. This, in itself, is a challenging research question for them to address. In our view, entropy, as described in the "Entropy and Precognition" chapter, appears to play a vital role in this process.

The bigger challenge is the nature of the information carrier. At this point in the process of retrocausal information, the question of a carrier and its information content is largely dependent on a carrier that can be perceived by the human perceptual systems. This in itself may provide a clue to the problem. May and Depp also provide clues, or at least plausibility arguments, as to how this might work—time-entangled states allowing information to flow through wormholes that provide a bridge between acasually separated points.

Neuroscience Domain

Stage 1 of the neuroscience domain (ND) addresses the question of how external information is acquired by the human perceptual systems. This problem lies largely within the domain of psychophysics, and researchers from that discipline would need to address the observable, as illustrated in the qualitative example given here.

Stage 2 of the process involves cortical processing of the information obtained from the external world. This problem rests squarely within the expertise of neuroscientists and allied disciplines. The problems that need to be solved here are: (1) How is this information processed by the brain? (2) Which regions are involved? (3) What is the special characteristic of this region that permits it to process the information from a carrier/bandwidth that may be different from those seen in the other senses? (4) Are there genetic factors that make this region different from the others? (5) If there is a difference in the cortical structure, what are the associated characteristics of this difference? (6) How can these be identified?

Contrary to the signal transmission model discussed so far are the quantum mechanical models of psi. The question raised for an experimentalist here is what is the process that permits the "retrocorticocausal" (brain-to-environment) interaction of the brain/consciousness/awareness with the external world? This is a particularly challenging question that scientists of all hues need to address. Yet, the challenge of environmental decoherence, which rapidly destroys entangled quantum systems, puts the burden of proof on the experimenter to demonstrate how in special cases decoherence does not operate. However, maybe jumping into the multidimensional spaces provided by Bernard Carr may provide a way around the decoherence problem.

Stage 3 of the process refers to cognitive processing of information. As we discussed in the multiphasic model of precognition, in our view, this stage is as it is for other sensory inputs. Aside from understanding normal cognitive processes, for experimentalists interested in this stage, the challenges are determining the role of intention, attention, and expectation on the perception of psi information, which ostensibly has a weaker "signal" than other sensory inputs. Further, the role of medication, drugs, and meditation in enhancing/weakening the psi information is another challenge, as it helps to determine ways to augment the ability.

Further, experimentalists interested in this area following the quantum mechanics models need to determine the role of psychological factors in bringing about the collapse of the wave function, and it must be pointed out that just because a small minority think consciousness can affect a wave function does not, in principle, make them wrong. The history of science keeps reminding us that sometimes, the minority swimming against the tide of the majority opinion prove to be right after all.

These are just some of the broad research questions that psi researchers need to address. In implementing these studies, many intermediate questions will also occur to the experimentalists and theorists. These studies require the formation of specific research programs directed toward addressing the question as a research goal. While it is an exhaustive task to present the specifics for addressing these questions, in the following section, we provide basic guidelines for organizing a research program.

DEVELOPING A RESEARCH PROGRAM

Screening for Participants

The most important aspect of any future research program is to identify a collection of individuals with psi ability who may or may not have developed specialties in the various psi categories. It may turn out that the only way to find these people is through a multilayer screening procedure, that is, gather groups and have them collectively attempt remote viewing for a single randomly selected target stimulus. This, of course, goes against statistics rules because of the stacking effect; that is, because of cultural, psychological, or physical reasons such as winter, groups of people when asked to free associate often will have significant overlap in their collective experience due to non-psi factors. If, however, such stacking also happens by chance to provide a good match to the target stimulus, then researchers can be misled into thinking psi happened when it did not. Nonetheless, such group sessions can be valuable to screen 50–70 people at a time. Using qualitative methods of comparison, the top 10% of the group, for example, can be picked. This group can then be tested in the lab for a series of trials that meet scientific standards of excellence and provide a threshold that must be exceeded to join the psi-abled group.

One could, of course, assess the lower 10% and confirm their lack of ability in a similar laboratory series for each of them.

Then there could be two rather large groups of people, one psi-abled and the other not. This opens the door wide to exploring a host of variables to determine what, if anything, characterizes the differences between the groups.

Finally, we must note that even with these two groups, the psi-abled people may not have control over when they experience psi. Thus, researchers need to be mindful of this when designing experiments for the two groups.

An Approach for Developing a Research Program

There are two approaches to conduct research in general:

- *Academic.* All topics are entertained under the rubric of academic freedom.
- *Industrial.* Highly focused approach to invent or improve a product depending upon the industry.

Both approaches have strengths and weaknesses. A strength of the academic approach, which, of course, has been remarkably successful, is that it optimizes the creativity of a large number of researchers within many different disciplines. The advances we enjoy in medicine, biology, physiology, and physics, and so on have come about, in part, because of this approach. However, there are drawbacks.

The industrial approach has also been highly successful. Steve Jobs at Apple Corporation is one example. Conceptually, Jobs wanted to accomplish a very specific goal: *It just works!* His design team and engineers set about to achieve this from the very beginning of the Corporation. These people did not have the luxury of just doing anything that they wanted—it is legendary in the organization as described in Steve Jobs's biography (Isaacson, 2011) that Jobs was at times vigilant and ruthless in keeping his teams on the mission. It was not always successful (e.g., the Apple Newton computer), but eventually, this approach "changed everything." Obviously, this goal-oriented technique is necessary for product-oriented businesses of any kind.

Determining a Research Goal

A proper five- to 10-year mission should be established. That is, what would we like to know at that future time about psi that we currently do not know now? This goal is not necessarily easy to set. One approach is first to determine what would be done within a number of disciplines, as discussed earlier in this chapter. To accomplish this, it is necessary to involve scientists from disciplines related to the research goal, for instance, by hosting a series of "mini" conferences, with two or three individuals from a given discipline. In a two- to three-day meeting, the first day would be devoted to one or two established and knowledgeable psi researchers presenting the best data the field has to offer—Yes, examine the white crow! During that day, the invited mainstream scientists are invited to ask clarification questions, but at the end of that day, they are to *assume* that everything they just heard was 100% true. During the next day or two, they are asked to suggest what specific experiments *within their discipline* they would recommend to shed light on the possible mechanism(s) for the research question they heard the day before.

Such mini conferences would be held separately for disciplines including neuroscience, pharmacology, medicine, physiology, psychophysiology, physics, information engineering, psychology, general philosophy, and philosophy of science in particular. Over a year or so, the small conferences would provide clear missions for the next five to 10 years.

How to Use the Suggested Activity?

Any organization would insist that each proposal for research activity be specific as to how it fits into this overall five- to 10-year plan, that is, specifically how the proposed research would help reach that goal. This approach has the distinct advantage of being extremely efficient at reaching the stated goal.

A Metric to Determine Success

To determine whether the results from the research are appropriate, we need to develop a proper metric. The usual scientific metrics used to assess scientific activity do not apply to psi research mainly because it is difficult for even the best research to appear in mainstream journals. However, we can develop our own much more sensitive metric in a rather straightforward way.

Based upon the mission statements (i.e., five- to 10-year goals) and upon the usual applications of the scientific method, a universal set of elements (USE) can be developed. A USE is simply a list of possible items or concepts in accordance with the missions and rules of science. Thus, each research activity could be scored against the broader set of USE to create a fuzzy set representation of that research. Fuzzy sets and their applications are deeply embedded in our collective culture. Invented by Zadeh in 1965, they are now part of Internet search engines and reside in nearly all smart electronics, from mobile phones to televisions. In this way, fuzzy sets can be used to assess each proposal, and a threshold could be set to winnow out the least relevant proposals.

As the results of the funded projects become available, they can each be scored against the same USE. Then develop a simple (and probably weighted for importance on an element-by-element basis) fuzzy overlap between a given set of results and the fuzzy sets associated with the various missions. This may seem complex, but the computations are rather straightforward, and spreadsheets or more sophisticated methods can easily provide the metrics.

What if the mission does not appear to be productive as gauged by the fuzzy set metric? Then the mission must be revised or abandoned as a "blind alley," and a replacement should be developed.

At the end of 1995, not all goals of the Star Gate program had been met, but many had been. A few (among many) successes include:

- A fundamental testable model of experimenter psi
- A thermodynamic model that might lead to an understanding of precognition
- A research methodology to illicit high-quality psi nearly on demand
- A host of practical applications of psi

A few examples of goals that were not met are:

- Did not develop a psi training methodology
- Did not develop a successful confidence-calling procedure
- Did not identify personality factors that were predictive of psi performance

The idea on how to move forward in psi research can be summarized as follows:

- Develop a set of goals for research in a five- to 10-year period.
- Require that in-house research projects show how the work leads to accomplishing these goals.
- Use a metric to determine if the research is on the correct path.
- Modify the goals as needed.

We have outlined an approach to move forward efficiently with psi research. At least conceptually, such an approach contributed to the success of a government-funded research program. Because of the obvious controversy surrounding the area of investigation, the government did not want to be embarrassed and, thus, wanted assurance that the end goals were realized.

The answers provided and questions raised in these two volumes should suffice to set the tone for a new phase in psi research—process-oriented research. As a concluding statement, we emphasize that for process-oriented research, it is essential to use people with known and tested psi abilities.

REFERENCES

Bem, D. J., & Honorton, C. (1994). Does psi exist? Replicable evidence for an anomalous process of information transfer. *Psychological Bulletin, 115*(1), 4–18.

Bem, D. J., Palmer, J., & Broughton, R. S. (2001). Updating the ganzfeld database: A victim of its own success? *Journal of Parapsychology, 65*(3), 207–218.

Bösch, H., Steinkamp, F., & Boller, E. Examining psychokinesis: The interaction of human intention with random number generators. A meta-analysis. *Psychological Bulletin, 132*(4), 497–523.

Broderick, D., & Goertzel, B. (Ed). (2015). *Evidence of psi: Thirteen empirical research reports.* Jefferson, NC: McFarland.

Cardeña, E., Palmer, J., & Marcusson-Clavertz, D. (Ed.). (2015). *Parapsychology: A handbook for the 21st century.* Jefferson, NC: McFarland.

Chabris, C. F., & Simons, D. J. (2010). *The invisible gorilla: And other ways our intuitions deceive us.* New York: Crown.

Honorton, C., Ferrari, D. C., & Bem, D. J. (1998). Extraversion and ESP performance: A meta-analysis and new confirmation.*Journal of Parapsychology, 62,* 255–276.

Isaacson, W. (2011). *Steve Jobs.* New York: Simon & Schuster.

Krippner, S., Rock, A. J., Beischel, J., Friedman, H. L., & Fracasso, C. L. (Eds.). (2013). *Advances in parapsychological research* (Vol. 9). Jefferson, NC: McFarland.

May, E. C. (1988). *An application oriented remote viewing experiment: Electron accelerator,* Project 8339. Menlo Park, CA: SRI International.

May, E. C. (1989). *An application oriented remote viewing experiment: Microwave device,* Project 8339. Menlo Park, CA: SRI International.

May, E C. (2014/2007). Advances in anomalous cognition analysis. In E. C. May & S. B. Marwaha (Eds.), *Anomalous cognition: Remote viewing research and theory,* pp. 80–88. Jefferson, NC: McFarland.

May, E. C. (2014/2011). Toward a classical thermodynamic model for retrocognition. In E. C. May & S. B. Marwaha (Eds.), *Anomalous cognition: Remote viewing research and theory,* pp. 327–338. Jefferson, NC: McFarland.

May, E. C., Hawley, L., Chaganti, V. K., & Ratra, N. (2014). Natural anomalous cognition targets: A fuzzy set application.*Journal of Parapsychology, 78*(2), 195–208.

May E. C., & Lantz N. D. (2014/2010) Anomalous cognition technical trials: Inspiration for the target entropy concept. In E. C. May & S. B. Marwaha (Eds.), *Anomalous cognition: Remote viewing research and theory*, pp. 280–298. Jefferson, NC: McFarland.

May, E. C., & Marwaha, S. B. (2014a). *Anomalous cognition: Remote viewing research and theory.* Jefferson, NC: McFarland.

May, E. C., & Marwaha, S. B. (2014b). Section: Entropy. A fundamental model of anomalous cognition. In E. C. May & S. B. Marwaha (Eds.), *Anomalous cognition: Remote viewing research and theory*, pp. 279–350. Jefferson, NC: McFarland.

May, E. C., & Marwaha, S. B. (2014c). Section: Research methods in anomalous cognition. In E. C. May & S. B. Marwaha (Eds.), *Anomalous cognition: Remote viewing research and theory*, pp. 17–116. Jefferson, NC: McFarland.

May, E. C., Rubel, V., & Auerbach, L (2014). *ESP Wars: East and West.* Palo Alto, CA: Laboratories for Fundamental Research.

May, E. C., & Spottiswoode, S. (2014/1994). Managing the target-pool bandwidth: Possible noise reduction for anomalous cognition experiments. In E. C. May & S. B. Marwaha (Eds.), *Anomalous cognition: Remote viewing research and theory*, pp. 48–56. Jefferson, NC: McFarland.

May, E. C., Spottiswoode, S. J. P., & Faith, L. V. (2014/2005). A search for alpha power changes associated with anomalous cognition. In E. C. May & S. B. Marwaha (Eds.), *Anomalous cognition: Remote viewing research and theory*, pp. 172–194. Jefferson, NC: McFarland.

May, E. C., Spottiswoode, S. J. P., & Utts, J. M. (2014/1995). Applications of decision augmentation theory. In E. C. May & S. B. Marwaha (Eds.), *Anomalous cognition: Remote viewing research and theory*, pp. 244–267. Jefferson, NC: McFarland.

May, E. C., & Spottiswoode, S. J. P. (2014). Anomalous anticipatory effects in the human autonomic nervous system. In E. C. May & S.B. Marwaha (Eds.), *Anomalous cognition: Remote viewing research and theory*, pp. 152–157. Jefferson, NC: McFarland.

May, E. C., Utts, J. M., Luke, W. L. W., Frivold, T. J., & Trask, V. V. (2014/1990). Advances in remote-viewing analysis. In E. C. May & S. B. Marwaha (Eds.), *Anomalous cognition: Remote viewing research and theory*, pp. 57–79. Jefferson, NC: McFarland.

May, E. C., Utts J. M., & Spottiswoode, S. J. P. (2014/1995). Decision augmentation theory: Toward a model for anomalous mental phenomena. In E. C. May & S. B. Marwaha (Eds.), *Anomalous cognition: Remote viewing research and theory*, pp. 222–243. Jefferson, NC: McFarland.

May, E. C., Utts, J. M., Trask, V. V., Luke, W. W., Frivold, T. J., & Humphrey, B. S. (1989). *Review of the psychoenergetic research conducted at SRI International, 1973–1988,* SRI International Technical Report, March 1989. Menlo Park, CA: SRI International.

Mossbridge, J., Tressoldi, P., & Utts, J. (2012). Predictive physiological anticipation preceding seemingly unpredictable stimuli: A meta-analysis. *Frontiers in Psychology.* doi: 10.3389/fpsyg.2012.00390

Parker, A. (2000). A review of the ganzfeld work at Gothenburg University. *Journal of the Society for Psychical Research, 64*, 1–15.

Radin, D. I., May, E. C., & Thomson, M. (1980). *Psi experiments with random number generators: Meta-analysis. Part 1.* Menlo Park, CA: SRI International.

Rock, A. J. (2013). *The survival hypothesis: Essays on mediumship*. Jefferson, NC: McFarland.
Schmidt, H. (1969). Precognition of a quantum process. *Journal of Parapsychology, 33*, 99–108.
Seaberg, M. A. (2011). *Tasting the universe: People who see colors in words and rainbows in symphonies. A spiritual and scientific exploration of synesthesia*. Pompton Plains, NJ: New Page Books.
Storm, L., Tressoldi, P. E., & Di Risio, L. (2010). Meta-analysis of free-response studies, 1992–2008: Assessing the noise reduction model in parapsychology. *Psychological Bulletin, 136*(4), 471–494.
Thalbourne, M. A., & Storm, L. (Eds.). (2005). *Parapsychology in the twenty-first century: Essays on the future of psychical research*. Jefferson, N.C: McFarland.
Vassy, Z. (1978). Method for measuring the probability of 1 bit extrasensory information transfer between living organisms. *Journal of Parapsychology, 42*, 158–160.
Zadeh, L. A. (1965). Fuzzy sets. *Information and Control, 8*(3), 338–353.

Appendix 1:
General PK Protocol

There is a major definitional problem with psychokinesis (PK) studies; that is, the negative definition—PK is what happens when nothing else could or did happen. Unlike ESP studies, this problem manifests as a significant and expensive problem. This becomes especially so the more sensitive the apparatus.

The first exemplar resulting from the negative definition comes from a PK study that was carried out over a two-year period at SRI International (Hubbard & Isaacs, 1986). The idea was straightforward. Incorporate a sensitive piezoelectric (PZT) strain gauge that was affixed to a thin piece of metal in an environment such that any known physical disturbances would be detected and ruled out as an example of PK. Over the two-year period of the investigation, approximately US$500,000 was spent mostly on engineering details and specialized personnel familiar with the apparatus.

Since it was impossible to anticipate every possible source of data that arose from an artifact, Hubbard and Isaacs elected to use two PZT sensors operating in differential mode as an additional method of artifact rejection. (Artifact in this context means a change in the PZT sensors that could be attributed to known interaction effects such as the housing in which they were contained shook.) In this mode, the absolute value of the difference between the outputs of the two sensors was defined as the signal of interest. An event above threshold would be detected when one of the sensors was perturbed to a greater degree than the other. The intent of this approach was to reject any unshielded transients (e.g., low-frequency magnetic fields, wide area acoustic artifacts, or building movements) that could presumably influence the sensors in a nearly equivalent manner.

Each of the two PZT crystals are suspended from a lead mass. Each of the lead masses contains a charge-sensitive preamplifier that drives a fiber-optic link. The PZTs were coated with a silicone insulator to provide electrical insulation and silver paint to provide EMI/RFI (electromagnetic interference/radio frequency interference) shielding.

The two PZTs/preamps/drivers were housed in a Hoffman EMI/RFI shielded enclosure of dimensions $20 \times 16 \times 6$ inches.

Rechargeable batteries supplied the power for all the PZT instrumentation within the shielded enclosure.

Based upon the 1986 pilot work, Hubbard et al. (1987) made substantial improvements to the isolation of the PK target PZT system, which included:

- Attaching a three-axis accelerometer to the Tempest enclosure housing the PZT apparatus so that any overall motion of the enclosure could be detected.
- During any session the self-contained enclosure was levitated on an air table.
- Calibrated pressure-sensitive microphones were mounted in the room.
- Because the electric company shared with the research team the details of the electric mains, the apparatus could not be closer than 1 meter to any wall containing electric mains—the research team was surprised to learn that the probability of observing a 50 kV, one μs pulse in any given minute was close to unity; such a short pulse radiates EM energy and *could* interact with a sensor, but obviously does not disturb the usual appliances connected to the mains.

There were a number of other technical details, but the few shown above demonstrate some of the complexity required to rule out non-PK influences. All the above PK systems were secured in a classified room where independent monitors assured there were no unintended entrances into the room. If one walked by the closed room and simply knocked gently, the system could identify the source of the noise and show that it came from the closed door.

Because of the complexity to attend to the negative definition of PK, the SRI team eventually pleaded with their U.S. government sponsors to stop any further PK tasking because it was too costly and no perturbations could be seen that could not be attributed to known physical effects in a large number of different studies. That pesky negative definition was too costly to carry out further research.

Another, far less expensive, example will illustrate the problem of separating PK from artifacts that might mimic PK. Charles Honorton worked with Ms. Felicia Parise, a research hematologist at Maimonides Medical Center in Brooklyn, New York, in 1971 (Honorton, 1993). Following the work of Ms. Nina Kulagina, a putative Russian PK agent, Parise apparently learned to move, ostensibly by PK, small objects under a large glass bell jar. Honorton made an 8 millimeter film of one of the sessions, and it is rather impressive to see the small objects move while Parise placed her hands on either side of the glass bell jar. The event was filmed in winter on a cold afternoon. A straightforward computation showed that since the spatial gradient of an electric field may assert small forces even on nonconducting material, we could not rule out EM as the cause of the movement. The origin of the electric field was assumed to be the electrostatic potential difference between Parise's hands. Anyone who has reached for a metal doorknob on a cold dry day only to see a spark jump between your hand and the doorknob knows how strong that field can be. Fifty thousand volts is not out of the question.

Does this anecdote provide evidence against the PK hypotheses? No. What it does do, however, is to demonstrate that the next time one should evaporate a transparent conductor in the inside of the bell jar and ground it to eliminate this possibility.

The protocols, then, for PK are driven by the test circumstance. On one hand, since it is a reasonably good assumption that PK interactions might be small, one might consider using extremely sensitive measuring gear. But doing so exposes the apparatus to all subtle environmental influences and requires tracking down each one and demonstrating that each did not account for the putative perturbation of the apparatus.

PK divides cleanly into a number of different categories:

- Inelastic change of a target system; that is, the PK target is perturbed permanently and does not require inferential statistics to see the perturbation. PK metal bending under appropriate protocols is one such example. For example, either the metal rod is visually bent or it is not.

- Elastic change of a target system is trickier in that it means the perturbation happens but rapidly returns to its original condition. Suppose the rod in the example above bent but in seconds straightened.

- Micro changes of the system, often called μPK. In this class of studies, inferential statistics are required by definition. The problem here, however, as is pointed out in decision augmentation theory, is that the door is open for experimenter and/or participant ESP-mimicking causal effects. Because of this, it is likely that the body of laboratory data involving putative PK influence upon random binary bits from an appropriate source of randomness has been shown to be informational in that the devices were not perturbed at all (May, Spottiswoode, & Utts, 2014/1995).

Beside RNG PK, the analytical difficulty remains in any study of PK, regardless of its complexity, as long as an effect occurs in the effort *and* control condition and thus requires inferential statistics to determine what was happening.

In summary, then, PK research poses substantial difficulty in two domains. The first is the negative definition in that it becomes too costly to rule out alternatives. The second relates to the application of inferential statistics. There is good news, however. By applying a proper protocol, it is possible in many circumstances to determine whether the observed effects are informational or arise from influence of some sort.

Finally, a word of warning. Even in this last case above, which may show influence and not informational effects, we are back to the pesky negative definition again, and ruling out "normal" effects becomes paramount before one can claim paranormal effects.

REFERENCES

Honorton, C. (1993). A moving experience. *Journal of the American Society for Psychical Research, 87*(4), 329–340.

Hubbard, G. S., Bentley, P. P., Pasturel, P. K., & Isaacs, J. (1987). *A remote action experiment with a piezoelectric transducer*, Final Report-Objective H, Tasks 3 and 3a Covering the Period 1 October 1986 to 30 September 1987. Menlo Park, CA: SRI International.

Hubbard, G. S. & Isaacs, J. D. (1986). *An experiment to examine the possible existence of remote action effects in piezoelectric strain gauges*, Final Report, Project 1291. Menlo Park, CA: SRI International.

May, E. C., Spottiswoode, S. J. P., & Utts, J. M. (2014/1995). Applications of decision augmentation theory. In E. C. May & S. B. Marwaha (Eds.), *Anomalous cognition: Remote viewing research and theory*, pp. 244–267. Jefferson, NC: McFarland.

Appendix 2:
Precognition/Remote Viewing Protocol

The areas covered by the general term "psi" involve information phenomena generally called ESP and interactional phenomena generally called psychokinesis (PK). In this appendix, we will cover issues with regard to protocols for information processes.

In experimental terms, ESP and PK share the same definition problems. The first is that the definitions are negative; that is, ESP and PK happen when nothing else could or did happen in an experiment. A second type of definition, which is in common use, is operational; that is, we define a protocol and what happens in the study we simply label as ESP or PK. Neither of these definitions tell you what ESP or PK is. As a result, the negative definition has profound implications with experiment design and, of course, the protocol. A working definition for precognition can be stated as:

- *Precognition* is a person-centered perspective that generally refers to information perceived about future events, where the information could not be inferred by ordinary means. Or more formally, precognition is *an atypical perceptual ability that allows the acquisition of noninferential information arising from a space-like separated point in spacetime.*

- For two points in spacetime to be space-like separated, insufficient time has elapsed between them to allow for any causal relationship. Procedurally in AC experiments, it means that target stimuli are randomly generated *after* data collection is complete. Associated concepts include rectrocausation, remote viewing, presentiment, and precognitive dreams.

Regardless of the particular ESP study, there is an overarching concept to which the study *must* adhere: all target stimuli must be chosen randomly. Otherwise, the potential exists for fraud because of some collusion between the participant and target selector or more likely, if they know each other, the participant can respond knowing what the target selector likes. For example, suppose the target selector lives and breathes boats and is an avid sailor. If that person can chose the target by preference, then the result from a trial is tainted.

A second concept to which a study must adhere involves *blinding*; that is, no one who is in contact with the participant can know what the particular target stimulus is. This includes the experiment monitor and witnesses. Since the participant is, obviously, also blind to the stimulus target, this circumstance is called double-blind condition. Additionally, any analysis for the trial must be blind to the intended stimulus, and anyone in contact with this analyst must also be blind to the stimulus.

A violation of the double-blind conditions, including for the analyst, renders the trial invalid.

In this appendix, we provide a brief outline of the stimulus-response technique and free-response method of a standard remote viewing (RV) protocol, details of which can be found in May, Marwaha, and Chaganti (2014/2011). We realize that there are many ESP protocols aside from remote viewing, but many of the concepts provided here may translate to these other protocols.

NUMBER OF PARTICIPANTS

Determining the proper number of participants in a study may be a complex procedure. It primarily depends upon the primary purpose of the study. For example, if the aim is to replicate previous work, it is important to use the reported effect size to set the statistical power; that is, given the effect size, how many participants does the study require to reach a given level of statistical significance?

The number of participants also depends upon the overall goal of the study. We provide two examples for illustrative purposes only:

1. There are obviously many possible designs for an anomalous cognition (AC) study, but a typical one might have 30 participants each contributing only one trial. Such a design might examine the so-called first time effect (Puthoff & Target, 1976; Houck, 1983; Marrs, 2007). It has been observed in many experiments that a novice trying for the first time does well; however, subsequently for the next few trials, the performance is substantially less—this might be simply

because of performance anxiety. This observation is known as the first time effect.

2. If the investigator is interested in finding individuals who possess an inherent AC skill, then 20 participants could contribute five trials each, and their five trials are evaluated separately. These numbers are meant as only guidelines, since the protocols allow for considerable flexibility.

SET AND SETTING

In this section, we list seven items that are important considerations for set and setting for two different AC protocols.

1. The setting is rather business-like.
2. An experimenter (a.k.a., monitor) sits opposite the participant across a table. Generally, they are present in an office-like setting (e.g., in a laboratory); however, this arrangement is flexible depending upon the participant's availability. In preparation for the arrival of the participant, pens, pencils, and sufficient plain white paper are made available.
3. There is no special participant welcoming ritual other than friendly greetings and small talk before entering the laboratory.
4. Before the session begins, especially with a novice participant, she is told the details about what will happen in the trial and what the experience might be like, or more accurately, what the experience is most likely *not* to be like. For example, she is informed that vivid and specific internal experiences are more likely to be incorrect and is advised not to report them. Rather, the experience might be more accurately described in terms of feeling like a guess and/or a hunch rather than specifics. These points are emphasized in that the vivid internals often include direct logical inference or at least a more subtle form of logical inference, and that logical inference of any kind cannot, by definition of the protocol, lead to accurate data. This is not to say that a vivid internal experience can never be psi mediated; however, as experience has shown, especially with unselected participants, vivid internals come mainly from imagination and memory.
5. Some institutions and/or funding organizations require the use of an institutional review board (a.k.a., human use committee, ethics review board, etc.) and its associated informed consent form. This requirement is fulfilled during the presession activity.
6. Before the session begins, the participant is asked to jot down any mental activity he is currently experiencing. It is emphasized that

no one but she will see what is written. The purpose of this preliminary exercise is figuratively to "empty" the mind of the internal dialogue that we humans are constantly engaged in. Four to five minutes are given to complete this process, which may require a few sheets of paper to complete. When finished, the participant is asked to crumple the sheets of paper and toss them aside and should be taken by the participant after the session.

7. When the session begins, the participant is provided with fresh sheets of paper and asked to write her name, the date, and the time on the upper right portion of the page and number the page as page one. No other participant preparation is required.

COLLECTION METHODS

The two principal collection methods—stimulus-response technique and the free-response method—assume a random selection of a target and assume that the participant and the monitor are blind to that choice (i.e., double-blind conditions), as described above. It is not assumed that both individuals are blind to the target pool in general. However, often there is a preferred laboratory rule, in that no lab personnel are engaged as participants in the experimental procedure. This may assist in lessening experimenter expectancy and unconscious use of experimenter psi as hypothesized in the decision augmentation theory (DAT). (DAT holds that participants or experimenters use their unconscious psi ability to enhance the outcome of studies by augmenting decisions toward favorable outcomes [May, Utts, & Spottiswoode, 1995].) We raise the issue of DAT in that some critics correctly question who may be the source of the psi in such studies. It is recommended that the choice made in this regard be noted in the methodology of a study.

Stimulus-Response Technique

The primary idea behind this method is analogous to a word association test in psychology. In a psychological setting, a therapist asks a client to respond rapidly, without thinking, with the first word that "pops" up after hearing the therapist's key word. For example, the therapist might say "fat," and an immediate response from the client might be "big" or "thin." The rationale for this is to limit the participant's time to respond as much as possible so that he or she does not have enough time to invent a reasoned or socially acceptable response.

Similarly, in the AC arena, it is assumed that the quickest response is likely to be the most genuine AC information. This is because the participant does not have enough time for logical inference or psychologically driven responses, neither of which can lead to the correct material because precautions against sensory leakage ensure that necessary prior information for such inference is not available. The general method is listed below for computer-based studies:

1. When the session begins, the monitor gives the following instructions to the participant: "A few minutes from now, you will be shown a picture on that monitor. Please access and describe that photograph now. Access to that photograph is through the key word 'target.' When you are ready, place your pen on the page."

2. When the participant hears the stimulus word, she is to rapidly write the word "target" and then *immediately* scribble words and/or a brief sketch of the first impressions that come to mind. Participants are informed that spelling and neatness do not count.

3. They are also told that if they hesitate—usually indicative of an attempt at logical inference—the monitor will say "break." The participant writes "break" on the page also. They are informed that if they register a quick response, the monitor will also say "break" to momentarily end the anomalous cognition. In this way, the target/break couplet is regarded as analogous to having an opaque screen between the participant and the intended photograph, and each couplet is like punching a hole in the screen to reveal a small amount of the scene.

4. Part of the monitor's responsibility is to make sure that the responses are noted on the paper—often a novice participant will describe in words and gestures rather than in writing, which if unchecked could mean that essential information is not available to the independent judge. The monitor may interrupt and ask that those words be added to the paper. The monitor may also seek clarification. Suppose that the participant draws some waves but does not label them. The monitor can then ask if there are any words associated with the sketch. At no time should the monitor ask leading questions or provide interpretation of what the participant has written or drawn.

5. After each target/break couplet, the monitor engages the participant with small talk for a few seconds or many minutes. The purpose of this is to prevent the participant from pondering on the nature and content of the target or from analyzing the response that they have provided. About 8 to 10 such target/break couplets are taken in a single session. If there is a long break (e.g., the participant needs a bathroom break) or the break has lasted many minutes with small talk, the monitor repeats the tasking as mentioned above.

6. Before the final response set, the monitor may change the instructions by inviting the participant to summarize the impressions when the key word "target" is given. For instance, the monitor might state, "Access to the summary of your impressions is through the key

word 'target.' " The participant is encouraged to summarize her fragmented impression across the 8 to 10 target/break couplets and to label any sketches she has provided. More advanced participants are encouraged to provide information that will help the analyst differentiate among a number of competing target possibilities.

7. After the summary, the monitor says "break" one last time, and the participant is instructed to write "EOS" after the last entry to indicate end of session.

Free-Response Method

The free-response method was developed and used in the early days of remote viewing research (Puthoff & Targ, 1976). This method shares similarities with others used in the field (Sinclair, 1930; Ullman et al., 1973; Warcollier, 1948); however, it differs substantially in that the experimenter interacts with the participant.

Much of the approach had the same goals in mind as in the stimulus-response technique, that is, to reduce expectation, logical inference, and psychologically driven responses. In the laboratory, the participant is given the following instructions: "Please access and describe a photograph that you will see in about 10 minutes." (If the target is chosen from a number of physical locations, the phrasing and timing should be suitably adjusted.) "What can you tell me about it now?" The participant is encouraged to write and draw his or her impressions.

In an attempt to reduce the cognitive expectations and other sources of incorrect information, the stimulus–response method is replaced by changing the participant's perspective. Thus, in the free-response approach, there is more of a participant/monitor dialogue:

1. If the participant draws what appears to be a building, the monitor might ask the participant to place her back against it, look outward, describe what she sees, fly to the top and look out, punch it and describe what it feels like, what it tastes like, each time describing immediate impressions.

2. If a response includes a relatively formless rural scene, the participant may then be asked to view the scene as when floating 1,000 meters in the air over it, rotate rapidly 360 degrees, and describe what is seen.

3. An important point in these attention shifting methods is to ensure that the monitor avoids using the participant's or his own interpretation. For example, even though the participant labels something as a building, the monitor might instruct the participant to place his or her back to "it" rather than against the "building." Some participants

may have difficulty with this attention shifting in their mental landscape; therefore, the monitor is challenged to induce the shift in psychologically acceptable ways for the given participant.

This kind of dialogue exchange should not go on for more than 15 minutes. Five or 10 minutes is more typical. Longer sessions tend to provide additional irrelevant and incorrect information that is referred to as noise.

When the participant and monitor agree that the session is complete, the participant writes "EOS" on the page to denote the end of the session.

Important to Both Collection Methods

The decision to end the session is made by the monitor when he or she feels that no new information is being provided or more and more complex responses are being provided, which would probably involve imagination, confabulation, or elaboration creeping into the response process. The monitor has the option to indicate that the session is nearly complete and it is time for the participant to wrap up the session by concluding with any remaining impressions. Other considerations include:

1. For security's sake, the responses should be photocopied and the original should be stored in a secure place.
2. All analyses use only the original responses.
3. The copy is used for providing feedback to the participant while showing the correct target photograph and when positive correspondence can be emphasized.
4. This feedback and emphasis does not constitute an analysis. But providing positive and re-enforcing feedback is a good idea even in the case of a poor response. This, of course, may once again challenge the experimenter. For example, there may not actually be any correspondence whatsoever, but finding any correspondence provides a positive experience, which appears to be important.

ANALYSIS METHODS

We describe two approaches for the analysis of remote viewing. Both methods differ from the ganzfeld in an important way. The participant is never shown anything but the intended target, and resultantly, cannot do the judging. We feel this is an important aspect of the methodology because of possible precognitive leakage from material other than the target.

Rank-Order Analysis

In a rank-order method, a blind analyst (not the participant) is presented with five photographs, one of which is the intended target, which is chosen by a random process.

Regardless of the quality of the response material, the analyst is obligated to pick one of the five in the set as his or her own subjective assessment as the best match to the response. Having completed that task, the analyst then continues to choose the second best match, the third best match, and so on. In principle, this matching must proceed even if the response is a blank page! (Such ranking may introduce the possibility of experimenter psi; however, we retain the measure for historical relevance as well as allowing a ranking that is independent of the quality of the response.)

In any human-oriented research, we can never assume that a participant's response is random under the null hypothesis; yet, as noted above, it is a hard requirement that one element be random in this process. The choice of target can be shown to be that random choice.

Thus, the probability of a judge assigning the correct target to the response is exactly equal to 20% regardless of that judge's biases, biases that may exist in the judging set of five photographs, or response biases by the participant. Like anomalous cognition itself, the judging should not be one of deep consideration and pondering. There are no specific methods for the analyst to use; however, the following set of guidelines have proved to be successful:

- Focus on any cognitive surprises. For example, the response might be mostly about a city, but in the middle, the participant says, "Wait a minute, what is all this sand doing here?"
- Do not focus on any single detail. For example, one detail might lead you to one photograph, but another might lead to a second one.
- In general, try to emphasize the drawing over the words. This is a general rule; however, some participants are not too visually oriented, hence preference may need to be given to their verbal responses.
- Often it is easiest to eliminate the worst match first.
- If two photos contend for first place, opt for the picture that appears to be accurate at the first impression.

Statistical Considerations

At the end of a study consisting of M trials, the analysis should also include the computation of an effect size and an equivalent z-score as:

$$ES = \frac{\dfrac{n+1}{2} - \bar{R} \pm \dfrac{0.5}{M}}{\sqrt{\dfrac{n^2-1}{12}}},$$

where n is the number of possible ranks (five in this case) and $\bar{R}$ is the average rank over M trials. The last term in the numerator is a continuity correction, which comes into play only for a small number of total trials. The z-score based upon this effect size is given by:

$$z = ES \times \sqrt{M}.$$

The rank-order method is popular because of its simplicity and its independence of bias under the null hypothesis of no AC. Yet, the method may downgrade how good the AC might be. Consider two cases.

In the first one, suppose a participant's response is "noisy" in that it contains much information that is not relevant to the intended photograph. Yet, there is enough information to allow the independent analyst to pick the correct photograph as a first-place match.

In the second case, suppose that the response is a nearly perfect description of the target photograph with little or no wrong information. Using a ranking analysis, both responses are given a first-place hit, but obviously, much of the information in the second case is lost. Additionally, the ranking procedure is strongly dependent upon the degree to which the judging pack of photographs are different from one another, and this induces a confound in that the orthogonality of the judging pack of photographs is totally unrelated to the quality of the AC response. This problem has been noted in the literature (Kennedy, 1979; May, Spottiswoode, & Faith, 2000; Parker, Frederiksen, & Johansson, 1997).

Fuzzy Set Assessment and Figure of Merit

Fuzzy set assessment can be used both for ranking and rating to find a quality assessment of a given response that overcomes these problems. Details of fuzzy set development can be found in May and Faith (2014/2012) and May, Hawley, Chaganti, and Ratra (2014).

Based on the fuzzy sets, the data at hand are:

- A consensus fuzzy set of the intended target
- A fuzzy set representing the single response in the session

From these two fuzzy sets, a computer program creates the accuracy, reliability and figure of merit. The accuracy is defined as the fraction of the target material that was described correctly and is formally given by:

$$Accuracy = \frac{\sum_{k=1}^{n} \min (T_k, R_k)}{\sum_{k=1}^{n} T_k},$$

where n is the number of elements (24) in the USE. T_k and R_k are the fuzzy set membership values in the target and response, respectively. The accuracy ranges over the closed interval [0,1] in steps of .1. The accuracy is not a good measure of anomalous cognition by itself because if a response were long enough (e.g., using the Encyclopaedia Britannica as a response), then the accuracy would always be high and could easily approach 1 (its maximum) by chance alone. To guard against this artifact, the reliability is computed.

Reliability is defined as the fraction of the response that is correct and is given by:

$$Reliability = \frac{\sum_{k=1}^{n} \min (T_k, R_k)}{\sum_{k=1}^{n} R_k}.$$

where the reliability ranges over the closed interval [0,1] in steps of .1 also. Reliability by itself, however, is not a good measure of AC. Suppose a response consisted of a single element, outside, then for many targets, this response would have a reliability of 1 (its maximum value) by chance alone.

The figure of merit, defined as accuracy × reliability, turns out to be a more sensitive measure of anomalous cognition. Since both accuracy and reliability range over the closed interval of [0,1], the figure of merit ranges over the same interval.

Experience with these metrics has shown that a good "rule of thumb" is that about a third of any response will match about a third of any target by chance. So a "chance" figure of merit is about .1.

Before we can compute meaningful accuracy and reliability, we must consider one last item. Anomalous cognition has not yet progressed to the point where a participant not only can correctly identify whether an element is present in the target but also the degree to which it is visually impacting—the metric on which the target fuzzy sets were constructed. To address this point, it is specified that all elements in a target with a membership value of .1 be set to zero and all membership values of .2 or larger be set to one. (Setting these elements to zero membership value has the effect of cutting out low impact visual noise in the target.) This is called an alpha cut in fuzzy set parlance and, in this case, removes all aspects of visual relevance of target elements from the analysis.

The figure of merit approach is positive in one sense and negative in another. As we noted above, the success of the rank-order method of analysis strongly depends upon something that is independent of any putative psychic ability; namely, how different from one another are the photographs in the judging pack. Formally, this is called the orthogonality of the photographic set—the more different the photographs, the easier the judging and vice versa. Using a rank-order method while searching for correlates to AC is a mistake in that there is a large orthogonality confound and a threshold effect. For example, suppose the decoy targets in a rank-order assessment are not too different from the intended target. "Noise" is introduced into the judging because it becomes all too easy to pick a similar, but incorrect, target as the best match. However, the threshold effect is more problematic. Suppose we are testing for a correlation of anomalous cognition with some personality variable such as extraversion. In one case, let us suppose that the participant's score is mediocre on an extraversion test and produces a good enough AC result that a judge can, with difficulty, assign the intended target as the best match (i.e., a rank of one). Consider a second participant who is a high-scoring extravert and provides a near-perfect match to the intended target. But that near-perfect match still only receives a rank of one. Therefore, substantial information is lost using ranking in correlation tests. So, using an absolute rating system, which is independent of any target in the pool except the intended one and has no threshold effects, is a major advance over the rank-order method in correlation studies. The figure of merit system is one such example. But the figure of merit is only a single number, so it is difficult to obtain a meaningful test statistic. If, however, it is possible to provide an estimate of what a null distribution of figures of merit might look like, then it would be possible to use that distribution to assess the statistic even from a single trial (May, 2007).

Now that we can compute an absolute assessment of a given response to its intended target, we can revisit the idea of rank-order analysis, except this time, the ranks are computed on the value of the figure of merit instead of the visual rating shown above. Haste and Dawes (2010) explored decision making by humans and computers and found that humans are much better than computers in determining the decision criteria; however, once the criteria have been set, computers are significantly better at making decisions based upon those criteria. Thus, the ranks based upon the figure of merit may improve the results. As of this writing, we can only say it is a laboratory anecdote that the figure of merit is more successful at ranking than those provided by a human judge. Should this prove to be correct, then it is entirely consistent with Haste and Dawes's finding: humans determined the universal set of elements (i.e., the judgment criteria), but the computer ranks according to the figure of merit, which is now devoid of human input.

CONCLUSION

We have described two different approaches to collecting data in a free-response methodology for anomalous cognition. In addition, we outlined two approaches to arriving at a statistical analysis of the results. Of course, we hope that these descriptions will inspire others to replicate this form of anomalous cognition. It is important to keep in mind that the methods outlined here should be used only as guidelines for research. Of course, two aspects of the protocol should never be changed. They are (1) the requirements of a randomly selected target for the session and (2) all individuals who might come in contact with the participant or the analyst must be blind to the target choice.

The details of the fuzzy set approach, for example, will depend upon the targets being used and the skill level of the proposed participants (May & Lantz, 2014/2010). Furthermore, to obtain a meaningful test statistic, one should collect a large number of trials in studies to create a meaningful estimate of the effect size.

With regard to the free-response method of data collection, there is considerable leeway in how a monitor might target and guide a participant toward a correct response.

To standardize the test procedure for future AC studies, we suggest the following steps be included:

- An approximate sample size based upon a statistical power analysis
- A minimum of 10 sessions of either the stimulus-response or the free-response method per participant
- The presentation of a single target as feedback
- The time period for each session, including analysis, should not exceed 30 minutes, from start to end of interaction between the monitor and participant
- Analysis of results from the ranking method and overall effect size and its meaning (Cohen, 1988; Rosenthal, 1991).

We finish by emphasizing an important point in research using human participants. In this appendix, we have provided an account of two anomalous cognition protocols that have been refined and used for over 20 years; however, besides a basic minimum, a successful experiment that includes many participants and sessions must be flexible in its design. Of course, once the design is set, it must be adhered to throughout the study. As is well known in social science research, experimenters should first avail themselves of extensive pilot studies to work out the "kinks" in the design before embarking on a formal study.

REFERENCES

Cohen, J. (1988). *Statistical power analysis for the behavioral sciences* (2nd ed.). Hillsdale, NJ: Erlbaum.

Haste, R. K., & Dawes, R. M. (2010). *Rational choice in an uncertain world: The psychology of judgment and decision making.* Thousand Oaks, CA: Sage.

Houck, J. (1983). Conceptual model of paranormal phenomena. *ARC ARCHAEUS, 1*(1).

Marrs, J. (2007). *Psi spies: The true story of America's psychic warfare program.* Franklin Lakes, NJ: Career Press.

May, E. C. (2007). Advances in anomalous cognition analysis: A judge-free and accurate confidence-calling technique. *Paper presented at the Parapsychological Association, Winchester, UK.*

May, E. C., & Faith, L. (2014/2012). A target pool and database for anomalous cognition experiments. In E. C. May & S. B. Marwaha (Eds.), *Anomalous cognition: Remote viewing research and theory,* pp. 38-47. Jefferson, NC: McFarland.

May, E. C., Hawley, L., Chaganti, V., & Ratra, N. (2014). Natural anomalous cognition targets: A fuzzy set application. *Journal of Parapsychology, 78*(2), 195–208.

May, E. C., & Lantz, N. D. (2014/2012). Anomalous cognition technical trials: Inspiration for the target entropy concept. In E. C. May & S. B. Marwaha (Eds.), (2014). *Anomalous cognition: Remote viewing research and theory,* pp. 280–298. Jefferson, NC: McFarland.

May, E. C., Marwaha, S. B., & Chaganti, V. (2014/2011). Anomalous cognition: Two protocols for data collection and analyses. In E. C. May & S. B. Marwaha (Eds.), *Anomalous cognition: Remote viewing research and theory,* pp. 18–37. Jefferson, NC: McFarland.

Puthoff, H. E., & Targ, R. (1976). A perceptual channel for information transfer over kilometer distances: historical perspective and recent research. *Proceedings IEEE, 64*(3), 329–354.

Rosenthal, R. (1991). *Meta-analytic procedures for social research.* Newbury Park, CA: Sage.

Sinclair, U.B. (1930/2008). *Mental radio.* Forgotten Books. www.forgottenbooks.org

Ullman, M., Krippner, S., & Vaughan, A. (1973). *Dream telepathy: Experiments in nocturnal extrasensory perception (3rd ed.).* Newburyport, MA: Hampton Roads.

Warcollier, R. (1948/2001). *Mind to mind.* Charlottesville, VA: Hampton Roads.

Appendix 3:
Research Organizations and Journals

ARGENTINA

Instituto de Psicologia Paranormal (IPP), Buenos Aires, *www.alipsi.com.ar/*

AUSTRALIA

Australian Institute of Parapsychological Research, Sydney: Gladesville, New South Wales, *www.aiprinc.org/index.asp*

Australian Society for Psychical Research and UFORUM: Pert, Western Australia, *http:/members.ozemail.com.au/~amilani/ufo.html*

QUIP Group: Quality Investigative Psi Projects: Hobart, Tasmania, *http://www.qipp.com.au/index.html*

AUSTRIA

Austrian Society for Parapsychology and Border Areas of Science, Vienna, *www.parapsychologie.ac.at/eng-info.htm*

BRAZIL

Instituto de Psicologia, Sao Paulo, *www.ip.usp.br/portal/*

DENMARK

Danish Society for Psychical Research (DASPR), *http://parapsykologi.dk/index.php/our-history*

FRANCE

Institut Metapsychique International (IMI) Paris, *www.metapsychique.org*

GERMANY

Gesellschaft für Anomalistik e.V. (Society for Anomalistics), Freiburg, *http://www.anomalistik.de/informationenglish*

Institut fur Grenzgebiete der Psychologie und Psychohygiene (Institute for Frontier Areas of Psychology and Mental Health) (IGPP) Freiburg i.Br., *www.igpp.de/english/welcome.htm*

HUNGARY

Eötvös Loránd University

Open University Szintezis (OUS), *http://www.szintezis.info.hu*

ITALY

Associazione Italiana Scientific di Metapsichica (AISM), Rome, *www.metapsichica.it/*

Centro Studi di Parapsicologia, Bologna (CSP), *http://cspbo.altervista.org/b/storia.htm*

Laboratorio Interdisciplinare di Ricerca Biopsicocibernetica, Bologna, *www.biopsicocibernetica.org/*

JAPAN

International Society of Life Information Science (ISLIS), Chiba, *www.islis.a-iri.org/*

Japanese Society for Parapsychology, Tokyo, *http://j-spp.umin.jp/english/jspp_e.htm*

THE NETHERLANDS

Dutch Society for Psychical Research (DUSPR), *http://dutchspr.org/spr*

SWEDEN

The Center for Research on Consciousness and Anomalous Psychology (CERCAP), Lund University, Lund, *www.psy.lu.se/research/networks/cercap*

The Swedish Society for Parapsychological Research, *www.parapsychology.se/*

UK

Anomalistic Psychology Research Unit (APRU), Gold Smith University, London, *www.gold.ac.uk/apru/*

Centre for the Study of Anomalous Psychological Processes (CSAPP), The University of Northampton, *www2.northampton.ac.uk/portal/page/portal/SocialSciences/sshome/psychology-homepage/ research#csapp*

Perrott-Warrick Research Unity, University of Hertfordshire, Hertfordshire, *www.psy.herts.ac.uk/res/para-magic.html*

Psi Research Centre, Glastonbury, *www.psi-researchcentre.co.uk*

Psychology of Paranormal Phenomena, University of Derby's Centre for Psychological Research,

www.derby.ac.uk/science/research/centres-groups/psychological/clusters/psychologyof paranormalphenomenacluster/

Society for Psychical Research (SPR), London, *www.spr.ac.uk/main/*

UNITED STATES

Boundary Institute, San Jose, California, *www.boundaryinstitute.org*

Center for Consciousness Studies Tucson, Arizona, *www.consciousness.arizona.edu/*

Division of Perceptual Studies, University of Virginia, Charlottesville, Virginia, *http://www.medicine.virginia.edu/clinical/departments/psychiatry/sections/cspp/ dops/home-page*

Global Consciousness Project, Princeton, New Jersey, *www.noosphere.princeton.edu/*

Institute of Noetic Sciences (IONS) Petaluma, California, *www.noetic.org*

International Consciousness Research Laboratories, Princeton, New Jersey, *www.icrl.org/*

Laboratories for Fundamental Research, Palo Alto, California, *www.lfr.org*

Monroe Institute Faber, Virginia, *www.monroeinstitute.org/*

Pacific Neuropsychiatric Institute Seattle, Washington, *www.pni.org/research/ anomalous/*

Parapsychological Association Inc., Columbus, Ohio, *www.parapsych.org/home.aspx*

Parapsychology Foundation New York, *www.parapsychology.org*

PEAR Laboratory (1979-2007), Princeton, New Jersey, *www.princeton.edu/~pear/* International Consciousness Research Laboratories (ICRL), Princeton NJ, *http:/icrl.org/*

Psiphen Lab, University of Colorado, Boulder, *www.psiphen.colorado.edu/*

Rhine Research Center, Durham, North Carolina, *www.rhine.org*

Society for Scientific Exploration (SSE): USA, *www.scientificexploration.org*

SKEPTIC ORGANIZATIONS

Committee for Skeptical Inquiry Amherst, New York, *www.csicop.org*

James Randi Educational Foundation, Fort Lauderdale, Florida: USA, *www .randi.org*

Skeptics Society (The), Altadena, California, *http://www.skeptic.com/*

Skeptics Society, Greenford, UK, *http://www.skeptic.org.uk/*

JOURNALS

Australian Journal of Parapsychology a peer-reviewed journal on the topics of extrasensory perception (ESP), psychokinesis (PK), and life after death; *aiprinc.org/journal.asp*

European Journal of Parapsychology (published between 1975 and 2010) focuses on experimental and theoretical aspects of parapsychology; back issues available at *http://ejp.wyrdwise.com/*

International Journal of Parapsychology focuses on experimental, theoretical, and philosophical aspects of parapsychology; *http://www.parapsychology.org/dynamic/070100.html*

Journal of Near-Death Studies, a peer-reviewed scholarly journal (ISSN 0891-4494) devoted exclusively to the field of near-death studies; cross-disciplinary and published quarterly; *http://iands.org/publications/journal-of-near-death-studies.html*

Journal of Parapsychology, a publication of the Rhine Research Center focuses on experimental and theoretical aspects of parapsychology; *http://www.parapsych.org/section/17/journal_of_parapsychology.aspx*

Journal of the Society for Scientific Exploration publishes original research on consciousness, quantum physics and biophysics, unexplained aerial phenomena, alternative medicine, new energy, sociology, psychology, and more; *http:/www.scientificexploration.org/journal/*

Journal of the Society for Psychical Research has been published continuously since 1884, promoting the Society's aim of examining "without prejudice or prepossession and in a scientific spirit those faculties of man, real or supposed, which appear to be inexplicable on any generally recognised hypothesis." The Journal's contents reflect the wide range of our contributors' specialisms and interests and include reports of current laboratory and fieldwork research, as well as theoretical, methodological and historical papers with a bearing on the field of parapsychology; *http:/www.spr.ac.uk/page/spr-publications-parapsychology*

Glossary

3D space: Three-dimensional space is what we all are most familiar with–up/down, east/west, and north/south. It takes only three points to locate something in this space. For example, to find the office, move 15 blocks east, 2 blocks north, and it is up on the 18th floor.

accuracy of response: Accuracy is defined as the fraction of the target material that was described correctly.

advanced waves: Since the EM Maxwell wave equations are all quadratic in time they have two solutions—waves traveling forward in time of which we see every day (i.e., retarded waves) and an equivalent set of waves moving backward in time. These are called advanced waves.

alpha waves: A distinctive, high-amplitude brain rhythm or brain wave that occurs mainly in the occipital region of the cortex and is associated with feelings of drowsiness, relaxation, and disengaged attention. It has a frequency range of between 8 and 13 Hz (cycles per second).

analyst: An individual who provides a quantitative measure of AC. This individual must be blind to experimental conditions and the intended target.

analytic philosophy: A tradition of twentieth-century Western philosophy deriving primarily from the work of G. Frege, G. E. Moore, B. Russell, and L. Wittgenstein. A central focus of this tradition is the analysis of language, the use of the analysis of language to understand philosophical problems, and the utilization of the tools of mathematics and science to conduct philosophical investigation.

anomalous anticipatory effects: Anomalous anticipatory effects usually refer to psychophysical responses in advance of randomly chosen stimuli.

anomalous cognition (AC): The perception and cognition of information that is blocked from the usual sensory systems by distance, shielding, or time and that emerges from a distant point in spacetime. In this process, some individuals are able to gain access to information from events outside the range of their senses by a currently not understood mechanism. Several synonyms for this phenomenon are in useremote viewing (RV), precognition, clairvoyance, and ESP.

anomalous mental phenomenon (AMP): A term developed by May, Utts, and Spottiswoode (1995) during the Star Gate era to refer to anomalous phenomena, or psi phenomena, that occur when nothing else should, at least as nature is currently understood. They include anomalous cognition and anomalous perturbation.

anomalous perturbation (AP): A form of interaction with matter in which all known physical mechanisms are absent. In other words, some individuals are alleged to be able to influence matter by an as yet unknown process. This phenomenon is also known as psychokinesis (PK).

anomaly: An observation that appears to be inconsistent with our current understanding of nature.

artifacts: Data that may either mimic or mask those anticipated from the primary hypothesis.

associative remote viewing (ARV): This form of remote viewing was designed to answer questions that are not easy to answer by more traditional forms of remote viewing. Suppose you wanted to determine the result of a future coin flip—heads or tails. An assistant randomly assigns one, say, photograph to one potential outcome and a second and entirely different photograph to the other outcome. We ask a viewer to please describe a photograph they will see shortly—the viewer and the monitor are totally blind to any photographs and are therefore blind to which picture has been associated with which coin toss outcome. Which picture is shown to the viewer is determined by the outcome of the coin toss.

autoganzfeld: A laboratory ganzfeld technique in which many of the key procedural details, such as selection and presentation of the target and the recording of the evaluation of the target-response similarity given by the percipient, are fully automated and computerized so as to reduce, as far as possible, errors such as motivational errors that could bias the manual operations.

beacon: An individual who, while receiving direct sensorial stimuli from an intended target, acts as a focus of attention for the receiver/remote viewer in AC experiments.

Bell's theorem: Famous for drawing an important line in the sand between quantum mechanics (QM) and the world as we know it classically. In its simplest form, Bell's theorem states that no physical theory of local hidden variables can ever reproduce all of the predictions of quantum mechanics.

bio-PK: Term used to refer to psychokinetic effects on living systems such as those involved in psychic healing and PK effects on germination of seeds and growth of bacteria. It is also labeled as DMILS, or direct mental influence on living systems.

Bloch's law: A temporal summation law that states the visual threshold is reached when duration times luminance is constant. If brightness is halved, then duration needs to be doubled. Also called Bunsen-Roscoe law, it applies to very low light brightness.

causal: A relationship between two events. For example, when I drop a hammer on my foot, that event causes pain in my foot.

chance: A state characterized by complete unpredictability.

clairvoyance: Generally refers to information received from a distance, beyond the reach of the ordinary senses. It refers to the anomalous cognition (AC) of objects and events as distinguished from AC of thoughts and mental states of individuals. Procedurally it means that the target stimuli in experiments are occurring in real time, and are randomly generated *before* data collection is initiated. In contrast, in a precognition protocol, the target is generated *after* data collection is complete. Using a double-blind protocol is standard for all such experiments.

cold reading: A set of statements claiming to be anomalously received, which are in fact no more than information gleaned from facial gestures, clues in conversation, etc. of the person seeking the reading.

collapse of a wave function: In quantum mechanics, the wave function for any system, in principle, contains everything that can be known about that system. In other words, it is a statement of all possible outcomes of a measurement. When a measurement is made, one possible outcome is seen. This process is called the collapse of the wave function; that is, a collection of possible outcomes collapses to only one actualized outcome.

control: The management of all external circumstances and factors in an experiment—often called the null hypothesis—so that any modification in the dependent variable may be attributed to an alternative hypothesis.

CPT symmetry: In physics, C means charge, P means parity, T means time. In any given situation, any of these may be individually symmetric. However, both theory and experiments show it is the product of these three symmetries that must remain constant in all known physical processes.

decision augmentation theory (DAT): A phenomenological model, DAT holds that AC information is included along with the usual inputs that result in a final human decision. In statistical parlance, DAT says that a slight systematic bias is introduced into the decision process by AC to bias the process toward a favorable outcome. In psychokinesis/anomalous perturbation experiments, DAT assumes that the underlying parent distribution of a physical system *remains unperturbed*; however, the measurements of the physical system are systematically biased by an AC-mediated informational process. The domain in which DAT is applicable is when experimental outcomes are in a statistical regime (i.e., a few standard deviations from chance).

decline effect: A strong trend of decreasing scores over time.

direct mental interaction with living systems (DMILS): A term used to describe instances in which a person tries to mentally influence a biological system.

displacement effect: AC response to targets other than the intended target.

dual aspect monism: The view that the concrete world is ultimately comprised of one kind of stuff that inherently has both physicalistic and mentalistic properties. Modern term for panpsychism.

dualism: In mind-body philosophy, the view that "mind" and "body" are two distinct *things* ("structural dualism") and/or are comprised of two different kinds of stuff ("hylic dualism")

dynamic targets: Consist of video clips or natural scenes with lots of activity.

eigenstate: In quantum mechanics, a state of the system whose probability does not change with time.

electrodermal activity: Refers to changes in the skin's ability to conduct electricity.

electroencephalography (EEG): A technique for amplifying and recording the fluctuations in electrical voltage in a living brain using electrodes attached to key positions on the person's head. Recordings of the electrical frequencies and intensities of the living brain are typically recorded over relatively long periods.

electromyography (EMG): The measurement of the electrical potentials associated with the activity of skeletal muscles.

EM theory: In 1865, James Clerk Maxwell wrote a complete (classical) theory of electricity and magnetism. Even today, the four equations from Maxwell hold precisely.

energy: In classical physics, energy has a precise definition—the capacity for doing work. Energy is conserved; that is, it can change form but is neither created nor destroyed.

entropy: A thermodynamic quantity that is a measure of randomness or disorder of the molecules of the system. For example, ice exists in a state of lower entropy than does water because the molecules in ice are relatively lined up, whereas in water, these molecules are randomly jostling about.

entropy change during phase transition: The change of matter from one state (solid, liquid, or gas) to another is called phase transition. Such changes occur at definite temperatures such as melting point (solid to liquid), boiling point (liquid to vapors), etc., and are accompanied by absorption or evolution of heat.

entropy gradient: In general, a gradient implies a change, and vector calculus and numerical analysis provide techniques to compute gradients. Thus, entropic gradients are a quantitative measure of how the entropy is changing.

entropy limit to AC: Recent results in AC studies, which have shown a correlation of AC with gradients of entropy of target systems, suggest that there may be a statistical limit imposed by entropy considerations on the ultimate quality of a given AC response.

epistemology: The study of what knowledge is and how we can obtain it. Also, models of the kinds of knowledge that are possible. Epistemological models postulate how we can come to have knowledge of what exists, what is possible, and how things behave. Instances of epistemologies are science, hermeneutics, and mystical revelation.

EPR paradox: At a visceral level, we believe that matter possesses properties independent of observation. For example, a 1-pound ball in a light-tight box still weighs 1 pound. In the quantum world, however, this is not the case. Systems have properties only when they are measured. Therefore, the analogy would be the ball's weight is undefined until it is put on a scale. Because this idea was not understood in the early days of the development of quantum theory, Einstein, Podolsky, and Rosen pointed out that if quantum theory were valid, it would lead to inconsistent results.

ESP: *See* Extrasensory perception.

event-related desynchronization (ERD): Roughly speaking, the brain in an "idle" state produces large amounts of alpha activity. Any external stimulus, an attempt to move a muscle or have a thought, will interrupt this process. This is called event-related desynchronization because these events stop or momentarily interrupt the synchronized alpha rhythm.

event-related field (ERF): Any stereotyped electrophysiological response to a stimulus, whether external or internal, as measured by an external magnetic field usually with a magnetoencephalograph. *See also* magnetoencephalography.

event-related potentials (ERP): Any stereotyped electrophysiological response to a stimulus, whether external or internal, as demonstrated by electric potentials on the scalp.

expectation artifact: An artifact that arises because of the participant's expectation of some future stimulus. Here we generally mean in the context of skin conductance experiments. *See also* Artifact.

expectation bias: *See* Expectation artifact.

expectation effects: An experimental outcome that results not from manipulation of the variable of interest per se, but rather from some aspect of the particular experimenter's behavior, such as unconscious communication to the participants —lack of blinding conditions, or possibly even a psi-mediated effect working in accord with the experimenter's desire to confirm some hypothesis.

experimenter psi: In most experiments, there is a subject/participant/volunteer and someone who is in charge, called the experimenter. This person makes all kinds of decisions that help guide the individual trials. There is no reason the human experimenter is restricted from unconsciously using his own psi to affect the outcome of individual trials or studies. This effect is called experimenter psi. *See also* Decision augmentation theory.

extrasensory perception (ESP): The acquisition of information about, or response to, an external event, object, or influence (mental or physical; past, present, or future) otherwise than through any of the known sensory channels; used by J. B. Rhine to refer to such phenomena as *telepathy, clairvoyance*, and *precognition*. *See also* Anomalous cognition.

falsifiability: This idea was proposed by Karl Popper. A notion, hypothesis, model, or theory is only as good as there is a way to show that it is wrong. If there is no measurement that can tell whether the idea was correct, then the idea is just that but does not generally contribute to the knowledge base.

feedback: After a response has been secured, the information about the intended target that is displayed to the receiver or agent.

figure of merit (FoM): The product of accuracy and reliability; indicates the assessment of the AC trial. It is a sensitive measure of a cognitive anomaly. *See also* Accuracy of response; Reliability of response

forced-choice method: Method wherein the participant is constrained to respond within a limited set of possibilities.

force-like connection/force-like interactions: In considering all anomalous mental phenomena, some are purely informational, such as anomalous cognition (ESP, remote viewing); however, there is a class of phenomena called anomalous perturbation or a direct action on the physical world. This can happen only with forces.

frame entropy: The frame entropy of a photograph is derived from the pixel values in each of the three digital primary colors (red, blue, green) taken from the photograph in total as opposed to some part of it.

free-form/free-response method: Technique in which the participant is free to report anything at all that comes before his mental landscape. In this method, a blind monitor may ask structured questions of the participant to elicit as much AC information about the randomly selected target as possible.

fuzzy set technique: Technique used to obtain a rating of the quality of the match. In this approach, all the targets in the pool should have previously been consensus-encoded with regard to their cognitive content. The analyst, who is blind to the encoding of the intended target for the session, encapsulates the response with the same set of potential cognitive elements that were used in the coding of the target pool. From these data, a simple calculation constructs the accuracy (i.e., how much of the intended target was described correctly) and the reliability (i.e., how much of the response was correct).

ganzfeld technique: Literally, "whole field." In AC research, it refers to a technique for homogenous, unpatterned sensory stimulation. Audiovisual ganzfeld may be accomplished by placing halved ping-pong balls over each eye of the subject, with diffused light focused on the eyes and unstructured sounds (such as "white" or "pink" noise) fed into the ears. Placing the subject in such an environment creates an altered state of consciousness in the subject. Sometimes, subjects report a total blank out consequent to the deprivation of patterned sensory input.

geomagnetic activity: *See* Geomagnetic fluctuation.

geomagnetic fluctuation (GMF): The earth's magnetic field fluctuates slowly and with a very small magnitude primarily due to the flood of charged particles from the sun. These small fluctuations are tracked worldwide (their values are available online).

goal-oriented AC: Goal orientation simply means that individuals use their innate AC ability to accomplish some perceived or unconscious goal. Rex Stanford's psi-mediated instrumental response (PMIR)—a precursor to DAT—is one example.

gradient of Shannon entropy: Gradients mean change, so a gradient of Shannon entropy describes how the Shannon entropy changes as a function of distance across a photograph.

grandfather paradox: Would arise if it were possible for someone to travel back in time. If that individual did so and killed his grandfather when he was a small child, how could that be, since that individual would have never been born, but he was! Thus, the paradox.

Haussdorff dimension: In mathematics, an extended nonnegative real number associated with any metric space. Generalizes the notion of the dimension of a real vector space. That is, the Hausdorff dimension of an n-dimensional inner product space equals n. This means, for example, the Hausdorff dimension of a point is zero, the Hausdorff dimension of a line is one, and the Hausdorff dimension of a plane is two. There are, however, many irregular sets that have noninteger Hausdorff dimension.

Hilbert space: In quantum mechanics, the vector space spanned by all of the eigenvectors of a given operator. The operator is usually assumed to be the energy operator (Hamiltonian) of the system. A Hilbert space may have either a finite or infinite number of dimensions.

hits: In AC experiments, when a participant gets the correct target stimulus as determined by blind analysis, is called a hit.

hylic dualism: The view that the concrete world is comprised of two kinds of stuff such that there is at least one causally effective property they do not have in common.

hylic monism: The view that the concrete world is comprised of only one kind of fundamental stuff.

idealism: The view that what exists most fundamentally has only mentalistic properties.

influence model: Within the context of anomalous mental phenomena, refers to psychokinesis.

informational entropy: Like entropy, a measure of how far something is from an ideal random state, information entropy is the equivalent for a sequence of numbers, but today physicists make no distinction between informational entropy and thermodynamic entropy other than a constant of proportionality.

information theory: A discipline founded by Claude Shannon that tries to understand how information is generated, stored, and transmitted. Information theory, in some sense, is the basis of much of our digital world.

intuition: The ability to acquire knowledge without inference and/or the use of reason.

intuitive data sorting (IDS): The earlier term for the decision augmentation theory (DAT).

judging: The process whereby a rating or a rank-score (that is, "1st," "2nd," "3rd," and so on) is awarded to one or more responses produced (or *targets* used) in a free-response test of ESP, in accordance with the degree of correspondence obtained between them or one or more targets (or responses); also, the attempt to match, under blind conditions, a set of targets with a set of responses.

laws of thermodynamics: First law of thermodynamics: Change in internal or thermal energy is equal to heat added and work done on system. (Same as law of conservation of energy.) Second law of thermodynamics: Heat flows only from region of high temperature to region of lower temperature, which is equivalent to saying entropy can never decrease in an isolated system. Third law of thermodynamics: It is impossible to reduce the temperature of a system to absolute zero in a finite number of steps.

local sidereal time (LST): Sidereal time, at any moment (and at a given locality defined by its geographical longitude), more precisely local apparent sidereal time (LAST), is defined as the hour angle of the vernal equinox at that locality; has the same value as the right ascension of any celestial body that is crossing the local meridian at that same moment. At the moment when the vernal equinox crosses the local meridian, local apparent sidereal time is 00:00. Greenwich Apparent Sidereal Time (GAST) is the hour angle of the vernal equinox at the prime meridian at Greenwich, England. Local sidereal time at any locality differs from the Greenwich Sidereal Time value of the same moment, by an amount that is proportional to the longitude of the locality.

macro-PK: A form of anomalous perturbation that does not require inferential statistics to observe an effect. Bending rods of metal by mental means alone is an example.

macropsychic state: A human conscious state, such as seeing a painting, feeling velvet, or tasting wine is said to be macropsychic because it is the kind of conscious state that a human can have. Macropsychic states are simply the conscious experiences that humans have that come to them as being unified as time passes.

magnetoencephalography (MEG): An imaging technique that measures the magnetic fields by highly sensitive measuring devices that are generated by electrical activity in the brain.

materialism: The ontological view that everything that exists in a concrete way is comprised of matter, i.e., it is constituted of stuff that has energy. Since the middle of the twentieth century, different from *physicalism*, which is the view that all matter that actually exists is *physical* matter. The view that there are kinds of matter that also or instead have inherently mentalistic or other nonphysical properties is called *broad materialism*.

materialization: Using macroscopic PK to make some material object appear from apparently nothing. *See also* Macro-PK.

Maxwell's theory: James Clerk Maxwell developed a theory of electromagnetism between 1861 and 1865. His four equations stand today as the basis of EM theory.

mean chance expectation (MCE): The most likely chance score in an anomalous cognition/perturbation test.

meta-analysis: A way of combining many experiments into a single statistical melting pot so that the strength of the whole database can be ascertained.

metaphysics: The study of the fundamental nature of world; models on the fundamental nature of world. Metaphysical models embrace a specific ontology and then postulate how the relevant particulars can behave. Examples of metaphysical views are *naturalism* and *supernaturalism*.

micro-PK: A form of anomalous perturbation that requires inferential statistics to observe an effect. Random number generators are considered examples of micro-PK. *See also* anomalous perturbation.

micropsychism: A view defended by the philosopher Galen Strawson; related to panpsychism. Panpsychism holds that consciousness exists at the fundamental level and that it is to be found everywhere. Micropsychism holds that only some entities at the fundamental level are experiential/conscious. These micropsychic properties or elements are the kinds of things out of which conscious human experiences can be built. A macropsychic state must at least involve micropsychic elements or properties, regardless of whether it involves some nonpsychic elements.

mind-body dualism: Mind-body dualism is a view defended by René Descartes (1596–1650). It holds that there are two distinct substances in nature. Material substance is essentially extended. Mental substance is essentially conscious or involves thinking.

monitor: An individual who monitors an AMP session to facilitate data collection.

Monte Carlo method: A way to estimate the true likelihood of an observed effect by randomly trying all possible outcomes to see how rare (or not) the observed effect is.

naturalism: The *metaphysical* view that everything that exists in a concrete way (i.e., has causal powers) is located in space and time and only changes in proportionate ways or only cause proportionate changes. These characteristics make it possible for science to work out the mechanisms behind observed changes and postulate what exists most fundamentally. Science is therefore the *epistemological* counterpart of naturalism. The *ontological* counterpart of naturalism is materialism. Naturalism has several important variants. *Standard naturalism* denies the existence of supernatural particulars. *Strict naturalism* denies both supernatural particulars and fundamental substances with mentalistic properties. *Broad naturalism* denies supernaturalism but accepts that fundamental particulars can have mentalistic properties.

near-death experience (NDE): Supernormal experiences reported typically by some people who go through a period of significant physical or emotional crisis. The NDE typically includes an out-of-body experience with attendant psychical abilities (e.g., telepathy or remote viewing), experiences of a transition to a transcendental realm followed by encounters with spirit beings and deceased relatives, and/or unitive mystical experiences. NDEs typically are transformative experiences such that NDErs afterward have no fear of death and are more prosocial and ethical. A significant number of NDErs have enhanced psychic abilities after their NDE. NDEs appear to be a kind of universalist phenomenon, as it exhibits significant phenomenological consistency across demographic and historical divisions.

neutral monism: A view defended by William James (1842–1910) that there is one substance and that substance is intrinsically neither mental nor physical.

Newtonian physics: Physics up to the time quantum mechanics and general and special relativity updated the concepts. In a Newtonian world, there is no uncertainty, waves are waves and particles are particles, and there is no confusion. Given a set of Newtonian laws and the initial conditions, the behavior of such a system is completely determined through time.

Newton's laws: Law I: Every body persists in its state of being at rest or of moving uniformly straight forward, except insofar as it is compelled to change its state by force impressed. Law II: The change of momentum of a body is proportional to the impulse impressed on the body and happens along the straight line on which that impulse is impressed. Law III: To every action there is always an equal and opposite reaction or the forces of two bodies on each other are always equal and are directed in opposite directions.

noise: The cognitive disturbance (whether internal or external) in the background that interferes with processing of information. This is similar to trying to read with the TV playing in the background at a loud volume, which interferes with your ability to understand what you are reading, and you may find that even after reading a passage, you are unaware of what you have read. In the acquisition of AC information, a similar process possibly occurs, leading to "noise" or incorrect elements in an AC response.

nonlocality: A term that has different meanings depending upon the circumstances. One definition of a force is the spatial gradient of some potential; a local force is one where that gradient is evaluated at a single point at which a test particle resides. A nonlocal force is one in which that gradient must be evaluated over some volume surrounding the test particle. The strong nuclear force is nonlocal. In psi research, the term has taken on a different meaning and simply describes the acquisition of information from some distant spacetime location or some psi-mediated action across space and time. Some researchers put forward the notion that consciousness itself is nonlocal in that it is capable of action and acquisition across spacetime.

NS-SCR: Non-specific skin conductance response is an observed deviation of skin conductance that is not associated with any known stimulus.

null hypothesis: In statistical inference of observed data of a scientific experiment, the null hypothesis refers to a general or default postulate that there is no relationship between independent variables and dependent variables. The null hypothesis, for example, in proof-of-principle psi research is that psi does not exist.

observational theories (OTs): Observational theories (OTs) of AC and AP/PK draw upon the measurement problem of quantum mechanics, according to which the central axiom is that the act of observation by a motivated observer of an event influences the outcome.

ontology: The study of what exists "ultimately" or "most fundamentally." Also, models of what so exists. Terms used in expressing ontological models represent "particulars," i.e., irreducible subjects of predication, and thus provide the basic conceptual building blocks for constructing theories about the nature of the world (instances of such proposed ultimate particulars are, e.g., physical particles, spirits, and wave functions).

out-of-body experience (OBE): An experience in which the world is perceived as if from a perspective outside the body.

panpsychism: The view that consciousness is a fundamental feature of the universe and is to be found everywhere.

phenomenological models: Based upon observations rather than upon fundamental theoretical principles.

physicalism: A restricted version of materialism, according to which the only kind of matter that exists is physical matter, and hence every material thing is a physical thing.

Planck's law: In the nineteenth century, a theory existed (Wien's law) that accurately described the amount of EM radiation emitted by a black body as a function of its temperature and wavelength (i.e., color) of the radiation. Near the turn of the twentieth century, the measured amount of EM radiation at short wavelengths was dropping rapidly, whereas Wien's law suggested it should increase rapidly. This discrepancy was called the ultraviolet catastrophe. Planck invented quantum mechanics and suggested that the light emitted at all wavelengths came in chunks (called photons), and the equation he developed was a perfect fit to EM radiation emitted at all temperatures and wavelengths. It is now known as Planck's law.

PMIR: *See* Psi-mediated instrumental response.

precognition: A person-centered perspective that generally refers to information perceived about future events, where the information could not be inferred by ordinary means. Or more formally, precognition is an atypical perceptual ability that allows the acquisition of noninferential information arising from a space-like separated point in spacetime. For two points in spacetime to be space-like separated, insufficient time has elapsed between them to allow for any causal relationship. Procedurally in AC experiments it means that target stimuli are randomly generated after data collection is complete. Associated concepts include rectrocausation, remote viewing, presentiment, and precognitive dreams.

presentiment: Concept postulating that present physiological states are correlated with near-term future affective experiences.

prestimulus: A period of time prior to administration of a stimulus. In AC research, prestimulus responses have been observed because of a startle stimuli (i.e., those that are surprising to the participant) and affective cognitive stimuli, called presentiment.

process-oriented research: Focuses upon possible mechanisms of anomalous mental phenomena both from a theoretical perspective as well as procedural ones. This differs from proof-oriented research.

proof-oriented research: Focuses exclusively upon demonstrating the existence of some anomalous mental phenomenon.

protocol: A template for conducting a structured data collection session.

pseudo stimuli: Synonym for control stimuli.

pseudo-random number generator: Generates random numbers from an algorithm rather than from an external sourced of randomness.

psi-hitting: *See* Hits.

psi-mediated instrumental response (PMIR): Posits that persons can use a combination of ESP and PK in the service of their own needs, even when they are not consciously intending to do so—a precursor to DAT.

psi missing: Term used to describe the circumstance in which a participant gets the wrong answer far more than chance would predict. For example, in guessing the number of heads in a future 100 flips of a fair coin, the expected number of heads is 50. Suppose a participant predicts only 40 heads. This leads to a significant ($p = .01$) example of psi missing.

psychokinesis (PK): Refers to the direct influence of mind on a physical system that cannot be entirely accounted for by the mediation of any known physical energy. *See also* Anomalous perturbation.

quantum coherence: In quantum mechanics, all objects have wave-like properties. For effects to be seen, these waves must all be in step with each other; that is, they are coherent.

quantum decoherence: Occurs when a quantum system interacts with the environment. As a result, the waves that were in step are no longer so. More formally, quantum decoherence or as described in the literature, *environmental decoherence*, suggests that entangled quantum states are fragile and thus it is very difficult to isolate quantum systems from any environment. As of 2014, the current record is 500,000 rubidium atoms in a single quantum state; however, to do so these atoms (too small to see with an unaided eye) had to be cooled to 0.00002 of a degree above absolute zero.[1]

quantum mechanics/theory: The study of properties of matter using its wave properties. The study of physical systems whose dimensions are close to or below the atomic scale, such as molecules, atoms, electrons, and protons. Quantum mechanics is a fundamental branch of physics with wide applications.

quantum Zeno effect: One of the oddities of quantum theory that suggests that if you have a radioactive particle and measure it continuously, it will never decay. This happens because each of the measurements finds the particle in the same state and not one that would be required for it to decay. Also known as the Turing paradox.

random event generator (REG): Synonym for random number generator.

random number generator (RNG): An apparatus (typically electronic) incorporating an element (based on such processes as radioactive decay or random "noise") and capable of generating a random sequence of outputs; used in tests of AC for generating target sequences. In tests of PK, RNGs may itself be the target system that the subject is required to influence, that is, by "biasing" the particular number or event output; a binary RNG has two equally probable outputs. The term "RNG" is increasingly being used to refer to any system that produces naturally random outputs, such as bouncing dice, radioactive decay, or even, perhaps, the brain.

---

[1]Behbood, N., Ciurana, F. M., Golangelo, G., Napolitano, M., Tóth, G., Sewell, R. J., & Mitchell, M. W. (2014). Generation of macroscopic singlet states in a cold atomic ensemble. *Physical Review Letters*, 113, 093601.

rank-order analysis: The most common form of AC analysis, in which an analyst (not the participant) is presented with a single response and five photographs, of which one is the intended target for the session. The analyst's task is to pick which photograph best matches the response, the second best match, and so on. This matching procedure is independent of the quality of the putative match.

receiver: An individual who attempts to perceive by AC and report information about a sensorially isolated target. Also known as a subject, percipient, or viewer.

reliability of response: *Reliability* is defined as the fraction of the response that is correct.

remote viewing (RV): Refers to the methodological procedures used in an experimental design in which a percipient attempts to describe a target stimulus (e.g., photograph or natural site) that is distant in time and space. In cases wherein the target stimulus is generated *after* the response has been generated and secured, it is, by definition, precognition.

replication: Repetition of an experiment that has been carried out before. In human sciences, it is impossible to conduct an exact replication because moment-to-moment humans are different, so also the sample population is different between studies. Often, repeating a human-oriented study is called a conceptual replication in which the details may differ substantially. In the physical sciences, it may be possible to conduct an exact replication in which *all* the experimental details are *identical* to those in the original study.

retarded waves: *See* Advanced waves.

retroactive PK (retro-PK): An example of the future influencing the present. For example, a participant tomorrow is given feedback from a binary sequence generated today and that effort then "causes" deviation when the sequence is generated in real time.

retrocausation: The proposition that the future affects the present, and it is not that the present can influence the past. The past is the past. The manifestation of retrocausation in human experience may be seen in the phenomenon of precognition. The term retrocausation (RC) and rectrocausal-signals (RC-signals) refer to a temporal, information-centered perspective for putative signals that originated from a distant, future spacetime point (i.e., space-like separated).

retro-PK: *See* Retroactive PK.

RNG-PK: Random number generator PK uses that physical device that generates random sequences of numbers (usually binary) as a target for psychokinesis.

runs: A collection of trials in a psi experiment is often called a run.

Schrödinger paradox: The laws of quantum theory suggest that unlike classical systems, quantum systems do not possess properties, such as mass and charge, until they are measured. This did not make sense to Schrödinger. To illustrate how silly he thought this to be, he posed the now famous circumstance in which a cat is both dead and alive at the same time.

search: The inverse of AC. That is, given a known target, determine its location.

sender: An individual who, while receiving direct sensorial stimuli from an intended target, acts as a putative transmitter of that information to the receiver in AC experiments.

session: A time interval during which AMP data are collected.

Shannon entropy: Shannon defined the entropy for a given system as the weighted average of the probability of occurrence of all possible events in the system. Entropy, used in this sense, is defined as a measure of our uncertainty, or lack of information, about a system. Shannon entropy is also devoid of meaning, i.e., there is no cognitive content to it.

signal-to-noise ratio: All signals contain some kind of distracting noise. The ratio of how much signal there is compared to that noise is called the signal to noise ratio (SNR). Trying to detect a radar signal sent to Mars and back represents a (single-pulse) SNR considerably less than zero; however, detecting a flashing light in the dark is usually accomplished with an SNR much larger than one.

source-of-psi problem: An important issue in psi research, as it asks the question whether the experimenter or the subject is using his precognitive ability to derive the response. Either way, it still indicates the existence of precognition.

space-like separated: Two points in spacetime are called space-like separated when there can be no causal relationship between them because not enough time could elapse to affect that relationship.

spacetime: In classical physics, space and time are considered separate things. Space is three-dimensional and can be divided into a three-dimensional grid of cubes that describes the Euclidean geometry familiar from high school math class. Time is one-dimensional in classical physics. Einstein's theory of special relativity combines the three dimensions of space and one dimension of time into a four-dimensional grid called spacetime. Spacetime may be flat, in which case Euclidean geometry describes the three space dimensions, or curved. In Einstein's theory of general relativity, the distribution of matter and energy in the universe determines the curvature of spacetime.

Star Gate: The U.S. government funded a 20-year, $20 million anomalous mental phenomena program, best known by its last code name Star Gate, spanning from 1972 through 1995, at SRI International and Science Applications International Corporation. The primary objective of the Star Gate program was to investigate the phenomenon of remote viewing (RV) as an aid in gathering intelligence during the Cold War, to assess the Soviet threat to the United States in their use of RV and to conduct basic and applied research to improve RV as an intelligence asset. At its peak, it had 12 full-time scientists on its roll. The principal investigators were Dr. Harold E. Puthoff (1972–1985), Russell Targ (1972–1982), and Dr. Edwin C. May (1976–1995).

state vector collapse: In quantum theory, a mathematical representation of all possible outcomes of a measurement is called the state vector. Upon a measurement (in jargon, a projection operator), some outcome from the state vector can be observed. This implies that the outcome may depend upon time. This process is called state vector collapse.

static targets: AC targets that do not change as a function of time.

stimulus: In the context of an experiment, one of the independent variables. It might consist of a light flash, an acoustic signal, or any other sensory input.

stimulus-response method: Within the context of AC research, AC information retrieval is obtained immediately after a trigger word such as "target."

structural dualism: In mind-body philosophy, the view that "mind" and "body" are distinct *things*, without an entailed commitment about their comprising substances being of ultimately distinct kinds.

supernaturalism: The metaphysical view that at least some particulars exist that can produce unconstrained and/or disproportionate change in the concrete world. The ontological counterpart of supernaturalism is immaterialism.

super-psi hypothesis: The retrieval of veridical information that is extensive and highly specific acquired via a generalized psychic information channel. It is generally thought to be an alternative to the data seen in survival research.

survival research: Many spiritual traditions hold that some aspect of us survives the death of our bodies. What survives is known by a number of names, including soul, ātman, nonmaterial consciousness. Investigating this notion, including reincarnation, falls under the term "survival research."

Szilárd's information theory: Szilárd's great contribution to information philosophy is his connecting an increase in thermodynamic entropy with any increase in information that results from a measurement.

target: An item that is the focus of an AMP task (e.g., person, place, thing, event).

target designation: The method by which a specific target, against the backdrop of all other possible targets, is identified to the receiver (e.g., geographical coordinates).

target-pool bandwidth: The number of different elements in the target picture.

telepathy: The acquisition of information concerning the thoughts, feelings, or activity of another conscious being; the word has superseded earlier expressions such as "thought transference." However, we think that the only form of anomalous acquisition of information is precognition, as one cannot determine whether a percipient has acquired information telepathically or has precognitively determined the information. Procedurally, it is difficult to determine exactly what the target is, as one has to either rely on a pre-recorded note of the target stimulus (a clairvoyant condition) or rely on a post-session narration of the target stimulus (a precognition condition).

time-like separated: Two points in spacetime are time-like separated when enough time has elapsed so that a causal relation between the two points is allowed. Most events in our everyday lives are connected in time-like fashion.

time loop paradox: *See* Grandfather paradox.

time symmetry: *See* CPT symmetry.

trial: The smallest unit of data to be analyzed.

universal set of elements (USE): A list of potential elements that define a set. For example, the USE for a set of dogs might include large, brown, black, spotted, noisy. Any given dog may possess some of these elements but is not required to have all of them.

wave function: A concept born in quantum theory. It describes everything that can be known about a quantum system as contained in its energy function (Hamiltonian operator). That is, its terms contain all possible outcomes of a measurement. *See also* Collapse of a wave function.

Zener cards: Also known as ESP cards; a set of 25 cards with five each of the following symbolssquare, circle, wavy lines, cross, star (☆ ○ + 〰 ▢). Designed by Karl Zener for ESP experiments, they were used extensively from the 1930s into the 1970s.

Acknowledgments: We express our sincere thanks to David Rousseau for his assistance in preparing this glossary.

About the Editors and Contributors

Sonali Bhatt Marwaha, Ph.D., is a research associate with the Laboratories for Fundamental Research. She received her master's and MPhil degree in clinical psychology from SNDT Women's University, Mumbai, and a doctorate in psychology from Andhra University, India.

Edwin C. May, Ph.D., is the president and founder of the Laboratories for Fundamental Research, Palo Alto, California. Formerly, he was a scientist with the U.S. government's classified extrasensory perception (ESP) program popularly known as Star Gate from 1976 to 1985, and was its contractor director from 1985 to 1995. He received his doctorate in experimental nuclear physics from the University of Pittsburgh.

Carlos Alvarado, Ph.D., Visiting Scholar, Rhine Research Center; Assistant Professor of Research at the Division of Perceptual Studies, University of Virginia.

Loyd Auerbach, M.S., Director of the Office of Paranormal Investigations; Professor at both Atlantic University and JFK University; Creator and Instructor of the Certificate Program in Parapsychological Studies, HCH Institute in Lafayette.

Dick J. Bierman, Ph.D., Professor, Department of Brain and Cognition, University of Amsterdam.

Denny Borsboom, Ph.D., Professor, Psychology Department, University of Amsterdam.

James Carpenter, Ph.D., a clinical psychologist (Board Certified, ABPP), research parapsychologist, and Adjunct Professor of Psychiatry, University of North Carolina, Chapel Hill, USA.

Bernard Carr, Ph.D., Professor in Mathematics and Astronomy, University of London, UK.

Richard Corry, Ph.D., Lecturer in Philosophy, University of Tasmania, School of Humanities, Hobart TAS, Australia.

Joseph G. Depp, Ph.D., Founding president and CEO of Accuray Inc., where he led the team that developed the first Accuray Cyberknife.

Michael Duggan, Ph.D., independent researcher, Birmingham, UK, formerly Nottingham Trent University, UK.

James H. Fallon, Ph.D., Professor Emeritus, Anatomy & Neurobiology School of Medicine, and Professor, Psychiatry & Human Behavior School of Medicine, University of California at Irvine.

Christopher C. French, Ph.D., Professor and Head of the Anomalistic Psychology Research Unit in the Psychology Department at Goldsmiths, University of London.

(Late) Charles Honorton, parapsychologist.

Rogier Andrew Kievit, Ph.D., postdoctoral research fellow at the MRC Cognition and Brain Sciences Unit in Cambridge, UK.

Joseph W. McMoneagle, retired Chief Warrant Officer with the US Army, Research Associate, Laboratories for Fundamental Research.

Brian Millar, Ph.D., experimental parapsychologist.

Dominic Parker, currently an undergraduate student based in Northern California.

Michael A. Persinger, Ph.D., Professor, Departments of Psychology and Biology Behavioural Neuroscience, Biomolecular and Human Studies Programs, Laurentian University, Sudbury, Ontario.

Dean Radin, Ph.D., Chief Scientist, Institute of Noetic Sciences, Petaluma, CA, USA.

Adam J. Rock, Ph.D., School of Psychology, Deakin University, Burwood, Victoria, Australia.

David Rousseau, Ph.D., Director of the Centre for Systems Philosophy based in Surrey, UK, and a Visiting Fellow of the Centre for Systems Studies in the University of Hull, UK.

Adrian Ryan, Ph.D., independent researcher.

Daniel P. Sheehan, Ph.D., Professor of Physics, University of San Diego, USA.

Richard Shoup, Ph.D., co-founder of the Boundary Institute, San Jose, CA, USA. The Boundary Institute is a small non-profit research group for the study of the foundations of physics, mathematics and computer science.

Sheila Smith, B.S. (Biology), independent researcher.

S. James P. Spottiswoode, a physicist and long-time researcher in psi.

Lance Storm, Ph.D., School of Psychology, University of Adelaide, Adelaide, Australia.

Patrizio Tressoldi, Ph.D., Dipartimento di Psicologia Generale, Università di Padova, Italy.

Jessica Utts, Ph.D., Professor of Statistics at the University of California at Irvine. She is elected to serve as the 111th president of the American Statistical Association, with her term as President-Elect to commence in January 2015, followed by her term as president in 2016.

Anand Jayprakash Vaidya, Ph.D., Associate Professor of Philosophy, Director of the Center for Comparative Philosophy, Department of Philosophy, San Jose State University, San Jose, CA, U.S.A.

Han L.J. van der Maas, Ph.D., professor and chair of Psychological Methods group at the University of Amsterdam. Since 2008 he is also director of the Graduate School of Psychology at the University of Amsterdam.

Zoltán Vassy, Ph.D., Department of Affective Psychology, Eötvös Loránd University, Budapest, Hungary.

Walter von Lucadou, Ph.D., Senior Lecturer at the Furtwangen Technical University, Germany.

Eric-Jan Wagenmakers, Ph.D., professor at the Psychological Methods Unit of the University of Amsterdam.

Ruud Wetzels, Ph.D., postdoc at the Informatics Institute (University of Amsterdam).

Nancy L. Zingrone, Ph.D., Psychology, University of Edinburgh. She is a two-time past President of the Parapsychological Association.

Index